The Acquisition of Written Language

Response
and
Revision

Writing Research

Multidisciplinary Inquiries into the Nature of Writing

edited by Marcia Farr, University of Illinois at Chicago

THE
ACQUISITION
OF
WRITTEN LANGUAGE:

Response and Revision

SARAH WARSHAUER FREEDMAN, Editor

University of California, Berkeley

ABLEX PUBLISHING CORPORATION
NORWOOD, NEW JERSEY

Library of Congress Cataloging in Publication Data
Main entry under title:

The Acquisition of written language.

    (Writing Research)
    Bibliography: p.
    Includes index.
    1. Rhetoric—Study and teaching—Addresses, essays, lectures. 2. Editing—Data processing—Addresses, essays, lectures. 3. Language acquisition—Addresses, essays, lectures. I. Freedman, Sarah Warshauer.
P301.A28 1985   808'042'07   85–13427
ISBN 0–89391–227–1
ISBN 0–89391–324–3 (pbk.)

Ablex Publishing Corporation
355 Chestnut Street
Norwood, New Jersey 07648

Contents

PART II: COMPUTERS: REVISION AND RESPONSE

PART III: THEORIES OF AND RESEARCH ON REVISION

To my parents

Miriam and Samuel
Warshauer

Writing Research

Multidisciplinary Inquiries into the Nature of Writing

Marcia Farr, series editor
University of Illinois at Chicago

PREFACE

This series of volumes presents the results of recent scholarly inquiry into the nature of writing. The research presented comes from a mix of disciplines, those which have emerged as significant within the last decade or so in the burgeoning field of writing research. These primarily include English education, linguistics, psychology, anthropology, and rhetoric. A note here on the distinction between field and discipline might be useful: a field can be a multidisciplinary entity focused on a set of significant questions about a central concern (e.g., American Studies), while a discipline usually shares theoretical and methodological approaches which may have a substantial tradition behind them. Writing research, then, is a field, if not yet a discipline.

The history of this particular field is unique. Much of the recent work in this field, and much that is being reported in this series, has been conceptualized and funded by the National Institute of Education. Following a planning conference in June 1977, a program of basic research on the teaching and learning of writing was developed and funded annually. The initial research funded under this program is now coming to fruition, providing both implications for educational improvement and directions for future research. This series is intended as one important outlet for these results.

Acknowledgments

To my husband Bob and my daughter Rachel, I owe special thanks for the many times they have put up with my absorption in matters professional. Rachel, as a developing writer with plentiful opinions on how children acquire written language, unknowingly guides me to attack those issues in the acquisition of written language that matter not just to researchers but also to the learners that we study. How others respond to students' writing and how students can best revise certainly touch on some of those issues.

I next would like to thank the chapter authors who agreed to publish some of their newest work in this edited volume, and who, in all cases, provided outstanding efforts.

For many years, my colleagues in the Bay Area, at Berkeley, at Stanford, and at San Francisco State have helped me think about the role response and revision play in the learning process. This book was nourished by conversations with Bob Calfee, Bill Robinson, Jo Keroes, Jim Gray, Doug Campbell, Miles Myers, Lily Wong Fillmore, John and Jenny Gumperz, Melanie Sperling, and Cynthia Greenleaf, to name only a few. Equally as important has been the stimulation provided by many devoted writing teachers from the Bay Area Writing Project.

Finally, Marcia Farr encouraged me to begin this book. Without her support, the project never would have come to fruition.

Sarah Warshauer Freedman
Berkeley
June, 1984

Introduction: Acquiring Written Language

Eudora Welty (1983) describes the internal response that cues her revisions: "When I write and the sound of it comes back to my ears, then I act to make my changes. I have always trusted this voice" (p. 12). The contributors to this volume are ultimately concerned with how writers acquire trusted inner voices and with understanding the roles schools and teachers can play in helping student writers in the learning process.

Underlying all the chapters is a theory of how writing is acquired. To set up a framework for the book and for studies of the acquisition of written language, I will first explicate that theory. To do so, I borrow from theories of oral language development and intellectual skill development. Writing, although closely related to oral language, is not just speech written down; it is a more conscious activity than speech, and for most, it is largely learned in school rather than at home. Thus, the perspectives of oral language acquisition and intellectual skill acquisition seem appropriate. The authors in this volume view writing at once as a form of language learning and as an intellectual skill.

In oral language development, children "use what people say to form hypotheses about how different ideas are expressed in the language they are acquiring." They test "how well they are understood by others" (Clark & Clark, 1977, 336–337). Children, it seems, use the speech of others as a model, and, when others' speech consists of a response to their own utterances, as a guide to the effectiveness of their own communication. If children employ similar hypothesis testing strategies to learn written language, they need to know how experts write, and they need to know how their readers understand and respond to their writing. By using this information, they can revise their hypotheses about how written language is produced. Just as the listener–speaker interaction is crucial to hypothesis testing when children learn to speak, the reader–writer interaction must be crucial when children learn to write. This reader–writer interaction takes into account both the writer as a reader of others' writing and the writer in interaction with his or her reader, at some times literally and at other times imaginatively.

In theories of the acquisition of schooltype intellectual skills, from Vygotsky's (1978) to Anderson's (1982), response or feedback plays a central role. As when developing other intellectual skills, learning writers need to distinguish when they are performing well from when they are not, and they need to know how to take corrective action when their writing is not proceeding well. They must gain metacognitive skills (Brown, 1981) which help them know what and how to revise. The notion that writers solve composing problems (Hayes & Flower, 1980) grows out of the problem-solving literature that is built around how learners solve problems in other domains (Newell & Simon, 1972). Theories of intellectual skill acquisition imply a level of conscious control of cognitive processes that is not implied by theories of oral language acquisition.

For the acquisition of written language, theory in both oral language learning and intellectual skill development indicates that response stimulates revision in the form both of somewhat unconscious hypothesis testing and of conscious problem solving. These theories lead to many questions about written language acquisition, but the two central ones to be addressed here are: How can response or feedback best serve the pedagogical end of helping writers increase their skill in writing? And what role does revision play in skill development?

A review of the literature on response to student writing reveals that in order to help students learn, response has to lead to revision in three ways: it must help students consciously identify and solve their composing problems; it must stimulate practice—students must use the response (reading or hearing a comment may not in itself lead to practice or use); and the practice must help students transfer their skills to new writings (Freedman, 1984).

Definitions of response and revision provide a framework for organizing the chapters in this book, for each chapter stresses a slightly different aspect of response or revision, each aspect being important in written language acquisition. Looked at broadly, *response* includes feedback or reaction to something the writer has already produced. It is important to remember two points: (a) response to nonwritten plans and ideas for writing is as much response as response to writing itself, but (b) teaching, in preparation for writing before the writing process begins, although also key in learning and related to response as it lays the groundwork for how response will be understood, is not, in itself, commonly defined as response.

Traditionally, the term *revision* has been used in several ways. First, a revision is a change a writer makes in a piece of writing. The writer makes the changes because the writer re-sees (or in Welty's case rehears) and decides the changes are needed. Such changes may or may not be traceable to the text the writer produces. A second kind of revision involves changes a writer makes in the procedures for producing writing. Again the writer decides to make the changes. Changes in procedures for producing writing may or may not be visible in the writing itself. The third sense in which revision is used is in reference to that part of the composing process during which changes are made. The cognitive processes included during the revision subprocess may be partially inferred through tracing the changes in the written product and through observing changes in procedures for writing. Finally, in its most fundamental sense, the term revision implies a revision of cognition itself. Revision becomes a part of the learning process that involves the reorganization of the rules for text production. This revision of cognition or cognitive reorganization spans across the production of different texts.

The authors in this volume use revision in all senses, but the underlying concern is to lead to an understanding of the last type of revision, the cognitive reorganization that must take place for transferable learning to occur, a reorganization that stems from response. When one considers how revision leads to cognitive reorganization or transfer, it is important to abandon the mechanistic view of a response–revision cycle that operates within a given text. Rather, what is important is how both response and revision span across a writer's learning, across different pieces of writing, written for different purposes, in different contexts.

Response and revision then are linked by a special type of response: self-response, or Welty's "inner voice." Response from others, augmented by one's reading experiences and the teaching-learning environment, shapes internal or self-response. It is this key part of the writing process that determines the nature of revisions in cognitive organization. Self-responses tell writers whether they understand external response and other input relevant to learning to write. It might be argued that response is basic to the process of teaching written language and that revision is basic to the process of learning.

The Language of Instruction—Classroom, Peer Group, Writing Conference

The six chapters in Part I examine the language of instruction to see how response and revision are accomplished in instructional settings. As a group, the chapters illustrate a range of ways that linguistic ethnography and text analysis, as research methodologies, can be used to shed light on the acquisition of written language. With the exception of Ammon (Chap. 4), the authors' linguistic analyses focus primarily on the oral language of teaching and learning. Heath and Branscombe (Chap. 1), and Gere and Stevens (Chap. 5) supplement their analysis of teaching with analyses of students' written language. Ammon focuses first on how the written language changes across a year's time and then looks back to the classroom to try to understand why those changes occur.

The six chapters cover a range of types of response to student writing and suggest how different types of response might engender the kind of revision that is associated with the cognitive reorganization that accompanies learning. Heath and Branscombe (Chap. 1), Dunn, Florio-Ruane, and Clark (Chap. 2); Cazden, Michaels, and Tabors (Chap. 3), and Ammon (Chap. 4) focus on whole class interactions. Gere and Stephens (Chap. 5) look at peer groups, and Freedman and Sperling (Chap. 6) at individual conferences. Cazden, Michaels, and Tabors and Freedman and Sperling demonstrate the extra complexity involved in the teaching–learning process for traditionally low-achieving students. Together these first six chapters illustrate how different types of response provide instructive feedback for writers, or in Cazden, Michaels, and Tabors's chapter, how emerging writers revise their speech to elicit positive response from their listeners.

All authors in this section would agree that the *coordination* of a variety of types of response is necessary for learning to occur. But most basic, writers first must learn from their respondents how they are communicating or making meaning, how they are being understood. Included in this concern with communication is more than the communication of propositional meaning; in addition, writers want to communicate an "intended impression." This impression is similar to what we communicate about ourselves through the clothes we choose, the house we live in, the friends we select. Once writers perceive a mismatch between what they intend to communicate—either with respect to meaning or impression—and what an audience understands, they then revise. At first, they revise a particular piece of text; this revision of text may demand a revised set of procedures. Further, it may or may not lead to a revision of cognitive structures. The chapter authors all suggest that a writer's first goal is to attend to the reader's needs by revising in order to communicate more effectively. In order to achieve this goal, they learn to control the written structures they need to accomplish their ends.

Computers—Response and Revision

Besides response to writing that is embedded in the language of the classroom, computers are now being programmed to respond to student writing and to help students revise. Furthermore, the computer, which is often anthropomorphized with its command structure, gives the appearance of interacting with the writer during composing. Some have suggested that the computer itself, because of how it works, helps young writers think of an audience that will read their writing as they compose (e.g., Daiute, 1983). Above and beyond what the computer does by its existence, the text editors and word processors that writers use allow them to revise differently than they do with pencil and paper. For this reason, composition researchers have speculated that the convenience of revising when using the computer might profoundly affect writers' composing processes.

The authors of the four chapters in Part II investigate the role of the computer as respondent and the usefulness of its aid during revision. Their findings are interesting, yielding sometimes unexpected results. Daiute (Chap. 7) and Levin, Reil, Rowe, and Boruta, (Chap. 8) show how elementary-age writers confront computers. Daiute's questions center on the effects of the computer on cognitive processing during writing. Her word processor prompts students to revise. Levin and his coauthors look at the responsive writing environments that can be encouraged by the computer and at the social effects of computer use. Bridwell, Sirc, and Brooke (Chap. 9) and Frase, Kiefer, Smith, Macdonald, and Fox (Chap. 10) turn to college-age writers. Bridwell, Sirc, and Brooke examine how the word processor itself affects these writers' revising processes whereas Frase, Kiefer, Smith, Macdonald, and Fox focus on the effects of the Writer's Workbench programs that are designed to aid writers during composing, especially with the mechanics of writing.

Daiute (Chap. 7) and Bridwell, Sirc, and Brooke (Chap. 9) look to see whether the computer itself facilitates more substantive revisions in texts and in the procedures for producing texts. They find that the computer exerts more of an effect on some students than on others. Daiute further finds that students use her computer prompts to help prompt themselves when they are composing on the computer. Levin, Reil, Rowe, and Boruta, (Chap. 8) and Frase, Kiefer, Smith, Macdonald, and Fox (Chap. 10) find the computer especially helpful for improving low-level editing skills. And Levin and his colleagues illustrate how the computer can be integrated into the classroom to assist in providing an environment conducive to the types of response described by the authors in the first section of this volume.

These four chapters on the computer as respondent and assistant to revision focus on different instructional settings, use different computer software, and use different research methods. It is not surprising that each sheds a different light on current knowledge about how computer response affects writers and about how that response relates to revision.

Theories of and Research on Revision

Taken together the three last chapters (Part III) challenge both traditional ways of studying revision and past assumptions about parts of the revision process. Indeed, they sketch a new perspective for studying revision and its relationship to response.

Danielewicz and Chafe (Chap. 11) suggest that it might be possible to understand how writers do or do not get the cues that they need in order to revise. These authors compare written and oral language, looking particularly at punctuation errors and relating them to oral intonation. On one level, the sounds these writers hear literally interfere with their writing. Matsuhashi and Gordon (Chap. 12) challenge the traditional expert–novice comparisons, showing that novices, when directed to do so, can revise globally in the ways that experts do. Witte (Chap. 13) offers a theoretical perspective for a new way of thinking about revision. He urges researchers to stop thinking of and studying revision as if it were a textbound process, and to be wary of the instructional implications drawn from research on the writing process without tests of those implications.

And So—

I have attempted to bring together a set of chapters that can help us begin to account both for cognitive processes underlying learning to write and the social context of schooling. Both perspectives are crucial to even a rudimentary understanding of the acquisition of written language.

References

Anderson, J. R. (1982). Acquisition of cognitive skill. *Psychological Review, 89,* 369–406.

Brown, A. (1981). Learning how to learn from reading. In J. Langer & M. Smith-Burke (Eds.), *Bridging the gap: A psycholinguistic and social linguistic perspective.* Newark, DE: Dell, International Reading Association.

Clark, H., & Clark, E. (1977). *Language and psychology.* New York: Harcourt Brace Jovanovich.

Daiute, C. (1983). The computer as stylus and audience. *College Composition and Communication, 34,* 134–145.

Freedman, S. (1984, April). *Response to, and evaluation of writing*. Paper presented at the annual meeting of the American Educational Research Association, New Orleans.

Hayes, J. R., & Flower, L. (1980). Identifying the organization of writing processes. In L. Gregg & E. Steinberg (Eds.), *Cognitive processes in writing*. Hillsdale, NJ: Lawrence Erlbaum.

Newell, A., & Simon, H. (1972). *Human problem solving*. Englewood Cliffs, NJ: Prentice-Hall.

Vygotsky, L. (1978). *Mind in society*. Cambridge, MA: Harvard University Press.

Welty, E. (1983). *One writer's beginnings*. Cambridge, MA: Harvard University Press.

PART I

Pedagogical Language: Classroom, Peer Group, Writing Conference

1

"Intelligent Writing" in an Audience Community: Teacher, Students, and Researcher

Shirley Brice Heath
Stanford University

Amanda Branscombe
Project Uplift, Auburn University

A recent historical examination of how American intelligence changed between 1750 and the mid-twentieth century posits that "intelligence is first of all a kind of social relation" (Calhoun, 1970, p. 28). This historical study argues that throughout the history of American schooling, the rhetoric of educators has maintained that teachers and tests judge the mental capacities of students on the basis of their performance as communicator and audience. Yet, the varieties of ways in which students could learn to respond as communicator and audience decreased sharply after 1870, when schools began to place more and more emphasis on standardized written tests as measures of intelligence. Techniques of performance and communication as calibrated through disjointed skills and mental activities replaced earlier emphases on holistic conceptions of communicator and audience in response to each other (Heath, 1981). Levels of testing teased apart certain areas of competence and expertise in communicating but left concealed ways of blending these to achieve the whole: an "audience community" (Calhoun, 1970, p. 340) sharing experiences through oral and written communication.

Social historians and critics of the development and role of formal schooling in industrialized nations have increasingly reexamined the content and methods of teaching and learning communication skills. Bourdieu (1973) and Graff (1980) point out that formal education systems tend to teach and promote the learning of only the barest of rudimentary skills for communicating. Proper spelling and grammar, varied vocabulary, and topic-sentenced paragraphs are not sufficient to make cohesive intelligent whole narratives or expositions. Schools teach and test to insure that students "absorb the automatic response and rule-of-thumb techniques," but neither teaching nor testing touches "the higher, active sense . . . [necessary to] set up an interchange between ideas, needs, and external reality" (Calhoun, 1970, pp. 130–31). Through mechanistic linguistic tasks, such as spelling tests and grammar drills, schools claim to impart communication skills. Yet, the academic discourse forms which lie at the heart of success in the higher levels of schooling—oral and written extended prose, sequenced explanations, and logical arguments—receive explicit identification and discussion. Those who are academically successful may assume either that schools teach these communication skills or that daily life outside the classroom will eventually instill these skills. However, certain social class positions (Bernstein, 1975; Bourdieu, 1973; Bourdieu & Passeron, 1979) or cultural backgrounds (Heath, 1983) may reward other types of communication skills and provide individuals relatively few opportunities for either extended discourse on a single topic or for step-by-step explanations or argumentation. Hence students' out-of-school experiences as responding communicator and audience using both oral and written language may have provided few models or occasions for the academic discourse forms the school expects.

But what can the school do? Some critics extol the view that schools should reform society and that they must be restructured to do so (e.g., Bowles & Gintis, 1975). Revisionist historians (e.g., Katz, 1968) and even moderates (Kaestle, 1980) have argued, however, that schools have served more to preserve the status quo than to rearrange the social structure of industrialized nations. Short of the revolutionary changes which might bring about a societal restructuring so that children formerly given limited opportunities at home could gain the cultural habits and extended practices necessary for formal schooling to "take," are there other moves the school can make? Are there ways the school can improve communicator-audience relations of students and thus advance the "intelligence"—i.e., the social-relation capacity—of those who have been judged by previous measures of school intelligence to be inferior or unacceptable communicators and audiences?

In this chapter, we describe the writing of students in a classroom in which they participated intensively as an "audience community" during one academic year. In their participation, they gained a willingness to communicate in writing, a desire for response to their writing, and an understanding of audience. As a result, they increased skills in both writing and talking about how, what, and why they learned through writing. The class was a 9th-grade basic English class of eighteen students (14 blacks, 4 white). All but three of these students had previously been in special education classes, which were courses for students judged mentally inferior who had an intelligence quotient on the Stanford–Binet Intelligence Test between 75 and 85. Since the end of their early primary grades, they had received their language arts instruction in these special education classes, which stressed remedial approaches to reading, arithmetic, and the mechanics of language. For all but three of the students, this 9th-grade basic English class was their first experience in a "regular lane" language arts class; only these three students had read through an entire book or had written extended prose, i.e., passages longer than 3 to 5 sentences. For all the students, most of their school work, even in classes such as social studies which were not designated special education, had allowed them to express their answers only in single words or short phrases and not in paragraphs or essays (cf. Applebee, 1981; Harste, Woodward, and Burke, 1984).

The Classroom as Community

The teacher of the 9th-grade basic English class described here was Amanda Branscombe,[1] who worked with Shirley Brice Heath during the academic year 1981–82 in a teacher–researcher relationship. Branscombe's class was in a high school in a town of 30,000 in the deep South of the United States. The school provided two academic tracks for grades 9 through 12: "general" for students who planned to attend college or technical school, and "basic" for those who had previously been in the special education lane or who scored below the 5th-grade level in reading and language arts skills.

Branscombe's emphasis was on making her classroom a community in which all students could use their diverse talents, personalities, and abilities to learn to read and write—and to think of themselves as readers and writers. Throughout the year, she and the students talked about their reading and writing—why and how they were writing, what they were gaining from writing and reading, and what sense these activities made in their daily lives outside the classroom. Branscombe stressed writing and reading as natural byproducts of each other, and in talking with students, she acted as though they were avid, capable writers and readers. She did not "teach" grammar or spelling, and she did not "red-pencil" written work. She began the year by telling students "All of you have A's in this class; now let's settle down and learn." Though there was an initial period of distrust, within the first six weeks students began to relax about being graded, to respond to the writing and reading opportunities of the classroom community, and to search out substantive evaluations of their writing from Branscombe and their peers. The class prepared an alternative school newspaper, and once class members determined the tasks which had to be done, they set about finding their own members who had expertise in the necessary areas: photography, design, news reporting, editorializing, copy editing, proofreading, etc.

During the first semester, on four days of the week, they worked through standard basic English materials for the class: fill-in-the-blank, matching, and spelling tasks which the district curriculum for special education required these classes to do. Branscombe did not grade these exercises; class members went over them in

---

[1] Branscombe had been an English teacher for 12 years in both public and private schools in the South. Her philosophy of teaching had evolved from her own experience, but she had been strongly influenced in her emphasis on writing as a window of students' personalities and intelligence by the work of Ann Bertoff, James Britton, Dixie Goswami, and Ken Macrorie of the Bread Loaf School of English of Middlebury College. Acknowledgment is here made of support from the Bread Loaf School of English for Branscombe to write up the results of her activities with the 1981–1982 9th-grade basic English class. The teacher–researcher relationship between Branscombe and Heath began in the summer of 1981 when Heath spent one week at Bread Loaf as consultant in D. Goswami's class on classroom research in writing in which Branscombe was a student. See Odell and Goswami, (in press) for other case studies of teachers as researchers.

small groups. In the second semester, the students moved rapidly through these exercises early in the week, so the rest of their class days could be spent on writing and reading to accomplish other tasks that members of the group decided upon. When students seemed to be nervous about grades, Branscombe consistently told them they were all "A students"; what mattered was whether or not their class-mates and others with whom they would communicate in writing during the year thought they "made sense," had something to say, and were responsible communicators.

As a teaching strategy, Branscombe set up letter-writing teams in September, 1981. Each team was composed of one member of the 9th-grade basic English class and one student in her 11th–12th grade general English class. The school was large enough and sufficiently segregated by the two-track system that students in the two classes had almost no chance of meeting. The upperclassmen had only the first semester of English (September–December) with Branscombe. In order for the ninth graders to have an audience and extended purposes for writing to an audience outside the classroom beyond December, Heath (who was located in California and did not meet the students until a two-day visit in early May of 1982) began corre-sponding with them as a class in the fall and continued throughout the spring. In addition, Heath's 15-year-old daughter Shannon wrote to the students as a class a few times during the spring term. Heath focused her letters on how the ninth graders could become "associates" in her interests as an ethnographer of communication in communities in different parts of the world.

Under Heath's guidance through her letters, the students began taking field notes on topics such as the types of questions used in their homes and communities; they interviewed family members about recollections of themselves learning to read and write and of their children's early language development. Branscombe and Heath explained their goal as wanting to compare the students' findings with research done in another part of the South, which was being prepared for publication as a book (Heath, 1983). Branscombe read portions of the book's manuscript to the class, so the students would have some idea of how field notes could be transformed into a final product.

During the fall term, at two-week intervals, Branscombe sent Heath copies of the 9th-graders' writings and her own field notes describing what she did in class and how the students were responding in their reading and writing. Branscombe and Heath talked by phone every two weeks, and Heath provided feedback on trends and patterns in individual students' writing. Branscombe had Heath as an audience with whom to discuss research on writing and its implications for classroom teaching.

In the second semester, Branscombe's central goal was to give the ninth graders several different audiences who would respond to their writing. The request that they act as ethnographers of their own and others' uses of language was intended to make them linguistically aware speakers and writers, able recorders of information to which they easily had access, and informed critics of their fellow students' reports and interpretations of information about which they all had a similar shared background. An important byproduct of these academic goals was the social skills the students developed as they cooperated as a class to accomplish the tasks requested.

Heath introduced students to the content of anthropology in order to allow them to see how others used the ethnographic tools of observing, recording, analyzing, and reporting information. The students developed as a community of ethnographers, criticizing, monitoring, and supplementing each other's field notes, questioning interpretations, and, most important, responding to each other's work with new challenges. They had access to knowledge someone else wanted, and the only way to gain and transmit that knowledge was to write so that their audiences could share their background information and develop with them new information and interpretations. Branscombe provided the class with films of ethnographers at work and read to them from ethnographers' writings, including Heath's; Heath prepared one videotape in which she talked about the place of ethnographic research within anthropology. As the class discussed these pieces, they came to accept Heath's implicit assumption: Their field notes and interpretations—their products—should measure up to the standards of the work they were seeing and hearing from other ethnographers.

In her letters, Heath asked individuals and small groups to research certain topics, but students often shared their information in class before they mailed it to her. Heath's letters and Branscombe's discussions with students repeatedly elicited questions from students on process: "How can I write fast enough to record everything being said in a conversation?" "How much detail do I have to give on the layout of the filling station where I'm describing the language the mechanics use?" "What's different about recording information and interpreting it?" The students came to know that a final product was in the distant future, after much discussion and many revisions, and their current pieces were part of a long and arduous process necessary before a finished product would result.[2] Though Branscombe and Heath occasionally pointed out mechanical errors or stylistic devices of writing (such as paragraphing), they did so in the context of the contribution of these bits and pieces to improved communication. Students were not asked to revise their fieldnotes, but they were encouraged instead to "write as much as possible as fast as possible" when they were recording data, and later to write essays of interpretation to explain to Heath what they thought their notes meant.

During the second semester, as the class spent more and more time writing and

---

[2] Throughout the year, Branscombe talked to the students of her hope that their work could be "written up" in some form: articles, newspapers, features, or a book. Heath stressed with the students her willingness to include them as associates in reporting their research; yet she cautioned them repeatedly that "real" authorship carried "real" responsibilities. For example, the class members agreed that any student whose work was used in a written report would have to go over the drafts of that report, correct errors of fact, and add interpretations. See Heath and Thomas (1984) for an article Heath coauthored with a member of the class who dropped out of school in November, 1981.

dropped the district-required worksheets altogether, some students asked "How come we don't *do* grammar, spelling, and things?" In response, Branscombe provided them numerous sources and worksheets and offered to work with students individually or in small groups with these materials. However, students soon turned back to what they came to call "writing for real." Near the end of the year, after taking a school-mandated minimal competency test, one student registered her recognition of the subtle learning which had been taking place by asking: "What else have we been learning this year that we didn't know we were learning?" (Field notes, May 10, 1982).

Assessing Written Language Development

Two students in the class—Cassandra Pitts and Eugene Spinks, both of whom had previously been in special education classes—were chosen for an analysis of their letters.[3] These two students were generally representative of their classmates in their background and development during Branscombe's class; they were selected because they produced more volume in their letter writing—both more letters and longer letters—than any other students in the class. Omitted from analysis here are the other types of writing they did during the year: field notes, field-site descriptions, autobiographical essays, personal narrations, and explanatory essays analyzing their field notes. The analysis of their letters is intended to illustrate ways in which each of these two ninth graders (as well as their classmates) developed written language through the interactive dyads of their letters—first to the upperclassmen and then to Shannon and Shirley Heath. In these letters, they became communicators, able to use written language for different audiences and purposes.

Cassandra began the year acting out feelings other ninth graders had learned to repress. Until November 16, she did not sit at a desk, but chose instead to sit crosslegged on top of a table in the back of the room, with her back turned to the class, often sucking her thumb. Later when she moved to a desk, she became a verbal warrior who lashed out at other class members when they made noise or mentioned subjects she judged unsuitable for discussion. Her mother's death the first week of school and the turmoil that followed caused Cassandra to live much of the year in grief and despair. Yet through the year she gradually began to function as a member of the classroom community. She changed her mode of dress, hairstyle, and behav-

---

[3] The unique nature of the agreement to engage the students as "real researchers" and "real writers" denied the usual research practice of making the "subjects" of research anonymous; these students were "participants of research." Thus, their names are used here with the full and written consent of Cassandra and Eugene and their parents. The two students have participated in the analysis of their writings and read and reviewed drafts of this article; their input in response to the initial drafts written by Heath and Branscombe has been included in the final version. In 1982–83, Cassandra went to another high school in the region and was placed in an honors English class. Eugene remained in the same school until graduation, and he consistently earned a grade of B in a regular-lane English class.

ior; not only was her writing more prolific than that of any other student in class, but she also became one of the class managers, stirring others to get more work done, to be quiet so she and her group could work, and to give their writing to someone else to read and evaluate. At the end of the school term, she was one of the students who chose to continue writing to Heath and to follow up on research begun during the year. Summative comments by class members (written in May, 1982) indicate that they had forgotten the earlier childish, unpredictable, and disruptive Cassandra. Instead, classmates evaluated her as a leader and a "nice person." One classmate wrote: "I would say that Cassandra is our number one leader in the group because of her knowledge and skill." Another student termed her someone who will "keep you on the right track."

Eugene was the class questioner—the "doubting Thomas." He saw himself in the role of clarifying points Branscombe made, explaining them to class members, challenging Heath to make her purposes and practices clear, and persisting in "getting things straight." His loud, grating voice loomed over those of other students as he continually interrupted teacher and students with "But wait, I want to know. . . ." As the year progressed, he became more restrained in some of his more abrasive tactics, but he moved his chair to the front of the room, a symbolic gesture asserting his dominance as the class questioner. In May, his classmates wrote of him: "There is one person that asks so many questions: his name is Eugene Spinks. He asks about 50 questions a hour." "If it wasn't for Eugene, I wouldn't know answers to questions that I was scared to ask." "Eugene is smart too. And when he is talking he gets right to the point, and he don't care who it hurts. And you know people like for him to get to the point."

Like the rest of the class members, both Eugene and Cassandra were paired with upperclassmen for the exchange of letters during the fall term (September through December). Eugene was paired with M, a 17-year-old 12th grader. Cassandra was paired with two girls, J and A (because there were more students in the upper-level class than in the 9th-grade class). Branscombe asked the upperclassmen to write to the 9th graders once each week; she told the upperclassmen only that she hoped the letters would help the 9th graders improve their writing. She asked students to introduce themselves in brief essays, and she then paired students on the basis of interests indicated in these introductions. During the semester, she transferred the letters from class to class each Monday; only rarely did she orally transmit messages between the students.

Over the course of the year, Branscombe expected increasing evidence in the ninth-graders' letters that they could envision the audience of their writing and accommodate their writing to the audience. She expected the ninth graders would, in differing degrees, see the upperclassmen as models of general behavior and as model writers. She also wanted the younger students to recognize that when face-to-face interaction was not possible, any writing represented a challenge to the audience, and response from the audience would be a judgment of both writer and writing. In short, Branscombe expected the exchange of letters to enable the ninth graders to:

1. see the upperclassmen's writings as models of acceptable personal letters;
2. become engaged with a distant audience known only through written communication—and to accept that "somebody cared" about their writing other than the teacher;
3. recognize writing as communication: writing in school did not have to be simply a way of completing an assignment; it could also be an occasion for practicing widely used communicative skills needed to reach varied and distant audiences;
4. participate willingly—and with a notion of a responsibility to "make sense"— in types of writing which had different functions;
5. move beyond initial response in writing to engagement with ideas: to be willing to explain and question their own ideas in writing, and to set up hypothetical situations in writing to assist their audiences in understanding their meanings.

Branscombe frequently discussed specific strategies for accomplishing these goals with the class. The students received almost no direct instruction on the mechanics of writing of these letters, unless they asked questions directed to these skills.

In his essay introducing himself to M, Eugene wrote that he had been told before school opened that he would get lost and not know where to find his classes. M responded that he did not think getting lost was a problem, but that he had had a problem getting his "ID [identification] card." He asked Eugene about sports and closed his letter with the following paragraph:[4]

The only problem I see in your writing is run on sentences but besides that it looks like you right pretty well.

Eugene responded with a letter which placed the salutation in the same place in which M had placed his and took up the points covered in the upperclassman's letter in turn.

No I did not have any problem getting my I.D card back. I got mines back the second day of school. I haven't played any sports this year but I have been thinking about it. I am glad you told me about my run on sentence. I will work on it. If you decide to play any sports let me know. Some of my hoddies are playing football, basketball, baseball and a lot of card games. Tell me some of your hoddies.

Eugene's letter "answered" each of M's points in turn and then initiated a topic in which Eugene was interested—hobbies ["hoddies"].

Eugene did not paragraph his letter as M did, and Eugene used a period in the term "I.D card" though M had written only "ID card" in his letter. Eugene gave a compliant nod to M's mention of his run on sentences, but Branscombe saw or

---

[4] Letters written by students are given just as they were written. Bracketed materials are added when necessary to clarify meaning.

heard no evidence in the next few weeks of class that Eugene knew what was meant by M's term. As their correspondence progressed, Eugene moved on from simply *responding* to M's topics or questions to *restating* the topic and using it as transition to a subject he wished to write about. He often ended his letters with questions he wanted M to answer or extended commentary on a topic he himself had introduced.

In his fourth letter to M, Eugene explained that he had not written the previous week because he was not in school. He had fallen and hurt his leg. M opened his next letter with an expression of concern about Eugene's leg and asked if he had to go to the hospital. M then described a fight he had recently had with a fellow student. His postscript to this letter noted: "You spell here like her. Please correct that. Look on your last letter, I'll circle it." In his next letter, Eugene responded by telling M his leg was still swollen and his mother wanted him to go to the hospital, but he did not want to go. He thanked M for "showing me my mistake," but he did not use either "here" or "her" in his letter. (In subsequent letters, he used these words but he spelled them correctly; he did not discuss these spellings with Branscombe, and there is no evidence of follow-up from anyone else on this error after M's mention of it.)

M responded with a long detailed letter explaining to Eugene why he should go to the doctor if his leg still hurt. He then described an injury he had had once which had not gone away, and he cautioned Eugene that his injury could get worse if he did not see a doctor. The theme of injuries runs through the remainder of the boys' letters: M's old injury required surgery, and Eugene had to go into the hospital for surgery on his leg, so the boys swapped hospital stories in long letters in which they focused on fewer and fewer topics—hospital visits, their hopes for recovery, and their plans to resume sports and hobbies. At the end of the semester, M closed his final letter to Eugene: "Well maybe I will see you around somewhere. Try to do good in school and stay out of trouble, its the easiest way. Your friend, M."

Cassandra's introduction of herself to J and A reads as follows:

My name is Cassandra. There's not much too say, except that I have a lot of ups and down's. I love to play sports, especially volley ball. I hope who ever reads this letter finds the personal Cassandra. We'll are you going to the game Friday. Well as for me, I'm not sure. My boyfriend want's me to go with him, but with things like they they are now, I'm not sure what my next move is. Oh and did you [know] who my boy friend is. (J O). And if you're not worrying about [it] then excuse me. I would appreciate if you wouldn't inform me about this letter. But it's o. k. because most of this stuff is just in the head. Well so-long kid. And have a nice day.

P.S—Hope that you don't mind me saying kid.

J and A responded with the confession that there were parts of the letter they did not understand. They mentioned specific points: "What do you mean by I hope whoever reads this letter finds the personal Cassandra?" They closed their letter by signing off as Cassandra had: "Well so-long kid. Have a nice day."

Cassandra opened her responding letter with a salutation, and launched immediately into a response to each point J and A had raised. She reminded her correspondents that she too had questions: "We'll [Well] I'm answering your letter back, and I have question's that I want to explain and maybe ask some." To remind J and A of each point in turn as she explained it, she opened each clarification with a brief restatement; for example, "We'll [Well] for the up's and down's. . . ." J and A responded to the next few letters by asking more and more questions about Cassandra, her family, her schoolwork, and her after-school activities. Though Cassandra complained to Branscombe that the older girls asked "too many questions," she tried to respond to each query. However, she frequently omitted words, inserted mysterious statements, and did not tie her response clearly to the queries of J and A.

The fourth letter from J (written on a day when A was absent) was an explosive protest against Cassandra's apparent failure to care about "making sense." The opening salutation was simply "Cassandra."

Hello. I just discovered you haven't written me a letter this week. I guess I'll have to struggle through this without your letter of response or A, shes not here today. Although your letters never were much to begin with. I'm probably better off talking to myself because your always so *damn* confusing. Maybe if you re-read or proof read your letters your might catch some of the strange things youve been saying. I think you probably try to say things with good intentions but it just comes out awkward with no meaning. Getting off the subject and forgetting the point your trying [to] make can happen to anyone every now and then but your constantly doing this. I have to give you credit for your handwritting and spelling, that's not the problem. Next letter try to make all of your sentences *clear*. Don't *assume* I know what your talking about. *Explain* everything.

I'm not trying to "get down on you" or "get on your case." But, before we become friends I have to know what your saying or asking to respond.

The letter was signed simply "J." Cassandra answered this outburst with a letter which contained no salutation and to which she signed her full name. After opening her letter with an apology for not writing the previous week, she gave J her philosophy of communication.

But you and I are to different person's you know. And I've tried to explain myself as much as I could, but somewho you just don't get the message. What do you mean about my letters being confusing. I explain the things I write about the best I know how. Maybe they are confusing to you but I understand what I write. I don't think that it's confusing to you. I think that you just felt like getting me told a little. And as for A. I know that she wasn't here, but I would like to know those [does] she feel the same as you. We're still friends in my book. and if it's something you want to know I'll try and make myself clear. I hope that this is not so *damn confusing*. And if it is the Hell with the stuff.

In her next letter, J indicated she realized her earlier letter had been "hard" on Cassandra, but she hoped that Cassandra had "learned something from it."

The remaining letters between the girls became longer, were more involved, and took up a wide variety of subjects. Cassandra began to anticipate points in her letters which might be confusing for the girls and asked them to let her know if they did not understand her.

As Thanksgiving and Christmas drew near, Cassandra's letters talked more and more about how she missed her mother and about the loneliness she would feel this holiday season. J responded by telling Cassandra about the loss of her own mother through divorce and by sharing her eventual conclusion that the loss had made her a strong person, depending on herself "mostly for everything." By the end of the term, the girls concluded they knew "plenty" about each other. For the final letter exchange, Cassandra wrote not a joint letter to J and A, but an individual letter to each girl. She indicated that the two girls were the "only friends" she had had all year; she singled out J as "the best friend of the year." At the top of her letter, she added the note "Maybe one day we will meet up as strangers, and become friends all over again."

Analysis of all of Cassandra's and Eugene's letters is illustrated in Figures 1 and 2, and Table 1. Letters to upperclassmen are marked simply by numerals; those to Shannon Heath are marked S1; those to Shirley Heath are designated H1, etc. After the year ended, we examined with the students their writings for evidence of ways in which they had achieved the five general goals set by Branscombe for the class and ways they had changed their uses of language as they became more active members of an audience community. Our focus in this analysis is on "discourse topic"—not a simple noun phrase, but "a proposition about which some claim is

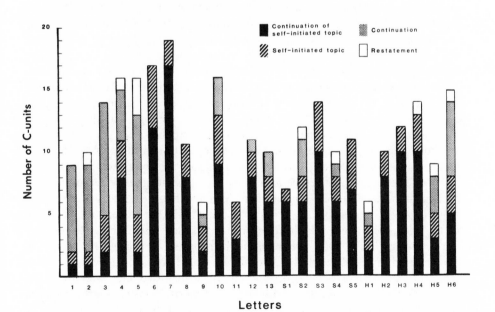

Figure 1. Eugene: Topic analysis.

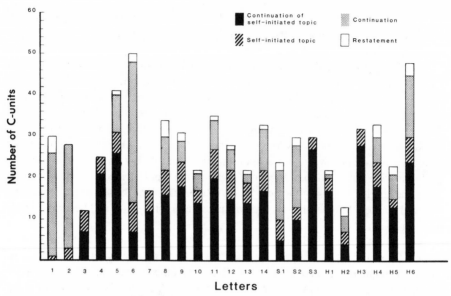

Figure 2. Cassandra: Topic analysis.

made or elicited'' (Keenan & Schieffelin, 1976, p. 380). Figures 1 and 2 illustrate
the extent to which Eugene and Cassandra shifted from a pattern of simply responding to their correspondents' topics—often without a restatement of the topic—to
initiating topics and providing sustained commentary on them. We interpret their
shifts as evidence of increased concern with "making sense" as well as engaging
the audience. Of the total number of communication units (groups of words that
cannot be further divided without loss of the essential meaning of the unit; cf. Loban
1963, 1976; Watts, 1967) in each letter, the percentages indicate the proportion the
student used to: (a) simply respond by continuing a topic introduced in their correspondent's previous letter (Continuation); (b) restate the topic introduced in their
correspondent's previous letter (Restatement); (c) introduce a new topic (Self-initiated topic); and (d) continue the self-initiated topic (Continuation of self-initiated
topic). In their early letters, Cassandra and Eugene usually answered the upperclassmen's letters without restatement of the topic, as though their responses were
contiguous parts of an oral conversation: M asked Eugene "Did you go to the
football game?" Eugene wrote "I did not make it to the last game, but I plan to go
to the game this week." In later letters, they added restatement: "About my
Thanksgiving. . . ." "Do you remember when you asked me about . . . ?" When
they initiated topics of their own choosing, they asked questions, recounted problems with teachers or homework, and described their activities with friends at
extracurricular events. As they made more and more comments on these topics,
their syntax became more mature, and they increased the numbers and types of
cohesive connectives by which they tied together their propositions and established

Table 1. General Features of Letters

	Eugene			Cassandra	
Letters	N of words	N of format features	Letters	N of words	N of format features
H6	166	4	H6	370	4
H5	88	1	H5	213	4
H4	112	2	H4	274	4
H3	118	2	H3	254	2
H2	106	4	H2	102	2
H1	55	2	H1	171	3
S5	116	4	S3	226	3
S4	97	3	S2	211	4
S3	164	5	S1	223	1
S2	112	3	14	246	1
S1	62	4	13	143	2
13	116	5	12	205	2
12	100	1	11	273	2
11	47	6	10	166	2
10	112	6	9	263	2
9	45	5	8	245	2
8	111	3	7	99	1
7	154	4	6	336	2
6	131	4	5	272	2
5	131	3	4	196	1
4	141	3	3	83	2
3	109	3	2	214	1
2	91	2	1	223	1
1	81	2			

continuity within a single letter and across letters.[5] Initially, they used primarily additive and adversative connectives (such as *and* and *but*), but by their fourth and fifth letters to the upperclassmen, and consistently in their letters to Shirley Heath, they made more use of connectives of the causal and temporal types (such as *so that* and *when*) (Halliday & Hasan, 1976).

Indications of the two general features of length and inclusion of format features in the letters of Cassandra and Eugene are given in Table 1. The bare feature of

---

[5] "Mature" syntax has, since the work of Harrell (1957), Hunt (1964), Loban (1963), and McCarthy (1964), been judged as containing more subordination, "movables," and compound predicates with a single subject than "less mature" syntax. In the past decade, linguists (e.g. Brown & Yule, 1983; Halliday & Hasan, 1976) have contributed ways of analyzing texts to illustrate how writers use these surface features to handle given and new information and to provide cohesion and coherence within texts. This recent work informs our interpretation here of the processes of writing the students used. Provided in this article, however, is only an analysis of communication units (cf. Loban, 1963), because we wanted a method of analysis in which Eugene and Cassandra could participate and through which they would gain practice in grammatical analysis which would readily transfer to their ongoing study in the high-school English curriculum.

length is, no doubt, far less meaningful as an indicator of writing maturity than other features included in our analysis. However, since neither Eugene nor Cassandra had previously written extended prose, we interpreted their increasing voluntary lengthening of their letters as indications of their general growth of engagement with both writing and audience. With each correspondent (upperclassmen, Shannon Heath, and Shirley Heath), the first letter was brief, and subsequent letters in which they built on shared background were longer. To be sure, certain pushes and pulls affected the length of specific letters. For example, Eugene's 4th, 5th, and 6th letters described his knee accident and detailed the progress of the injury and its effects on his participation in sports. His 7th letter was all about a motorbike he had borrowed; he described his adventures with the bike in detail. Letters 12 and 13 described his knee surgery; he included the procedures and descriptions of the equipment. Eugene's letter 11 was, however, short; it was in response to a very despondent letter from M, who had learned that he would no longer be able to participate in sports activities, because an old injury to his hand was not healing. In Eugene's words: "I don't know what to say." Clearly we cannot expect a consistent increase in length of letters over the term or year. The students' letter were *responses* in the fullest sense of that word, and the appropriate response was sometimes short and sometimes long.

Since Branscombe gave no specific instructions on format features of letters, the students had to learn how to format their letters by imitating the letters of the upperclassmen, or, in Cassandra's case, letters written in her first-year typing class, begun in the second semester. Though both students indicated in a writing inventory at the beginning of the year that they wrote and received letters very rarely, they used bare rudiments of standard letter format in their opening letters to the upperclassmen. Credit is noted in Table 1 for the inclusion in each letter (in correct place and with appropriate content) of entry of date, salutation, closing, signature, postscript, notice of enclosure with letter, and paragraphing. Cassandra opened and closed her letters to the upperclassmen as though she were in an oral conversation: "hello, J" and "Goodby." Only in the first letter to Shirley Heath, which she typed in typing class, did she use a "Dear——" salutation, and in subsequent letters to Heath, she closed routinely with "Cassandra Pitts." In all her letters to Heath, she used the formal format for letters, and when appropriate, she included the notation of "enclosure" to indicate her fieldnotes were enclosed.

Eugene did not paragraph any of his early letters, but M, in his sixth letter to Eugene, wrote: "you need to use paragraphs on your paper. If you don't know how, Mrs. Branscombe will show you how." Eugene did not ask Branscombe, and in his 9th letter to Eugene, M noted that Eugene had not reformed his writing: "You need to start using paragraphs. Try to make your paper look something like this." M's "model" letter had three paragraphs, each on a different topic. In Eugene's next letter, he began paragraphing conventionally; he wrote one paragraph about his weekend activities, another about career night, and a final one about the Christmas dance. He subsequently used paragraphs in all his letters which exceeded 80 words.

Throughout the year, voluntary reading increased along with the volume of the students' writing. As the students read more, they also introduced new topics from their reading into their writing. During the first semester, they read letters from the upperclassmen and Heath, as well as news clippings, magazines, and short stories. Branscombe also read aloud to the students and provided audiovisual materials on ethnography. In the second semester, members of the class read four novels. Though only three of the students had previously read through an entire book, Branscombe introduced the assignment of the novels as a natural sequence in their learning. The class read some portions aloud, just as they often read aloud letters from the upperclassmen and Shannon. Branscombe photocopied Heath's letters for each member of the class, and they read these orally together, negotiating meaning and interpretations as a community.

In the final month of class, the group carried out a community reading inventory—a questionnaire designed to collect information about the reading and writing habits of members of their communities. Before attempting to use the inventory elsewhere, the students practiced collecting information from each other in class; in the process, they critiqued the form and content of the questionnaire (which had been obtained from an international agency for use in developing nations). They read aloud to fellow classmates passages of the questionnaire and talked about its questions and possible responses. Their group reading followed the pattern of social interaction and group cooperation for negotiating meanings of texts described elsewhere for adults in a community similar in many cultural traits to their own (Trackton, Chap. 6, Heath, 1983). One member read aloud, others commented on the meaning of single words or sentences, and together, at the conclusion of the reading, they discussed the meaning of the text. For example, students often had questions about vocabulary and sentence meaning in Heath's letters. Specific vocabulary items prompted definition by members of the group; for example, Eugene responded to a fellow classmate's general nondirected request for an explanation of "avert" with "Avert mean to look away" (Field notes Feb. 18, 1982).

During the year, the students became increasingly aware of the need to step back from talking and writing and to make comments about how the sounds and words themselves were working. Since the students wrote their letters in the midst of a great deal of classroom talk by Branscombe and other class members about language, we expected the students to demonstrate an increased awareness of "language as such" (Olson, 1984) in their writing. We take their comments to indicate not only metalinguistic awareness, but also a sense of the limits and possibilities of writing as compared with speaking. For example, their comments included the following: "I would tell you her name, but I don't know how to spell it" (Eugene, letter 4); "I am sorry I did not wright you back. The top part is what I started wrighting on the 5 of the mounth. But it will go good with the last letter you wrote" (Eugene, letters 5, 6). Casssandra frequently commented that she hoped her handwriting and her spelling were correct or that she had made herself clear.

The growth of complexity in writing as responder and communicator noted here should be viewed with the understanding that in the first semester, Branscombe gave the students only one class period (50 minutes) each week to read letters from the upperclassmen and to write their letters in response, with no time for revising or copying. The increase in voluntary extended prose length, use of format features, idea initiations, types of conjunctions, and metalinguistic comments came not through teacher-directed revisions of the same pieces, but through "natural" needs that evolved as the ninth graders developed more topics on which they wanted to share information with the upperclassmen and as they became more inquisitive about how the upperclassmen felt about issues and ideas. Their only way of maintaining this social relation was through letters, since they did not see their respondents. Thus their development as writers came about for one of the primary reasons writing in the real world occurs: when direct face-to-face interaction or oral communication by telephone is not possible.

Decontextualizing Communicator–Audience Relations

In January, when letter writing to the 11th and 12th graders was no longer feasible, the 9th graders began writing to Shannon and Shirley Heath. This change of correspondents prompted new types of writing tasks. Near the end of the first term, Branscombe gave the 9th graders a list of questions and asked that they write autobiographical essays which could provide a substantive introduction of themselves to anyone. However, Heath would be receiving these before beginning the regular letter exchange in January. In this task, for the first time since their introductory essays written before the pairing for letter exchanges with the upperclassmen, they had to focus on presenting background information about topics on which their readers had very little or no shared experience. These essays were 3 to 10 pages in length and included answers to the following questions:

1. Who am I? Who are my family members? How does it feel to be a member of my family?
2. Where do I live? Where have I lived? Which did I like best and why?
3. Have I ever lost someone? How did it feel?
4. What do I want for myself?
5. What's my oldest relative like? Who is he/she? What does he/she do? Does he/she give advice? Tell a story about this person.

These essays forced the students to write about certain topics, and students had choice only of ways to orient the topic in response to each question. Neither Branscombe nor Heath gave any direct feedback on the essays (yet Cassandra apparently conceived Branscombe as her specific audience, since the response to nearly every question contained a vocative to her teacher.) Illustrations of the ways in which she and Eugene handled parts of this assignment follow.

Cassandra—in answer to the question "How does it feel to be a member of my family?—wrote:

It's just wonderful. I thank God for letting each of us have our lives together every night. I don't care how much we argue I still love them dearly. There's no telling where I might be if I didn't have the family that I so much love. My dearly-beloved mom's gone, but there are all that I have left. So I will pray that we stay together for as long as I'm a teenager. And longer if possible, but I no that someday we will have to grow up and depart. and I'm quite ready to take that step. All I need is just a little more adjustment's. You never no how it really feels to lose a love one until it's to late. And then it's to late. Well I no how its feels and I need the family that I have left. So help me pray to be a success in life, Miss Branscombe.

Cassandra began the answer to each question on a separate sheet of paper, opening the page with the question. In answer to the opening question about who her family was, she listed the name, relation, and age of each member of the family before discussing her relationship with each.

Eugene chose to answer the questions in only three pages, beginning the first page with the all-encompassing question, "Who am I?" In answer to the question about his vocational plans for the future, Eugene wrote:

When I finish High school I plan to go to college. When I finish college, I want to join the Navy Aviation and become a pilot. They make a good money. But the only thing I don't like is the years I have to put in. I guess that's the price you have to pay. But that is not all I would like to do I would all so like to own some different business such as car lots, oil wells, grocery stores, farms, and a lot of other things. After I have come out of the navy aviation if I am lucky I can go into commercial flying. And I promise my self not to fall short of my goals. Each time I reach my goal I will set a higher. But I will never just think about my self when I am a sucess I will always help other people to become a sucess to. I do plan to get married and have children and name my son after me. I do not really know where I want to live but I was thinking about Las Vagas.

Eugene was quick to question any piece of writing which did not have an immediately identifiable purpose and audience. He ruled out Shannon and Shirley Heath as audiences for his autobiography, because he wanted them to get to know him just as he would have to learn about them—through letters. Thus he felt that his autobiography had to contain only the bare essentials of facts about him and his feelings.

Throughout the second term, Branscombe asked the students to write paragraphs about certain topics. She sometimes asked the class to negotiate the topics; on other occasions, she assigned them. However, students saw no purpose or audience for these paragraphs, and they rejected these assignments because they "don't teach us anything."

In their correspondence with the upperclassmen, the ninth graders had focused on topics of the here-and-now, such as school dances, local hangouts, and school sports; these scenes and events had been familiar to their readers, and they had needed to write few detailed descriptions. With the exception of Cassandra's discussions of past holidays with her mother, their letters had contained almost no references to events in the distant past or to abstractions, such as hopes, plans, or assessments of people or activities not directly and currently involved in their lives.

Branscombe saw the autobiographies, paragraphs, and letters to Heath as occasions to force the students to communicate to distant, unknowing audiences the following types of information: (a) detailed explanations and assessments of past events, (b) descriptions of current scenes, actions, and people, and (c) arguments defending their course of action, point of view, or interpretation. Writing in the second term was designed to enable students to move beyond the highly contextualized personal and immediate topics they had addressed in their letters to the upperclassmen. They wrote letters to Shannon Heath (S1–5), letters to Shirley Heath (H1–6), field notes, field-site descriptions, and data interpretations in essay form. In addition to different functions, forms and content, these writings had different audiences; moreover, feedback and response varied greatly. Figure 3 graphically represents the role of students as initiators in the four phases of their writing during the year.

Letters between Shannon Heath and the class as a whole were a bridge between the letters to the upperclassmen and those to Shirley Heath. After the ninth graders responded to the autobiography and paragraph assignments with little enthusiasm, Branscombe reasoned that writing to a young peer would be a useful transition from the personalized individual responses the upperclassmen had given the ninth graders to the nonpersonalized letters Heath would be writing to the class. Each member of the class wrote Shannon, but she responded with a letter to the class as a whole; her topics were similar to those of the upperclassmen: boy–girl relations, weekend activities, etc. However, since Shannon's site was different from theirs, the students quickly realized that there were topics for which neither she nor they had any context. Thus they had to describe scenes, actions, and people in their school and town to Shannon, and they asked that she tell them about her school—its physical layout, privileges, and academic program. Moreover, in her first letter to the students, Shannon told them that she often traveled with her mother when she did her anthropological fieldwork, and the ninth graders picked up this topic and asked many questions about where, when, and how Shannon traveled, what she did about school, and how she felt about travel to foreign places. In turn, the students explained the kinds of travel possible to them in and around their home town.

Shannon was, however, an unsatisfactory correspondent in comparison with the upperclassmen: she did not write often (only three letters during the semester), she almost never answered the students' questions, and she did not personalize her responses. For example, she did not respond to Eugene's request for more information about competitive swimming, her major extracurricular activity, nor did she acknowledge in any way a lengthy letter he wrote about his own swimming. The ninth graders, in their initial letters to Shannon, tried to get her to respond to them individually. When it became clear that she was not writing to the class on a regular basis, their goal shifted to getting her to respond at all. They tried the same tactics with Shannon that the upperclassmen had used with them: asking many questions and picking up and extending topics known to be of interest to her. For example, in

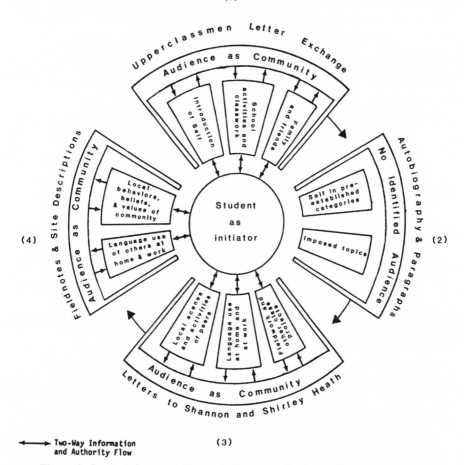

(1)

Figure 3. Student Opportunities as Information Initiator: The Four Phases.

his first letter to Shannon, Eugene asked 5 questions, and all his subsequent letters to her, with the exception of the final letter, included questions. Eugene asked about the rules of Shannon's school, whether or not the school had drink machines, and what she did in her spare time.

Cassandra asked more personal information, following the style she had established in her correspondence with J and A. Cassandra wanted to set up a girl-to-girl friendship; her questions revolved around boyfriends, views of proper sexual behavior, and rules for dating. In an attempt to get Shannon to respond to these, Cassandra also asked questions about Shannon's views and commented on her own background experiences as a "black girl": "we has entirely too many girls pregnant (and they are all black and unmarried). I would like to no, is it that bad where you live? Do they not care, or is just young & need a good parent, friend to talk to them and tell them all better. Well I've thought about that, and that doesn't work. Some of the parents do talk, and it comes in one ear and flies out the other.'' After this letter, to which Shannon did not respond, Cassandra did not try again to open correspondence with Shannon. However, she did not indict Shannon. Instead, in her final letter to Shirley Heath, she spoke of Shannon as a distant other in a positive way and avoided comment on Shannon's failure to be a responsive letter writer: ''I can see that you are so proud of Shannon. So am I. She's something special. May be because of the wonderful parents that kicking her in the rear end. I hope that Shannon will pass the test [AP History Test]. But with your help, and her father, she will. Even if she doesn't, I know she would have tried her very best.''

Eugene, on the other hand, indicts Shannon in his final letter to her and comments on the futility of writing to a nonresponsive audience. He indicates he knows she will not write again; the year is ending, and she has no time to write: ''when I wrote to you I talked about swimming but you did not comment on the letter but it's too late to know. I would ask you what you are going to be doing this summer but you could not answer.''

Writing to Shannon had bridged the highly contextualized letters of the upperclassmen and the more decontextualized, nonpersonalized letters to Heath and ultimately the standard classroom assignments of interpretive essays. Shannon had not tied her responses directly to the interests of the students; she had written as though to a nonpersonalized general audience, and she had addressed topics which were not directly translatable into the experiences of the ninth graders.

Shirley Heath's letters continued the transition from the here-and-now familiar personal-needs-directed writing to composition tasks which focused on distant unfamiliar depersonalized topics. Heath wrote her letters on a word processor, often printing them without proofreading for typographical errors or incoherent sentences. The letters were usually long—literally and figuratively, since they were printed on running computer paper. Most were more than forty inches in length; on standard-sized paper, they would have been 3 to 4 pages. Heath wrote on only 3 topics: her background as an anthropologist interested in language (giving minimal information about her family and daily life); previous travels and a trip to Brazil which took place in mid-March of 1982; and her reactions to the students' letters and tapes of their interviews with members of their community. Within the first topic, she focused on methods of the anthropologist: how to get to know people in social groups, how to observe and record language and accompanying behaviors, how to interview informants, and how to analyze and compare data.

When Heath went to Brazil, she had to postpone a tentative trip to visit the ninth graders. Several class members, especially Eugene, saw this postponement as an indication of lack of interest and commitment on Heath's part. Eugene wrote: ''I would like to know why you are doing this what are you doing to gain by doing this and the way things are going I believe you have changed you're mind about coming and don't want us to know and I don't believe you are coming if you are not coming you are wasting our time'' (letter H3). The class discussed Eugene's comment, and while some classmates condemned him for being unfair and argued he was wrong, others admired his courage. During the trip, Heath sent postcards to individual students in the class, and on her return, she sent a package to the class with an individual present and brief message for each student. In Eugene's next letter, he tried to repair the damage: "I am sorry for the way I was acting when we first started writing these letters to you. If you will remember I got upset when you said that you would not be able to come and when I thought you were not answering my questions in the letters I proble caused some trouble with you." After the students received Heath's long letter describing what she had done in Brazil, Eugene wrote, trying to put into practice what he had learned about the kinds of questions anthropologists ask: "What did you eat there and How did the people act what were you looking for there and did you go the poor part of Brazil where the kids are stavering [starving]" (letter H5).

After the Brazil trip, Heath shifted the style of her letters to students by omitting vocatives and first and second person; she embedded directives in long depersonalized explanations, and omitted reference to why the materials or tasks she discussed would be important to either her or to the students. An early letter to the students had contained the following:

It is important to tell you why I am interested in these everyday things [daily habits of reading and writing], so you won't think I am just wanting to be sticking my nose in everybody else's business. Anthropologists collect field notes from people all over the world and look at what they do that is alike and what they do that is different. Your field notes, if you remember to tell me as much as you possibly can, will help me compare the things you tell me with the field notes I have taken in other parts of the world. I will know whether old people in your community and old people in Papua New Guinea start remembering things from their childhood at about the same time. I will be able to tell whether people in your neighborhood talk to babies the same way that people in Australia talk to their babies. Do people coo and talk baby talk to a young baby in your community? Have you ever thought about that? In some parts of the world, adults do that, and in other parts of the world, they don't. Do you think baby talk helps a child learn to talk faster or not?

In these early letters, Heath personalized her messages, explained the reasons for the tasks she asked the students to do, and gave examples of the kinds of questions and data she collected and wanted from them.

By midsemester, she wrote of her trip to Brazil entirely in the third person.

The churches are beautiful, because they were built 200 years ago and modeled on the big and beautiful churches of Europe. The people in the country are mostly Catholic. There are many celebrations there for Lent and Easter, but these celebrations are also heavily influenced by African traditions. Slaves were brought to Brazil 200 years ago to work the sugar plantations, and later the rubber plantations. In the northeast, there are today many African descendants who have continued to live there and have become landowners and businessmen. They have many celebrations which are very African, different kinds of dress for special occasions, and beautiful music and dance.

Often throughout the letters, Eugene spoke of the difficulties of "hearing" the speaker in letters, and of his desire to be "heard." In response to the first letter which reflected Heath's shift to a depersonalized style, Eugene said: "I don't hear her when you say it [when Branscombe or other class members read the letter aloud]. I don't hear her answer *my* questions when she sticks it up in the letter. Like when I ask her the question about coming—she'll say I'm sorry I didn't get to come. I see it but I don't know it or hear it. If she repeats the question that I asked then I know it's the answer to my question. I'll see this time cause I ask her some direct questions" (letter H6). Early in the semester, Eugene had tried to persuade Heath that she should write individual letters to each student:

I may be wrong but I don't think so. You see Miss Branscombe is having all of us write to you. But in your last letter you only said that you would only write to some of us and I think that you should write to all of us. Because all of us are writing to you. If you don't want to write to me than I want [won't] write to you or take any field notes. I think you will agree with me if you dont then put your self in our shoes and if you still dont then let me know. (letter H2)

Even though members of the class had individual photocopies of each of Heath's letters, and the group read them aloud (often many times), discussing each paragraph and stopping at confusing sentences, Eugene wanted a personal voice communicating to him, either through individual letters or specific acknowledgment that certain information was in response to the questions he had asked. He and others of the class resisted moving away from the highly personalized here-and-now written "conversations" they had had with the upperclassmen. Yet by the end of the term, they had learned to negotiate through oral discussion the meaning of the depersonalized and decontextualized passages of Heath's letters. Perhaps most important, they retained their questioning habits from their correspondence with the upperclassmen, continually asking Heath to explain herself, to clarify points, to add more information, and to relate points she made in her letters to points of information she or they had included in earlier letters. They also learned to select general information from Heath's letters and apply this to specific situations. They grew more confident about communicating with different audiences on a range of topics about which they either had knowledge or wanted to learn.

Acquiring Written Language

Numerous studies of young children learning to write (e.g., Ferreiro & Teberosky, 1982; Goelman, Oberg, & Smith, 1984) provide windows on the cognitive and social processes of young children using writing for social interaction and self-initiated expression. The yearlong project described here allows us to look at how two students, judged in their previous schooling as mentally inferior and needing special education, learned to write in an interactive cycle. We argue that previous schooling had in essence denied writing as a form of communication to these students; in many ways, this extended denial of a channel of communication by an institution is analogous to the severe and extremely rare cases of parents who shut their children off from verbal and social interaction at birth and prevent them from learning to talk (Curtis, 1976). However, the school's shutting off of written communication for students designated as not "intelligent" enough to write extended prose is an accepted event which occurs frequently. These ninth graders, denied early written language development, condensed into one nine-month period the learning about writing as communication which young children in regular classrooms acquire over several years. Although recent research (e.g. Graves, 1982; Harste, Woodward, & Burke, 1984) shows that primary-level classrooms in which extensive writing takes place are rare, students in the accelerated or regular tracks of the curriculum have many more opportunities to use written language for communication than children in special education classes do.

Within the rich and highly diverse communication network that Branscombe's basic English class gave them, these ninth graders were able to acquire fundamental concepts and skills of proficient writers. Although at the end of the year, many of the special conventions of writing, such as spelling, placement of periods, apostrophes, and other marks of punctuation still did not come naturally or consistently, the students had learned to communicate effectively—to extract information from others, to share their personal opinions and emotions, and to step into the reader's place sufficiently to be able to "hear" their writing as their readers would. Through modeling their letters after those of their correspondents, the students left behind many of the mechanical errors of their early letters, and with brief, specific instruction on certain points later in the year, they immediately changed these habits. For example, when Heath visited in May, she pointed out, in a long conversation with Cassandra about her fieldwork, the need to distinguish uses of apostrophes and the proper spellings of *to, two,* and *too,* as well as *no* and *know.* In a few minutes of illustration and explanation, Heath indicated when and why writers used apostrophes to show possession and when they used them to show omission, as in contractions. In subsequent letters to Heath, Cassandra made no further errors in spelling these words or using apostrophes. She commented about ways in which she reviewed her writing to check herself by the rules they had discussed, and she asked "Why hadn't anyone ever told me about apostrophes like this?"

Specific analyses in Figures 1 and 2 and Table 1 include only the personal writing of the students, and not their field notes, essays, fieldsite descriptions, etc. Analysis of these letters indicates how the surface structures of the earliest letters reflect the students acquiring a "writing voice" (Moffett, 1981). Describing young children acquiring oral language, Vygotsky (1978) maintained that internal speech and reflective thought of the young child arise from the social interactions between the child and others. Subsequently, language becomes internalized to organize thought and increasingly difficult mental functions. The child gradually learns to differentiate between himself as audience of his thoughts and others as audience. With this functional differentiation comes the realization that external, overt social speech, unlike internalized speech, must contain linguistic devices and background information in explicated form if the addressee is to understand the speaker. Similarly, the novice writer must learn to differentiate between egocentric writing and writing for social, communicative purposes. With "the writing voice" comes the ability to put oneself in the place of the reader and anticipate areas of confusion or misunderstanding and thus to express oneself after having "preplayed" the message as a listener (for example, J's early letter to Cassandra trying to get her to proofread her letters and Eugene's reminder to Heath that if she could not understand his argument for personal letters rather than class letters, she should put herself in "our place").

Mitchell and Taylor (1979, p. 250) emphasize the "integrating perspective" students gain from having a responding audience for their writing. They depict the cycle of communication as being from writer to written product through the writing process. The written product is then transmitted to an audience who either does or does not provide feedback through the responding process. Drawing on Moffett's application of Vygotsky's theories of the social interactive nature of early oral language development, we suggest that novice writers have to learn through dyadic writing interactions the social—and consequently the linguistic—prerequisites of written language as communication. This dyadic writing need not be in the form of letters, though across grade levels and subject areas, letters can serve multiple roles in the curriculum.

Student writers must, however, learn for written communication—just as they have learned for oral language—that communication is negotiation. When direct response is not possible through a return letter, the writer must play the role of writer *and* reader, anticipating and hypothesizing the kinds of information the reader will bring to the text and the questions which, therefore, the writer must explicitly answer. This social interaction is similar to the process through which children acquiring oral language move as they learn to handle discourse topics—to adjust, clarify, expand, or abandon their efforts to communicate with listeners. Crisis in communication is a natural part of this learning process; at some point in learning to write, students must have the experience of an audience which responds, "I don't understand you. What do you mean?"

Linguists who have studied child language acquisition have described the rules which children need to learn in order to be able to handle the notion of discourse topic in oral discourse; these rules parallel those which novice writers must learn to produce coherent prose.

Step 1: The speaker [writer] must secure the attention of the listener [reader]. The listener [reader] must attend to the speaker's [writer's] utterance [written message].

Step 2: The speaker [writer] must articulate his utterance [written message] clearly. The listener [reader] must decipher the speaker's [writer's] utterance [written message].

Step 3: The speaker [writer] must provide sufficient information for the listener [reader] to identify objects, individuals, ideas, events, etc. included in the discourse topic. The listener [reader] must identify those objects, individuals, ideas, events, etc., that play a role in the discourse topic.

Step 4: The speaker [writer] must provide sufficient information for the listener [reader] to reconstruct the semantic relations obtaining between referents in the discourse topic. The listener [reader] must identify the semantic relations obtaining between referents in the discourse topic (Keenan & Schieffelin, 1976, pp. 349–350).

These rules, which hold for young children who learn over several years of redundant repetitive interactions to handle discourse topics orally, are also those the novice writer must acquire. Occasions for multiple and redundant meaningful written interactions can enable novice writers to learn, for example, that in writing letters, if they wish to focus on a topic that has not been part of the previous written communication, they must be certain that the reader will realize what this topic is; they must therefore both alert the reader that they are addressing a new topic and introduce the presuppositions of the topic.

Without an interactive cycle of feedback and response, writers—especially those denied early access to productive and receptive uses of written information—cannot learn how to preplay the communicative cycle. Such writers need repeated, redundant, and long-term experience in putting themselves in the positions of both writer *and* audience by having experience in both writing and responding—both of which are inner intermediating processes. Students must not only be responded to, but they must respond themselves; by seeing how others fail to take them into consideration as audience in their writing, they learn to hypothesize themselves as audience. Shaughnessy (1977) indicates this interplay between expectations and "errors" when she points out that student "neophyte" writers make single propositions, but often do not know how to elaborate that proposition and thus move on to another. The neophyte writer leaves the intermediating process entirely to the reader. Shaughnessy thus sees a central instructional task of teaching writing to be one of making students aware of the needs and expectations of their readers.

In many respects, these 9th-grade students learning to write share many characteristics of the learning process which young children acquiring speech go through as they interact with their interlocutors. Moreover, the students' tasks in writing and their frequent oral and written responses to these tasks illustrate what "contextualization" and "decontextualization" meant to them in their writing. Scholars studying linguistic and cognitive processing frequently define and use these terms in connection with classroom learning; the ninth graders in Branscombe's class operationalized these terms from their own viewpoints.

The two students described in this case study began writing with a limited set of purposes, primarily as respondents to instrumental and regulatory language about here-and-now topics of others. In their early letters, they were passive links in a written conversational chain; they did not frequently initiate topics. They were like very young children hearing others speak to them but speaking little in return and communicating largely through the efforts of the parent or intimate who tries either to voice or to clarify their intentions and meanings for them (cf. Ochs, 1982). As the students began to initiate ideas themselves and to have content they wanted to expand, they used language for an expanded set of functions—interactional and personal, as well as heuristic and imaginative (Halliday, 1975). To accomplish these functions, they had, however, to learn to anticipate the presuppositions and intentions of their respondents. They could not rely on context, direct speech, or oral conversational supports such as "You know" to confirm that their respondents made sense of their writing. More and more, they used writing to establish and maintain interpersonal relations, exchange information, try to regulate the behavior of their respondents, and ask questions or seek information. Moreover, they began to play with language as such, and they commented on the limits of the written word. They created hypothetical situations and used conditional propositions in which they asked readers to put themselves in their places. In letter 11 to J, Cassandra ended a self-initiated discussion of her grades as follows:

I study true enough, but time that test is handed out to me, my mind go blank. I had this problem before my mother died, but now it's worst. Sometimes I think if I knew the teacher better I could do at least 5% better. What do knowing a teacher better have to do with my lesson or shall I say work.

Cassandra here anticipated her reader's reaction, and though she did not explain away what she felt might be viewed as a "stupid" statement, she acknowledged that her reader might be confused. She used language to show she could switch roles with her readers and express not only her concerns about a topic but also those they might have.

Once they shifted from writing the upperclassmen to writing Shannon and Shirley Heath, the students had to move from here-and-now topics on shared information available to both parties in the immediate environment. They had to explicate background information on the location of certain workplaces, their own communities, the layout of specific buildings in which they were describing language uses, etc. In their earlier letters, only a few topics, such as a hospital stay and surgery, had required extended explication of background. Even their alternative school newspaper had focused on current topics and issues known to all their readers—fellow high school students. Branscombe's list of questions for the autobiographical essays, written near the end of the first term, provided the first opportunity for the ninth graders to write to an "unknowing audience." In Heath's letters, she reminded the students that she was also "unknowing": she did not know what they knew, and they would have to explain in detail what they wanted her to understand.

During the second semester, Branscombe continued to ask the students to do more and more writing in which they had to explicate. She read parts of Studs Terkel's *Working* to the class and asked the students to watch someone working for two days and write a full description of his or her language at work. Heath's constant requests for field notes and field-site descriptions gave other opportunities for the students to address topics about which they had to provide presuppositions and also writing tasks which did not have an immediate respondent. For these field notes and site descriptions, Heath wrote detailed critiques of ways the students expressed detail, provided background data on speakers, and indicated the time, setting, and contexts of their field notes. To improve their next piece of work, the students had to read these critiques embedded in Heath's letters, connect the general information to their own writing, and infer the skills they should use in collecting and recording information; in Eugene's terms, the students had to "hear" Heath speaking directly to them. Numerous lapses of communication occurred. Heath was not patient, often insisting that a particular site or person be visited several times for data collection. Heath, moreover, often wrote incoherent sentences, and she usually did not directly answer students' specific questions. Branscombe could serve as an oral intermediary on only some topics, for she often did not know how to speak for Heath or interpret passages of her letters. Thus the students each week returned to their tasks and to their personal letters to Heath with renewed efforts to make themselves clear, express their distress about the miscommunications, and ask for clarifications from Heath. The fact that they could not communicate orally with her forced them to call on all their resources for making communication happen in their letters.

The students' maturity as writers developed in accord with situations similar to those of young children who want something, are misunderstood, and must use oral language to have their needs met. Over the year, the students had to learn, just as the child acquiring spoken language must learn, that their respondents did not have access to their thoughts and past experiences, and they had to share this knowledge and their emotions explicitly to be skillful in communicating. Cassandra, at the beginning of the year, clearly needed and wanted to talk with J and A about her mother's death. Her first reference to the death was, however, embedded in a one-sentence answer to their question about whether or not she played sports: "Well I'm sure about the volleyball team. But I do like volleyball. And my mind was on basketball until my mother passed about two weeks ago. But there's plenty of time before try-outs (letter 2)." By her ninth letter to J and A, she responded to their questions about her Christmas plans by talking at length about what was on her mind: "Well the problem is this will be my first Christmas without my *Mom!* And I don't quite no how to handle it. She's always on my mind. And last night I cryed my heart out thinking about her. I tryed calling my boyfriend but couldn't even find any words. I tried calling a friend and she was talking about all the fun that she and her Mother was going to share this Christmas. And I ended up hanging the phone up on her. She called back but I had already broke out into so many tears that there was no reason for me to try and hold them back" (letter 9). She followed shortly after this letter with a long essay on her mother in response to the autobiographical assignment in which Branscombe asked "Have I ever lost someone? How did it feel?" In letters to both Shannon and Shirley Heath, Cassandra wrote often of her mother, her current family situation, and her fears about her own future.

We maintain that just as the development of oral language depends on the context of the rich interaction between child and adults, so the development of written language depends on a rich responsive context. This context is especially critical for older students who have reached high school without opportunity to participate in any extended interactive writing. Young children acquiring language *search for units of symbolic behavior, construct systems of elements and relations, and try to match their production to those of selected others in recurrent situational contexts;* the new writer must follow similar steps to generate internal rules for writing to communicate. Responsive, interactive writing frequently occurring over a period of time provides the data from which students may search out meaningful units and systems in writing.

For example, both Eugene and Cassandra discovered in the upperclassmen's letters that openings and salutations were units of letters. Similarly, they gradually became aware of ways in which their correspondents restated topics introduced in previous letters, and they began adopting these units: e.g., "About my grades [etc.]. . . ." As they wrote more and more, they developed their own systems for restating topics from their respondents' letters, introducing topics, and continuing their own commentaries. To check their readers' understanding, they employed different strategies. Eugene used conditional propositions: "If you don't . . . , then . . ." Cassandra used rephrasings to make her point clear: "I can't make up my mind what to get my boyfriend for Christmas have any suggestions. And my father—I might have to decide that for myself, but what are some good things you would get your Father. Any advice will do." Moreover, their respondents often pointed out areas which did not match their own letter-writing. For example, M reminded Eugene that *here* was not spelled *her;* that paragraphing should follow the model of his letter; J and A reminded Cassandra to watch her spelling and to introduce topics with restatements so they could know what she was talking about. Both Eugene and Cassandra were reminded by the upperclassmen to read their letters over and "listen" to how they sounded and decide whether or not they made sense. As Cassandra and Eugene wrote more and more, they elaborated on the metalinguistic aspects of writing and the bonding roles which written texts play across the physical distance between reader and writer. In Cassandra's words, she had made friends of strangers through her letters to J and A; if they met again, it would be as strangers. Eugene's final letter to Shannon called attention to the closure of their communication now that the year was ending and that there would be no more letters.

Both *imitation and rule generation* played a part in the acquisition of written language by Cassandra and Eugene. With varied responses from different people writing for different purposes within a long-term relationship between writer and audiences, these students gained enough input to be able to *generate the needed internal rules or knowledge about how to make writing work* to communicate their feelings and knowledge. These two students and others in their basic English class had previously had only minimal opportunities for writing so much as a single paragraph. They had had drills and exposure to the deductive rules of grammar along with endless dictates about "good writing," but they had not come to *own* these given rules. In their interactive writing, they internally generated rules through repeated trials and errors in attempting to communicate. These students truly *acquired* writing instead of learning simply to imitate styles of a limited number of types of decontextualized academic writing.

In the case of most of the pairs of letters-writers—ninth graders and upperclassmen, ninth graders and Shannon and Shirley Heath—crises in communication occurred which had to be negotiated in writing. Resolution of these crises came in part through the ninth graders' learning, in Virginia Woolf's terms, to see the "face beneath the page." The communicator–audience relation thus developed only through a processs of mutual adjustment, just as oral conversation or any other form of give-and-take discourse does. Listeners seek clarification, register misunderstanding and disagreement, and question their conversational partner's information. In writing, the same "sidewise process of dislocation, failed communication, and then readjusted contact" (Calhoun, 1970, p. 29) occurs.

Historians such as Calhoun have argued that the "intelligence of a nation" depends upon communicator–audience relations. Creativity and intelligence increase in accord with audience reactions: "a form of creation, supposedly individual and private, would thrive if bound in a healthy audience relationship" (Calhoun, 1970, p. 31). Immediate and real responses enabled Eugene and Cassandra, and the other formerly "special education" students of Branscombe's basic English class, to become "intelligent" writers within such an audience community.

References

Applebee, A. (1981). *Writing in the secondary school: English and the content areas.* (Research Report No. 21). Urbana, IL: National Council of Teachers of English.

Bernstein, B. (1975). *Class, codes, and control. Vol. 3: Toward a theory of educational transmission.* (2nd ed.) London: Routledge, Kegan, & Paul.

Bourdieu, P. (1973). Cultural reproduction and social reproduction. In R. Brown (Ed.), *Knowledge, education and cultural change: Papers in the sociology of education.* London: Tavistock.

Bourdieu, P., & Passeron, J. C. (1979). *Reproduction in education, society, and culture.* Beverly Hills, CA: Sage.

Bowles, S., & Gintis, H. (1975). *Schooling in capitalist America.* New York: Basic Books.

Brown, G., & Yule, G. (1983). *Discourse analysis.* Cambridge, England: Cambridge University Press.

Calhoun, D. (1970). *The intelligence of a people.* Princeton, NJ: Princeton University Press.

Curtis, S. (1976). *Genie.* New York: Academic Press.

Ferreiro, E., & Teberosky, A. (1982). *Literacy before schooling.* Trans. K Goodman Castro. Exeter, NH: Heinemann.

Goelman, H., Oberg, A., & Smith, F. (Eds.) (1984). *Awakening to literacy.* Exeter, NH: Heinemann.

Goswami, D., & Odell, L. (in press). *Teachers as learners, teachers as researchers.* Montclair, NJ: Boynton/Cook Publishers.

Graff, H. (1980). *The literacy myth.* New York: Academic Press.

Graves, D. (1983). *Writing: Teachers and children at work.* Exeter, NH: Heinemann.

Halliday, M. A. K. (1975). *Learning how to mean: Explorations in the development of language.* New York: Elsevier North-Holland.

Halliday, M. A. K., & Hasan, R. (1976). *Cohesion in English.* London: Longman.

Harrell, L. E. (1957). An inter-comparison of the quality and rate of the development of oral and written language in children. In *Monographs of the Society for Research in Child Development, 22*(3).

Harste, J. C., Woodward, V. A., & Burke, C. L. (1984). *Language stories and literacy lessons.* Portsmouth, NH: Heinemann.

Heath, S. B. (1981). Toward an ethnohistory of writing in American education. In M. F. Whiteman (Ed.), *Variation in writing: Functional and linguistic cultural differences.* Hillsdale, NJ: Lawrence Erlbaum.

Heath, S. B. (1983). *Ways with words: Language, life, and work in communities and classrooms.* Cambridge, England: Cambridge University Press.

Heath, S. B., & Thomas, C. (1984). The achievement of preschool literacy for mother and child. In H. Goelman, A. Oberg, & F. Smith (Eds.), *Awakening to literacy.* Exeter, NH: Heinemann.

Hunt, K. W. (1964). *Differences in grammatical structures written at three grade levels.* Report on Cooperative Research Project. Washington, DC: USOE.

Kaestle, C. (1980). Literacy and mainstream culture in American history. *Language Arts, 58*(2), 207–218.

Katz, M. (1968). *The irony of early school reform.* Cambridge, MA: Harvard University Press.

Keenan, E., & Schieffelin, B. (1976). Topic as discourse notion: A study of topic in the conversations of children and adults. In C. Li (Ed.), *Subject and topic.* New York: Academic Press.

Loban, W. D. (1963). *The language of elementary school children.* Champaign, IL: National Council of Teachers of English.

Loban, W. D. (1976). *Language development: Kindergarten through grade twelve.* Urbana, IL: National Council of Teachers of English.

McCarthy, D. (1964). Language development in children. In L. Carmichael (Ed.), *Manual of child psychology* (2nd ed.). New York: John Wiley.

Mitchell, R., & Taylor, M. (1979). The integrating perspective: An audience-response model for writing. *College English, 41*(3), 247–271.

Moffett, J. (1981). *Coming on center: English education in evolution.* Montclair, NJ: Boynton/Cook.

Ochs, E. (1982). Talking to children in western Samoa. *Language in Society, 11,* 77–104.

Olson, D. (1984). ''See! Jumping!'' Some oral language antecedents of literacy. In H. Goelman, A. Oberg, & F. Smith (Eds.), *Awakening to literacy.* Exeter, NH: Heinemann.

Shaughnessy, M. (1977). *Errors and expectations.* London: Oxford University Press.

Vygotsky, L. S. (1978). Interaction between learning and development. In M. Cole, V. John-Steiner, S. Scribner, & E. Souberman (Eds.), *Mind in society: The development of higher psychological processes.* Cambridge, MA: Harvard University Press.

Watts, A. F. (1967). *Language and mental development of children.* Toronto: Harrop & Co.

2

The Teacher as Respondent
to the High School Writer*

Saundra Dunn
Susan Florio-Ruane
Christopher M. Clark
Michigan State University

Introduction

Many teachers and theorists would accept as a truism the statement that the relationship between teacher and student matters a great deal when the business at hand is learning to write. Yet while it seems obvious that student writing and teacher response would be at the very heart of any successful writing curriculum, many of us find the task of responding to our student writers unwieldy and difficult. In addition, many of our students experience confusion about the purpose and meaning of the writing they do in our classrooms. Moreover, these problems seem greatest in the secondary school, often our last opportunity to ensure access of our students to written literacy by means of formal instruction. Here the roles of teacher and student in the writing process can be complex. Moffett (1983) asserts, for example, that for the high school teacher to act as audience is "a very delicate matter fraught with hazards that need special attention" (p. 193).

It is the aim of this chapter to explore the relationship of one teacher to his high school writers in one high school creative writing class. By means of the case study that follows, we hope to support and instantiate the assertion that the relationship between teacher and students matters a great deal when written literacy is at stake. We also hope, by portraying one teacher's approach to the role of respondent to his student writers, to encourage teachers to think about the many alternatives available to them when they work with young adult writers.

Elsewhere, we have written about constraints on the teacher's planning and instruction that are imposed by district mandates and policies and about the way these are managed by Mr. Jameson[1] in teaching his freshman English classes

---

* The work reported here is sponsored by the Institute for Research on Teaching, College of Education, Michigan State University. The Institute for Research on Teaching is funded primarily by the Teaching Division of the National Institute of Education, United States Department of Education. The opinions expressed in this publication do not necessarily reflect the position, policy, or endorsement of the National Institute of Education (Contract No. R-400-79-0046).

[1] Pseudonyms are used throughout this case study.

(Florio, 1982). In creative writing, we see Mr. Jameson exercising considerably more autonomy in determining what will be taught and when and how it will be taught. In the next section of this chapter, we will examine an overview of the curriculum for creative writing and begin to consider several facets of the teacher's role in response to the student writer. These facets of his role include the creator of an environment for writing, model of the role of writer, motivator and resource person, and coach of the writing process.

The Study

Guided by concerns about the relationship between student writers and their teachers, we identified a high school teacher noted for his effectiveness in motivating writing among his students. We spent one semester documenting the planning and teaching of Mr. Jameson and eliciting students' perspectives on the writing they did in his high school creative writing class. Our intention in this study was to learn more about the socially negotiated nature of school writing and to identify ways in which the teacher supported the acquisition process.

By taking multiple vantage points on the process of writing in high school, we developed the following case study. The focus of this case study is on Mr. Jameson's perspectives about writing and its instruction and on the interpretations of his students about what happens in their class. Data collected in the course of this study included the following:

1. field notes of classroom participant observation;
2. journals kept by Mr. Jameson containing his thoughts on the teaching of writing;
3. samples of naturally-occurring student writing in the creative writing class; and
4. dialogue journals in which six student volunteers wrote with a researcher about their perceptions of the creative writing class.

We used these data to test and provide evidence for an evolving set of assertions about the variety of ways that Mr. Jameson enacts the role of teacher as he responds to student writing. Excerpts from these data will be used to instantiate our assertions in the case study presented here.

School and Community

Creative writing is a multigrade elective class taught by Mr. Jameson in the community of East Eden. East Eden is a moderate-sized suburb of a state capital in the Midwest and is also the home of a large, land-grant university. Many, if not most, of Mr. Jameson's students reflect the community's high value on educational achievement. Almost none, for example, denied that "going to college" was a major goal when surveyed by Mr. Jameson in September. The concern for school achievement on the part of students and parents is not without its costs, however. In early interviews and journal entries, Mr. Jameson spoke of the difficulty of teaching writing to young adults so concerned with achievement and the pleasing of authority. Writing in his journal on September 14, 1982, Mr. Jameson noted, for example:

> When you mentioned that the "lack of skills" is not an impediment to student writing at EEHS, you're essentially correct. Except for a few students who have been identified as learning problems and for the most part are receiving more help here at EEHS than at many other places they might be going to school, most EEHS students could be exciting, creative, original writers if you could map an entry space into a territory which valued personal expression as much or more than "standard" writing. Real writing is such a joy, but like all arts, it is indulged in only at the risk of engaging yourself in what you have to say. It is a difficult step for anyone to take. One of the reasons I've remained in secondary teaching is that I've always thought it was a step that students made more easily than adults. Perhaps this isn't so any longer.

A day later, Mr. Jameson made the following observations in his journal about what had gone on in his class:

> Had students read aloud today and was impressed for the most part by their reading skills. However, one curious impression emerged. A number of students were technically proficient readers. The words were all recognized and pronounced correctly, taking into consideration punctuation, but there was no magic, no celebration in their voices. No recognition of the imaginative role of language. No wonder at making another world come alive in their minds. How to help kids this year enter more animatedly into the world of imagination is a major goal for me.

These journal entries not only highlight problems that Mr. Jameson perceives among his would-be writers, but they begin to identify his values and commitments as a teacher of writing. One particularly rich context in which to observe Mr. Jameson working to realize those values and commitments was his creative writing class.

Creative writing is an unusual course at East Eden High School for several reasons. First, it is taken by a diverse group of students. As one of the few remaining electives in the curriculum, students from the upper three grades take it. In addition, it is taken by different students for different reasons. Some take it to augment their English curriculum with more opportunities to write. Others take it because they are particularly interested in fiction writing. Still others find themselves in creative writing because it is one of the few classes that would fit their schedules.

After nearly a decade of electives and relative openness to student curricular choice, the curriculum in East Eden has been narrowed in recent years. English I, II and III are required at East Eden. Beyond these three courses, there are few electives available to students through the English department. Creative and expository writing are the notable exceptions.

Classroom and Curriculum

Mr. Jameson's classroom was a visual buffet. Not only were there samples of his own photographs and paintings throughout the room, but charcoal sketches, airbrush designs, and oil paintings done by his students hung from every wall. The classroom had five bulletin boards which Mr. Jameson changed often, sometimes to reflect the theme of a unit in one of his classes, sometimes to display student work, sometimes to share interesting newspaper or magazine articles, and sometimes to relieve his boredom with the previous display. Artwork even lined the space between the top edge of the chalkboard and the ceiling. He used the bulletin board near the chalkboard to post announcements, especially concerning writing contests. Figure 1 offers a map of the classroom, highlighting the locations of the visual displays.

This was our first impression of life within Room 10. This was also the scene that greeted Mr. Jameson's students on the first day of school. The creative writing class met in the late morning, five days per week. During the term that we observed, 18 young men and 6 young women were enrolled. Many of the students shared their work and ideas with us during class time, and six of them volunteered to keep

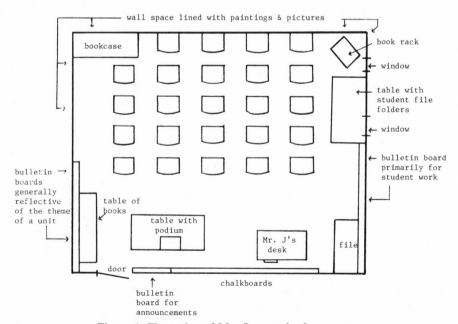

Figure 1. Floor plan of Mr. Jameson's classroom

dialogue journals with us outside the class. Three broad areas of creative writing were discussed during the first semester: poetry, the short story, and the play. Poetry was the focus of the first ten weeks of the semester. Creative writing in prose form was the focus of the remainder of the semester, building up to the major project of writing a short story or a play.

Within the poetry section of the semester, several topics were discussed and written about. A time line of the poetry topics has been laid out in Fig. 2. Each week, two or three topics were discussed by the class. Mr. Jameson prompted discussions of new topics in any of several ways, among them, reading aloud the poetry of other authors, listening to poetry set to music, or presenting slides and photographs related to the topic. The number of class periods dedicated to each topic varied from one to several.

Figure 2 illustrates the curricular decisions made by Mr. Jameson for the creative writing class. Like other teachers we have studied, Mr. Jameson's teaching provides for an extensive amount of framing of the activities that make up the first half of the semester. In our fieldwork in this class as in others, we have found that Mr. Jameson and his students use the framework to give meaning to an otherwise endless flow of written tasks—both to parse that flow into topical units that they can name (e.g., spiders, fences, hands) and to bind those activities together into logical sets that enable writing to be sustained across frequent interruptions from outside the classroom (Florio, 1982).

What makes the framing observed in the creative writing class unique among the classes we have observed, however, is Mr. Jameson's relative freedom to identify and label the units and to link them over time by means of foreshadowing and referring back to other units. Framing is thus the first area in which Mr. Jameson can work responsibly with student writers. Framing of time and activity not only helps to structure the interactions of class members, but can be done reflexively in terms of those interactions. Basil Bernstein (1975) has written in this regard about the framing of subject matter within the curriculum. He distinguishes between curricula with reduced insulation between contents ("open curriculum") and what he calls "closed curriculum," where the borders between contents are strictly defined and frequently punctuated by activities "where the learner has to collect a group of favored contents in order to satisfy some criteria for evaluation" (Bernstein, 1975, p. 87).

Bernstein's distinction suggests that the degree to which the writing curriculum is framed from outside either by teachers or for them by district mandates is related to the kind and amount of writing which will be asked of the student as "academic performance." Aiming to open up the facets of the author's role that can be played by student writers in the creative writing class and freed somewhat from district mandates by the elective nature of this course, we shall see Mr. Jameson working to negotiate a more open curriculum with his students. That curriculum is typified by extended and related writing activities not artificially segmented by tests or other evaluative activites that would render the relation between student writer and teacher respondent one of student as performer for grades and teacher the sole audience.

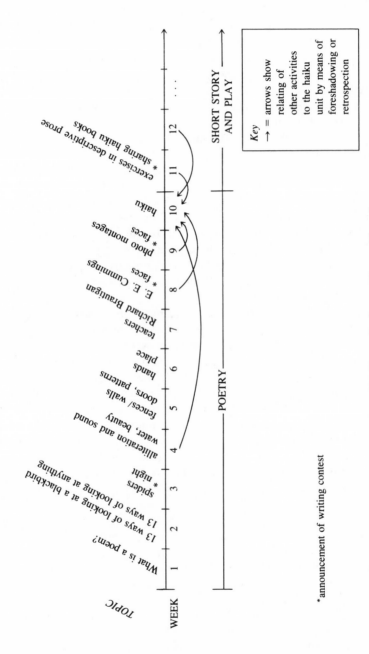

Figure 2. Weekly topics in creative writing class.

*announcement of writing contest

WEEK

TOPIC

1 — What is a poem?

2 — 13 ways of looking at a blackbird
    13 ways of looking at anything

3 — *
    spiders
    night

4 — alliteration and sound
    water, beauty

5 — fences/ walls
    doors, patterns

6 — hands
    place

7 — teachers
    Richard Brautigan

8 — E. E. Cummings
    *
    faces

9 — photo montages
    *
    faces

10 — haiku

11 — *
    exercises in descriptive prose

12 — sharing haiku books

...

POETRY

SHORT STORY
AND PLAY

Key
→ = arrows show
    relating of
    other activities
    to the haiku
    unit by means of
    foreshadowing or
    retrospection

Teacher Response in Context: The Haiku Unit

Introduction

In what follows we will describe in detail several scenes from the haiku unit to illustrate the range of Mr. Jameson's responses to his student writers. We hope to show in the description that Mr. Jameson negotiated his role as teacher in a variety of ways with his students. By means of such negotiation he was able sufficiently to distance himself from the putative role of "teacher as evaluator" to enable his students to take greater power and responsibility for their roles as authors. Before offering this analysis, however, just as Mr. Jameson foreshadows topics for his students, we would like to make preparations for what is to come through an introduction to the haiku unit of the creative writing class.

The haiku unit, in many aspects, represents the culmination of the writing experiences which preceded it. One theme common to the poetry section of the creative writing class was the exploration of new ways of viewing and experiencing the events, objects, persons, and situations of everyday life. In this respect, the creation of haiku poetry—valued for its simplicity and its capturing of intimate moments from the real world—was an appropriate finale for the poetry section of the creative writing class.

Another sense in which the haiku unit was a culminating experience of the first part of the creative writing class was in its connection to a writing contest. As early as November 2, Mr. Jameson began to introduce opportunities for his students to enter writing contests. The writing contests not only served as a motivator or stimulus to student writing, but powerfully communicated to students the effectiveness of writing and the prospects of writing for audiences other than the teacher and outside of the classroom walls. In addition, Mr. Jameson, himself a photographer, well known in the state and nationally for his work and the participant and winner of many contests, did considerable modeling of the problems and opportunities of being a working artist by means of the writing contest.

During the week before the haiku unit, Mr. Jameson announced to the class the details of a haiku writing contest. Announcements of writing contests were a frequent occurrence in Mr. Jameson's class. Earlier in the year, there was not much dialogue following Mr. Jameson's announcements of the various writing contests. Whether the students became more competent in their writing, more eager to seek other audiences, or more tolerant of Mr. Jameson's announcements is hard to say, but as the semester progressed, the students interacted more with Mr. Jameson regarding these writing contests. Mr. Jameson announced that the prize for this writing contest was a trip to Japan. Kevin asked, "What's haiku?" Mr. Jameson described haiku as poetry which has three lines, is arranged in 5/7/5 syllabication "though not necessarily," and presents one image to the reader—that is, gives a vivid picture with a deeper meaning, without saying it in so many words. He went on to say that the difference "between an O.K. haiku and one that's really exceptional" is how well the author presents that image (Field Notes, 11/2/82).

Mr. Jameson discussed this contest in some detail, encouraging the students that they have "everything to gain, nothing to lose" by entering the contest. The class then moved to a more general discussion of writing contests and photography contests. Mr. Jameson shared some of his own experiences in photography contests throughout his career, answering questions from the students about various types of contests. He ended the discussion with a warning against entering contests in which you surrender all rights to your work. Later in the period, Mr. Jameson came back to the topic of the haiku writing contest, announcing that the class would be discussing haiku poetry in more detail the following week.

Mr. Jameson often foreshadowed events in this way. It may be helpful to refer back to Fig. 2. The assignment on which the students were working as Mr. Jameson made this announcement was a project called photo montages. Having just finished writing about "faces," the students were now asked by Mr. Jameson to make a statement by combining a picture of a face with other pictures. Besides bringing in magazines, scissors, and glue, Mr. Jameson also brought in several examples of photo montages done by former students. Thus, not only did Mr. Jameson foreshadow the haiku section by announcing the haiku contest, but he encouraged them, via the photo montage assignment, to begin to use visual images rather than words to make statements about the world around them.

Thus, in structuring the curriculum as he did, Mr. Jameson enacted his role as a teacher in a variety of ways that both supported the writing process and redefined school writing such that students were writing for purposes other than academic performance and for audiences other than Mr. Jameson. In addition, he modeled for them in his planning for related activities the artistic process that he undertakes when, as a working photographer, he decides to work to communicate in his medium and, ultimately, to share his work with others through contests. Taking a closer look at the facets of the teacher's role played by Mr. Jameson in the haiku unit, the following sections describe four ways of teaching offered to us by Mr. Jameson and his students. We have labeled these ways of teaching, "motivating," "creating the space for writing," "coaching," and "modeling." These labels, some actually used by Mr. Jameson and others of our own deviation, refer to aspects of the teaching observed in Mr. Jameson's class and described by both teacher and students in their journals. In the following sections, we hope both to instantiate each way of teaching and to offer evidence from field notes and journals to support our assertions.

Social Identity and the Teaching of Writing

As we begin to think about Mr. Jameson's role as respondent to student writers, it is useful to consider social roles and the ways that they are negotiated in face-to-face interaction (Goodenough, 1969). Goffman (1961) and others have usefully distinguished between a "status," or the position one occupies in social space, with its relation to others in the form of reciprocal ties, rights, and duties; "role," or the activities incumbent on a person who acts solely upon the normative demands of his/her social status; and "role enactment," which is "the actual conduct of an individual while on duty in his position'' (Goffman, 1961, p. 85). Goffman argues that, in role enactment, one has considerable leeway in how to manage the rights and duties attendant to one's status and that enactment is negotiated with others in the context of face-to-face interaction. In addition, how one enacts one's role has implications for the reciprocal roles of others in the same social situation.

In Mr. Jameson's classroom, his status predicts certain rights and obligations. However, how the teacher enacts his role is negotiated between him and the students and is sensitive to the instructional purposes and context at any given time. How Mr. Jameson enacts his teaching role thereby, of necessity, has implications for the rights and duties that his students will experience in their roles as student writers.

In the process of such role enactment, a teacher may at one time "embrace" the teacher role, taking the power to initiate student writing, determine its content and format, and be its sole audience and evaluator. Such embracement, Goffman (1961) notes, is typical of baseball managers during games and traffic police at rush hour— in short, of "anyone occupying a directing role where the performer must guide others by means of gestural signs" (p. 107). When the teacher assumes such power and responsibility for student writing, it is clear that s/he can greatly limit the student's role to mere task completion and academic performance for a grade.

In contrast to such role embracement, teachers often distance themselves from the full expression of the putative teacher role according to their curricular and instructional goals and to the needs and purposes of their students. In what Goffman calls "role distance," teachers separate themselves somewhat from their role, thereby opening up interactional options to others in the social scene. In doing this, the teacher (or other person with potentially great situational power) "apparently withdraws by *actively* manipulating the situation . . . the individual is actually denying not the role but the virtual self that is implied in the role for all accepting performers" (Goffman, 1961, pp. 107–108).

In the descriptions that follow it is apparent that Mr. Jameson distances himself from the "virtual self" of the teacher as initiator/framer/evaluator of student writing in a variety of ways. By an "active manipulation" of the instructional situation, he is able both to support the writing process among his students and to make more of that process available to them.

Teacher as Motivator

Mr. Jameson, in reflecting upon his own journal writing, wrote:

> After rereading this entry, it occurred to me that my main concern as a writing teacher for ninth graders—in fact writers of any age—is to motivate. To get people into spaces where they are really thinking about what they have to say and are being honest. For me, this is the space where good writing originates. (Teacher Journal, 9/8/82)

Just as Mr. Jameson's room was a visual buffet, so also did he lay a rich and varied table for his students as he tried to get them interested in and thinking about writing.

The ways in which Mr. Jameson chose to motivate his classes were varied. He attracted different students with different lures, casting his line often to try to attract student interest. In the haiku unit, for example, Mr. Jameson attempted to motivate students in several ways. He introduced the unit with a filmstrip about haiku poetry and passed out a handout on haiku.[2] In addition, he offered many books from his own collection that were related to haiku poetry.

Although Mr. Jameson selected several other items for his motivational buffet (e.g., records, slides, photographs, oral readings) here we will describe some of the roles that books in particular played in this buffet. We will describe the ways he used these books to motivate his students to write, demonstrating how he drew on the many varied characteristics and facets of the books and their production to interest a variety of students in his class. The books allowed Mr. Jameson an opportunity to share with his students a closer look at several facets of the author's role.

The first 35 minutes of the period were spent discussing the kinds of poetry and artwork within each book. Mr. Jameson began by discussing an anthology of haiku poetry that a teacher in the high school brought back with her following a visit to China. This book helped the students to experience the spectrum of topics about which these haiku poets chose to write.

The next two books were written by authors from this state. These books provided an impetus and a foundation for class discussion. As was often the case during these motivating activities, dialogues between Mr. Jameson and a student were held out loud so that other interested students could listen and participate. For example, Steve asked if either of the local authors made their living as writers. Mr. Jameson talked briefly about the lives of each of the authors, explaining that both of them have other jobs to support their writing careers. He talked about his own life, explaining that when he is teaching he gives his all, but that making artwork was his primary career. When asked which was more important to him, he responded, "How can you separate the two?" He felt that if he couldn't make artwork, he couldn't teach.

The next of the books was a collection of image poems. These are short poems, though not exactly haiku, that "capture a moment." Mr. Jameson described them as a photograph with words. He went on to say that they are like little windows on the world, and that when you've read enough of someone's haiku or image poems, you have a better idea of how that person views the world.

---

[2] Although the purpose here is to highlight the various strategies and resources Mr. Jameson uses to motivate his students to write, it is interesting to note the features about haiku which he has chosen to highlight by his handout as an introduction. The handout gave a brief history of the development of the genre of haiku from its seventeenth century origins in Japan to its recent adoption into English and other languages. The word *haiku* translates to "playful phrases." Originally, these simple statements were calligraphied in ink-brush ideographs, often accompanied by a sketch or design. The finished product was called a *haiga*. The handout focused on the relationship of reading and writing haiku poems to living life more fully, tracing the links of poetry to Zen Buddhism. The handout concluded by recommending books for beginners interested in learning more about this art form.

Mr. Jameson used the books to illustrate potential facets of an author's role beyond the actual writing of poetry. For example, one of the books had a lot of illustrations, and Mr. Jameson commented to Craig that he would be able to do some stuff with his artwork. He reminded Craig of a drawing Craig had done earlier in the year for one of the assignments and said that perhaps Craig could write a haiku to fit it and print the haiku beside the drawing. In this way he was able to make connections to the interests of some of the students who enrolled in the course more for scheduling convenience than for the desire to increase their writing opportunities.

Mr. Jameson also used the books as bridges to discussions of other available resources. Some of the books were about Zen Buddhism. He encouraged the students that when they write their first haiku that really worked, they would have had their first Zen moment. He told the class of a man in East Eden who was "very into Zen" and recommended that anyone interested should talk to him. He also noted that the Center for Asian Studies at the local university had a lot of information about Zen. He encouraged the students to read all that they could about Zen to help them with their haiku writing. But he added that the most important thing the students could do to help them with their haiku writing was to read a lot of haiku.

The books were also used as models for the class's project. Most of the books Mr. Jameson displayed were collections of works by a single artist. One book was completely made by the artist—"written, illustrated, and stapled together." This led Mr. Jameson to a discussion of the project for the haiku unit. Each student could experience many facets of the author's role by making his/her own book of haiku poetry. He told the class that this is generally the best project of the year. He had none of the books left from previous years to show them, but felt that was a good sign that people had wanted them back. He talked about some of the books which had been done. One was only 1½ × 3 inches. He said that one had a very intimate feeling while reading it.

With the broader goal of the haiku book project in mind, the assignment for the rest of the period was that the students read haiku from the books or the handout and work on writing some haiku of their own. He planned for them to spend the rest of the week working on their haiku books.

Teacher as Creator of the "Space" for Writing

The assignment for the rest of the period was to read haiku, read about haiku, or try to write haiku. Mr. Jameson said that haiku works best outside and proposed that students could go outside to write if they would like. He looked out the window at the rainy, grey sky and commented that today was a good day for haiku. He talked a little about getting into a "haiku state of mind," looking for interesting details or intimate moments. One haiku feeds the next until you can't get them down quickly enough. The important thing, he noted, was to get the moment written down. "Worry about the syllables later." He also told the class that they need not be strict in their 5/7/5 syllabication.

Many of the students in the class understood what Mr. Jameson meant when he spoke of getting into a frame of mind conducive to writing. Devon, in his first journal entry, wrote:

> The space my teacher talks of can only be entered when I feel like writing true feelings and not what people want to read. (Student Journal, 1/21/83)

The students became active as Mr. Jameson finished talking about getting into a "haiku state of mind." Four of the students headed to the library to have their photo montage assignment laminated. Three students turned their desks to face the window. Dan announced that he was going to try to write outside. Some students went up to the table at the front of the room, picked out one of the haiku books, and took it back to their seat. Other students stood around the table, waiting to talk to Mr. Jameson.

The room quieted as the students began reading and writing. There were 20 minutes left in the period. Dan came back in, announcing that it was too cold to write haiku out there. He was looking for haiku moments, but all he could think of was how cold he was. Mr. Jameson remembered two haiku books on the bookrack in the back corner of the room. He opened one of the books, reminded us that haiku didn't have to be serious, and read two funny haikus from the book he had found. One of these was "Xerox Candy Bar" by Richard Brautigan:

Xerox Candy Bar[3]

Ah,
You're just a copy
of all the candy bars
I've ever eaten.

The class became active again as the period neared its end. People began to return the haiku books to the front table and put their notebooks away. As the period ended, people began to leave the room. One student stopped at the front table to tell Mr. Jameson that he had felt more inspired by the photographs in the book he had looked through than by the haiku poems in the book.

Teacher as Coach

Another facet of the teacher's role we observed Mr. Jameson enact was that of "coach." Each of these facets we describe is clearly related to the other facets. All are dimensions of the role of teacher which we believe are important to Mr. Jameson and his students. One of our goals in observing and experiencing the creative

---

[3] "Xerox Candy Bar" excerpted from the book *The Pill Versus the Springhill Mine Disaster* by Richard Brautigan. Copyright © by Richard Brautigan. Reprinted by permission of Delacorte Press/Seymour Lawrence.

writing class so extensively was to take the perspective of those involved, to discover the ways they were making sense of the writing process in this class. Though coaching and motivating are similar aspects of the teacher's role, we have chosen to distinguish them here because they look and sound different in the classroom and are distinguished by the participants themselves.

The "teacher as coach" assumes that the students are motivated to write. As coach, Mr. Jameson supported students *in the process* of writing. This support was generally offered individually, while motivating activites were generally geared to the entire class. Even when Mr. Jameson spoke to individuals during the motivating activities, it was out loud, for anyone in the class to hear, if they were interested. Coaching was most often a one-to-one situation, in a quiet voice, at the desk of either Mr. Jameson or the student. Mr. Jameson's coaching of the student writers took many forms—sometimes aimed at offering technical assistance; at other times aimed at encouraging the students to be persistent in their writing efforts. We saw an example of each of these forms of coaching during the haiku unit.

Mr. Jameson often walked around the room, talking to students who motioned for his attention. In these situations, his coaching took the form of technical assistance to the student writers. For example, Jeff asked him to look over a haiku he had been working on. Mr. Jameson spent several minutes talking to Jeff, explaining that haikus are attempts to capture a moment and leave it up to the reader to interpret it. Jeff contended that he wanted to make a statement in his haiku and he felt that he had done so. Mr. Jameson suggested that another strategy Jeff might try if he still wanted to lead the reader in some direction would be to present an image in the first two lines of the haiku, followed by a dash, and end the haiku with a question. In closing, Mr. Jameson reminded Jeff that traditionally, "the subject matter of haiku has never been heroic, but humble."

In other cases, his coaching was more in the spirit of encouragement than in the offering of technical assistance. One student alluded to this type of coaching when she wrote in her journal that "Mr. Jameson is a great teacher because he puts on no pressures . . . he understands that creativity doesn't always come fast" (Student Journal, 1/23/83). This type of coaching—encouraging students to continue to write, even during difficult periods—can also be illustrated by describing a brief conversation Mr. Jameson had with Tony during class. Tony was one of the students who had enrolled in creative writing because it fit his schedule. He had become one of the "invisible students" in the classroom, so rarely did he talk in class. Yet he had asked questions about the haiku contest. Two weeks after the haiku unit, he asked Mr. Jameson to help him pick his three best haiku to enter in the contest. Mr. Jameson read over the haiku Tony had given him, commenting that he thought he had the knack of writing haiku. He suggested to Tony that since there was no real rush (the contest deadline was six weeks away), he might "just crank out tons of them" so that a couple of weeks before the deadline "we can choose from 120 to 150 haiku, not just 15 or so." Mr. Jameson reminded Tony of the comment he had written at the end of Tony's haiku book: "More, Tony, give me more."

Teacher as Model

Mr. Jameson modeled his love of artwork and his belief in the importance of practice in the decor of his classroom, his class discussions, and his own life style. He often talked of "doing" as the most important part of art, giving examples about his own life and his own persistence, especially regarding photography. Two evenings a week, Mr. Jameson taught photography at a local arts workshop, and from these experiences, he shared with the class his amazement at the adults who sit through his class without ever taking a photograph. They assume they can "learn" to take photographs by listening attentively and understanding the mechanics. Mr. Jameson doesn't believe that you can learn to take good photos that way and emphasized the importance of getting out and taking many, many photos, "even if 99% of them are awful."

Discussion

One way to think about Mr. Jameson's teaching is in terms of the way he structured the learning environment and negotiated his role as respondent to student writing. The haiku unit vignette illustrates that Mr. Jameson was not the sole audience for student writing, nor was he its formal evaluator. As teacher, he served as motivator, coach, and model. Using the writing contest as an "occasion for writing" (Clark & Florio, with Elmore, Martin, Maxwell, & Metheny, 1982), Mr. Jameson helped students to write for audiences other than the teacher and for purposes beyond academic performance.

It has been argued that students learning to write are beginning to perform a complex balancing act that includes their expressive intentions, the expectations of their audience, and the subject matter about which they intend to communicate. In addition, they are managing all of this in the medium of the written symbol system with its attendant conventions.

In some sense, student writers are learning to manage written discourse in school much as they learn to manage oral discourse in early childhood. However this time the task may be far more difficult. The catalog of reasons for this difficulty is long and pertains both to writing as a way of communicating and to schools as places in which to write. Not only are students now managing a new, second-order symbol system, but they are communicating with an often absent interlocutor. In addition, they are learning to write not in the circle of the family where feedback and response of adults is immediate, meaningful, and supportive, but in classrooms where adult feedback and response are commodities shared among twenty or more students and where evaluation, competition, and abstractness may infuse even the most rudimentary oral and written exchanges.

By the time the student reaches secondary school all of the above complications may be intensified because, as Moffett (1983) points out,

Although younger children often want to write for a "significant" adult, on whom they are willing to be frankly dependent, adolescents almost always find the teacher entirely *too* significant. He is at once parental substitute, civic authority, and the wielder of marks. Any one of these roles would be potent enough to distort the writer-audience relationship; all together, they cause the student to misuse the feedback in ways that severely limit his learning to write.(p. 193)

The acknowledgement of this difficulty in relations between student writer and teacher respondent highlights the socially negotiated nature of school writing. Face-to-face interactions around writing in school are ultimately concerned with negotiating the roles of student and teacher in the composing process. These negotiations concern the relative rights of students and teachers to identify the purpose, audience, and format of writing done in school (Florio & Clark, 1982).

Studying oral language in classrooms, Mehan (1979) observed that teacher–student interactions are often of the form, "Teacher Elicitation—Student Response—Teacher Evaluation." It has been observed that this structure carries over into the teacher–student relationship in writing (Staton, Shuy, Kreeft, & Reed, 1982). Here the teacher typically determines the subject matter and form of the writing. The student writes as an academic performance to be evaluated by the teacher. This pattern is atypical of most writing that goes on in the world outside classrooms (Varenne, Hamid-Buglione, McDermott, & Morison, 1982). Rarely does one person play the roles of initiator, audience, and evaluator. Rarely is writing's purpose to earn a grade.

Some theorists who have addressed issues of writing curriculum and teaching methods (Emig, 1981; Graves, 1983; Moffett, 1983) have implied that if one approaches learning to write as the acquisition of multiple forms of discourse rather than merely as mastery of technique, sensitivity to the relations between student writer and teacher respondent become critical. If the teacher remains the sole initiator and audience, particularly with older students, the assymetry inherent in ordinary teacher–student discourse potentially stymies and distorts the role of student writer.

Moffett (1983) has argued that a "trinity of discourse" underlies all writing (p. 11). In this idealized triad, the author writes about his/her intended topic for an audience removed in time and space. In many classrooms, the triad is modified as follows:

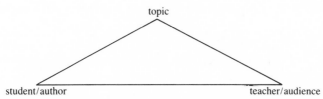

Figure 3. Relationships among student, teacher, and topic in many classroom writing assignments

In this triad, the student as author is seen primarily as communicating for the purposes of academic performance. The teacher as audience participates as the offerer of direct instruction in the writing process and the evaluator of the quality of student writing produced. The subject matter about which students write is largely teacher-determined, tightly framed, and almost exclusively expository (Applebee, 1981; Shuy, 1981). This triad limits the range of potential relationships among authors and their audience, authors and their subject matter, and the audience and their subject matter.

School writing is but one expressive alternative that might have been chosen from a greater repertoire available (Basso, 1974). Its negotiation potentially distorts our ordinary ways of thinking about the author, subject, and audience. The outcome has implications not only for the kinds of writing skills acquired in practice but for the values and attitudes learned by students about what it means to take the role of the author. The outcome of such occasions for writing in school is too often one in which, as Moffett (1983) describes, the student now

> may write what he thinks the teacher wants, or what he thinks the teacher doesn't want. Or he writes briefly and grudgingly, withholding the better part of himself. He throws the teacher a bone to passify him, knowing full well that his theme does not at all represent what he can do. (pp. 193–194)

Another way to think of this triad is in terms of what might be called "writing for the real world." Here our ordinary expectations involve relationships as represented in Fig. 4. This figure more closely resembles the writing situation in Mr. Jameson's class. Mr. Jameson intentionally gave away several key rights typically assumed by writing teacher—those of determiner of the author's subject matter and evaluator of the author's written product. Thus, he helped to define for the student author an audience and subject matter that lie outside the classroom and the teacher–student relationship.

In Mr. Jameson's classroom, the teacher serves to motivate writing, to provide support and technical assistance, and to act as a proxy for the student's intended audience when necessary. This is a move from school writing to "real world"

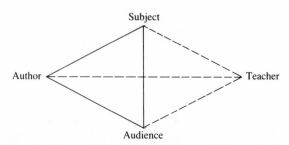

Figure 4. Relationships in writing in Mr. Jameson's class

writing where, although relations among author, topic, and audience will vary depending on the functions of literacy motivating the writing act (e.g., scholarly papers, business letters, friendly letters, personal journals, fiction), the author has considerable leeway to negotiate both the subject matter to be written and the audience for whom the writing is intended. In this case, it is the job of the author to select the subject matter and to decide the format in which to write about it, just as it is the audience's responsibility to receive the written work and to participate in its meaning through the act of reading comprehension.

By rethinking the roles of student and teacher in the writing class and by reconstruing the audience and the purpose of school writing, it might be possible to open up not only the range of responses that teachers can make to support student writing, but the range of purposes to which writing can be put and the range of written topics and forms that can be used and practiced by students. Thus, Fig. 4 combines the more ordinary relationship among author, audience, and subject with the special relationship between student, teacher, and subject. Figure 4 demonstrates that many ways of teaching are important in preparing students to write for the real world. In this kind of writing, the student as author exercises considerably more authority to determine the subject matter and can identify a variety of audiences or a range of significant others to whom s/he intends to write for various purposes. Occasionally, the audience might be solely the teacher but most often the audience might be peers, parents, other members of the community, and audiences more distant in time and space. As a coach and provider of resources, the teacher offers students ideas about subject matter and serves as a proxy audience responding to the student's writing as one of the intended audiences might. In this way, the teacher role is enacted in several ways, including foreshadowing or providing context for the writing act, modeling the role of a writer, motivating and providing resources to the student writer, creating the "space" within which writing can happen, and coaching by offering rhetorical strategies and encouraging responses to student efforts.

References

Applebee, A. L. (1981). *Writing in the secondary school: English and the content areas* (Research Report No. 21). Urbana, IL: National Council of Teachers of English.

Basso, K. H. (1974). The ethnography of writing. In R. Bauman & J. Scherzer (Eds.), *Explorations in the ethnography of speaking*. Cambridge, England: Cambridge University Press.

Bernstein, B. (1975). *Class, codes and control* (Vol. 3). London: Routledge & Kegan Paul.

Clark, C. M., & Florio, S., with Elmore, J. L., Martin, J., Maxwell, R. J., & Metheny, W. (1982). *Understanding writing in school: A descriptive case study of writing and its instruction in two classrooms* (Research Series No. 104). East Lansing, MI: Institute for Research on Teaching, Michigan State University.

Emig, J. (1981). *The composing processes of twelfth graders* (Research Report No. 13). Urbana, IL: National Council of Teachers of English.

Florio, S. (1982). *Written discourse in the classroom*. Paper presented at the annual meeting of the American Anthropological Association, Washington, DC.

Florio, S., & Clark, C. (1982). The functions of writing in an elementary classroom. *Research in the Teaching of English, 16*(2), 115–130.

Goffman, E. (1961). *Encounters: Two studies in the sociology of interaction.* New York: Bobbs-Merrill.

Goodenough, W. (1969). Rethinking "status" and "role": Toward a general model of the cultural organization of social relationships. In S. A. Tyler (Ed.), *Cognitive anthropology.* New York: Holt, Rinehart, & Winston.

Graves, D. H. (1983). *Writing: Teachers and children at work.* Exeter, NH: Heinemann.

Mehan, H. (1979). *Learning lessons: Social organization in the classroom.* Cambridge, MA: Harvard University Press.

Moffett, J. (1983). *Teaching the universe of discourse.* Boston: Houghton-Mifflin. (Originally published 1968)

Shuy, R. (1981). A holistic view of language. *Research in the Teaching of English, 15*(2), 101–111.

Staton, J., Shuy, R. W., Kreeft, J., & Reed, L. (1982). *The analysis of dialogue journal writing as a communicative event.* Final report to the National Institute of Education (NIE-G-80-0122). Washington, DC: The Center for Applied Linguistics.

Varenne, H., Hamid-Buglione, V., McDermott, R., & Morison, A. (1982). *I teach him everything he learns in school: The acquisition of literacy for learning in working class families.* New York: Columbia Teachers College, Elbenwood Center for the Study of the Family as Educator. NIE Technical Report, Contract No. R-400-79-0046.

3

Spontaneous Repairs in Sharing Time Narratives: The Intersection of Metalinguistic Awareness, Speech Event, and Narrative Style*

Courtney B. Cazden
Sarah Michaels
Patton Tabors
Harvard Graduate School of Education

Children, like adults, spontaneously repair their utterances in the course of speaking. Clark and Anderson (1979) have demonstrated with extensive evidence that "children monitor what they say from the very early stages of language acquisition" (p. 1), and that spontaneous self-repairs are excellent evidence of that monitoring. They found two kinds of repairs in the speech of 26–43-month-old children: Corrections of pronunciation, morphological endings, and word order that they call "repairs to the system"; and replacement of one word with a preferred alternative, often a pronoun with a more informative noun phrase, that they call "repairs for the listener." Our protocols come from primary school-age children several years older than Clark and Anderson's preschoolers, and so it is not surprising that aspects of their phonological, morphological and syntactic systems are no longer problematic, and that new kinds of repairs for the listener appear.

Our protocols consist of the narratives of personal experience told at Sharing Time (ST) by first- and second-grade children in four classrooms: one in Berkeley, California (Michaels, 1981) and three in the Boston area (Michaels, 1983; Michaels & Cazden, in press).[1] All four classrooms were ethnically mixed, with the proportion of black children ranging from one half to one tenth. For the analysis of self-repairs, we selected narratives of the "star sharers" for which we had good quality recordings. Star sharers are children in each classroom who shared frequently and

---

* An earlier version of this paper was presented at the Boston University Child Language Conference, October 8, 1983. We are grateful to John and Jenny Cook Gumperz, Alyssa McCabe, and other members of the audience for their questions and comments, and to Val Hinderlie for suggestions on an earlier draft. We are also grateful to the National Institute of Education and the Spencer Foundation for support of the research during which these narratives were collected.

[1] Sharing Time, sometimes called Show and Tell or News, is a nearly universal speech event in U.S. kindergarten and first-grade classrooms, at least weekly and often daily, when children are called on to tell about some out-of-school experience to the rest of the class.

willingly, and who were considered good sharers by their peers—as evidenced either by attentiveness at the moment or by comments in interviews.

We selected for detailed analysis 14 narratives of 10 star sharers—6 white and 4 black, distributed among the four classrooms—that contained repairs for the listener. All our analyses and all the examples in this chapter come from these 14 narratives. Children are referred to by pseudonyms and their ethnicity identified by (W) or (B) before each example. The narrative titles are ours. We first describe the kinds of repairs for the listener that these children made and the metalinguistic awareness we believe that their presence demonstrates; second, we detail the features of ST as a speech event that make ST narratives a specific genre; finally, we show how the form and function of the repairs relate to cultural differences in narrative style.

Self-Repairs as Evidence of Metalinguistic Awareness

Repairs for the listener in these narratives are of two kinds. One kind are lexical replacements exactly like the ones Clark and Anderson found in the speech of younger children. For example, instead of using the word *ramp* in retelling the movie *ET,* Joe corrects *ship* to an empty subject noun *thing* plus a relative clause *that you walk up on* (1). In a longer narrative about her puppy, Leona pronominalizes *puppy* to *he* and then repairs the next *he,* changing it to the full nominal *my father,* and makes the referent *father* clearer (2).

(1) Joe (W):   . . . and the ship was closing / the um ship /
                 the thing that you walk up on / was closing /
(2) Leona (B):   . . . and / my puppy / he always be following me /
                 he said / uh / my father said / um you can't go //[2]

Many such lexical replacements are scattered through the narratives, but their presence is not news, and we will say no more about them.

A second kind of repair, not found by Clark and Anderson, we call "bracketing": the insertion of material, as if in brackets or parentheses, in the middle of an otherwise intact sentence.[3] Examples (3) and (4) show bracketing in the context of

---

[2] In our transcriptions of children's narratives, in order to highlight the fact that this is actual speech, we use the following notations: a single slash (/) indicates the end of an intonational phrase or breath group, but signals "more to come," akin to a comma; a double slash (//) indicates final closure, akin to a period; . . . indicates a measurable pause; . . indicates a brief break in timing; a colon (:) following a vowel indicates a vowel elongation, the bracket ([) across speaker turns indicates overlapping talk.

[3] We have found two discussions of this kind of self-repair in adult speech. Shimanoff and Brunak (1977, pp. 137–140) use the term "bracket" for the same phenomenon, and point out that in writing such inserted material is set off by commas (most common), parentheses, or dashes (often criticized by composition teachers). Polanyi (1978) also describes the same phenomenon, but explicitly argues against Shimanoff and Brunak's repair interpretation. Naming her paper 'False starts can be true," Polanyi

the child's entire text. (Words immediately preceding and following the bracketed material are italic.)

A Hundred Dollars

(3) Carl (W):Well / last night / my . . father / . . was at work /
    ⌐ *he* / . . . every Thursday night / they have this thing /
    | that . . . everybody has this dollar /
    | and it makes up to a hundred dollars /
    | ⌐and . . . *my* / and . . you've gotta pick this name out /
    └ └and *my father's* name got picked /
    └ so *he* won a thousand dollars //
       a hundred dollars // (child self-corrects)

In this example, Carl wants to tell the class that last night his father won a hundred dollars, but to explain where that money came from he inserts a description of a lottery. As we later diagram in (3a), this insert actually itself contains an embedded bracket (which we counted together as one instance).

In (4), Leona tells a much longer story with shifting scenes:

(4) Leona (B):   *Bad Luck Day*

        Uh today / is . . . the . . it's Friday the thirteenth / and it's (breath) bad luck day / and my grandmother's birthday is on / back luck day / / and . . my mother / my mother / my mother's bakin' a cake / and I went up to my grandmother's house / while my mother was bakin' a cake / and my mother was bakin' a chee:se cake / my grandmother was bakin' a whipped cream cup cakes / / and . . my / we both / went over my mother's house / . . . and then my grandmother / had made a chocolate cake / and then we went over my aunt's house / and she had made a cake / and everybody had made a cake for Nana / so we came out with six cakes / /

Class: Ohmigaw (sighs of amazement)

Leona: and / every last ye— / last night / my grandmother snuck ou:t / and she ate all the cakes / and we hadda make mo:re / she knew w-we was makin' cakes / *and she* / and we was sleepin' / *and she* went in the room / and gobbled 'em up / / and we hadda bake a who:le bunch more / / . . . she said mmmmmm / she had all chocolate on her face / crea:m / stra:wberries /

Class: (giggles)

Leona: she said mmm⌐mmmmmm

Class: └mmmmm⌐mmmm

Leona: └that⌐was good

Class: └that was goo-

Leona: And then / and then my gran (each) all came out / and my grandmother had ate all of it / she said / what's this cheese cake doin' here / she didn't like cheese cakes / and

---

(1978) says, 'The force of this paper is to establish such a mistake-making strategy as one of the devices a speaker has at his/her rhetorical and interactional command' (p. 637). Intuitively, Polanyi's analysis makes sense to us as adult speakers, but we retain the more conservative interpretation of repair for our child narrators.

she told everybody that she didn't like cheese cakes / / . . . and . . we had a:ll / and
then she— then she / and we kept makin' cakes / and she kept eatin' 'em / and / and
last night / and we finally got tired of makin' the cakes / and so / and so / we a:ll
ate 'em / / . . . (long pause) and no:w / now today's my grandmother's birthday /
and only one . . person . . is— / a lot of people's makin' a cake again / but my
grandmother . . is . . goin' to get her own cake / at her bakery / / . . . and she's
gonna come out with a cake / that we didn't make / / 'cuz she likes chocolate cream
/ / . . . and I went to the bakery with her / and we had /and my grandmother ate cup
cakes / and and she finally got sick on / on today / / and she started / she was
grow:ling like a dog / 'cuz she ate / she ate so many cakes / / and that's why / t— / I
told her / and I finally told her today was / Ap— April— it was— / . . . I finally
told her that it was . . . it was Friday the thirteenth / bad luck day / /

In the first episode of "Bad Luck Day," family members are all making cakes for
grandmother's birthday. Then the scene shifts, and grandmother becomes the agent
of the narrative action as she sneaks out to eat the cakes, with inserted material
explaining that this happened while the rest of the family was sleeping.

These bracketings, and the difference in their structure, can be shown diagram-
matically:

(3a) ┌ he—
     │   (insert: ┌my—
     │   │   [insert]
     │   └my father's name got picked)
     └ he won a hundred dollars
(4a)   and she
            (insert)
        and she went in the room and gobbled 'em up

Bracketing, by our conservative definition, has three criterial features:

1. There is a break in an utterance, either within a clause or at the end of a
    dependent clause.
2. Some material is inserted that minimally contains a noun phrase and a verb
    phrase, i.e., is a clause.
3. The speaker then repeats one or more words spoken before the break (with
    change only from noun to pronoun or vice versa) and completes the original
    sentence.

We call the original sentence that is broken off and then resumed the "host", and
the bracketed material the "insert." Examples of constructions that do not fit these
criteria may make the definition clearer: (5) has no syntactic break in the host; (6)
has no verb in the insert; (7) has both a break and a clausal insert, but the host is
never resumed.

(5) No syntactic break:

Carl (W):   *So the sheriff comes* / and you know how sometimes /
            uh / . . . like um . . . uh / T.V. guys put their hands
            on concrete / they do that / *so the sheriff* shot 'em /

(6) No verb:

Sandy (W): My mother said / um / *on* / before Thursday /
            on maybe Monday / Tuesday / or Wednesday /
            I might be goin' to my mother's work /

(7) Break, plus inserted clause, but no return to interrupted segment:

Joe (W):   It's / like / this little boy / *he finds* /
            well / this / nn / this little boy he has this
            brother / and they're / and his brother has friends
            over / and they're all having a party / . . .

We have maintained this conservative definition to rule out cases that could be analyzed in other ways. In our 14 narratives, there are 19 instances of bracketing so defined:

	white	black
No. of children	6	4
No. of narratives	8	6
No. of bracketings	9	10

We interpret bracketing as evidence of two aspects of children's communicative competence. First, structurally, the insertion of bracketed material within the host sentence is evidence of the speakers' syntactic resources being used in a particularly complex way—evidence, that is, of syntactic competence in all 10 children.

Second, functionally, the bracketings are evidence of the children's ability to "monitor, check, and repair," as Clark (1982) argues for younger children, but here at the level of discourse rather than the sentence. These children are not just replacing one word with another within a sentence, nor solving a problem of anaphoric reference across adjacent sentence boundaries. They are making repairs for the listener at the level of organization of thematic content of the narrative as a whole. They are thinking about the information the listener needs in order to understand part of the story not yet told and making a midstream repair to provide needed orientation. In this way, these children are showing their ability to do more than retrospectively monitor what has already been said, and more than provide local repairs if something does not come out quite right; they are thinking ahead and monitoring against an internalized sense of what information is shared by the audience or not. This is what we mean by metalinguistic—or better, metapragmatic—awareness.

The Influence of Sharing Time as a Speech Event

Bracketing as we define it is a category of utterances defined in formal terms. Usually, the preferred sociolinguistic research strategy is to start with a functional category—a communicative problem—and look for all formal solutions. To look at the functional problem to which bracketing is one solution, we have to consider ST as a speech event, and the conventions that are implicitly adhered to in all our classrooms for how ST narratives are to be constructed.

Any narrative requires an integration of multiple levels of information. Labov (1972), in his article on "The Transformation of Experience in Narrative Syntax," identifies six elements of a narrative (some of which are optional): abstract, orientation, narrative action, evaluation, resolution, and coda. ST narratives, one particular narrative genre, always evidence at least two of these: narrative action and orienting information needed to understand that action and appreciate its significance. Thus all our sharers face the problem of providing, and integrating, narrative and nonnarrative (orienting) clauses. Because the expected topic of ST narratives is personal out-of-school experience, these young narrators—called upon to talk about their home lives in the public forum of the school—face this problem in an acute way.

Furthermore, ST narratives have a characteristic genrelike format that constrains, or at least influences, easy solutions to this rhetorical problem. The narratives tend to begin with temporal and spatial location, introduce a key agent, and then get right into the action—typically all in the first sentence (almost always spoken with a marked rising intonation that we have come to call "sharing intonation" [Michaels, 1983]). In previous research, we have found that over 90% of ST narratives start with time marker + information on scene if not home + agent of action. Here are some typical opening sentences:

At Thanksgiving/ when I went to my grandma and grandpa's/ we

Yesterday/ me and my father went out for a sundae/ and then we came home/ . . . and we

Last Christmas/ my mom

When I slept over my mother's/ the cat/ in the middle of the night/ she

When we went down the Cape once/ my mother

Last Friday/ my mother and grandmother went out/ and they

Yesterday/ I was walking and this man was walking beside me/ and we

"A Hundred Dollars" (3) starts the same way:

Well/ last night/ my . . father . . . was at work/ he

That entire narrative could consist of just one orienting clause, *Last night my father was at work,* and one narrative action clause, *He won a hundred dollars.* The inserts add important background information, but they also stretch out the story and delay the punch line about the hundred dollars. (It was this story that called bracketing to our attention and became our prototypical example.)

Of course, bracketing is not the only way to insert background information into an ongoing narrative. Menig-Peterson and McCabe (1978) found in their larger sample of elicited narratives from 3–9-year-old children in rural Ohio that children regularly supply orienting information in both dependent and independent clauses, and our sharers do too. (8) contains a dependent clause, and (9)—from (5)— contains two independent clauses. (Background information is italic.)

(8) My big sister said / Deena you have to keep that away /
    from Keisha / *'cuz that's my baby sister* / and I
    said no / . . .

(9) So the sheriff comes / *and you know how sometimes* /
    uh / . . . *like um . . . uh* / *T.V. guys put their*
    hands on concrete / *they do that* / so the sheriff . . .

As we said earlier, we have isolated for analysis one formal solution—bracketing, because it is such a transparent indication of cognitive processes at work. The implicit ST convention to get immediately into the action may make it a more common solution here than elsewhere. But because we know of no other analyses of bracketing in children's narratives, we cannot say for sure.

The Relationship of Bracketing to Narrative Style

In our previous research in Berkeley and the Boston area, we have analysed both cultural differences in ST narratives and differences in teacher's responses. We will summarize those findings, and then discuss their relationship to bracketing.

Michaels, in her original (1981) research in Berkeley, found that white children were more apt to tell narratives she termed "topic-centered," while black children were more apt to tell narratives she termed "topic-associating"; and we found that difference again in the Boston area research (Michaels, 1983; Michaels & Cazden, in press). Examples (1) and (2) exemplify that contrast: "A Hundred Dollars" is about a single event at one time and place, whereas "Bad Luck Day" shifts time and place several times. Recently, we have substituted the term "episodic" for topic-associating, meaning by that the dictionary definition of "proceeding by a series of episodes.''[4] Black children do not always tell episodic narratives, and white children occasionally do so, but a marked differential tendency has been found in all studies.

In the present set of 14 narratives, 2 of the 8 white narratives and all of the 6 black narratives are episodic. One of the white episodic narratives, ''ET'' (from which examples (1) and (7) are taken), is a movie retelling, and it seems likely that all narrators—child or adult, white or black—are more likely to retell a movie or TV show in an episodic style. (Labov, 1972, found other significant qualitative differences between vicarious TV narratives and narratives of personal experience.) If we exclude ''ET,'' then the contrast among narratives of personal experience is even more marked: only one of the seven white children's narratives but all six of the black narratives are episodic.

We make no attempt to explain these differences in narrative style and are not even sure of the ethnic labels. We originally identified them as black/white differences simply because that aspect of children's identity was obvious. We have since found other similar descriptions of black rhetorical style. For example, Afro-American scholar, Gineva Smitherman (1977), speaks of black adult narrative style as ''concrete narrative . . . [whose] meandering away from the 'point' takes the listener on episodic journeys'' (pp. 147–148). But in these urban classrooms, as in American life generally, ethnicity is confounded with social class and with experience with what is loosely referred to as oral versus literate cultures.

Closely related to this difference in the children's narrative style are differences in teachers' responses.[5] We have analyzed these responses during ST itself, and we also conducted an experiment in which we played mimicked versions of typical white and black narratives—all spoken by the same voice—to an ethnically mixed group of graduate students at Harvard, and to three groups of white educators in New Zealand where Cazden was on leave (Michaels & Cazden, in press). All the white adult informants, like the white teachers in the original classrooms, had a harder time following the episodic narratives. Moreover, white adults in the experiment tended to infer lower academic ability on the part of the narrators. Black adults in the experiment responded differently: As is so often the case, they were more bicultural—recognizing differences but valuing both styles.

---

[4] Alyssa McCabe warns that our use of the term *episodic* is open to misinterpretation because of its use by story–grammar researchers with a different meaning (personal communication, October, 1983). It still seems to us the best name for narratives such as (4), and we can only repeat our (and the dictionary's) meaning.

[5] We have been asked why we attribute such importance to the teacher's understanding of these stories when the sharers may be speaking more to their peers. Of course there is a peer audience as well as the teacher, and Sharing Time as an activity may be justified as much for its contribution to a sense of community among children as for the opportunity for oral language development. The fact of the dual audience may itself add to the rhetorical problems faced by the child speakers, just because teacher and peers may hear stories very differently. But in the Sharing Times that we have observed, it is the teacher who responds verbally, and often in an evaluative way. More generally, we suggest that in all official school speaking and writing assignments, no matter who the ostensible ''audience'' may be, it is the teacher's response that counts.

Considering just our 14 narratives, we have no evidence that any of the 8 narratives told by white children were hard for the original teachers to understand. But there is evidence in their on-the-spot responses that 3 of the 6 black narratives posed problems. Two others were told when teachers were not present (one in a classroom where ST was regularly conducted entirely by children [Michaels & Foster, in press] and the other in a classroom where the teacher had briefly left the room); and our tape for the sixth stops before the teacher's response.

We have tried to determine what features make the episodic narratives harder for white adults to understand. The fact that bracketing occurs—with the careful monitoring for the listener that it evidences—rules out any general explanation of cognitive egocentricity (that is, inability to take the audience's perspective) on the part of the children. But because successful communication in a ST narrative requires integration of action and orientation, and bracketing is one formal means used by all the children, it seemed possible that the way bracketing was done, and the way orienting information was set apart, might provide clues to the answer. So we looked more closely at the bracketings, in both functional and formal terms.

Functionally, one important feature is the relationship between information supplied in the host and the insert. The modal pattern is a host clause that describes narrative action (defined by Labov, 1972, as one of at least two clauses that appear in a fixed order) and an insert that explains something about the physical scene or social setting, as in (3) and (4). Six of the nine bracketings in white children's narratives fit this pattern, and seven of the ten black children's bracketings also do, if we extend the categories of orienting information to include time and scene change. And both groups occasionally insert one kind of orienting information into a host that is itself an orienting clause. In both (10) and (11) the host is an orienting clause about the social situation; in the first, the insert is about a participant, while in the second the insert is about a prop. (Inserts are italic.)

(10) Joe (W):   This little boy / he has this brother / and they're /
                and his brother has friends over / and they're all having a
                party / . . .

(11) Leona (B): Yesterday / when uh / m-my father / in the morning /
                and he / *there was a hook* / *on the top of the stairway* /
                and my father was pickin' me up / . . .

Formally, one potentially important feature is the relationship between verb tense in the host and verb tense in the insert. Contrasting tenses should make it easier for the listener to hear the insert as orienting information rather than as the next segment of narrative action. The modal combination for our 14 narratives is past tense in the host and either present or past progressive in the insert. These patterns are exemplified in (13)—past/present, and (14)—past/past progressive. (Contrasting verbs are italic.)

(13) Rene (B):   he said / . . . um . . . he *said* /
                  he*'s* at the kitchen table /
                  he *said* / when your father was your age /

(14) Leona (B):   she knew w-we was makin' cakes /
                  and she— /
                  and we *was sleepin'* /
                  and she *went* in the room /

Six of the nine white and five of the ten black children's bracketings fit one of these patterns.

In the cases that do not fit the modal pattern, some ethnic differences appear. Among the white children, all of the three exceptions do incorporate some shift in tense (for example, where the host is future and the insert perfect progressive). Among the black children, there are five exceptions and, of these, three have the same (past) tense in host and insert—as in (15). (Verbs in host and insert are italic.)

(15) Deena (B):   and / . . . when— /
                  um / and I *got* it ye:sterday /
                  and when . . . I *saw* it / . . . on the cou:ch /

While these numbers are too small to say anything definitive, they suggest that there may be proportionally fewer lexical cues signaling the distinction between orienting information and narrative action in black children's narratives.

To pursue this hypothesis, we looked for lexical cues at the beginning of an insert that could mark it for the listener as a shift in the kind of information about to be heard. Words that are unlikely to begin a narrative clause can serve as lexical cues that mark the forthcoming clause as orientation. In addition to *every* and *everybody* and *you've* in ''A Hundred Dollars'' (1), we included the following:

(W)	(B)
well (3x)	well
there's	there was
like	see
I have	it was (pleonastic *it*)
if	because
you know	

Of the 19 bracketings, six of the nine white and four of the ten black children's bracketings include one or more of these cues at the beginning of the inserted material. Interestingly, if we now go back to the three cases in the black children's narratives where there was no tense distinction between host and insert, we find that two of these cases include other lexical cues that might help highlight the shift where the verbs do not.

From these analyses of the bracketings, we conclude that while there are cultural differences, they do not seem large enough to account, by themselves, for differential comprehensibility by the teachers. However, these small differences become more important when we see them in the context of differences in more global thematic characteristics of the narratives as a whole.

Consider (16) and (17) (with insert verbs italic):

(16) Evan (W):   *Stamp Pad*
Last Christmas / . . . my mo:m / she— . . . I . . . I *was telling* my mom / that I wanted a stamp pad / and so / on Christmas / I mean on my birthday / . . . she got / . . . a stamp pad / and a stamp for me //

(17) Deena (B):   *Deena's Coat*
Um / . . . in the su:mmer / . . . I mean / . . . w-when um / I go back to school / I come back to school / in September / . . . I'ma ha:ve a new coat / and I already got it // . . . and / . . . it's / . . . u:m . . . got a lot of bro:wn in it // . . . a:nd / . . . when— / um / and I got it ye:sterday / . . . and when . . . I saw it / my um . . my mother *was* . . *was going* some . . where / when my . . when I saw it / . . . on the couch / and I showed my si:ster / and I was readin' somethin' out on . . on the ba:g / and my bi:g sister said (. . .) my big sister said / Deena you have to keep that away / from Keisha / 'cuz that's my baby sister / and I said no // . . . and I said the plastic ba:g / . . . because / . . . um / . . . when / . . . u:m / . . sh-when the um . . she was u:m (with me) / wait a minute / . . . my / cou:sin and her⌈(. . .)

Teacher: ⌊wait a minute// you stick with your coat now // I s-said you could tell one thing // . . . that's fair //

In both cases, the verb in the insert should have been in a perfective tense: Evan *had been telling* his mother what he wanted for Christmas, and Deena's mother *had gone* somewhere before Deena showed her baby sister the plastic bag. In the absence of that tense marker, the listener can't tell from syntax alone that the inserted action had been completed before the host action took place.

Moreover, the fact that the bracketing in (17) occurs at the end of a dependent clause—*and when I saw it*—is another potential source of confusion. The bracketed material can be heard as an independent clause—the well-formed fulfillment of a syntactic expectation. The one other instance of an insert at the end of a dependent clause begins with a lexical cue, *well,* which probably helps avoid the wrong hearing.

But we believe the more important reason why (17) is harder to understand than (16) is a significant difference in the extent to which listeners can clarify the relationship among actions from extratext knowledge. Requesting and getting Christmas presents (16) constitute a widely shared script in this culture, and we know those actions can be sequenced in only one way. That is not true of the actions in (17). There is no conventional script that sequences a mother going out and a child showing a potentially dangerous plastic bag to a baby sister; yet that sequence is critical to the unfolding story.

The same contrast holds between narratives (3) and (4). Carl's explanation about lotteries has extensive problems of vague words: *this thing, this dollar, it makes up to, this name.* But adult listeners would get enough cues to some kind of lottery to clarify the vagueness on their own. Leona's story of how her grandmother's birthday became in reality, as well as on the calendar, a "bad luck day" (4) has a much more elegant structure, with an evaluative ending that ties right back to the beginning. But, in between, the narrative is about a series of unique family events, and the listener has to rely solely on Leona's words. (It is interesting to note that "Bad Luck Day" is an episodic story that happened to be told while the teacher was out of the room. So, while Leona got appreciative back channel comments from her peers, there were no interpolated and potentially disrupting questions by the teacher. Coincidentally or causally, it is her best structured story.)

A further cultural difference in thematic content is exemplified by (18) and (19) (Words before and after the insert are italic.)

(18) Sandy (W):   *Book Report*

My sister / . . . she's in sixth grade / and *she's gonna ask her teacher Miss . . Miss Richardson / to um . . get---* / she's been doin' a book report every week / *and she's / gonna ask Miss Richardson to get one bla:nk to bring home* / so I have to do it //

(19) Deena (B):   *Tooth Story*

Today I gon' put my tooth under my pillow / and and I been puttin' my tooth under my pillow every night / *and I st---* and I was gettin' money / *and still / have my um tooth* //

Teacher: You still have your tooth? (said wistfully) // Well maybe the fairy will come get it tonight / Stick it under there //

. . .

Here, both narratives are about future action, and both involve familiar scripts: writing book reports for which a special form is needed, and putting a tooth under the pillow for an expected reward. (19) is the first part of a short episodic narrative, and the teacher does not hear the child's intended meaning. While the child's implicit evaluation is of a magically wonderful tooth that keeps producing money, the teacher infers disappointment that the tooth hasn't disappeared as it should. "Tooth Story," in short, is a familiar script with a novel ending. (One of the black children's narratives included in our experiment but not analyzed here because it contains no bracketing also had a counterintuitive ending that only the black adult informants heard correctly [Michaels & Cazden, in press]).

In conclusion, we believe that black children's preferred narrative style poses more complex rhetorical tasks for the narrators, and more problems in comprehension for the listener—particularly listeners for whom this style and choice of theme is less familiar—in three ways. First, structurally, the narratives are more frequently episodic and therefore require repeated juxtaposition of action and orientation. Second, thematically, they tend to be about less widely shared scripts, or familiar scripts with a novel, counter-to-expectation ending. Third, whereas narratives with these characteristics require more explicitly stated orientation information in order to communicate successfully to a teacher who is unfamiliar with both this style of story-telling and with the story content, the black children are apt to supply somewhat less.

Since egocentricity is eliminated, we suggest three alternative explanations:

1. Black children may not have experiences (either at home or at school) in which they learn specific solutions to the complex rhetorical tasks they give themselves that would satisfy a school standard that emphasizes lexical and syntactic explicitness in narrative presentations (Michaels, 1981).

2. The more complex tasks arising in episodic stories may require the integration of so many verbal devices, no matter how well learned each one might be, that few children of this age, black or white, could successfully manage the task. (Shatz, 1977, makes this cognitive load argument with respect to other communication tasks.)

3. Black children may be using systematic intonational and rhythmic cues to highlight shifts between host and inserted material. However, because teachers (and we white researchers) are not familiar with these cues, we miss their signalling potential and assume that differentiating cues are absent. More research with both black and white informants, along the lines of our small experimental study, is needed to support or refute this third explanation.

While this analysis has focused on a small, and only occasionally occurring, part of one genre of children's narratives, we believe the pieces of our analysis have a wider generalizability. Any analysis of children's language should look for expressions of universal cognitive processes, consider the relationship of speech to the structure of the situation of which it is a part, and be open to considering cultural, as well as individual, differences in style.

But What About Writing?

We have not studied the relationships between the oral phenomena discussed in this paper and children's writing. However, we suggest that three aspects of children's school writing could be explored in the light of our findings: ethnic differences in the structure and thematic content of children's compositions; how orienting information is provided in first drafts or revisions; and differential success of teacher-child interactions during writing conferences.

References

Clark, E. V. (1982). Language change during language acquisition. *Advances in Developmental Psychology, Vol. 2* (pp. 171–195).

Clark, E. V., & Anderson, E. S. (1979). Spontaneous repairs: Awareness in the process of acquiring language. Stanford University Department of Linguistics: *Papers and Reports in Child Language Development 16* (pp. 1–12).

Labov, W. (1972). The transformation of experience in narrative syntax. In W. Labov, *Language in the inner city: Studies in the Black English vernacular* (pp. 354–396). Philadelphia, PA: University of Pennsylvania Press.

Menig-Peterson, C. L., & McCabe, A. (1978). Children's orientation of a listener to the context of their narratives. *Developmental Psychology, 14,* 582–592.

Michaels, S. (1981). "Sharing time": Children's narrative styles and differential access to literacy. *Language in Society, 10,* 423–442.

Michaels, S. (1983). Influences on children's narratives. *Quarterly Newsletter of the Laboratory of Comparative Human Cognition, 5,* 30–34.

Michaels, S., & Cazden, C. B. (in press). Teacher/child collaboration as oral preparation for literacy. In B. B. Schieffelin & P. Gilmore (Eds.), *Acquisition of literacy: Ethnographic perspectives.* Norwood, NJ: Ablex.

Michaels, S., & Foster, M. (1985). Peer-peer learning: Evidence from a kid-run sharing time. In A. Jagger & M. Smith-Burke (Eds.), *Kid watching: Observing the language learner* (pp. 143–158). Urbana, IL: National Council of Teachers of English.

Polanyi, L. (1978, Feb. 18–20). False starts can be true. *Proceedings of the Fourth Annual Meeting of the Berkeley Linguistics Society,* 628–639.

Shatz, M. (1977). The relationship between cognitive processes and the development of communication skills. In C. B. Keasey (Ed.), *Nebraska symposium on motivation, 1977* (pp. 1–42). Lincoln, NE: University of Nebraska Press.

Shimanoff, S. B., & Brunak, J. C. (1977). Repairs in planned and unplanned discourse. In E. O. Keenan & T. L. Bennett (Eds.), *Discourse across time and space* (pp. 123–167). Southern California Occasional Papers in Linguistics, No. 5. Los Angeles, CA: University of Southern California, Department of Linguistics.

Smitherman, G. (1977). *Talkin' and testifyin': The language of black America.* Boston: Houghton Mifflin.

4

Helping Children Learn to Write In English as a Second Language: Some Observations and Some Hypotheses*

Paul Ammon
University of California, Berkeley

Much of the difficulty children have in learning to write can be attributed to differences between the demands of written communication and the kinds of oral communication skills children typically master during their preliterate years (Bereiter & Scardamalia, 1982; Olson & Torrance, 1981; Rubin, 1980). Because of these differences, young writers must acquire new linguistic forms that are associated specifically with written language, and they must develop new procedures for drawing upon their linguistic competence and their world knowledge to communicate effectively in writing. In addition, they must be able to resist interference from previously acquired forms and procedures where these are inappropriate for written communication. For children learning to write in a second language in which they are not yet fluent, the problems of acquiring and using new elements of communicative competence while inhibiting old ones can be greatly magnified. By definition, second language learners are still in the process of gaining control over basic linguistic forms in the second language (L2)—forms that would be taken for granted in many children who are native speakers of the same language. Also by definition, second language learners already have some knowledge of a first language (L1), and it can interfere with L2 writing in various ways that do not exist for monolinguals. In other words, the problem of moving from oral to written language is compounded for many second language learners by the problem of moving from L1 to L2, and it may be further compounded if the home culture is an essentially oral one (Cook-Gumperz & Gumperz, 1981).

The dual problem of acquiring productive literacy while also acquiring English as a second language is a critical one not only for the many individual learners who face it but also for our society as a whole. According to one demographic projection, the U.S. population in the year 2000 will include nearly 3.5 million children aged 5 to 14 with non-English language backgrounds and limited English proficien-

* The present research was supported by National Institute of Education Contract No. 400-80-0030 with the University of California at Berkeley. Linda Kroll, Kevin Delucchi, Marta Giegling, and Siew-Tin Beh-Bennett assisted in collecting and preparing the data cited here. Mary Sue Ammon, Sarah Freedman, and Leann Parker provided useful comments on drafts of this chapter.

cy (Oxford et al., 1981). Finding instructional strategies that are effective in dealing with the problem is, therefore, a matter of some urgency. In principle, one might contemplate the possibility of addressing the two parts of the problem separately, either by postponing instruction in writing until the learner attains fluency in oral English, or by teaching writing in L1 before teaching it in English (Cummins, 1979). In practice, however, neither of these alternatives seems viable as a general solution, although each may have some specific applications. Resources and/or support for writing instruction in L1 are often lacking, and English literacy skills are generally deemed too important for writing instruction in English to be postponed for very long. Consequently a typical case is one in which children are expected to begin learning how to write in English when they are still limited in their facility with oral English, and when their literacy skills in L1 are also limited or even nonexistent.

In considering how to help children move from spoken to written language and, simultaneously, from a first language to English, one might naturally expect to be guided by what is known about the teaching of writing to native English-speaking children and about the teaching of English as a second language. But, aside from the fact that our knowledge in both of these more familiar areas still has its limitations, it also seems advisable to be cautious about extrapolating from them to the problem at hand. Fostering the development of English writing among second language learners may need to be treated as a distinct problem in its own right, and the nature of the problem may depend on age and other learner characteristics. If so, it would be useful to investigate the problem directly, by observing the writing development of different groups of second language learners in a variety of instructional settings and by generating hypotheses as to why they make better progress in some settings than in others.

My purpose in this chapter is to offer an exploratory analysis along these lines by drawing upon data from a large study that is concerned with the acquisition of school-related English skills among language minority children (Wong Fillmore et al,, 1983). After presenting an overview of the available data and outlining my strategy for generating hypotheses from them, I will focus on two children in each of two third-grade classrooms in order to determine how their English writing improved in the course of one year and to suggest possible reasons for these gains.

The Available Data and a Strategy for Generating Hypotheses

Briefly, the design of the larger project on which the present analysis is based included 13 third-grade classrooms that contained groups of children learning English as a second language. In 6 classes their first language was Cantonese, and in 7 it was Spanish. Within each of these two language groups, some classes were designated as bilingual classes, while in others English was the only language of instruction. The group of target subjects in each class consisted, on the average, of 9 children who had had 2 to 3 years' exposure to English in school prior to third grade and had usually been in the same type of classroom (bilingual or English only) before. All of the target subjects had been identified as limited- or non-English-speaking children when they first entered their schools. Information on the language learning environments in their classrooms was gathered throughout one school year by means of formal and informal observation and on video and audio tape. We used a variety of speaking, listening, reading, and writing tasks to assess the target subjects' English proficiencies in the fall and spring, so that we could look at language learning outcomes in relation to instructional features and individual differences. Whenever possible, parallel tests of language proficiency were administered in L1 as well. (See Wong Fillmore et al., 1983, for more detail regarding the language proficiency measures and classroom sites.)

Because the larger study was designed to examine the acquisition of a variety of language skills, the data on writing per se do not have as much depth as one might wish when writing is the focus. On the other hand, the available data are quite broad—both with respect to the range of language skills assessed and with respect to the information gathered on instructional settings and learner characteristics—and this breadth may prove to be advantageous, since writing development surely reflects much more than effects of instruction aimed directly at writing. In the analyses that follow, I have tried to take advantage of the breadth in the available data, or at least I have tried to do so in a preliminary way, as I have yet to do much more than scratch the surface of what is ultimately possible.

In using the data for present purposes, I first asked which of the third-grade classrooms stood out with respect to the gains our target subjects had made in writing during the year of the study. If the target group in a particular class had large gains relative to the target groups in other classes, this would suggest that certain features of the instructional program or classroom environment were especially conducive to progress in writing, and I could then try to determine what those features were. Second, I asked which individuals in the classroom's target group showed particularly large gains, so that I could focus on children who gave particularly good examples of kinds of gains that occurred more generally in their class. It would also be interesting to investigate the question of *why* those children had especially large gains—by examining their individual characteristics and by relating them to the distinguishing features of their classroom—but that is beyond the scope of the present analysis.

Selection of Classrooms and Individual Children

The principal criterion I used in selecting classrooms and individual cases for closer scrutiny was the occurrence of a relatively large gain in ratings of the English writing samples we collected in the fall and spring of the school year. Two writing samples—a story and a descriptive comparison—were elicited by means of standard picture prompts and instructions in individual interviews at each testing. The focus of our writing assessment was on the child's ability to communicate clearly in writing by producing a text that would be "autonomous" (Olson, 1977) in the sense that it could be readily understood by a reader without benefit of special knowledge about the topic or the writer, and therefore the children were instructed to write stories and comparisons that someone else could read and understand without ever seeing the pictures used as prompts. Each writing sample was rated from 1 to 5 on six dimensions relevant to text autonomy: use of genre, cohesion, clarity of reference, coverage of basic content, elaboration of basic content, and conventional usage. The score of interest here is the sum of the ratings across these six dimensions. This dimension sum has been found to correlate highly ($r = .95$) with a rating of overall text autonomy, but it also appears to offer more resolution in detecting differences between levels of writing proficiency than the latter, more global score (Ammon, Kroll, & Cann-Ortiz, 1984).[1] Because different prompts were used in the fall and spring testings and because of remaining uncertainties regarding their relative difficulty, it is potentially misleading to measure writing gains in terms of absolute differences between fall and spring scores.[2] Thus I have chosen to look at gains in relative terms, by transforming the raw dimension sum for each writing task into a standard score (z), by computing a mean z score for the two writing samples each subject produced at a given testing, and by then comparing the z score means from the fall and spring testings.

The left side of Fig. 1 displays the means of the z scores attained in the fall and spring by target subjects in each of the 13 third-grade classrooms involved in our study. Each classroom group is identified by a letter indicating the first language of the target subjects (Cantonese or Spanish) and by a classroom number, which is essentially arbitrary (e.g., C1 identifies the first of the classrooms in which the subjects spoke Cantonese as their first language). It can be seen that there was a wide range of differences between classes with regard to the target groups' levels of English writing proficiency in the fall. The difference between groups C6 and S3 in the fall was about 2.6 standard deviations, which corresponds to about 13 points out of a possible 30 per writing task. It is also apparent in Fig. 1 that the Chinese subjects generally scored higher than the Hispanic subjects. The extent of this difference is exaggerated somewhat by Fig. 1, because it cannot be seen from the classroom means that several Hispanic subjects scored high and that several Chinese subjects scored low. On the whole, however, the Chinese subjects did tend to score higher, and therefore it seems advisable to limit comparisons between classrooms to those cases in which the target groups had the same first language.

Turning now to the main question of differences in gain between classroom groups, Fig. 1 indicates that dramatic shifts in relative standing between fall and

---

[1] The dimension sum may not be sensitive to actual gains in some cases, because of trade-offs between gains on some dimensions and "growth errors" on others. But it should suffice for the purposes of the present analysis because it is unlikely to *over*estimate the amount of improvement in writing, i.e., to result in false positives.

[2] The use of different prompts to elicit the fall and spring samples of English writing was necessitated by a decision to use the same prompts for both English and L1 within a given testing. Otherwise, the subjects would have had to respond to the same pictures on four different occasions overall.

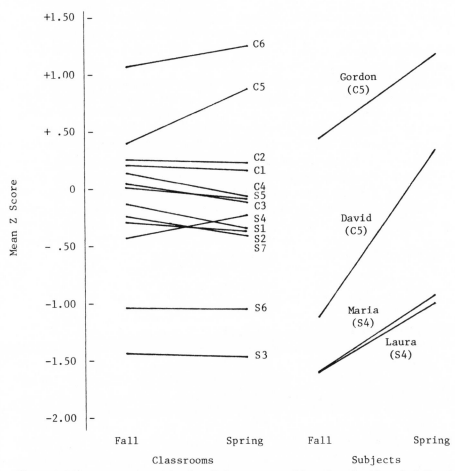

Figure 1. Mean *z* scores in writing for all classrooms and for selected subjects in fall and spring.

spring generally did not occur. Nevertheless, three groups did improve their relative positions. One of these groups, C6, had by far the highest mean to begin with. The fall writing scores of this group, together with their performance on other measures of language proficiency, suggest that most children in the group were not significantly limited in their facility with English at the outset, and therefore were not representative of the kind of second language learner this chapter is about. Consequently this group will be excluded from further consideration. The two remaining groups with positive gains, C5 and S4, had fall writing scores that seemed comparable to other groups with the same first language, and their writing often gave evidence of limited facility with English. These, then, are the two groups from which I have selected individual subjects for the present case studies.

The right side of Fig. 1 shows the fall and spring writing scores of the four children I have selected. All four improved more than the average for their respective classroom groups. One of these children, from classroom C5, scored near the mean for his group in the fall, while the other three children were initially well below average. With regard to these latter three, one must consider the possibility that the striking improvements indicated in Fig. 1 are more apparent than real, as they could reflect the phenomenon of regression toward the mean. That is, it might be argued that their actual writing proficiencies at the time of the fall assessment were underestimated by their low scores. If this argument were correct, then any attempt to explain the improvements shown in Fig. 1 would be meaningless, since little or no improvement might actually have occurred. But other evidence, such as parallel gains in reading, suggests that the writing gains observed in all four of the present cases were real rather than artifactual, so that it is meaningful to ask what caused them. As a first step toward an answer to that question, it is necessary to examine some of the writing samples the four children produced in the fall and spring, in order to see exactly how they were writing initially and how they improved.

A Look at Some Writing Samples

In the fall writing assessment all subjects produced stories in response to a series of pictures showing the following sequence of events:

1. A man stealthily taking a lady's purse from her shopping bag as she looks at some hats in a store window;
2. The lady chasing the thief down the street toward an old man who is sitting on a bench;
3. The old man using his cane to trip the thief, who drops the purse while falling to the ground;
4. The lady, purse again in hand, thanking the old man as the thief is led away by a policeman.

Before writing, all subjects had shown their understanding of these events through their spontaneous and elicited comments on the pictures. Nevertheless, the stories produced by the two children I have selected from classroom S4 are far from complete in their coverage of basic content, and they display a variety of other problems as well.

Maria (Fall)

The men gat The prrs he rn en. The stit (street)
The old men put sitic nu hi fit (stick in his feet)
hTi sicrim (hit screaming) The old men he gat gr
prs The polismen gat hem The polismen Tuc he Tu The hel

Laura (Fall)

woman is wall (walking) and the men said guimo (give me)
my puros said the woman if the not guimo my puros
I call the pulismen.

Maria covers most of the basic events in her rendition of the thief story, but she never explicitly mentions the victim of the theft, and the very occurrence of a theft can only be inferred from what she has written. Laura's rendition is even more fragmentary, apparently ending just after the theft has occurred, and also requiring the occurrence of the theft to be inferred. With regard to use of genre, neither writer does much to structure or mark the text as a story. For example, there is only the barest hint of a setting in Laura's first clause, and Maria's story begins with no setting at all. Problems with reference are also apparent in both thief texts; neither writer uses the indefinite article to introduce characters, and Maria uses some pronouns whose referents are difficult to assign correctly (e.g., The policeman got him). Cohesion is minimal in both texts, as Maria is particularly remiss in failing to tie parts of her text by means of conjunction or anaphora (e.g., the last two clauses). Finally, both writers depart significantly from conventional English usage with respect to grammar, lexis, spelling, and punctuation.

In the spring, Maria and Laura wrote stories that contrast in several ways with the ones I have just discussed. In this case, they were writing in response to a set of pictures showing the following events:

1. A little boy and girl playing with blocks on a sidewalk, as an older boy and girl approach on bicycles;
2. The older boy riding so close to the little children that they and their blocks are sent sprawling;
3. The older girl pointing out to the older boy what he has done;
4. The older boy reassembling the blocks as the older girl comforts the younger children.

Because the prompts used here are different from before, we cannot see how Maria and Laura expressed exactly the same content on both occasions, but we can compare their performances on analogous aspects of the two story writing tasks.

Maria (Spring)

two littls boy and a gril whis playn blacs
in the sanwac (sidewalk) and den a boy and
gril whis Ride a bik and den the boy rand his
dak (bike) and den the gril sed sori bot you
did not mub out the way and den the two kem
(came) end helpl them.

Laura (Spring)

It was a boy and a girl who was playing
with stis (sticks) them a big boy came and
made fell the boy who was playing with the girl
them he said that he sorry about he have doun
(done) wiht the stis them the boy said that he
was go and fixe them the big girl said I sorry
them they play togethor with the girl and
the boy.

It is obvious that Maria and Laura both give more complete coverage to the basic
content of their spring stories, despite the fact that the content is perhaps more
complex than in the fall. Both writers establish settings before the real action of
their stories begins, though neither makes use of such formulaic story-telling devices as "One day . . . when suddenly. . . ." Except for "the big girl" in Laura's
story, all characters are appropriately introduced by indefinite determiners, and—
while other aspects of reference are not free of problems—Laura makes a particularly valiant effort to be clear as to which character she is writing about at a given
point in the text, using adjectives and even a relative clause to distinguish referents
from one another. Greater cohesion is brought about by more effective use of
anaphora than before, and by the use of "then" or "and then" to mark temporal
relations between parts of the text. And, while there are still departures from
conventional usage, words and sentences are generally easier to recognize as English. Thus it seems that the stories Laura and Maria wrote improved along several
dimensions. Though I will not go into them here, parallel changes can be found in
their descriptive comparisons, and in the stories and comparisons written by other
children in classroom S4.

The children in classroom C5, while generally performing at a higher level,
showed similar initial difficulties and subsequent improvements, as illustrated by
writing samples from the two boys selected from that class, David and Gordon.

David (Fall)

The man ROOB (rob) the p (purse)
and thin the man ran.
and thin the and thin the man saw him.
and thin he tiep (trip) him
and thin the man fall Dowen.
and thin The gril tank him.

Gordon (Fall)

When the woman was buying a hat, a man
was running to stil (steal) the woman's purse,
and the man run away. and they is a old man

sitting on a bench and he saw the man was
stoling the purse that time, now and he got
a stick, then he trip the robber down,
then he drop the purse. and then the woman
thank him for helping her and the old man
call the police and the robber was caught
by a police.

It can be seen that David wrote a thief story which has much in common with the responses of Laura and Maria to the same task. David's rendition begins with no story opener or setting, and several elements of the story's content are omitted. Problems with reference occur throughout the text: (a) all characters are first introduced by means of "the"; (b) the thief and the old man are both called "the man"; and (c) the referents of some pronouns can only be disambiguated on the basis of substantial inference. Aside from the use of "and then" and some anaphoric pronouns, there is little to give the text cohesion, and departures from the conventions of written English are sufficient to impede comprehension still further.

In contrast, Gordon's thief story already shows more of the features that make a text autonomous. Most notable in that regard are his nearly complete coverage of basic content and his generally conventional spelling, but he also makes use of the indefinite article to introduce story characters, and he attempts to establish a setting in the first clause and to mark some temporal relations by means of adverbials and progressive aspect. Nevertheless, there are still fundamental inadequacies in Gordon's use of the story genre, in clarity of reference, and in cohesion, and his verbs are often ungrammatical by conventional standards.

Both boys show substantial improvement in their spring stories:

David (Spring)

there are two children are makeing a cales
(castle) and there are two children riding a bike.
And the boy nock the blocks down. And the girl
say pick the block back. And the girl pick the
children up. and the boy put the block back.

Gordon (Spring)

Once upon a time, there were one little girl and
a little boy. They were making a track for a
train by the street. Suddenly there is a big boy
ride on a big bicycles. The boy saw the little
boy and the girl and the boy think they are not
soppose to play by the street, and then the boy
had to trip the boy first. so the boy fell down
and they beginning to cry. Then there came a

big girl. She saw everything and she go to the
boy's bicycle and tell him you and they were wrong
and tell that you shouldn't do that. And the big
girl pull the little boy up and tell them you
shouldn't play here and the big boy will help
you fix it, OK?

David provides a setting for his bike story, and also attempts to introduce the
characters in a more appropriate way. His coverage of story content is more adequate than before, and his English usage is more conventional, especially with
regard to spelling and lexis. Gordon's use of the story genre is enhanced now by the
markers "once upon a time" and "suddenly," and he elaborates on the basic story
content by having his characters think and talk. All characters in Gordon's bike
story are now appropriately introduced, although other aspects of reference are still
problematic, as in the ambiguity as to which boy did the tripping and which fell
down. Gordon's bike story also contains nearly conventional sentence punctuation,
but the sentence structures themselves become somewhat tangled toward the end of
the story, when dialogue is introduced.

In describing the stories written by these four subjects, I have focused on the
inadequacies of their fall stories as autonomous texts and on the ways in which their
spring stories seem more adequate. Before proposing some hypotheses as to the
causes of the initial inadequacies, and of the improvements that ensued, I first want
to lay out some theoretical assumptions that have guided them.

A Theoretical Perspective on Writing Performance and Proficiency

Any attempt to generate hypotheses from data is both data-driven and theory-
driven, as theoretical assumptions determine what one chooses to notice and how
one chooses to interpret it. In the present instance, the hypotheses I will propose
reflect a theoretical view of proficiency in second language writing that is concerned
as much with the process of writing performance as with the linguistic or communicative competence underlying performance. My thinking in this regard has been
influenced most directly by a general model of cognitive behavior and development
known as the theory of constructive operators (Pascual-Leone & Goodman, 1979),
but it also seems consistent with many current ideas about the writing process
(Scardamalia & Bereiter, in press), about second language acquisition (Canale &
Swain, 1980; Cummins, 1981), and about learning to write in a second language
(Edelsky, 1982).

From the present perspective, a writer's performance depends not only on the
availability of task-relevant knowledge regarding acceptable linguistic forms and
their appropriate uses in context, but also on the writer's ability to access such
knowledge, along with knowledge of content, and to monitor its application to the
task at hand. This ability depends, in turn, on several other variables, including: (a)
the extent to which relevant knowledge is activated directly by the task environ-

ment, or indirectly by virtue of its involvement in well-consolidated or automatized structures; (b) the extent to which *ir*relevant knowledge is also activated, either directly or indirectly; (c) the extent to which the writer has the mental attentional capacity to activate relevant knowledge as needed when it is not strongly activated by other means; and (d) the extent to which the writer possesses executive plans and controls for mobilizing and coordinating relevant knowledge while inhibiting irrelevant knowledge. A given writing performance results from the interaction of all of these variables in response to the writing situation and the motives with which the writer approaches it.

In principle, deficiencies in a particular child's English writing performance might be attributed to any of the aforementioned factors or to some combination of them. It is possible, for example, that the child simply does not know how certain things are done in English or, more generally, in written discourse. On the other hand, it is also possible that the child actually has the requisite competence (in some form) but has not applied it in performance. Such a failure to draw upon existing knowledge can come about in several ways. The knowledge itself may not be in a form that permits it to be accessed easily in the task environment, being as yet poorly consolidated or tied strongly to some other context. It may also be outweighed by knowledge that is associated with L1 or with oral language use, but is irrelevant to the immediate task. The writer may also lack executive procedures for orchestrating the performance, or may have insufficient attentional capacity to carry out such procedures, so that some requirements of the task are neglected, or are met inappropriately by default. Finally, the writer may fail to use existing knowledge because of motivational considerations, such as the desire to avoid making errors in L2 writing.

It follows from the preceding analysis of theoretically possible obstacles to effective writing performance that a similar list of possibilities might be invoked to account for improvements in performance. That is, the writer may have acquired new linguistic knowledge or modified old knowledge into more usable forms. Interference from task-irrelevant knowledge may have decreased. Increases in the writer's repertoire of executive procedures, or in basic attentional capacity, might allow the writer to coordinate previously acquired knowledge in new and more powerful ways. And, finally, the writer may now be motivated in ways that are more conducive to full use of existing competence. Thus increased proficiency in writing can result from a variety of changes that have occurred in the writer, either singly or in combination. I will come back later to the question of what might cause these changes to occur. At this point I wish to return to the inadequacies observed in the fall writing samples discussed earlier, to consider the question of what might have caused them.

Theoretical Interpretation of the Fall Writing Samples

All of the theoretically possible obstacles to effective writing mentioned earlier appear to have been operative to some extent in the fall writing performances of the four subjects, though the particulars varied from one child to another. With regard to possible gaps in underlying competence, it is difficult to infer these from gaps in observed performance, since it might be the case that other, unobserved performances would have revealed the knowledge in question. Nevertheless, there are instances in the present data where it seems reasonable to conclude that the child just did not know a particular linguistic form. For example, in referring to the instrument with which the old man tripped the thief, Maria used the word "stick" rather than the more appropriate "cane." When writing the same story in Spanish, however, she used the word "baston," which fits the object in question better than stick does in English. Thus it seems likely that Maria did recognize the old man's cane as a particular kind of stick, but did not have a good word for it in her English vocabulary.

Other examples of possible gaps in linguistic or communicative competence are more ambiguous than this one, because we can easily see how existing competence might have been masked by interference, by motivation, or by limitations of the writer's executive repertoire or attentional capacity, and because we can also find positive evidence that these performance factors were operating elsewhere in the data. Evidence of this sort comes from variation in a subject's performance from one context to another—that is, where a given element of competence appears in some contexts that call for it but not in others. In the latter case, it is usually possible to see how the deficit in performance might have resulted from one or more of the performance factors, which may often have worked in combination to "overdetermine" the error in question. (See Pascual-Leone and Goodman, 1979, for discussion of overdetermination in performance.)

Consider, for example, the absence of an introduction in Maria's thief story. When writing the same story in Spanish, she began "un dia una sejora (senora). . . ." Thus it is clear that she knew something about the conventional way to introduce a story, and it also seems likely that she knew the English necessary to begin with "One day a lady . . ." when writing in English. Her failure to demonstrate this competence may have resulted from the added attentional demands of constructing a text in a relatively unfamiliar language, which might have led Maria to proceed directly to the most salient events of the story, so as to make the writing task more manageable. This shortcut could also have been motivated by a desire to write as little as possible in order to minimize errors. Finally, it might reflect interference from well-learned habits associated with oral language use. That is, in view of these other considerations, Maria may have been more easily led to approach the writing task as a continuation of the conversation she had had with the examiner about the picture prompts, in which case it would have been unnecessary for her to reestablish a context for the actions in the story by means of an introduction to her written text.

Although it seems plausible that a number of performance factors could have been operating simultaneously in the preceding example, it is difficult to say that any one of them was definitely involved. In other cases, however, it is possible to isolate one or another of them. For example, it seems clear that Maria's spelling of "her" as "gr" in the thief story reflects interference from her knowledge of spelling in Spanish, where the letter *g* is pronounced something like /h/ in English. It also seems clear that, in a sense, Maria knew better than to spell "her" as she did, because in the same text she began her spellings of "he" with the letter *h*. The occurrence of L1 interference in the spelling of "her" may therefore have resulted from additional complications. Perhaps it was a spelling that Maria "invented" on the spot because she had not previously learned the spelling of "her" as a unit. In trying to generate a spelling from her knowledge of sound-to-letter correspondences, she might have fallen back on relatively well-learned correspondences in Spanish, perhaps because she pronounces English with a slight Spanish accent.

The topic of invented spellings raises a more general question about the degree of automaticity in a writer's knowledge of the more "mechanical" aspects of writing and about its effects on other aspects of writing performance. Writers who must invest a lot of time and effort in spelling and the like may begin to tire earlier in the text they are constructing, or they may feel that they have already used up the time available for writing before they have gone very far. Either of these effects might account in part for the omissions that occurred in some children's writing samples— with respect to basic content, for example. But aside from inducing fatigue and consuming time, a lack of automaticity in writing mechanics can be debilitating in other ways too. While laboring over a particular mechanical problem, the writer must also keep track of the general course he was on before the immediate problem arose. Failure to do so can result in unwanted discontinuities or redundancies in subsequent text, both within and between sentences. For example, what appears to be a run-on sentence in Laura's thief story may have resulted from difficulty she had in spelling "give me." In general, then, if a writer's knowledge of mechanics is in a form that does not lend itself to automaticity in performance, he may be forced into trade-offs between attention to mechanics and attention to organization at higher levels of discourse structure.

Even when the more mechanical aspects of writing are highly automatized, the need for coordination between different parts or levels of a text is still inherent in the writing process. And it is also generally problematic, due to built-in constraints on human attentional capacity, or "working memory." Mature writers work around their attentional limitations by employing a variety of executive procedures that make the writing task more manageable. Under the control of these procedures, text production is not so much a matter of beginning at the beginning and letting the text unfold, but more a matter of planning ahead, reviewing what has already been done, and shifting systematically from one aspect of the emerging text to another. Child writers are at a double disadvantage in this regard. First, their attentional capacities appear to be more limited than those of adults (Case, 1972; Pascual-Leone, 1970), so that the availability of efficient executive procedures is all the more important for them. But, second, their executive repertoires also appear to be more limited, so that their use of whatever they have in the way of attentional capacity is less efficient than it might otherwise be.

It seems likely that many of the inadequacies found in the fall writing samples resulted from failures on the writer's part to attend simultaneously to different parts of the text under construction—failures which were due, in turn, to limitations in the writer's attentional capacity and/or executive repertoire. If so, one would expect in general to find a higher incidence of such failures in places where the writer's attention was occupied by other aspects of the writing task. To give but one example from the present data, it is interesting to note in Gordon's thief story that his clarity of reference breaks down when it becomes necessary for him to coordinate the conflict in the story with its resolution.

In sum, the problems displayed in the fall writing samples may stem from a variety of underlying causes, including gaps in L2 linguistic competence, interference from L1 and oral language, lack of automaticity with regard to writing mechanics, and inadequate or absent procedures for deploying attention to the different parts of a text that must be coordinated with one another. This list of possible causes of the problems observed implies a similar list of possible solutions, and therefore in a general way amounts to an assessment of the children's instructional needs with respect to writing during the year of the study. It is with these needs in mind that I approach the available data on the learning environments in the children's classrooms in hopes of determining how their needs were met.

First, however, it is important to note that effective instruction not only addresses areas of need but also builds on abilities that have already developed, and the fall writing data speak to the latter issue as well. In spite of all their inadequacies, the fall writing samples constitute clear evidence that the children had already learned enough English and enough about written language to produce something in the way of an English text. What the writing samples do not show is the latent competence in English and in written language (including relevant knowledge associated primarily with L1) that was not manifested in the children's English writing performance, for the various reasons that have been discussed. The existence of this competence can be inferred from other data sources, as I demonstrated earlier when I cited evidence of Maria's knowledge regarding the story genre in her Spanish writing. But in order to assess the extent of such hidden competence, it would be necessary to explore the data on individual students in greater depth than is possible here, where the focus is on classroom learning environments and their effects on gains in writing.

Classroom Learning Environments

In many ways, the two third-grade classrooms with superior gains in writing seemed more different than alike. Classroom C5 was a place where the students generally remained in their seats during periods of instruction. Their teacher, a middle-aged man whom I will call Mr. Allen, spent a major portion of each day teaching the whole class, or working simultaneously with subgroups of students who were at different levels of proficiency. Although a teacher's aide was present much of the time, Mr. Allen relied rather little on her for actual instruction. All teaching was done in English, as Mr. Allen does not speak Cantonese, but the students sometimes spoke to each other about their work in Cantonese as well as English, as a certain amount of quiet talk was permitted among students when they were not involved in teacher-centered activities.

In contrast, classroom S4 was a place in which students moved around more freely and spoke to one another a great deal, often in Spanish. Their teacher, whom I will call Ms. Zamora, was a younger woman who spoke fluent Spanish as well as English. In comparison with Mr. Allen, Ms. Zamora was somewhat more likely to be found working with one group of students while her aide worked with another, with still other children working more or less on their own. Ms. Zamora's class was designated as a bilingual class, and she did occasionally speak Spanish while teaching, though not nearly as often as she spoke English. Her aide provided some language arts instruction in Spanish, but that was confined mainly to students who were regarded as fairly proficient in English.

It is tempting to speculate that the global differences between these two class-rooms were congruent with culturally based differences between the two groups of students in them, so that learning was enhanced in each case by virtue of the congruence. While this sort of optimal match hypothesis may have merit, what I want to emphasize here are those features of instruction that had to do specifically with writing or with related aspects of language and language use. This emphasis is motivated not only by the immediate goal of accounting for gains in writing, but also by the finding that—relative to other classrooms—Mr. Allen's and Ms. Zamora's did not have as high gains in some other areas of achievement, which suggests that their unusually high gains in English writing resulted from specific features of instruction pertaining to writing and language and not just from the overall ambiance in each classroom.

With regard to writing and related activities, similarities between the two class-rooms were more striking than differences. First of all, the writing of texts longer than a single sentence was a frequent, almost daily activity for students in both classes. This observation will hardly surprise anyone who believes that the way to help children learn to write is to "let them write," or that practice makes perfect, but exactly why frequent writing should be associated with gains in writing is a question I will come back to later. The point I want to make here is that frequent writing per se does not suffice to explain the gains made by Mr. Allen's and Ms. Zamora's students, because students in some (but by no means all) of the other classes wrote about as often, but without making as much progress between fall and spring. Thus we must look beyond sheer frequency for other, more qualitative features of writing instruction that might have distinguished classrooms C5 and S4 from the others, and we must consider the possible contribution of other language activities as well.

In neither of the classrooms did the approach to writing instruction seem particu-larly revolutionary, at least not by current standards. However, the two writing programs did have some features in common that seem noteworthy in relation to the observed gains in writing. Both Mr. Allen and Ms. Zamora treated writing as an act of communication about content that is important to the writer and to the reader.

That is, both teachers favored writing assignments in which children were given opportunities to write about something of personal interest, and they helped students develop their topics through such prewriting activities as discussion and drawing. Both teachers also expressed their own genuine interest in content when reading what students had written. Moreover, they sometimes indicated that they thought others would be interested too, by posting student writings on their bulletin boards, for example. Occasionally Mr. Allen would share his enthusiasm for a piece of writing in a very immediate way, by saying to the class "Hey! Listen to this!" whereupon the piece would be read aloud by Mr. Allen or the student.

Along with this clear concern for the content of student compositions there was, in both classes, an equally clear concern for the formal aspects of writing as well. For the most part, matters of form were not addressed through how-to-write lessons, except insofar as spelling, punctuation, and the like were taught as separate subjects in the standard language arts curriculum for third grade. But both teachers gave students informative feedback on their writing mechanics and, more generally, on how well they had communicated their intent in writing. Students in both classes were usually expected to make immediate use of teacher feedback in producing more presentable revisions of what they had written. In general, then, form was approached as something to think about after content. Mr. Allen expressed this attitude succinctly in some instructions he gave his class on one occasion when they were putting the finishing touches on letters they had written to friends in another class. He said, "Read all your sentences, make sure each one makes sense, and then make sure each one ends with a period."

It seems likely that students would have profited in a number of ways from the writing instruction they experienced in Mr. Allen's and Ms. Zamora's classrooms. First, their motivation to engage in writing is likely to have increased in response to the teacher's attitude toward writing as something to take pleasure in, but also as something to work at in order to enhance both the writer's and the reader's appreciation of the product. With regard to possible effects on the ways in which students approached the work of writing, several currently popular notions about writing and writing instruction come to mind. It might be said, for example, that students in the two classrooms were assisted in developing a sense of audience, a sense of text as artifact, and a sense of text production as a craft that includes prewriting, writing, and rewriting. To translate these notions into the kind of theoretical terminology I used earlier, it might be said that the children were guided toward constructing executive procedures for planning and reprocessing text—procedures for thinking about what they would say in writing and how they would say it; for evaluating what they had written (or thought about writing) to see how it would read; and for shifting their attention between form and content while they were engaged in these planning and reprocessing activities. In addition, frequent production of English in the context of writing presumably would have given the students more automaticity in using their knowledge of English, and it would have established a closer association between that knowledge and the task of composing a text. All of these effects of the writing instruction that occurred in the two classrooms would have served to make relevant aspects of linguistic and communicative competence more accessible to students in the context of writing. They also would have helped to make writing performance more resistant to the debilitating effects of information overload and interference from irrelevant knowledge associated with L1 or oral language use.

A number of other language activities observed in both classrooms seemed to support and supplement what was done with respect to writing. Both teachers gave their students many opportunities for extended production of oral English in the form of narratives, descriptions, explanations, and so on. This contrasted sharply with some of the other classrooms, in which students were seldom called on (or permitted) to produce utterances of more than a word or two. Students in Mr. Allen's and Ms. Zamora's classes also received a good deal of second language input, in the form of teacher talk, student talk, and reading. This input was likely to have helped students fill gaps in their basic knowledge of English, because both teachers seemed fairly adept at monitoring student comprehension and at providing sufficient context for the language being used to enable students to figure out what meanings were being expressed. Again, this kind of input compared favorably, both in quantity and in quality, to what was observed in some of the other classrooms, where language input to students often seemed to be dominated by routine questions ("What page are you on?") and directives ("Turn to page 12"). Finally, there was, in both classrooms, a fair amount of reflection on and talk about language itself. Mr. Allen, for example, frequently paused in the middle of a lesson to comment on a particular word or way of saying something, and Ms. Zamora was observed teaching a lesson on the concept of a sentence in which students were asked to make judgments as to whether or not a particular statement was a complete sentence, to explain why it was or was not, and to suggest ways of making incomplete sentences complete. "Metalinguistic" activities such as these probably helped students learn to reflect on their own writing and to interpret teacher feedback on it.

In their use of these other language activities, and in their approach to the teaching of writing, Mr. Allen and Ms. Zamora seemed to build effectively on abilities their students already had, such as the ability to begin producing English text and the ability to reflect on language and communication in ways that appear to become possible developmentally by about age 8 or 9. They also seemed to go a long way toward addressing the whole range of their students' needs, as I described them earlier. In fact it may be this breadth, more than anything else, that accounts for the successes the two teachers enjoyed in helping their students learn to write in English. My impression from preliminary inspection of the data on the other teachers is that, while each may have attended to *some* of the prerequisites for gains in English writing, none was as comprehensive as Mr. Allen or Ms. Zamora.

If breadth of instruction is as important as I have suggested, then it also seems important to speculate as to how Mr. Allen and Ms. Zamora managed to achieve such breadth without sacrificing depth, i.e., without giving only superficial attention to some of the needs they addressed. One way both teachers seemed to avoid this pitfall was by individualizing instruction, so that different children were involved in different activities that built upon their own particular abilities and addressed their own particular needs. For instance, the one-on-one writing conference, which was used often by both teachers, is a prime example of an instructional strategy that lends itself to individualization. Ms. Zamora, especially, seemed to adjust her demands for conventional English in writing according to what she thought the individual child could manage. But neither Ms. Zamora nor Mr. Allen seemed to work as hard at individualizing their teaching as some teachers do, and there may be practical limits as to how much teachers can rely on individualization to meet all of their students' needs anyway. It is not always possible to determine exactly what a given child's needs and abilities are at a particular time, and even if it were, the child's needs might well be so varied that there would still be the problem of somehow attending effectively to all of them within the time available for instruction.

Perhaps the principal solution to this problem lies in the "richness" of the instructional activities a teacher employs. A rich activity is one in which students can increase their knowledge and skills in a variety of relevant ways all at the same time. Better yet, it is also one that children at different levels of developed ability can profit from more or less equally. Writing itself is a very rich activity, especially under conditions of the sort that prevailed in Mr. Allen's and Ms. Zamora's classrooms. With appropriate support, writing provides students with opportunities to practice component skills and to coordinate them in the ways that are required for writing at more advanced levels. Activities other than writing can also be rich with regard to the kinds of learning that are needed for progress in writing. Reading, for example, can be used as a basis not only for acquiring new linguistic forms but also for reflecting on language and for practicing oral production, as when students are asked not merely to read a text aloud but to interpret what they have read and to explain their interpretations. Drama and poetry can be instructionally rich activities too, as Ms. Zamora demonstrated in her class when she helped each student study and rehearse a student-selected poem, in English, for recording on a class tape. When the tape was completed and the class listened to it together, there was rapt attention (and unusual silence) as each familiar voice, in turn, was heard reciting eloquently in a still somewhat unfamiliar language whose possibilities the students were coming to appreciate.

To summarize this discussion of classroom learning environments, I will propose a hypothesis that seems to account for the observations I have reported. It is that success in helping children learn to write in English as a second language hinges primarily on the use of instructional activities that are rich in opportunities for exposure to, production of, and reflection on English discourse, and that such activities must include frequent writing, with guidance and feedback, on topics of personal interest.

Conclusion

In the introduction to this chapter, I suggested that helping children learn to write in English as a second language might be a unique problem, and that it might not be sufficient just to borrow solutions from current thinking about the teaching of writing and about the teaching of English as a second language. Yet a direct look at some data on the problem of interest has led me to some hypotheses which might well have been derived from existing theory and research on writing development (e.g., Bereiter & Scardamalia, 1982; Graves, 1983) and on second language learning (e.g., Canale & Swain, 1980; Ramirez & Stromquist, 1979), and which also seem consistent with recent ideas about the teaching of writing in English as a second language (e.g. Valadez, 1981). It would be fair, then, to ask whether the present analysis adds anything new. By way of conclusion, I will offer a few responses to that question.

At the very least, the present analysis suggests strongly that children can learn to write in English as a second language through a program of instruction that emphasizes doing just that, even when the children's initial efforts at English writing seem quite limited. In the face of such limitations, some teachers may be inclined to retreat from English writing as an instructional activity and to focus instead on giving their students a firmer foundation for writing by working on spelling, vocabulary, and grammar. The problem with this sort of bottom-up approach is that it neglects the communicative purposes of writing and the higher-level composing procedures essential to effective communication. Moreover, it tends to involve students in activities that are not instructionally rich.

The present analysis has highlighted the concept of instructionally rich activities as a basis for explaining the superior writing gains that were observed in two classrooms. Richness is a concept that seems potentially important for all kinds of teaching, including the teaching of writing and the teaching of a second language, but it may be especially important for teaching second language learners to write in their new language, simply because they have so much more to learn. However, while richness may be a useful concept for instructional planning, it seems unlikely that just any instructional activity aimed at multiple objectives will necessarily succeed, and therefore a question for further research is exactly how instructionally rich activities work. Is there a principled basis for planning instructionally rich activities, or are they more dependent on the art of teaching, or on trial and error?

A limitation of the present analysis is that it did not include attention to the ways in which individual differences and their interactions with instruction might have affected the extent of the subjects' gains in writing. Not all children in the two classrooms gained as much as the four children who were selected for closer study. It may be that the needs of more children could have been addressed effectively had there been additional variations on the same instructional themes in response to individual differences. There were considerable individual differences among children in the present sample with regard to the nature and extent of their proficiencies in L1. A study of individual differences might therefore do more to indicate the various ways in which learning to write in English as a second language can be a unique situation. I have mainly characterized it as a situation that gives students double trouble, but perhaps—as others have suggested (Cummins, 1979; Edelsky, 1982)—it is also a situation that can give some students unique learning opportunities, both in writing development and in second language acquisition.

References

Ammon, P., Kroll, L., & Cann-Ortiz, M. (1984, April). *Dimensional analysis of children's writing*. Paper presented at the annual meeting of the American Educational Research Association, New Orleans.

Bereiter, C., & Scardamalia, M. (1982). From conversation to composition: The role of instruction in a developmental process. In R. Glaser (Ed.), *Advances in instructional psychology* (Vol. 2). Hillsdale, NJ: Lawrence Erlbaum.

Canale, M., & Swain, M. (1980). Theoretical bases of communicative approaches to second language teaching and testing. *Applied Linguistics, 1,* 1–47.

Case, R. (1972). Validation of a neo-Piagetian mental capacity construct. *Journal of Experimental Child Psychology, 14,* 287–302.

Cook-Gumperz, J., & Gumperz, J. J. (1981). From oral to written culture: The transition to literacy. In M. F. Whiteman (Ed.), *Variation in writing: Functional and linguistic-cultural differences.* Hillsdale, NJ: Lawrence Erlbaum.

Cummins, J. (1979). Linguistic interdependence and the educational development of bilingual children. *Review of Educational Research, 49,* 222–251.

Cummins, J. (1981). Four misconceptions about language proficiency in bilingual education. *NABE Journal, 5*(3), 31–45.

Edelsky, C. (1982). Writing in a bilingual program: The relation of L1 and L2 texts. *TESOL Quarterly, 16,* 211–228.

Graves, D. H. (1983). *Writing: Teachers and children at work.* Exeter, NH: Heinemann.

Olson, D. R. (1977). From utterance to text: The bias of language in speech and writing. *Harvard Educational Review, 47*(3), 257–281.

Olson, D. R., & Torrance, N. (1981). Learning to meet the requirements of written text: Language development in the school years. In C. H. Frederiksen & J. F. Dominic (Eds.), *Writing: The nature, development, and teaching of written communication: Vol. 2. Writing: Process, development, and communication.* Hillsdale, NJ: Lawrence Erlbaum.

Oxford, R., Pol, L., Lopez, D., Stupp, P., Gendell, M., & Peng, S. (1981). Projections of non-English language background and limited English proficient persons in the United States to the year 2000: Educational planning in the demographic context. *NABE Journal, 5*(3), 1–30.

Pascual-Leone, J. (1970). A mathematical model for the transition rule in Piaget's developmental stages. *Acta Psychologica, 32,* 301–345.

Pascual-Leone, J., & Goodman, D. (1979). Intelligence and experience: A neo-Piagetian approach. *Instructional Science, 8,* 301–367.

Ramirez, A. G., & Stromquist, N. P. (1979). ESL methodology and student language learning in bilingual elementary schools. *TESOL Quarterly, 13,* 145–158.

Rubin, A. (1980). A theoretical taxonomy of the differences between oral and written language. In R. J. Spiro, B. C. Bruce, & W. F. Brewer (Eds.), *Theoretical issues in reading comprehension.* Hillsdale, NJ: Lawrence Erlbaum.

Scardamalia, M., & Bereiter, C. (in press). Written composition. In M. Wittrock (Ed.), *Handbook of research on teaching* (3rd ed.). New York: Macmillan.

Valadez, C. M. (1981). Identity, power, and writing skills: The case of the Hispanic bilingual student. In M. F. Whiteman (Ed.), *Variation in writing: Functional and linguistic-cultural differences.* Hillsdale, NJ: Lawrence Erlbaum.

Wong Fillmore, L., Ammon, P., Ammon, M. S., Delucchi, K., Jensen, J., McLaughlin, B., & Strong, M. (1983). *Second year report: Learning English through bilingual instruction* (Contract No. 400-80-0030). Washington, DC: National Institute of Education.

5

The Language of Writing Groups: How Oral Response Shapes Revision*

Anne Ruggles Gere
Ralph S. Stevens
University of Washington, Seattle

Students in a fifth-grade class have been assigned to write descriptive essays comparing two pictures in a series called "The Changing Countryside." These pictures depict the same scene at different periods of time, and the assignment is to compare how the scene had changed. One student, Ellen, reads the following draft aloud to three others in the class:

It seemed just like yesterday; I remember it so well. The road was dirt; now it is cement. Now trains come by more than they used to. They tore down the old dock and put in pipes for the stream to run through. It looks like a whole new city. The town seems smaller and there is a railroad station. The bridge on the old road is gone. I wish it was like before.

Ellen reads the draft twice, stopping briefly between readings. After she finishes the second reading the three students, who have been listening and taking notes, begin making comments:

Lynn: I like that part where you said that you remembered it so well.
Kurt: When you said the town seemed smaller? They're, um, they're adding on and stuff so it would be bigger if there's a train station there now.
Ellen: What I meant was, was with the fog it seems smaller.
Kurt: Ok, um you should of . . . of . . . if you said, if you meant that, why didn't you put in because of the fog?
Ellen: Maybe I should change it.
Mick: Ok, um, . . . why do you wish it was like it was before? You should put like, you know, what you did, um, before to make it real fun and stuff.

These students are participating in a writing group, a small subdivision of the class that works independently of the teacher and is variously termed "reading group," "writing group," "peer response group," "writing circle," or "helping circle." Whatever the name, writing groups usually consist of from 4 to 6 students who meet during regular class periods to read and respond to each other's writing.

A great deal has been written about writing groups (Beaven, 1977; Benson,

* Support for this project came from the National Institute of Education, grant no. NIE-G81-0113.

1979; Bruffee, 1973; Buxton, 1975; Elbow, 1973; Gebhardt, 1980; Hawkins, 1976; Lagana, 1973; Macrorie, 1970; Moffett, 1968; Murray, 1968). This existing literature suggests procedures for establishing and maintaining writing groups, recommends them as an alternative to grading papers, points to their value for general intellectual development, and makes claims for the value of peer response for developing writers. However, this literature does not include any close examination of what actually occurs in writing group meetings or of how writing groups affect the writing process, particularly the revising which may take place subsequent to group meetings. Our study evolved in response to this perceived omission.

What we wanted to know can be reduced to two general questions: Can the oral response provided by writing groups be described as evaluation, and does it shape subsequent revisions of the writing? To answer the first question we need to analyze the responses of students in writing groups. What do students tell each other about their writing? What is the apparent function of these responses? Our answers to these questions are based on tape recordings of writing group meetings, interviews with students and teachers, drafts of papers read in writing group meetings, and subsequent revisions. A total of 9 groups and 46 students were involved, representing six teachers and nine classes. Elementary, middle school, and high school were included, with 2 groups from fifth grade, 4 from eighth grade, and 3 from grades ten through twelve. We recorded from 3 to 6 meetings of each of these groups over a six-month period. Thirty-nine transcripts, ranging in length from 3 to 35 pages, contain the language recorded in these meetings. Typically, each transcript contains responses to drafts of all group members. The comments on Ellen's draft which appear at the beginning of this chapter are excerpted from a transcript which contains responses to the writing of Lynn, Kurt, and Mick as well.

The teachers whose classes participated in this study had all been teacher-consultants in the Puget Sound Writing Project, an experience which had included participation in writing groups. The procedure they were familiar with is based on what Elbow (1973) terms the "teacherless writing group," and follows these steps at each meeting:

1. The writer reads the same selection twice, taking a short break between the two readings.
2. The writer does not comment on, or apologize for, the selection read.
3. Listeners, who have no copy of the manuscript, make notes between readings and during the second reading, but not during the first.
4. After the first reading, listeners briefly record their strongest impressions of the writing, noting the language and ideas they found most striking. During the second reading, they take more detailed notes on their responses to the selection, usually recording language that they particularly did or did not like.
5. After the second reading, each listener in turn comments on the writing with the purpose not so much of evaluating it as of communicating to the writer the impression her/his language has made. (As we shall see, this does not mean that responses do not have an evaluative function.) The writer does not speak during these comments, except to ask for clarification.

6. The total time available to the writing group is divided by the number of members so that each member has an opportunity to read and receive response.

As you can see from the fifth-grade excerpt, these procedures are not always strictly observed. For instance, Ellen "violates" the rule that writers should not defend their pieces when she responds to Kurt's comment by "explaining" that she was talking about the effect of the fog rather than the literal size of the town. In some cases teachers modified these procedures to suit their own purposes or because they felt changes were necessary for particular students. One senior-high teacher, for example, sometimes gave writing groups specific features to watch for, features reflecting the purposes of the assignment. Two other high school groups regularly engaged the writer in dialogue concerning the text in order to develop and refine both content and style. What the procedures describe is a common point of departure for all the teachers in the study; the procedures actually followed by their groups are variations on this one theme. The following account of the most notable variations should also provide a general sense of how the groups worked.

One of the two eighth-grade teachers, who felt that junior high students have a tendency to abuse each other and was concerned that they might use the writing group to take advantage of one another, did not allow any negative statements. Students were instructed to say what they liked about each other's writing, and to indicate things they did not understand in it, but they were not to say anything about what they did not like. In an interview this teacher explained that she believed the value of group response was that it gives the students a chance to see how their writing affects other people so the students can "internalize" that information and make whatever judgments they deem necessary. Maybe a student would listen to all these people responding to the writing and think, "Gee, I really was able to make the point I was trying to make." For this teacher the purpose of the group is not so much to influence the writing of a particular paper as to influence the writer's overall attitude toward writing, as well as to internalize general criteria for effective writing.

In other cases, students, like Ellen, took the procedures into their own hands, modifying them to use the resources of the group most effectively. While Ellen's "explanation" can be seen as defensive and even argumentative, her comment prompts Kurt to offer more specific advice on how she could improve her writing. We found this kind of exchange occurring frequently in writing groups. Occasionally it led to antagonistic exchanges such as the following from another meeting of the same fifth-grade group.

Ellen read a draft of a story titled "Renting the Castle." Students had been given a scenario and asked to write a narrative based upon it. The scenario had a character, Duke, whose castle was for rent, and who was approached by some vampires who wanted to rent it. Students were expected to decide whether the duke rented the castle, and why, giving at least one reason for and one against the decision. The group made initial comments on Ellen's draft and then continued with the following:

Kurt: You didn't tell the reasons for letting and not letting the vampires.

Ellen: Oh you want to make a bet, then what's this?
Kurt: Yeah, how much?
Lynn: Okay, 58 thousand dollars.
Ellen: Okay.
Kurt: Ain't got that much.
Ellen: Okay, one reason for not letting 'cuz they were looking for a treasure and
         one reason for it was because they um, killed people.
Kurt: Yeah, but you didn't say that in your story.
Ellen: I did too. It says they killed people. See it says . . .
Kurt: Yeah, but it doesn't say the reason . . .
Ellen: "The ragged old man said they killed people and turned them into bats and
         so they wouldn't rent it to them."
Kurt: But you said the guy was telling rumors.
Ellen: Rumors, yeah.
Kurt: Yeah, you didn't say anything about letting or not letting, right?
Ellen: Oh, I skipped the rumor part.
Mick: No, you didn't.
Ellen: Well where's the rumor part then?
Mick: It's in the very beginning.
Kurt: Read your story over.

(Ellen reads her draft to herself and rereads portions of it to the group. Some
group members ask to see the paper for themselves, so Kurt takes it and reads a
section aloud.)

Ellen: I also told them. I told the rumors and the reasons against, and the reasons for it.
         There, there, there. So give me my story. Good.
Mick: I just put it back by your . . .
Ellen: My mother went over it and she's better at language than you, she should know, I
         mean.
Kurt: Well, she doesn't.
Ellen: She does too. It says the reasons for it and the reasons against it and everything.
         Come on, can't you ever be satisfied?
Kurt: No, not with your junk.
Ellen: It's a good story.
Kurt: Oops, I'm sorry, I didn't mean that.

(Kurt realizes that his statement about "your junk" is an attack on Ellen and is
embarrassed because his comment has been recorded. The discussion continues for
some time, ending when one group member goes to get clarification about the
assignment from the teacher.)

Although this kind of degeneration into personal attack and vigorous argument
about a piece of writing does occur, it is relatively rare. In discussion of 163 pieces
of writing, we found approximately 7 such exchanges. Most often the questions or

explanations from writers served, as did Ellen's statement about the fog, to elicit more specific response from group members.

A notable example of students modifying procedures for their own purposes occurred in two high school groups in junior "Challenge English" classes, courses for particularly able students. These students frequently participated in lengthy interchanges about their writing, asking for advice on how to approach topics or how to phrase a particular idea. The following excerpt is typical of these groups. The students were working on junior essays, 500-word expository interpretations of *The Red Badge of Courage*. Although the assignment contained guidelines for the form of the paper (admonitions about complete sentences, support for ideas and absence of errors), students were free to select their own topics. The teacher had helped them to decide on topics by asking them to write what they would remember most about the book. Danny read a summary statement from his paper:

"All through *The Red Badge of Courage* Henry tries to become a man and when he finally does, he finds it is not what he expected."

Tom:	Do you think that was what he was trying to do though?
Danny:	Yeah.
Tom:	Do you?
John:	I don't think . . .
Danny:	Of course . . .
John:	I don't think he set out with that purpose in mind.
Danny:	No.
Tom:	To say "I'm going to be a man."
Danny:	No, but he is just kind of trying to prove himself to able to say, "I'm a man." Well, you know.
John:	I . . . I got the idea he . . .
Tom:	He may have felt this way when he made it through a battle.
John:	Yeah, and like he, he was saying he wanted stories to tell his kids.
Tom:	Yeah.
Danny:	OK.
John:	That sort of deal. He wanted to be a hero. He wanted to be looked up to.
Tom:	Yeah, he wanted to be a hero, that's what it was.
Danny:	Oh, so Henry tries to be a hero when he finally becomes a——Ok, can I see your pencil?
Tom:	Sure.
Danny:	Thanks.
John:	So what are you going to use to back it up?
Danny:	Well, there, I am going to talk about first, how he's talking about ummm the brok . . . vision of broken bladed glory, and you know, talking about men were too sophisticated now to have battles and war and then you, the end where he's just fighting instinctively.
John:	OK.

Danny: You, where they, when . . . the battle where they said that he was a war demon or
          something like that.
Tom: Un huh.
John: OK.

The group worked with a relatively short piece of prose and spent most of its
energy on the term "man" versus "hero." The writer participated actively in the
discussion, asking and answering questions designed to help him amplify the idea of
his initial statement. Although the group might be accused of spending an inordinate
amount of time on one detail, the discussion led Danny to an enlarged understanding of his topic as is evident in his explanations at the end of the excerpt. This kind
of freewheeling discussion occurred frequently in this writing group. Often, as here,
the discussion seemed to fuss a particular word or phrase to excess (on one occasion
the second group spent nearly five minutes debating whether the phrase "out-
rageous extent" should be used), but as Danny's concluding comments indicate, the
less structured discussion was often very helpful to group members. In interviews
the students asserted that the writing group had given them a new perspective on
their writing, and they claimed that the stated procedures, which they had used
originally, were not as useful for them as the collaborative procedure they had
evolved. Evidence of the effectiveness of the variant procedure came in an unre-
corded comment over heard as students came into class one day. A member of this
group asked if writing groups were going to meet and continued, "We have to
meet; I *need* some help from my group."

As is evident from variations in procedures, whether introduced by the teachers
or by students, the writing groups in this study were not subject to strict controls.
All groups did adhere to the principle of reading work aloud twice and of making
oral responses to work read, but the quality and delivery of those responses and the
role of the writer in the group varied considerably. However, since this study was
designed to be descriptive rather than experimental, these variations provided additional information rather than confounding data. We began from the premise that
the most useful starting place in the uncharted language of writing groups would be
to describe it as it occurs naturally rather than to impose artificial constraints on it.

Because we were interested in naturally occurring language, we paid particular
attention to both the nature of the equipment and the introduction of it into classrooms. Participants in writing groups frequently interrupt one another or speak
while another person is talking, so we used a mixer to separate individual voices
during recording sessions, and we attached lavalier microphones to students'
clothing so equipment was neither encumbering nor particularly visible. To ensure
that the novelty of the equipment did not inhibit students, we brought it into classes
early in the year and recorded group meetings that did not become part of the data.

Perhaps the best testimony to the effectiveness of reducing the artificiality of
recording writing groups is found in the transcripts themselves. For example, although Kurt, the fifth grader who attacks Ellen's "junk," is embarrassed because

his attack has been recorded, the language he used in the attack cannot be described as anything other than naturally occurring.

What we learned from looking at that language can be described in quantitative and qualitative terms. All recorded responses were divided into idea units (Chafe, 1980), spurts of language marked by intonation (where pitch either rises or falls), by pauses, and by syntax (an idea unit is usually a single clause). The total 39 transcripts in which 163 students' papers were discussed yielded 11,264 idea units. These idea units were coded according to a three-part system which identified the language function, the general focus of attention, and the topic of the utterance. The following description explains the coding system in detail.

Code	Rubric

Inform

IGP   Inform re group procedures. Idea units in this category deal with such issues as the order in which students are to read and procedures for responding.

> "We need a writing group form."
> "Your turn."
> "Okay, I'm ready."

IGC   Informs re the group except for procedures for reading and responding.

> "We need Patty in here."
> "My thesaurus is at home."

IGX   An idea unit that informs re the context of the group. These would refer to topics related to the group, but outside it in time or beyond its existence as a unit meeting to discuss writing. IGX can also refer to the recording process.

> "I went to the basketball game Friday night."
> "Look, there's Mr. Morgan."
> "No, we're not gonna test (the microphones)."

IWC   An idea unit that informs re the content of the writing. This could be an evaluation or judgment, or simply a reference to something in the writing.

> "That's gross."
> "It's just a hole that goes back in time—a black hole."
> "Um, I like how you use 'appear,' and 'sun deck'."

IWF   An idea unit that informs re the form of the writing. This could be structure, length or style, anything that has to do with formal properties of the text.

> "It isn't in first person."
> "This is the prologue."
> "We have to watch our length."

IWX   Informs re the context for the writing, whether the writing assignment, or the form or content of the writing.

> "And it's just, you know, the way that (Stephen Crane) uses color it just shows that nature could really care less what's going on with man."

continued

Code	Rubric

Inform (*continued*)
IWX (*continued*)

    "Stream of—stream of consciousness became famous with James Joyce's *Ulysses*."
    "And (Hemingway) used really short sentences with really direct words, you know."
    "Cause I think Miss Spenard said that we had to have something like two sentences."
    "Well, I am considering writing on that one."

IWP   Informs re the writing process. Idea units in this category will usually refer to the general experience of writing. Comments by the writer about how s/he intends to revise go under the DWP category.

    "But I usually, I usually write it, and then I cut it down."

IWR   Informs re another idea unit. This most often occurs in writing groups that give a lot of attention to revision, which leads to comments, about how to revise the text. These comments, rather than the text itself, often become the subject of discussion.

    "I like 'wafer.'"
    "Okay, 'cause then we are getting into things like 'insolent' and 'offensive' with 'outrageous.'"
    "He doesn't have to make it longer."

Direct

DGP   Directs re the groups procedures. This is commonly an idea unit that directs a student to read, or that keeps the group's attention on the task of responding.
    "Yeah, read the introductory paragraph."
    "You go first, Andy."
    "Say your comments."

Groups that deal with the written text direct its use.

    "Can I look at it?"
    "Let me see this part right here."

Note that questions can be directions.

    "Would you read your opening?"

DGC   Directs re a group activity not related to reading and responding to writing.

    "I say we write a group paper."

DGX   Directs re some activity related to the group but outside the group meeting.

    "Tomorrow we should talk about your draft."

DWP   Directs re the writing process. Idea units in this category are commonly suggestions to the writer about changes in wording, sentence structure or content.

    "That's a quote he could use."
    "The 'little' doesn't need to be in it."
    "Oh, I think that you might, you need—need to describe a little bit more and tell more about cuz . . ."
    "You might want to make it longer."
    "I'll just have to erase it from . . ."
    "I don't know—I'll just keep it like that."
    "Come on, write your story."

Code	Rubric

Direct (*continued*)
DWP (*continued*)

"Well, finish it."
"OK, write one more sentence."

Elicit

EGP   Elicits information about group procedure.

"Are you done with your comments?"
"I have to read it again?"
"Do we have time?"
"Who's going first?"

EGC   Elicits information regarding the group but not related to procedures.

"How do you spell your name?"
"What do the initials of our group stand for?"

EGX   Elicits information re the context of the group. This could also concern the recording process.

"Are we gonna test (the microphones)?"
"What did you do this weekend?"

EWC   Elicits information about the content of the writing. Often asked of the writer, when a group member needs clarification of something in the writing. Includes questions by the writer about how group responds to content.

"What was that guy's name?"
"How do you spell 'concussion'?"
"What is the definition of determinism?"

EWF   Elicits information re the form of the writing. Includes questions by the writer about how groups respond to discourse/grammar—both in comments and the writing itself.

"Does the ending work at all?"
"Any slow spots?"
"How long was it?"

EWX   Elicits information about the context for the writing. This could be a request for information about the writing assignment.

"Is it supposed to be exciting?"
"That's a book?"
"Who wrote it?"
"You think 'nature is impervious' is the main theme of the book?"

EWP   Elicits information or directions/suggestions re the writing process. These will often be requests for suggestions about how a composition might be written or rewritten.

"And how are you going to lead her to saying that?"
"Um-m-m—so how are you going to end yours?"
"You haven't written one yet?"
"I need help on proof for that."
"I need one more (example), I think."
"Will that look bad if I use the quote she used?"

continued

Code	Rubric

Elicit (*continued*)
EWP (*continued*)

      "Could I say 'important theme'?"
      "Well, don't you think, don't you think going to a slumber party is—?"
      "Which one—do you like either one at all?"

EWR   Elicits re a response to the writing or writing process, that is, it asks a question about something someone in the group has said.

      "What do you mean, 'run-on'?" (Asking for clarification of what another student has just said.)
      "Just what do you all think: 'The belief that nature is impervious is given important position as the theme'?"

H   Phatic utterance. Contains no content but serves as placeholder.

      "Umm"
      "Well"
      "Okay"

/   Slash at end of idea unit indicated incompleted unit. May result from either an interruption or speaker's inability to complete thought.

      "Well it seems to me . . ."
      "But on this page . . ."

( )   Parentheses around idea unit indicate reflexive language, the writer talking about his or her own writing.

[ ]   Brackets indicate language of observer.

As Table 1 indicates, the greatest number of responses fell in the IWC category, language which informed the author about the writing under discussion. In quantitative terms, then, it is clear that students spend a majority of writing group time talking to one another about their writing. The more complex (and interesting) task is to determine the substance of these utterances. Applying the coding system to excerpts from transcripts offers a first step toward understanding the language in qualitative terms. The discussion of Ellen's writing is coded:

IWC   Lynn: I like that part where you said that you remembered it so well.
IWC   Kurt: When you said the town seemed smaller,
IWC   They're, um, they're adding on and stuff so it would be bigger if there's a train station there now.
(IWC) Ellen: What I meant was, was with the fog it seems smaller.
DWP   Kurt: Ok, um, you should of . . . of . . . if you said, if you meant that why didn't you put in because of the fog?
(DWP) Ellen: Maybe I should change it.
EWC   Mick: Ok, um, why do you wish it was like it was before? You should put like, you know, what you did, um, before to make it real fun and stuff.

This excerpt is typical in that the directing language and the eliciting language have similar functions. Kurt's question about the fog is similar to Mick's question

Table 1. Number of Each Type of Idea Unit

Function category	N of idea units concerning writing		N of idea units concerning group		Totals
Inform	IWC	3806	IGC	352	4158
	IWF	352	—	—	352
	IWX	862	IGX	243	1105
	IWP	329	IGP	331	660
	IWR	298	—	—	298
Totals	IW	5647	IG	924	6571
Direct	DWP	1340	DGP	672	2012
	—	—	DGC	28	28
	—	—	DGX	9	9
Totals	DW	1340	DG	709	2049
Elicit	EWC	557	EGC	54	611
	EWF	35	—	—	35
	EWX	88	EGX	61	149
	EWP	140	EGP	162	302
	EWR	121	—	—	121
Totals	EW	941	EG	227	1218
Phatic (H)					1424
Total idea units	Writing	7928	Group	1910	11264

about how it was before and to many other questions asked by writing group participants, questions such as: "Was it about this little boy who has to do all this to become a man and all that?" or "Can you tell me when he goes over to Philip's house?" These questions challenge the author to clarify, to provide more detail, and they indicate exactly where the listeners had difficulty understanding or felt something was missing. Likewise, the directing responses give authors (or authors give themselves) very specific instructions on what they should do to improve the writing. Ellen knows she should add the fog and explain what made the former scene more attractive. Other authors are given instructions such as: "You can describe the hole more, how big it is and, you know, what did it look like and stuff," or "You should change 'Scott said "My name is Scott"' to 'the boy said "My name is Scott"'." Students in writing groups do not feel obliged to follow all directions or to deal with all the questions raised by eliciting responses; as one student put it in an interview, "Sometimes I just write down what they say to make them feel good and then I revise the way I want to."

Responses which fall into the informing category are much more diffuse. One general category of informing response is *evaluative*. Some, like Lynn's "I like that part" provide reinforcement for the writer, indicating what sections of the writing worked well. A majority of informing comments fell into this category of praising specific features in the writing. (Even when we subtract data from the one eighth-grade teacher who insisted that all comments be positive, the largest number of comments still fall in this category.) Group members frequently make global comments such as "it was good" or "I liked it," but in almost every case these comments are accompanied by details as to why it was good or the specific language which the responder liked. Other evaluative comments point to less effective parts in the writing: "The part about the saber tooth was pretty gross," or "Where it said my name is Scott, it sounded funny," or "I don't know why they killed the pig." Here, as with positive comments, authors are given clear indications of the language in questions.

Another kind of informing language can be described as *collaborative*. Here group members pool intellectual resources to help one person develop an idea or find the right way to approach a question. The high school students who discuss *The Red Badge of Courage* provide an extended example of this kind of informing function. John's statements, "He was saying he wanted stories to tell his kids," "He wanted to be a hero," "He wanted to be looked up to," and Tom's statements, "He may have felt this way when he made it through a battle," and "Yeah, he wanted to be a hero, that's what it was," combine to help Danny see his topic in a new way. Sometimes this kind of collaboration occurs more fleetingly as in these comments in response to an eighth grader's story about a gang: "They should have to avoid their mothers because their mothers would think, y' know, well they're all beat up." The speaker is responding to the confusion of another group member who says, "Then they got beat up and stuff, but I don't really understand that," by suggesting a way to make the narrative less confusing.

Sometimes collaborative informing language comes in overlapping form where group members interrupt one another as they all work to develop an idea. Here is an example from a high school group:

Patty: But war is caused by a clash between people, between groups of people.
Mike: Right, it's not . . .
Patty: I mean it didn't start by, you know, a few men getting together.
Mike: Oh yeah.
Patty: And getting angry at each other . . .
Mike: That what she's saying . . .
Patty: It's caused because one, you know . . .
Mike: Yeah, I know what you mean . . .
Patty: Section of people disagreed with . . .
Mike: With another section, well that is what the civil war was . . .
Patty: With their traits or whatever . . .
Mike: Yeah.
Patty: How they like their life. I want to know what else you could . . .
Mike: Okay, since it's the civil war . . .
Patty: A war caused by . . .
Mike: Well, we'd be biased . . .

Although Mike and Patty interrupt one another continually throughout this exchange, the interruptions are supportive, aimed at developing the idea about war. We designate interruptions as collaborative if all speakers continue to elaborate upon the same topic rather than taking the discussion in another direction, and a significant amount of informing language took this overlapping collaborative form.

The language designated as informing, elicting, and directing has distinctive features, and we can learn something about the kinds of responses students make to one another's writing through considering these features. Yet, the language that takes writing as its topic has one feature in common: It tells the writer how the reader/listener makes meaning with what has been written. Students in writing groups tell authors what they think language says, they ask questions about the places which confuse them, and they suggest ways for the writing to do its job better. The term *response* means, literally, an answer or reply offered in reaction to a specific stimulus. The language of these writing groups is responsive in that it is sharply focused on the stimulus of the text, re-acting in a way that acknowledges the text and how the text is acting on the reader/listener. The significance of this can be appreciated by comparing writing group response with typical teacher comments. As we shall explain further on, teacher responses are highly generalized. They thus lack that focus on the text which we find in the language of writing groups and do not constitute a genuine reaction or response. That is, teacher comments give little account of how the text acts on the reader. To be considered genuine, a response should include some acknowledgement of the stimulus which prompts it, and by this definition, the language of writing groups is, for the most part, ''genuine'' response.

The power of writing group response manifests itself in a number of ways. One perverse example appeared in the eighth-grade class where students were instructed to make only positive comments. The following comments come from typical sessions of the writing group observed in this class:

Well, I like the way you used the German word, um *Blitzkrieg.*

I didn't really understand it very well.

Okay, well, I didn't really understand what you were talking about either.

I think the word *sludge* was kind of weird cuz I don't really know what you're talking about.

It sounds like you know what you're talking about. But some of the words you used I didn't really understand.

I think your words were kind of strong and might have got just a little bit carried away. And I thought it was pretty good.

First, you used ''Moral Majority'' a lot, a little too much, you know.

I don't know, for our age it's a little higher than we can comprehend . . . I mean you could probably explain it to us in a simpler way.

Ah, that ''green Peace''—I didn't really understand what that was.

I really thought the word "brutally" stood out.

I think you need to have, like more information in it.

Despite the injunction against it, there is criticism here, criticism specifically directed at helping authors convey their meanings more clearly. The group was nearly unanimous in telling Greg that his editorial needed to have "like, more information in it." All participants told Adam they were confused by or didn't understand his paper, and three of four listeners were quite emphatic in telling Kate the same thing about hers. To a writer intent on making meaning clear, these comments would carry clear messages: "add more information," "use simpler language," "explain your points more clearly." We feel that the spontaneous appearance of such language, despite instructions to the contrary, offers evidence of the power of this kind of response. We saw nothing to indicate that the students who "disobeyed" the teacher were challenging her authority; rather the force of the response itself seemed to take over, whether or not they intended it to.

A more negative example of the power of response appeared in a fifth-grade class, a class where personal attacks were frequent among members of the writing group. We have already seen, in the argument between Kurt and Ellen over her "Renting the Castle" paper, how even a group that works together constructively can lapse into personal abuse. Incidents of verbal violence were much more common in the other fifth grade group. And, unlike the argument between Kurt and Ellen, the hostility of this group was frequently incidental to the task of responding to the writing. Rarely was a disagreement over the writing itself the focus for an argument. Instead, the actual response was commonly perfunctory, even automatic. Students would take notes during the reading, and then read verbatim from these notes in a hurried robotlike monotone. A typical response would simply list words and phrases from the writing, with no predication, e.g., "far away, swamp, creature, walking, closer, bad, hurt, afraid, friends." In contrast with this lifeless language, verbal squabbles were energetic and meaningful, but rarely integrated with the reading/responding procedure.

It was clear that, in contrast with the other groups, these students did not find the group meetings purposeful. While we can only speculate about the reason for this, one explanation seems likely: Students in this class did no revising nor was there any precedent in the way the teacher handled writing assignments for what might be termed formative response. Even students in the eighth-grade class which had been enjoined against negative response had extensive experience with revising and with constructive criticism from the teacher. They thus had a model for what we have called genuine response. This fifth-grade class had no such model. Because they did all their writing in one draft, listener–response could have no power to affect the text. And because the writing read at group meetings had already been read and graded by the teacher, any further treatment was bound to seem anticlimactic. This seems to us a likely explanation for the routine, formulaic nature of the comments. By having students read work that had already been finished and graded, the teacher had undercut the genuine function of the group. And, without any significant purpose for meeting, the group degenerated into restlessness and bickering.

Of course, the most telling measure of the effect of writing group response lies in the changes it induces. Accordingly, we spent considerable time comparing drafts read in groups with writing produced subsequent to the group meetings. Students of all ages incorporated suggestions of their peers into their revisions. Ellen, the fifth grader who wrote about the changing scenes, took note of Mick's comment by writing "why" in the margin of her draft. In response to Kurt she added the words "with the fog" after the line about the town seeming smaller. The final draft which she submitted to the teacher for a grade read:

It seemed just like yesterday; I remember it so well. The road was dirt; now it is cement. Now trains come by more than they used to. They tore down the dock and put pipes for the stream to run through. It looks like a whole new city. The town seems smaller with the fog so low. There is a railroad station. The bridge on the old road is gone. I wish it was like before. It was more peaceful then.

While these changes do not represent radical revisioning of the subject, they do indicate that the writing group has had a positive effect on the writing. This draft makes Ellen's intentions more clear and offers an overview of the difference ("it was more peaceful then") she sees.

What Ellen has done is typical for the fifth graders we observed. Her revisions are relatively simple, and they are concrete (rather than abstract) in nature. We found that fifth graders tended to make literal statements (such as Kurt's "It would be bigger if there's a train station there now"), and the revisions were correspondingly concrete. While students in eighth grade and high school could debate precise meanings of words and question one another's interpretations, fifth graders, as might be expected from their level of cognitive development in Piagetian terms, focused on more concrete issues in their responding and revising.

In contrast, the revisions of high school students were more complex and, therefore, more difficult to document. Danny, who began from the premise that in *The Red Badge of Courage* Henry was trying to prove himself a man, met opposition in his writing group and was persuaded to change his mind: "Oh, so, Henry tries to be a hero when he finally becomes a . . . Unfortunately, Danny did not finish his sentence but instead asked to borrow a pencil and began writing notes to himself. When prompted, he explained his plan to move from Henry's visions of glory to the end where he's just fighting instinctively. The distance from "All through *The Red Badge of Courage* Henry tries to become a man and when he finally does, he finds it is not what he expected" and the brief sketch of supporting material to be included to the following paragraphs suggests the complexity of the revision which resulted, in part, at least, from Danny's session with the writing group:

Stephen Crane, the author of *The Red Badge of Courage* was a naturalist, meaning he felt Nature is impervious to man. No matter what a man does, he cannot alter the course of

Nature. Instead, Crane thought man should submit himself, and in so doing, let his instinct control his life, instead of trying to rationalize everything. Crane's philosophy is portrayed through the thoughts and actions of his main character, Henry Fleming.

At the beginning of The Red Badge of Courage, Henry is a romantic. He believes "he (is) master," (p. 89) and Nature must submit to his every whim. But immediately following his first battle, Henry is amazed to find "Nature had gone tranquilly on with her golden process in the midst of so much devilment." (p. 45) This astounding revelation causes Henry to conclude that, actually, Nature is not affected by the actions of humanity. In fact, Nature is in control of mankind. Henry "could now perceive himself to be a very wee thing," (p. 86) He feels himself "liable to be crushed," (p. 46) by Nature, and there nothing he can do about it. For probably the first time in his life, Henry begins to seriously doubt not only his own strength, but the strength of the human race as well.

But this spasm of philosophy quickly passes. Once safely back in camp, Henry's "self-pride . . . (is) entirely restored," (p. 89) "he . . . (returns) to his old belief in the ultimate, astounding success of his own life." (p. 90) Later, when Henry returns to battle, he changes his philosophy once again, from a cocky self-confidence to his former sense of helplessness. Although his comrades consider him an important hero, Henry realizes that, in reality, "he (is) very insignificant." (p. 104)

After his last battle, Henry discovers that ever since he first joined the army, "his mind (had been) undergoing subtle changes." (p. 130) He slowly learns to be less intellectual and more instinctive. In the afterthoughts of battle, Henry finds that, while fighting, "his usual machines of reflection had been idle," (p. 131) and that "he had been a beast, a barbarian . . . and it was fine, wild, and in some ways, easy." (p. 100) Henry discovers that he has become less deliberate and more impulsive, and he is surprised to find that he prefers himself that way.

Throughout the course of *The Red Badge of Courage,* Henry Fleming learns not to try to reason his way through life but, instead, to live by his inherent emotions. When he attempts to live by the teachings of his mind, "he (imagines) the universe to be against him, He (hates) it." (p. 97) But once he submits himself to Nature and learns to live by the guidance of his heart, he is pleased to discover that "the world (is) a world for him." (p. 134) Although *The Red Badge of Courage* is considered a classic by many, it can also be called just another prolixious pamphlet on the philosophy of Naturalism.

Danny has "re-seen" or "revisioned" his central point and moved from thinking of Henry as one who is proving his manhood to seeing him as a romantic turned naturalist. While we cannot "prove" that the comments made by members of the writing group were responsible for this shift, it does seem clear that the questions posed by his peers forced Danny to think more carefully about his assumptions.

We compared teacher comments with students' responses as another way of assessing the power of the responses, and we found marked differences between the two. As has already been demonstrated, student responses were focused and specific; if listeners did not like or understand something, they explained where or why: "I didn't know whether Cory was a girl or a boy until halfway into the thing"; "For a God to just come up to you and show you around, I mean, it's pretty weird."

Students frequently gave one another explicit or implicit directions for rewriting: "You need to explain that part about time travel"; "This part where he says, uh, ' "No!" shouted John, almost shocked at his own voice ' uh, I think it would sound better if you just said 'shocked at his own voice almost' "; or "I like the part where you said that you remembered it so well" (which contains the implicit direction to keep the opening sentence as it is).

In contrast, teacher comments were much more general and gave students few directions for rewriting. Comments such as: "Good organization," "Generally well-written," "Excellent job," "Good variety in sentences" and "Work on adding variety in your writing," "Vague and underdeveloped in parts," and "Try to be more clear" were typical teacher responses. Existing research on teacher comments indicated that our findings were not unusual. Searle and Dillon (1980) examined comments of intermediate school teachers and found that most evaluative comments were highly ambiguous. They cite examples such as "Very well done," "Good work," "Good composition," "OK," and "Excellent" (p. 236), and note that it was sometimes difficult to determine whether comments focused on content or form because they were so vague. Sommers (1982) examined comments of college instructors and found that the comments are not text-specific and "could be interchanged, rubber-stamped, from text to text" (p. 152). Sommers (1982) cites comments such as "Think more about audience, avoid colloquial language, avoid prepositions at the end of sentences or conjunction at the beginning of sentences, be clear, be specific, be precise, but above all, think more about what (you) are thinking about" (p. 152).

The one place where we did find specificity in teacher comments was in the area of mechanics. Misspelled words were circled (or in some cases corrected), punctuation errors were noted, and sentence faults were repaired. In some cases teachers took on more comprehensive editorial duties and rewrote phrases or sentences. For example, a student text read "This astounding revelation causes Henry to come to the shocking conclusion that . . ." and the teacher modified it to read "This astounding revelation causes Henry to conclude . . ." This finding is consonant with other research in the field (Marshall, 1971; Searle & Dillon, 1980). However, these specific comments (or marks) about mechanics did not seem to function as response; rather, they served to "justify" a low grade.

A further difference between teacher comments and student responses in writing groups derives from (apparently) different sets of assumptions. The teachers we observed seemed to begin from abstract criteria for "good writing" and their comments applied these criteria to the written text at hand. Students in writing groups, on the other hand, seemed to begin from what happened in their own minds when hearing another's language. The literature on evaluation of writing confirms our sense that much evaluation proceeds from abstract criteria, whether or not it is articulated by the teachers employing it.

Perhaps the most widely known criteria derive from the work of Diederich, French, and Carlton (1961) who, through factor analysis of responses by experts in various fields, identified five criteria for "good writing." These five—ideas, wording, organization, mechanics, and flavor—seem to be used in varying proportions by many teachers. Jones (1976) found that high school teachers' comments could be categorized under these five headings, and that responses were fairly balanced among the five. Not all teacher comments fall neatly into Diederich's five categories because they combine two or three.

While self-reporting may not be as reliable as examination of actual comments, Kline (1976) derived commenting priorities from a group of college teachers using this approach. The criteria reported by these teachers were: errors in use of words, representation of experience insufficiently precise, data not taken into account, inappropriate tone of voice or point of view, unclear thesis, lack of coherence, inaccurate or doubtful assertions, and inconsistency in reasoning or judgment.

Nold and Freedman (1977) employed multivariate analysis to identify features that predict favorable evaluations of writing. They limited themselves to agreed-upon features which could be counted easily, mainly syntactical features, and found that length (longer is better), final free modifiers, lack of modals (could, should) absence of "be" and "have" verbs, and avoidance of mundane vocabulary could predict a significant percentage of quality judgments. Although they do not claim these features as abstract criteria for teacher evaluators, we think they may be so described.

In an experimental study with student essays rewritten to emphasize certain features, Freedman (1979) found that scores of selected evaluators were more influenced by content and organization than by sentence structure and mechanics. However, the definition of content in this study—correct interpretation of quotation, exclusion of irrelevant ideas, lack of repetition, and development and clarification of ideas—likewise suggests abstract criteria.

We have taken this excursion into research on the criteria used by teacher evaluators to substantiate our point about the abstract criteria that seemed to be operating in the teacher comments we read, and to lay the ground work for discussing the larger implications of this difference between teacher comments and students' responses in writing groups. We think this difference hinges on different conceptions of meaning and that it has importance to all thought on evaluating writing.

Another way to account for differences between teacher comments and student responses is to consider the difference in context. Students in writing groups have the advantage of immediacy in time and space. They can address the writer in person rather than through the more distant medium of the red pen, and they can offer response as soon as the passage is read. Because response is oral and in person, it can be given without the elaborate explanatory structures of written communications. In a writing group, a student can say in one or two sentences things which, were they to be communicated in prose, would require a small composition, since prose must establish that elaborate context of writer and audience which already exists in the writing group. And, in contrast with written comments, oral response is simply much faster and hence a more economical form of communication. The greater specificity of group response may thus be attributed to context.

Another way to account for the differences between teacher comments and student responses is to look at the difference in function. After all, one might say, students are responding to a draft in process while teachers are commenting on a "finished" piece of writing. One functions as formative evaluation and the other functions as summative evaluation. While we acknowledge this difference, we feel that the differences between formative and summative evaluation are less distinct than the two terms imply. To the extent that it has instructional (as opposed to administrative or research) purposes, a teacher's summative evaluation is simultaneously formative, because it is designed to provide information which will enable the student to write better next time. Most teachers cite instructional purposes as the primary justification for spending hours, days, and weekends laboring over stacks of student papers. Teachers presume that their comments, like student responses have a formative function.

Yet, another way to look at the issue is in terms of the function, not of the response, but of the text itself. And it is here, we believe, that the difference between teacher and group response may have its most significant explanation. Although, as we have noted, both group response and teacher's summary comments have a formative function, there may still be a profound difference in what each set of responses is trying to form, either consciously or unconsciously. As we have seen in so many of the examples cited here, group response is often intent on forming the text by informing it, that is, it tries to realize the meaning of the text by informing the writer of its actual and potential meaning for each listener. Group response thus may be said to have as much an interpretive as a formative function. In contrast, teacher comments may be said to attempt to form student writing by conforming it, that is, by trying to realize its potential similarity to a paradigm text by asking the writer to conform to certain abstract characteristics of "good" writing.

What group response is trying to form, then is an actual text, one which communicates the meaning students find inherent in the text presented, a meaning which is often compounded of a variety of questions, comments and criticisms of quite different "interpreters" who may each find a different "meaning." What teacher response is trying to form is an ideal text, one which possesses certain abstract features of writing quite independently of any meaning.

In these difference between what the two set of responses are trying to form or determine, lie two different assumptions about the function of the text itself. By trying to form an actual text, one which communicates a particular meaning (or sets of meaning), writing groups unconsciously assume that the purpose of writing is rhetorical, that it is meant to have some influence or effect on a reader/listener. By trying to form an ideal text, one which conforms to certain features which can be abstracted from an indefinite number of exemplary texts, all with different meanings, the teacher assumes that the purpose of the writing is pedagogical, that it is an exercise meant to train the student in the use of certain rhetorical forms. Concerned with an actual text, writing group response might be predicted to show the features we have described here as genuine response: questions about meaning, directions about possible meanings, information about effective and ineffective passages, all of it highly specific. Concerned with an ideal text, teacher response might be predicted to show its well-documented concern with mechanical errors and highly generalized, interchangeable criteria.

We might summarize these findings, as well as our speculations about how to account for the differences between student and teacher response, in terms of meaning theory. As Gere (1980) has explained, current philosophical and linguistic debate centers on two theories of meaning. One, the "formal semantics" view, posits meaning as conventionalized in the sentences of a text. The other, the "communication intention" view, assumes that meaning is not the property of sentences but of the way those sentences are used. For those who take a formal semantics position, reading (or listening to) a text is a process of extracting the meaning from the page. For those who take a communication-intention view, reading is the process of engaging with a text, bringing to it whatever purposes, knowledge and values the reader may have. For the former a student paper is a code to be deciphered, and for the latter the paper is a musical score to be interpreted (Dillon, 1981).

As we compare teacher comments with student responses in writing groups, it appears that teachers proceed from the view that meaning is conventionalized in the text while students assume that meaning lies in the constructions they create in their minds while listening to one another read. When we look at teacher comments from this perspective, it is easy to understand why attention to mechanical errors (or as Joseph Williams [1981] calls it, the phenomenology of error) is dominant—the imperfections in the code interfere with the function. Likewise, the abstract criteria evident in teacher comments reflect the belief that the text must conform to certain prerequisites in order for its meaning to be extracted by any and all readers.

Student responses demonstrate, through their diversity, that not all readers take the same meaning from a given text. What is clear to one student is confusing to another, and the writer is thus provided with a representation of the meaning which several readers might make of the same piece of writing. Furthermore, student responses, with their specificity and directness, show the author how the score or text can be interpreted. They show that the text does, indeed, have a communicative, or rhetorical, function, and they provide the writer with an immediate account of the dynamics of reader–text interaction, such an account as teacher comments can at best imitate. If students wish to improve their writing, we can think of no better information to guide them.

We do not make these distinctions between teacher comments and student responses to say that student responses are "better." Rather we wish to demonstrate how one's theory of meaning has many implications for one's evaluation of writing. Further, by pointing to the differences between teacher comments and student responses, we wish to highlight *how* these oral responses shape revision. They shape writing by interacting with its meaning.

References

Beaven, M. (1977). Individualized goal setting, self-evaluation, and peer evaluation. In C. R. Cooper & L. Odell (Eds.), *Evaluating writing: Describing, measuring, judging.* Urbana, IL: National Council of Teachers of English.

Benson, N. (1979). *The effects of peer feedback during the writing process on writing performance, revision behavior, and attitude toward writing.* Unpublished doctoral dissertation, University of Colorado.

Bruffee, K. (1973). Collaborative learning: Some practical models. *College English, 34,* 634–643.

Buxton, E. W. (1958). *An experiment to test the effects of writing frequency and guided practice upon students' skill in written expression.* Unpublished doctoral dissertation, Stanford University, CA.

Chafe, W. (1980). The deployment of consciousness in the production of a narrative. In W. Chafe (Ed.), *The pear stories: Cognitive cultural and linguistic aspects of a narrative production.* Norwood, NJ: Ablex.

Diederich, P., French, J., & Carlton, S. (1961). *Factors in judgments of writing ability.* Princeton, NJ: Educational Testing Service.

Dillon, G. (1981). *Constructing texts.* Bloomington: University of Indiana Press.

Elbow, P. (1973). *Writing without teachers.* New York: Oxford University Press.

Freedman, S. (1979). How characteristics of student essays influence teacher's evaluations. *Journal of Educational Psychology. 71,* 328–338.

Gebhardt, R. (1980). Teamwork and feedback: Broadening the base of collaborative writing. *College Composition and Communication 31,* 69–74.

Gere, A. R. (1980). Written composition: Toward a theory of evaluation. *College English, 42,* 44–58.

Hawkins, T. (1976). *Group inquiry techniques for teaching writing.* Urbana, IL: National Council of Teachers of English.

Jones, B. E. (1976). *Marking of student writing by high school English teachers in Virginia in 1976.* Unpublished doctoral dissertation, University of Virginia.

Kline, C. (1976). I know you think you know what I said. *College English, 37,* 661–662.

Lagana, J. R. (1973). *The development, implementation, and evaluation of a model for teaching composition which utilizes individualized learning and peer grouping.* Unpublished doctoral dissertation, University of Pittsburgh, PA.

Macrorie, K. (1970). *Uptaught.* Rochelle Park, NJ: Hayden.

Marshall, B. (1971). *A survey and analysis of teachers' markings on selected compositions of average students in grades 10 and 12.* Unpublished doctoral dissertation, State University of New York at Buffalo.

Moffett, J. (1968). *Teaching the universe of discourse.* Boston: Houghton Mifflin.

Murray, D. (1968). *A writer teaches writing.* Boston: Houghton Mifflin.

Nold, E., & Freedman, S. (1977). An analysis of readers' responses to essays. *Research in the Teaching of English, 11,* 164–174.

Searle, D., & Dillon, D. (1980). The message of marking: Teacher written responses to student writing at intermediate grade levels. *Research in the Teaching of English, 14,* 233–242.

Sommers, N. (1982). Responding to student writing. *College Composition and Communication, 33,* 148–156.

Williams, J. (1981). The phenomenology of error. *College Composition and Communication, 32,* 152–166.

6

Written Language Acquisition: The Role of Response and the Writing Conference*

Sarah Warshauer Freedman
Melanie Sperling
University of California, Berkeley

Introduction

Although children generally learn written language in school and acquire spoken language at home, they depend on response from others for both types of language learning. Most evidence dealing with spoken language acquisition supports the theory that children acquire spoken language through hypothesis testing—by "testing their hypotheses about structure and function and by finding out how well they are understood by others when doing this" (Clark & Clark, 1977, p. 337). Although it is probable that the processes of acquiring written and spoken language differ in significant respects, it is likely that the responses of the receivers or readers of written messages give learners a foundation for testing hypotheses about the construction of written communication. Just as parent–child interaction is central to the process of hypothesis testing when children acquire speech, teacher–student interaction becomes central when students learn to write in school. Our research focuses on a key teacher–student interactive event in the teaching and learning of written language: the writing conference. We examine its potential role in the teaching and learning of written language.

From elementary school through college, the student–teacher writing conference has become a popular and seemingly effective pedagogical event (e.g., Duke, 1975; Graves, 1982; Murray, 1968). The conference occurs away from classroom activity so that teacher and student can interact one-to-one. Both participants have the opportunity to express not only academic but also personal concerns about any number of issues ranging from specific student papers to writing in general, and even to areas only tangentially related to writing. The conference gives the teacher a chance to address the student's individual needs in a way that cannot be duplicated in the classroom, and perhaps mainly for this reason, the conference has come to be

---

* This work was supported by grants to the first author from the Research Foundation of the National Council of Teachers of English, from San Francisco State University, and from the University of California at Berkeley.

regarded as a felicitous adjunct to classroom interaction, which often unavoidably demands that the teacher homogenize the student group being addressed.

In a sense, the conference is two things at once (Freedman & Katz, in press; Jacobs & Karliner, 1977). First, unlike most learning situations, it is a conversational dialogue. As such, it has what Gumperz (1982) calls "dialogic properties"; that is, among other things, meanings and interpretations are being continuously "negotiated by speaker and hearer and judgements either confirmed or changed by the reactions they evoke" (p. 5). In other words, both participants continuously engage in seeking and maintaining a mutually agreeable level of interaction. Characterized by turn-taking, the conference-as-conversation also allows each participant to raise issues, to shift topics, and to encourage or discourage topic elaboration.

But like most school-based learning situations, the conference is also a teaching–learning event, constrained by the teacher–student relationship and the relative status of the one to the other, as well as by an overall purpose that the teacher give something, that is, new knowledge, to the student.

This double-headed nature makes the conference particularly interesting to study and raises questions about teaching and learning that our research has attempted to begin to answer. Do, for example, high- and low-achieving students elicit different types of responses from the teacher during the writing conference? Do students themselves respond differently and can their responses be explained by the data? Can we develop hypotheses about the effects on learning of these writing conferences? Can we develop insight into the efficacy of individualized teacher–student interaction?

It has been recognized for some time that high- and low-achieving students and students from nonmainstream ethnic backgrounds receive differential instructional emphases, even within the same course, resulting in high-ability, middle-class students being given discourse strategies that can prepare them to participate in a literate, middle-class society (e.g., Collins & Michaels, 1980; Michaels, 1981). Low-achieving students from non-Caucasian ethnic groups often have difficulty adapting to the culture of the school and may unintentionally elicit differential treatment from their teachers (e.g., Au & Mason, 1981; Cazden, John, & Hymes, 1982; Cazden, Michaels, & Tabors, this volume; Cook-Gumperz & Gumperz, 1981; Michaels, 1981). These students also have difficulty acquiring the written language of the school, and once such students begin to have difficulty, their problems only increase (e.g., Weinstein, 1982; Wilkinson, Clevenger, & Dollogan, 1981).

The one-to-one writing conference allows us a close look at what has been observed by others in the classroom, in many ways being better open to scrutiny because of its focused, yet sustained, nature. That it is a one-to-one setting adds interest to the observation because it has at least the appearance of being spontaneous and personal behind its often somewhat planned (Ochs, 1979) and pedagogic nature. Teacher and student must operate at different levels—the conversational as well as the pedagogical—which may, ultimately, reinforce one another. Whether interaction is conversational or pedagogic, because it is interaction, what one party puts in influences what the other party puts out; that is, response by each is influenced by the other.

For this chapter, we examine student–teacher interactions in one college-level writing conference for each of four students: one high-achieving Caucasian, one high-achieving Asian-American, one low-achieving Caucasian, and one low-achieving Asian-American. With this small sample, we cannot make general claims about written language acquisition as it is affected by teacher–student interaction; however, we aim to suggest possible avenues to explore and certain analytic methods to use to help understand how best to study the acquisition process and, in the end, to help students in their efforts to acquire written language skill, which, we know, often depends on response and interaction. We have chosen to focus on the first conference of the semester for each student. We look closely not only at differences in how these four students interact with the same teacher, with implications about the interaction being more, or less, productive for the student, but also at how teacher and student initially establish the teaching/learning relationship.

Methods and Procedures

Subject Selection

Teacher (T). The teacher was selected from a pool of approximately 30 instructors at San Francisco State University (SFSU) who participated in a rigorous three-course training sequence for college composition teachers. The thirty were hired because they excelled in the training program.

All these instructors required regular teacher–student writing conferences of their writing students. The selected teacher was chosen because she represented the best teaching available. Student evaluation placed T in the top 90% of the staff as did supervisor evaluations based on class visits. We were interested in seeing how an excellent teacher works with what we would traditionally label higher- or lower-achieving students and with students from differing ethnic groups.

Students (Ss). Originally 8 students were chosen to participate in the study, 2 high-achieving Caucasians, 2 low-achieving Caucasians, 2 high-achieving Asian-Americans, and 2 low-achieving Asian-Americans. Those students designated as high-achieving scored above 500 on verbal aptitude as measured by the SAT, and those designated as low-achieving scored below 350. Deciding on the ethnic mix was the result of a demographic survey conducted in 1978 of students enrolled in composition courses at SFSU which showed an almost even mix of Caucasian-Americans (31%) and Asian-Americans (29%), a parameter that invited our studying the Asian-American student writer, about whom little work had yet been done.

The Asian-American students selected to participate were native English speakers whose parents spoke an Asian language; thus, they came from homes in which there was an Asian cultural heritage, but they were not expected to produce the writing errors typical of the nonnative speaker.

From these 8 students, everything they wrote during the semester was collected, including all drafts of their papers and all their notes. All their conferences were tape-recorded, a minimum of four across the semester for all students who completed the course.[1] Also collected were three investigator–student interviews about the students' at-home composing process.

Next, four students who were judged to have learned the most and to have had the most successful T–S interactions in the conferences were selected for our analysis, one from each original group: high- and low-achieving Caucasian and Asian-American. Selections were based on both student and teacher judgments. In this study, then, we look at these four students: (a) Jay, a high-achieving Caucasian; (b) Sherry, a high-achieving Asian-American; (c) Dee, a low-achieving Caucasian; and (d) Cee, a low-achieving Asian-American. While the group is split in two by ability level, we note that the four students are also listed in order of decreasing scores on the SAT: Jay scored higher than Sherry; Dee scored higher than Cee.

Database

Since we wanted to learn about how the relationship between T and S is established, we studied the first of the semester conferences for each of the four students. It was reasonable to believe that in this first conference differences and similarities in the students' interactions with T would begin to evolve. This conference had the added benefit of T's following the same specified format for each S. The conference covered, in sequence, discussion of (1) interview questions to S about course schedules, previous writing courses, and writing habits; and (2) certain diagnostic instruments that S had already completed, specifically, (a) the items on a questionnaire that had been given to the entire class about writing; (b) a writing sample done by the entire class; and (c) the items on a verbal skills test, also completed by the entire class.

Each conference was audiotaped and then transcribed. Conferences lasted from 30 to 45 minutes.

Data Analysis

Topics of Conversation. We first examined topics of conversation, a semantic concept (Agar, 1980; Covelli & Murray, 1980; Keenan & Schieffelin, 1976; Shuy, 1981). By analyzing *what* one talks about, that is, the topics one covers and the topics that concern students, one can see *how* (and if) conferences with different students vary, while at the same time discovering systematically what the key topics in a conference are.

Two independent coders identified topic shifts and achieved agreement approx-

---

[1] All except one student, a low-achieving Caucasian, completed the course.

imately 90% of the time. They noted whether T or S initiated a topic and whether T or S was continuing a topic. (For further discussion of procedures for analyzing topic shifts, see Freedman, 1981.) For each student, the coders then noted how often each topic was T-initiated, S-initiated, T-continued, or S-continued. Topics were labeled and classified as either *intellectual,* that is, dealing objectively with some aspect of the subject matter that came up, or *affective,* that is, dealing with either T or S feelings about different subjects (including feelings about each other), or *other,* that is, dealing with neither of the other classifications and generally unique to a particular student.

We followed Mehan's (1978, 1979) procedures for accounting for data:

1. "Retrievability of data" (Mehan, 1979, p. 19): The data should not be present-ed in a reduced or tabulated form when one presents research findings; ver-batim transcripts should be organized and included. In other words, the fre-quency counts of correlational research and the selected descriptions in the field report are not sufficient.
2. "Comprehensive data treatment" (Mehan, 1979, p. 20): A model for data analysis must include all the data. "This comprehensive data analysis is ac-complished by a method that is analogous to 'analytic induction' (Znanicki, 1934, 234–233; Robinson, 1951). The method begins with a small batch of data. A provisional analytic scheme is generated. The scheme is then compared to other data, and modifications are made in the scheme as necessary. The provisional analytic scheme is constantly confronted by 'negative' or 'disc-repant' cases until the researcher has derived a small set of recursive rules that incorporate all the data in the corpus" (Mehan, 1979, p. 21). This is similar to the procedure the linguist uses to explain the rules of speech, to show the organization inherent in spoken language (Chomsky, 1965).
3. "Convergence between researchers' and participants' perspectives" (Mehan, 1979, p. 22): The researcher must check his or her interpretations of the events against the perceptions of the participants.[2]
4. "Interactional level of analysis" (Mehan, 1979, pp. 23–24): "Since class-room events [and conference events] are socially organized, a constitutive analysis has the further commitment to locate this organization in the interac-tion itself. . . . Evidence for the organizational machinery of lessons [and conferences] is to be found in the words and in the gestures of the partici-pants." In other words, what the participants actually do and say, not what one guesses about their thoughts, is what will reveal the structure of the event.

Idea Units. To allow a closer examination of the discourse, we had certain portions of the talk transcribed into idea units. The theoretical basis for this division

---

[2] It should be noted that Mehan's guideline #3, "Convergence between researchers' and partici-pants' perspectives," can be questioned. Research in conversational strategy (Gumperz, 1982) has shown that what participants perceive is occurring in conversation can be different from what is actually occurring.

comes from Chafe (1980), who defines the idea unit as a segment of discourse that coincides with a person's focus of attention or focus of consciousness. Chafe (1980) notes, "A property of spontaneous speech that is readily apparent to anyone who examines it closely is that it is produced, not in a flowing stream, but in a series of brief spurts" (p. 13). These spurts are the idea units. The main criterion for deciding on an idea unit boundary is the intonational contour (that is, pitch either rises or falls). See Danielewicz and Chafe (this volume) for more detail on the idea unit or what they now call an "intonation unit."

By breaking the talk into idea units (numbering each unit and placing it on a separate line), we could measure the amount of conscious energy or focus devoted to each part of the conference conversation, compare the weight of the teacher's and student's focus on particular topics, and compare the weights across conferences. We could then develop hypotheses about the consequences of topic focus on the student–teacher relationship, and try to think of that emerging relationship as it might affect subsequent student writing.

This analysis also allowed us to hypothesize whether the amount of focus could be related to student ability or ethnicity, a topic that could be pursued in more extensive research that would make use of a larger S and T sample base.

Comparison of Cross-Conference Similarities: Backchannel Cues. We next looked at a segment of discourse that appeared to be the same across conferences to see if, on close analysis, an apparently similar incident might provide insights to add to the analysis of differences in topic focus across conferences that we had already found and identified. We selected the segment in each conference when T and S discussed the test of verbal skills that S had taken in class, since T followed the same format and covered the same items in this segment for each S. Our close analysis consisted of examining "backchannel" cues (signals) made by each S.

Backchannel signals are what Yngve (1970) calls interjections such as "OK," "right," "aha," and "uh huh," and are a common signal of conversational cooperation (Gumperz, 1982). Further, Gumperz explains that they are expected to be synchronous in conversation, coming at boundaries between clauses or tone groups. Rationale for analyzing these segments for backchannel signals comes from studies of interactive synchrony which show that asynchrony characterizes "uncomfortable moments" in conversational interaction (e.g., Erickson & Schultz, 1982). As Gumperz notes, because the timing of backchannels can reflect differing sociocultural conventions, it may unintentionally create, to use Erickson's phrase, "uncomfortable moments" in cross-cultural communication. Analysis of backchannels was, thus, a way to discuss "harmony" or "disharmony" between T and S and to discover possible differences among the four students that might fall into a pattern.

Consequences to the Student. Since our semantic analysis uncovered differences in both T and S behavior, we next looked for what we could call obvious consequences of these differences for the student. That is, since the student presumably is to come away from a conference having been given at least something from the teacher, we looked for what the students indeed came away with in these first conferences, which, occurring at the beginning of the semester, did not focus on current class work or class assignments and so could not contribute in an immediate or direct way to the student's work for the course.

We found two points worth noting: (a) expository modeling episodes, and (b) invitations to return to T's office, issued by T to S. As a way to measure the amount of "conscious energy" devoted to these segments of the conference, we counted the number of idea units devoted to each. For the modeling episodes, we also noted how frequently they occurred. These counts allowed us to compare conferences for patterns.

Results

Analysis

Semantic

Generalizations about self. When considering the semantic content of the data, we looked primarily for "focal" topics, those specified topics, both intellectual and affective, that T and S seemed to want to address most. In the analysis, however, we encountered an interesting sidelight: Throughout the conferences, students offer different generalizations about themselves, not necessarily "focal" as we have defined the term, but nonetheless informative statements volunteered spontaneously by S about S, not made in response to T questions. That the students make such generalizations is not in and of itself surprising—we all, during conversation, make them (I'm not any good at Scrabble, I'm an Agatha Christie fan, I don't water-ski very well, and so on). These kinds of generalizations lead whomever we are conversing with to make inferences about us, to get a picture of us. What we noticed with our four students was that these generalizations fell into distinctive patterns for each one. Because of this they deserve attention, and we discuss them first since they are one factor, albeit a subtle one, that we think influences the general quality of the conferences, lending support to our findings on focal topics.

The generalizations made by each S are as follows:

Jay

I could write long letters, but after I read it I can't stand them.

I really admire people who can write well.

People who write well are special to me.

I like to write well.

Sherry

I'm pretty weak in English

I'm really not good in math.

Dee

I hate libraries.

I still don't think I'm that good a writer.

I'm not really into writing . . .

I never did well on tests.

I have a terrible vocabulary.

Cee

My sister has a brighter mind than I do.

I enjoy working better than going to school.

I prefer to be educated in a company because I learn much faster.

I do not like lectures at all.

Jay's generalizations are positive, revealing his sympathy with writing—"people who write well are special to me"—and would no doubt please an English teacher. Sherry's, while critical about herself, are nonetheless mitigated criticisms—she says she is "pretty" weak in English, not "really" good in math, these appearing as statements of modesty as much as of self-deprecation. The patterns for the low-achieving students are strikingly different. Dee's remarks tend to be strongly negative—"I hate libraries," "I never did well on tests." Her notions of herself seem set in concrete and, in content, are not remarks that would guarantee positive T response. Cee's remarks, too, are not calculated to ingratiate an academic. She can learn, she says, but school's not the place—"I prefer to be educated in a company" (that is, the workplace). Their generalizations follow a kind of pattern from most teacher-pleasing to least, with Jay's most likely to lead to productive T response, as opposed to blind alleys.

The teacher, of course, responds to these generalizations. Her responses to Jay and to Dee are particularly revealing of the differentially productive nature of these exchanges, with both T and S influencing each other's remarks.

Jay: I really admire people who can write well. I think it's, it's hard, sometimes, so people who write really well are really special to me.

T.   Yeah, that's nice. Uh, do you feel like you're the kind of person who could write well? I mean, do you ever identify with, with that ability or do you kind of say that's a group out there. . . .

The teacher doesn't need to confront this statement in any way or clarify her stance toward writers—it's fairly safe to assume that she and Jay are on the same wavelength. She can take his statement about admiring writers and turn the experience around to Jay, personalizing it for him and getting him to explore his own sense of being a writer. Jay's statement triggers a conversation, by the way, that goes on for twelve more turns. He and the teacher "have something to talk about" that the teacher uses as a discovery tool for the student and as a teaching tool. In the course of this fourteen-turn segment, the teacher talks about the writing process, using that term; she talks about prewriting, feedback, writer's block, in a way that she doesn't do for any of the other three students.

The exchange with Dee is different.

Dee: I hate libraries.
T: I know. I always hated libraries too.

On the surface, T's response to Dee's "I hate libraries" is, as is her response to Jay, positive and sympathetic. In fact, the conversation goes on for five more turns in which Dee, essentially, elaborates on libraries being stuffy, big, and unpleasant, and the teacher interjecting a sympathetic "yeah" at appropriate junctures. What is interesting is that the teacher seems to have established a common experience with the student; however, we found out later in interviewing the teacher about this particular exchange that she was so taken aback by Dee's admission, that "I always hated libraries too" is what came out. She was trying to do the same thing as with Jay—establish common ground. Yet the substance could only lead to an anti-academic exchange.

It is interesting to keep these interactions in mind when looking at the different topics, both intellectual and affective, that T and S focus on during the conferences.

Types of topics. Table 1 illustrates the topic initiations for both the student and the teacher. Notice that the two Asian-American students initiate either significantly more or significantly fewer topics than the Caucasians. Sherry, the high-achieving student who is Chinese, follows the stereotype of the quiet Asian student, initiating only eleven topics. Cee, the low-achieving student who is Japanese, initiates significantly more topics than appears to be the norm. The teacher initiates approximately

Table 1. Topic Initiations

Student	Teacher-initiated				Student-initiated			
	Intellectual	Affective	Other	Total N	Intellectual	Affective	Other	Total N
Jay	58 (54%)	14 (13%)	35 (33%)	107	17 (47%)	9 (25%)	10 (28%)	36
Sherry	32 (43%)	8 (11%)	34 (46%)	74	7 (64%)	3 (27%)	1 (9%)	11
Dee	60 (50%)	4 (3%)	56 (47%)	120	29 (62%)	7 (15%)	11 (23%)	47
Cee	48 (47.5%)	6 (6%)	47 (46.5%)	101	42 (49%)	32 (37%)	12 (14%)	86

the same number of topics with all students except Sherry, with whom she initiates fewer topics. In all cases, the teacher initiates more topics than the student, an indication of her role as director of the conversation. None of the other trends in topic initiation appear noteworthy.

Focal topics: Intellectual. In each conference, the teacher focuses on an almost identical percentage of intellectual topics with each student. However, the substance of those topics varies for both the teacher and the student. The intellectual topics were subdivided into two categories: discourse and surface level. Table 2 illustrates the differences in concentration across the conferences. The different types of students express their intellectual energy differently, and T expresses different intellectual foci with the different students.

As Table 2 illustrates, of the topics T initiates with Jay, Sherry, and Dee, most are discourse-level topics. In fact, recent research (Ammon, this volume; Dunn, Florio-Ruane, & Clark, this volume; Freedman, 1979; Gere & Stevens, this volume; Heath & Branscombe, this volume; Sommers, 1982) indicates that feedback on discourse level topics is the most "productive" feedback for a S to get about writing; that is, when T and Ss make discourse concerns a priority, Ss are more apt to generate successful essays than when discourse concerns are subordinated to surface concerns. It is of note, then, that T does not emphasize discourse concerns for Cee in the way she does with the other three students. T initiates discourse and surface-level topics almost equally with Cee, neither one assuming priority over the other.

The two Caucasian students, Jay and Dee, initiate mostly discourse topics themselves. Here Jay thinks of global planning:

T: Can you remember the kind of steps you went through . . . when you had to write a paper?

Jay: I probably took longest thinking of an introduction, how I would introduce what I was going to write about.

Table 2. Intellectual Focal Topics

Student	Teacher-initiated			Student-initiated		
	Discourse	Surface	Total N	Discourse	Surface	Total N
Jay	43 (74%)	15 (26%)	58	15 (88%)	2 (12%)	17
Sherry	24 (75%)	8 (25%)	32	2 (29%)	5 (71%)	7
Dee	49 (82%)	11 (18%)	60	21 (72%)	8 (28%)	29
Cee	27 (56%)	21 (44%)	48	22 (52%)	20 (48%)	42

Here Jay brings up his changing the *content* of his essay:

T: I was interested in what you thought about your revision. . . . Did you feel like you
      changed a lot of the essay? What kinds of things did you attack?

Jay: I took a little, a different point to explain . . . mostly got rid of stuff about, the usual
      stuff that is obvious in college—you're exposed to a lot of new people and new ideas
      and stuff like that. I think I cut that down . . . but I went on to something different.

Later:

Jay: I think my endings are pretty vague and repetitive . . .

On the other hand, Sherry initiates surface concerns most, exactly the opposite of
what her teacher initiates with her. Cee splits her concern, a pattern again different
from the rest. Cee seems to see intellectual concerns as a flat set; she imposes no
hierarchy of importance on them, a fact that could have detrimental consequences
for her writing process. She seems to have difficulty distinguishing what is
important.

Here Cee tells T what in the course she finds helpful:

Cee: I did have trouble [in a past class] in some areas which you are going over right now.

T: Like what kind of areas so far?

Cee: Well, like when we were on fragments and clauses and phrases. . . .

On the steps in writing an essay:

T: What kind of steps and stages would you go through, um, when you were writing the
      three-page essay?

Cee: Well first, she gave us about three topics to choose from, and I chose one then. And
      then we had to choose a topic sentence. Sometimes she said the topic sentence
      doesn't come first; it comes last after you write your whole essay.

T: Oh, your thesis statement. Oh, okay, okay.

Cee: And then, uh, we'd write our thesis statement and then we'd start narrowing it down
      until we can no longer go no farther. And then we'd write the next one which has to
      be sort of on the basis of the first one.

T: The next draft, is that what you're saying? Or the next . . .

Cee: No, the next paragraph.

T: The next paragraph. I see. Okay, okay. And how long would that kind of process
      take you then?

Cee: Sometimes an hour. Sometimes up to three hours. It depends.

T: Okay. Then what would you do after that?

Cee: Well, then, I would retype it and then see where my errors are. Which I cannot always find. And see which ones I could take out. And see what I could add in.

T: Were you mostly like taking out or putting in sentences or were you like taking out and putting in whole paragraphs, or whole . . .

Cee: Sentences or words. If I want to change a word or not.

Cee allocates her composing energy on some parts of the task and then on others. At this point in the semester, the teacher does not appear to be leading her to concentrate mostly on one area as she does with the other students.

It is interesting that, during the conferences, the teacher asks whether English is the native language for both Asian-American students, an issue that never arises with the Caucasians. Both Asian-Americans evidence a certain amount of linguistic insecurity, which perhaps leads to their concern with the surface level of writing.

Students' own agendas. That the concern be shared between T and S, however, may be even more important than what the concern is. As we have noted, there is no match in focal topics between T and Sherry. With no match in focal concern, T and S may likely be talking at cross purposes and may not even be attending to what the other is trying to say. Freedman (1981) found that such cross-purpose talk manifests itself in a T–S conference when S and T each bring up a topic of concern over and over again, no matter what the other wants to focus on, indicating that T and S often have different agendas for what needs to be covered in the conference.

In this study, we found, in fact, that the students' own agendas surface subtly. For example, we found that students can initiate talk about their concerns by bringing up topics as if in extended response to T questions, but which really take the form of "quick answer to X, but now I want to talk about Y."[3]

T: Okay and you're not sure about some punctuation marks. Okay those are fairly technical concerns. Do you have any other .. areas in your writing like when you're sitting down to write an essay, that you really feel, . . . that are . . . difficult for you to do. Like does it seem difficult to organize, does it seem difficult to develop?

Sherry: No not really. Um . . . I sometimes my I guess tense, I have to say it out loud, and that's why I can't do it in class, cause you don't want to . . . start .. talking.

---

[3] Transcription conventions:

italics	interruption by other speaker
—	elongated syllable
–	speech hesitation
,	rising intonation
.	falling intonation
..	nonmeasurable pause
...	measurable pause

T wants to talk not about mechanics, but about organization and development, but Sherry brings the conversation around to her own concerns, verb tense. Another example, with Cee, follows:

T: (reading Cee's essay) See—when you break it down like that, you ... what .. what you have is the .. the first core, "person is able to experience," prepositional phrase, and, another verb phrase, "receive education, that is directly related" ... clause, and "not off the beaten path." Okay that you could have really ... um ... taken out, because it was almost redundant with this, particular statement there. "As it is taught in college, where the teachers teach the student, and ... the student finds." So ... you have all those joining words, and joining techniques, so that you never ... you never stop the sentence, and then start a new one, because you keep having these link words, these words that link all your ideas together.

Cee: It is true enough. (laughter) Well it is true. Like I took this Secretary Administration class, and I was working at Kaiser, as a personnel clerk, and I noticed that, I learned things much better .. and much faster, and ... my supervisor is much more patient with me, than the teacher, who expected more, and who didn't really give a darn, if you failed or not.

T talks about sentence structure, but Cee is more concerned with the topic itself, not as content for writing but as an anecdote to discuss anew, to lend support to her complaints about past experiences with teachers. Cee's is an affective, rather than an intellectual, concern (see next section) that she brings up over and over during the conference.

The quality of exchanges in which the students wedge in their own agendas is clearly different from instances in which there is a match between what T and S wish to discuss:

T: Um ... is there anything else, about starting to write, that seems really frustrating to you, or hard or keeps you from wanting to start a paper, aside from the thesis statement.

Jay: Um ... no u—m I'm just like ... like I said before, I'm afraid, that I'm gonna get too vague, if I ... if I'm writing a paragraph, and I don't have any ... you know to support I'm gonna start repeating myself, saying the same ... saying the same differently. So

T: Uhhum. Do you, is it, would you say that's one of the things that, a good writer would have to ... to be able to do is have ... choose the right ideas, that are defensible, right from the beginning, before they start to write?

Jay: Yeah. Yeah. That's ... that's choosing the right idea, and then having a thesis statement from there.

T: Oh, okay, good.

In later conferences, the importance of one's own agenda also manifests itself when T does not listen to or acknowledge S's topic of concern, but rather brings the discussion back around to something else. However, in these first conferences, T tends to play the role of good listener. (In later conferences, she has a clear-cut agenda of her own about the students' papers and does not have to shift topics subtly; instead, she may and usually does shift clearly and explicitly.)

Focal topics: Affective. Just one affective response, praise giving, is made by T, and it is distributed somewhat unevenly, with T initiating praise more with the higher-achieving students than with the low-achieving ones. Table 1 shows that T initiates praise for the two stronger students more than for the two weaker. Indeed, the percentage of times the teacher initiates praise (of the total number of teacher-initiated topics) is 13% and 11% for Jay and Sherry, respectively, and 3% and 6% for Dee and Cee, respectively.

Interestingly, the amount of praise the high-achieving students receive seems to reflect, in part, the substance of the affective topic that these students initiate. Both high-achieving students admit their insecurity about their writing and praise follows these admissions. It appears that these students are skilled at eliciting praise from the teacher. For example,

Jay: (On thesis statement) I worry .. sometimes,
T: If it's a good thesis statement.
Jay: Yeah.
T: Yeah .. well that's a good worry. I mean you're accurate, and you're on the right track, to be concerned, about a thesis statement, so that's good.

Further, the nature of the other affective focal topics initiated by the students differs, depending on the S's achievement level, with high-achieving students initiating teacher-pleasing comments, and low-achieving student initiating potentially teacher-alienating comments. Dee discusses at length her laziness as a student. Of the 47 topics she initiates, this one is the third most frequently initiated. Understandably, these admissions do not elicit praise. For example, in response to the teacher question, "Do you like to read?" she says:

I have friends, and my friends are really .. big readers, and they are constantly recommending books, and I just ... it's laziness, I just .. I mean reading takes concentration, whereas television viewing you just sit there, and they do all the work.

Cee, the low-achieving Asian-American, has a markedly different affective concern, how much she dislikes and distrusts teachers. She brings up this topic more than any of the other topics she initiates. She brings up her concern when she discusses her job and remarks that her "supervisor is much more patient with me than the teacher, who expected more and who didn't really give a darn if you failed or not." The conversation continues:

T: Hum. Have you found that to be true, a– at State too. In all your classes.
Cee: Yes, . . . As a whole. I found there is a lot of ... discrimination, going on, at this school, and I talked with other students, and they .. notice it too. Like .. I was

talking to this girl recently, I believe it was about two or three days ago, a—nd she took this psychology class, last semester. She got a B out of the teacher. But there was this other girl, who also had the same teacher, two s—semesters ago, uh received a D or an F. A—nd she found out that .. if the teacher likes you, she'll give you a good grade. If she doesn't like you at all, she'll give you a bad grade. That's why I've been feeling, I guess depressed, a—nd lost, because .. I sometimes ... there are not many people who .. who would give you confidence, and who would help you. Even though a teacher might say .. oh I'm always there to help you, but when you go to them, have this attitude .. of I don't want to help you. That happened to my business teacher; she always came to the classroom, and there's um ... two students she liked. She always said hi to them, directly, and then the other students she would just ignore.

Neither low-achieving student focuses on an affective issue that would indicate that she was "teacher-wise." Rather, both talk in ways by which they could easily alienate a teacher or at least not ingratiate themselves to the teacher.

Backchannel Cues. Analysis of semantic content was augmented by the finer-grained backchannel cue analysis. While the content of the segment analyzed, in which T talks to S about a test S has taken, appears similar in all the conferences, in fact the quality of one of the segments contrasts sharply with that of the others (Table 3) when one considers backchannel cues.

In each conference, this segment lasts just short of 7½ minutes, In all segments (that is, across conferences), T covers the same issues, in the same order. In each conference T does most of the talking, with S contributing only an occasional comment. Yet Cee's conference looks unlike the others when we examine back-channel cues. Cee produces approximately three to four times as many backchannel responses as the other students, and one third of her responses come at inappropriate moments, interrupting clauses or tone groups. Further, when listening to the tapes, we perceived that several of these responses are elongated, "uh—huu—h," serving to interrupt T simply because they "drag on." It is as if Cee wants to be a participant in the conversation but does not know how. The following examples help illustrate what occurs:

Table 3. Backchannel Cues

Student	Length of test episode segment	N of S backchannel cues	N of backchannel cues that interrupt tone groups
Jay	7 min 20 s	8	0
Sherry	7 min 20 s	8	0
Dee	7 min 20 s	12	0
Cee	7 min 30 s	30	11

T: Um you also did well, if we come back and look at the very beginning, ... the first
         two questions were asking you, if they if you knew how to limit the topic. Remember
         how we talked about /uh hum/ limit in class. And the first one was uh, in a two-page
         essay, which one of these categories. And in a 20-page essay, which one of these
         categories. And you got them both right, which is good, because it indicates at least
         according to this test, whatever a test /uh hum/ can indicate, that you have a sense of
         how much or how little you can say ... in a given amount of space.

Cee: That's true.

T: So that's, that's good. Now this part in through here, down throu—gh .. /oh that/
         Oh that. You remember /laughter/ the sentences. What they want what they were
         essentially testing here was your organizational ability. Um .. up through number 37.
         Which is right .. /um here/ here. Okay.

In contrast, note the appropriate placement of Dee's backchannel cues. The
teacher does not have to stop to address any interruptions; the conversation flows
smoothly, with synchrony.

T: They're testing your sense of how much you should limit .. a subject. It's better to limit a
         subject, and say .. a lot about it, and go in depth, and develop it. Than to chooses a hu—
         ge subject. And say very little about ... it. /Uh hum./ Cover all this area, and really say
         nothing. /Uh hum./ Okay so that's what they were testing, and you missed both of those.
         I don't know if it's because you didn't know, how much this was, or if you didn't
         understand what they were testing or what.

One has to ask whether Cee's backchannel cues reflect her place on the achievement scale, whether they are a product of ethnic background, or whether they are
simply idiosyncratic. Analysis of the language patterns of more students would be
required to answer those questions. Yet it is evident that, whatever the cause, Cee's
discourse strategy marks her as different from the other students, and that this
strategy, taken along with the kinds of topics she focuses on, as revealed earlier,
helps shape the quality of her conference.

Consequences to the Student

Expository Modeling

   Definition. Certain segments in T's discourse stand out for their length and
complexity. They appear, in fact, like "mini" essays, composed orally, on the
spot, and delivered to the student almost like formal lessons. We found that some of
these segments meet certain "expository writing criteria." The criteria are:

1.   that the piece of discourse contain a "thesis," that is, an overriding general
     idea that could be supported by facts, illustration, explanation, or other conven-
     tional development strategies that an essay writer would employ;

2. that it also be developed in some way, whether by a single sentence or several sentences; and
3. that it be able to "stand alone" as writing stands alone, with appropriate deixis, independent of exophoric reference (Halliday & Hasan, 1976).

Example 1 should make clear the kind of discourse that we included in our analysis, and example 2 the kind we excluded:

(1) *T speaking to Dee*
     There is a difference obviously between speaking and writing. There's a lot more communication that can go on in speaking. I can move my hands, or knit my brows or do something, and you're getting a lot more information, than my words, whereas the reader only has a piece of paper, and the words on it. So ... a lot of people, do tend to write the way they speak, until they suddenly ... learn ... principles or guidelines, that help them, manipulate, this artificial .. world called a piece of paper with words on it, or an essay, however you want to call it.

(2) *T speaking to Sherry*
     Of course the subject emphasizes, and what you need .. at least, to join these two .. complete ideas, is a semicolon. Hopefully, you'll be learning other joining words, like "but," and "and," and "or," "so," to show, how to join, the sentences, and indicate, the kind of relationships that exist between these two sentences.

In example 2, while T develops the idea of joining complete sentences with a semicolon or coordinating conjunctions, and while it might be argued that she begins with a topic sentence, she depends on exophoric reference to be understood, specifically, reference to the identity of the sentences that T and S are discussing. The use of the demonstrative "these," occurring twice in the discourse cited, is a clue to her depending on an external context. Thus, even though it has some of the marks of expository discourse, we do not count it as expository for our purposes. In contrast, example 1 contains all the criteria: It has a topic sentence which is deveoped and the text is internally consistent, with reference being endophoric.

After identifying all instances of expository discourse for each of the four conferences, we considered the following:

1. the number of times that such discourse occurs and the number of idea units within each occurrence,
2. whether the occurrences are characterized as highly colloquial or as academic in register,[4] and
3. what motivates the discourse.

---

[4] Let us clarify what we mean by "written" language features. Chafe (1980, 1982) describes certain language features as being prototypically spoken or prototypically written. Nominalization ("operation," not "operate"; "management," not "manage"), for example, is a prototypically written rather than spoken feature. We also designate as written, or academic, certain broad discourse strategies such as succinct thesis statement, clear supporting evidence, balanced sentences, and transitional devices such as "however." Such features will be identified as they come up in the discussion.

Frequency of occurrence. Over the four conferences, expository discourse appears as is illustrated in Table 4. At the extreme ends, the high-ability Caucasian, Jay, receives almost five times the number of expository discourse models from T as does the low-ability Asian-American, Cee.

Looking at idea units, one gets a slightly different picture. Although idea units devoted to expository discourse for Jay outnumber those for Cee by more than four to one and thus echo the ratio seen in Table 4, the linear progression across the four students does not recur. The two Caucasian students receive an almost equal number of total idea units devoted to expository discourse. However, because this is accounted for by one stretch of discourse in Dee's conference that is particularly long—96 idea units, as opposed to the average length for the four students which is 23 idea units—the results may simply reflect an anomaly.

Occurrence of written language features. We found some of these expository episodes to be more "written" or academic in register and some to be more colloquial. Example 3 illustrates what we mean. Italicized are elements that can be identified as belonging to a written rather than colloquial register:

(3)   *T to Jay*
      When we talk about prewriting in class, we talk about the whole process, and that Trimble book, talks a lot about feelings people have, and *assumptions* that are ... *either* accurate *or* inaccurate, about professional writer, *people who make their living writing,* and um ... maybe by reading that book, and doing some of your own thinking, um ... and I'd like students' feedback, as they go through the course of the semester, to see ... what kinds of things, you start realizing about yourself, as a writer, you know ... what ... what ... does seem to block you, what is really that fear, and can you tackle it. Is it just something ... that's ... kind of an arbitrary ... fear you have, or is it something that is really genuine, that ... where you lack a certain ability that you feel, is necessary, to be a professional writer. So hopefully, you know by going through this class *not only* do you learn *the techniques of expository writing, but* you'll learn something about yourself.

The written-like features include: an introductory subordinate clause, two instances of technical language, an instance of nominalization, two correlative conjunctions, and an appositional phrase. One should also note T's reference to authority, "that Trimble book," in support of her ideas that writing is a "process" whereby one discovers one's strengths and weaknesses as a writer, the overriding

Table 4. Expository Modeling

Language features	Jay	Sherry	Dee	Cee
N of incidents	9	6	4	2
N of idea units	166	84	157	42
Range of idea units across incidents	6 to 34	8 to 21	16 to 96	13 to 29

thesis of this stretch of discourse. These features, thesis and support from an outside authority, are, of course, characteristic of written essays.

Example 4 between T and Dee, although labeled expository since it contains "expository" features, contrasts sharply with example 3. One might argue that the expository model that Dee receives is different in kind from the one Jay receives:

(4)   *T to Dee*

That's really a great start, to come into .. a .. a writing class like this and have all those ... different ideas, plans and stages that you go through, you're really .. I think .. very far along in knowing, the whole *process,* that ... that .. um occurs when you have to write a paper. Most people think that you can just sit down and do all that at once, you can think and write and organize it, yeah ... and that's why most people have so much difficulty when they write.

One written-like feature (technical language) is italicized here. There is a thesis—that there's an advantage to knowing that writing is a process—but the support is anecdotal, a legitimate strategy for development but close to informal conversational strategy. So while both pieces appear more "spoken" than "written," containing hedges, hesitations, vagueness, and colloquialisms, example 3 is clearly denser in written features than is 4 and fits an academic register more than a colloquial one.

While T uses both colloquial and academic registers throughout the conferences, during these expository episodes, at least, she speaks in a strikingly more academic manner more of the time with Jay than with Sherry or Dee and even less with Cee. Perhaps for the reasons we found in our semantic analysis, perhaps for other reasons, T is motivated to use, and thus to model, an academic register differentially with these students. In general, the effects of this kind of interchange for students could well be that, even indirectly through modeling, some learn how to talk to a teacher, getting practice participating in an academic register with a guiding interlocutor, while others get no such practice.

The two high-achieving students seem to know how, although unwittingly, to get T to begin her expository episodes. As in the incidents of praise-giving, T generally responds to Jay in this expository way when he has expressed or implied uncertainty about writing. T seems to want to help him see things as writing teachers do, to let him in on her own perspectives about writing:

T: You—as long as .. and along with your classmates, will—see that, editing is very specific. It's not just sitting back, and saying, "Gee this seems nice, or it doesn't seem nice," and you don't know why, and you start ... when you're va—gue, you almost have to, it seems, attack the person personally, but if you're looking at specific things, . . . every single topic sentence, the thesis statement, the organization, how you decided to open up the paragraph, introductory paragraph. It's very ... technical really, when you get down to it, so that there isn't much room for va—gue generalities, va—

gue judgments, at least it shouldn't be. And I think by then too, once you see the kinds of things that other people are doing, you ... you won't be as threatened. Too—at least hopefully that's the experience you'll have. And by then you'll be ... you'll have written a lot of essays for the class, so you'll have a pretty good sense of, the things that are your strengths and weaknesses as a writer. So too, so it shouldn't come as some great shocker.

Her responses to Sherry and Dee are similarly motivated (although Dee's motivating statements tend to come across as complaints rather than uncertainty—e.g., "I have a terrible vocabulary"). T is not, however, motivated to give Cee the kinds of lessons and insights that she does with the other three. Of the two expository episodes that Cee is exposed to, the first Cee requests directly: "What exactly is an idiom?"—a question, incidentally, that comes somewhat inappropriately after T has asked Cee whether she has any questions about class procedure.

The second of these episodes with Cee comes as a way for T to divert an awkward situation in which Cee praises T's teaching abilities. So this low-achieving student, unlike Dee, and unlike the two high-achieving students, does not get "taught" by T during the conference in the same characteristically "expository" manner. Her own contributions to the conference helps prevent these lessons from occurring.

Invitations to Return. A sample of talk from the end of every conference proved particularly revealing in illustrating the disparities of the student–teacher interaction. This talk generally centers on the teacher's invitation to the student to return for additional individual meetings. On the whole, this teacher is exceptionally generous with her time and lets her students know about her generosity. However, these four students get different tastes of this generosity. Each idea unit is numbered.

Jay
T: (1)   if you think of anything,
      (2)   do feel free to come down,
      (3)   ... and talk with me,
      (4)   in the office.
      (5)   If I go through a lesson too quickly,
      (6)   .. or there're points that I ... didn't raise,
      (7)   that you really wanted,
      (8)   to ask about,
      (9)   and you didn't feel you had time in class to cover them.
     (10)   Always come down,
     (11)   .. or set up an appointment to ... to meet with me.
     (12)   .. Uhm—as a process class it's important,
     (13)   .. that you keep up with the work.
     (14)   Because you don't want to be thinking about thesis statements,

(15) when you're thinking about topic sentences.

(16) or topic sentences when you're thinking about paragraph development.

(17) Or—introductions and conclusions.

(18) You know ... when you can kinda tackle ... each part of the writing,

(19) itself,

(20) as its own,

(21) little ... what.

(22) ... As its own issue,

(23) and its own lesson.

(24) .. And you can kinda get clear,

(25) at least on the principle.

(26) It takes a while,

(27) to incorporate it into your writing.

(28) It takes practice.

(29) .. There's only so much I can teach you through,

(30) ... talking.

(31) Most of it comes from you,

(32) writing
        /Yeah/

(33) Um,

(34) but I think you'll find that,

(35) step by step,

(36) the essay will not be,

(37) a big blur,

(38) of issues that,

(39) ... you've already got a good sense of a lot of the factors and variables that go in.

(40) Hopefully this will clarify some of the techniques that you can use to accomplish those,

(41) .. those techniques,

(42) those variables,

(43) so if you have any questions,

(44) ... feel free to ask.

Sherry

T: (1) Well you know where my office is.

S: Yeah.

T: (2) And . . . if you . . . if after a class,

(3) on a thesis statement . . or something,

(4) you don't understand,

(5) do come down here.

(6) I try not to let . . . I really like people to get . . . keep up with the class,

(7) since it is a what do you call process-oriented class.

(8) You don't want to be thinking about thesis statements,

(9)   when you're down the road looking at . . how to join sentences,

(10) and develop sentences,

(11) or . . . you don't want to be thinking about topic sentences when we're looking at . . how to develop . . . paragraphs.

(12) So that if for some reason a particular lesson seems very confusing,

(13) or you have other ideas that you wanted to discuss,

(14) do come down,

(16) . . and make use of this time.

S: Okay

T: (17) Okay all right . . . and if you think of questions later,

(18) you'll feel free to come in.

Dee

T: (1) Uhm . . . all right like I said,

(2) if you have any . . . questions,

(3) . . . comments,

(4) things that you want to talk to me about,

(5) . . . do come down to the office,

(6) and keep up with the course.

S: Okay.

T: (7) Uhm feel free to come down now that you know where it is,

(8) . . . to visit,

S: All right.

(9) whatever.

T: Okay.

S: Is that it?

T: Yeah

        . . . that's all

        . . . I just essentially(. . .)

Cee

T: (1) I think it's very important that you . . . feel that you come and talk . . . with me,

(2) or even /uh hum/ your other students in the class

(3) and say . . . I didn't get this

(4) when she was talking about that

(5) or can you give me more . . . homework for this

(6) on . . . um . . . I di I disagree I—everybody in the class saying this about the paragraph

(7) but I really think that.

The number of teacher idea units devoted to the invitation varies from 44 for the strongest Caucasian student to 7 for the weaker Asian-American. Of note is T's depersonalizing Cee's "invitation" by creating a scenario in which Cee is given a strong option to speak to other Ss in the class rather than to T about what she doesn't understand. She invites Cee to ask her for homework, not for elaborate discussion. And whereas the invitations to the other three Ss occur at the end of the conference, Cee's is embedded in the middle. Her last remarks for Cee are:

T: I have to go to a class now.
Cee: Okay.
T: Uhm is there anything else you want to ask me? Any final observations?
Cee: Is there any extra credit work we could do?

It is notable that this is the same student, Cee, who admits that she feels discriminated against by her teachers. In fact, she is. But we also see why.

Conclusion

We have examined how the teaching–learning relationship is established between one teacher and four of her students in a college composition course. We have found that: (a) the different students wanted to focus on different types of topics (discourse-level topics for the two Caucasians and surface-level for the high-achieving Asian-American; the lowest-achieving student had no hierarchy of intellectual topics); (b) the teacher focused on different types of intellectual topics for the different students (discourse-level topics for all except the lowest-achieving Asian-American student); (c) the teacher gave more praise to the higher-achieving students who seemed to elicit that praise by expressing their insecurity about their writing; (d) the lower-achieving students initiated topics likely to alienate a teacher; and (e) the synchrony of the conversation broke down with the lowest-achieving Asian-American student, a native speaker of English, who inserted backchannel signals at inappropriate times in the conversation.

These differences in conversational interaction signal the possibility of differential instruction. Even in this first get-acquainted conference, we found that the teacher gave quantitatively and qualitatively different explanations to the four students, with the higher-achieving students receiving more expository explanations and with their explanations being delivered in a more formal, "written-like" register. Further, the higher achieving the student, the more likely she or he was to receive a more elaborate invitation to return for future conferences.

The teacher intended to treat all of her students equally and was surprised by the results of the analysis which bring to light much of what is unconscious in a T–S interaction. By highlighting the differences in a single excellent teacher's interactions with her different students and by making explicit the students' contributions to the interaction, we can begin to practice exerting conscious control over those aspects of the teaching–learning process that are likely to influence what a student learns, and we can focus on those aspects that are likely to lead to success. Our intent is to help teachers carry out their intents.

References

Agar, M. (1980). *The professional stranger: An informal introduction to ethnography.* New York: Academic Press.

Au, K., & Mason, J. (1981). Social organizational factors in learning to read: The balance of rights hypothesis. *Reading Research Quarterly, 17,* 115–152.

Cazden, C., John, V., & Hymes, D. (1972). *Functions of language in the classroom.* New York:

Chafe, W. (1980). The deployment of consciousness in the production of a narrative. In W. Chafe (Ed.), *The pear stories: Cognitive, cultural, and linguistic aspects of a narrative production.* Norwood, NJ: Ablex.

Chafe, W. (1982). Integration and involvement in speaking, writing, and oral literature. In D. Tannen (Ed.), *Spoken and written language.* Norwood, NJ: Ablex.

Chomsky, N. (1965). *Aspects of the theory of syntax.* Cambridge, MA: M.I.T. Press.

Clark, H., & Clark, E. (1977). *Language and psychology.* New York: Harcourt Brace Jovanovich.

Collins, J., & Michaels, S. (1980). The importance of conversational discourse strategies in the acquisition of literacy. *Proceedings of the Sixth Annual Meeting of the Berkeley Linguistics Society, 6,* 143–156.

Cook-Gumperz, J., & Gumperz, J. (1981). From oral to written culture: The transition to literacy. In M. F. Whiteman et al. (Eds.), *Variation in writing: Functional and linguistic cultural differences.* Hillsdale, NJ: Lawrence Erlbaum.

Covelli, L., & Murray, S. (1980). Accomplishing topic change. *Anthropological Linguistics, 22,* 382–389.

Duke, D. (1975). The student centered conference and the writing process. *English Journal, 64,* 44–47.

Erickson, F., & Schultz, J. (1982). *The counselor as gatekeeper: Social interaction in interviews.* New York: Academic Press.

Freedman, S. (1981). Evaluation in the writing conference: An interactive process. In M. Hairston & C. Selfe (Eds.), *Selected papers from the 1981 Texas Writing Research Conference* (pp. 65–96). Austin: The University of Texas at Austin.

Freedman, S. (1979). How characteristics of student essays influence teacher's evaluations. *Journal of Educational Psychology, 71,* 328–338.

Freedman, S., & Katz, A. (in press). Pedagogical interaction during the composing process: The writing conference. In A. Matsuhashi (Ed.), *Writing in real time: Modelling production processes.* New York: Academic Press.

Graves, D. (1983). *Writing: Teachers and children at work.* Exeter, NH: Heinemann.

Gumperz, J. (1982). *Discourse strategies.* Cambridge, England: Cambridge University Press.

Halliday, M, A. K., & Hasan, R. (1976). *Cohesion in English.* London: Longman.

Jacobs, S., & Karliner, A. (1977). Helping writers to think: The effect of speech rate in individual conferences on the quality of thought in student writing, *College English, 38,* 489–505.

Keenan, E., & Schieffelin, B. (1976). Topic as a discourse notion: A study of topic in the conversations of children and adults. In C. Li (Ed.), *Subject and topic.* New York: Academic Press.

Mehan, H. (1978). Structuring school structure. *Harvard Educational Review, 48,* 32–64.

Mehan, H. (1979). *Learning lessons: Social organization in the classroom.* Cambridge, MA: Harvard University Press.

Michaels, S. (1981). *Differential acquisition of literate discourse strategies: A study of sharing time in a first-grade classroom.* Unpublished doctoral dissertation, University of California, Berkeley.

Murray, D. (1968). *A writer teaches writing.* Boston: Houghton Mifflin.

Ochs, E. (1979). Planned and unplanned discourse. In *Syntax and semantics*. New York: Academic Press.

Robinson, W. (1951). The logical structure of analytic induction. *American Sociological Review, 16,* 812–818.

Shuy, R. (1981). Topic as unit of analysis in a criminal law case. In D. Tannen (Ed.), *Talk and text: The twenty-fifth annual Georgetown Round Table on languages and linguistics.* Washington, DC: Georgetown University Press.

Sommers, N. (1982). Responding to student writing. *College Composition and Communication, 33,* 148–156.

Weinstein, R. (1982). *Expectations in the classroom: The student perspective.* Invited address, Division C, annual meeting of the American Educational Research Association, New York.

Wilkinson, L. C., Clevenger, M., & Dolloghan, C. (1981). Communication in small groups: A sociolinguistic approach. In *Children's oral communication skills.* New York: Academic Press.

Yngve, V. (1970). *On getting a word in edgewise.* Paper presented at sixth regional meeting of the Chicago Linguistic Society.

Znanicki, F. (1934). *The method of sociology.* New York: Farrar & Rinehart.

Computers: Revision and Response

7

Do Writers Talk to Themselves?*

Colette Daiute
Harvard University

Introduction

Research on the writing process has shown that good writers do not create wonderful texts in one smooth step (Bridwell, 1980; Flower & Hayes, 1981; Matsuhashi, 1980; Sommers, 1980). Rather, writers plan, compose, revise, throw drafts away, rewrite, and sometimes seem to do nothing at all. These processes do not simply involve expression. People express ideas in writing, but they also react to their texts. Writers read and critique their texts. They talk to themselves about ways to improve their writing. One question in studies of the creative process is "How conscious is the creative process?" "How much creating is actually responding to ideas and to seeds of ideas?" The related question for studying production processes like writing is "Does it make sense to guide students in monitoring their thought processes as they write and revise?"

One reason why writing is more difficult than talking is that our partners in conversation guide our oral planning and revising as they listen, ask questions, or grimace. Writers have to give themselves cues for judging their creative processes and their texts as they compose and revise. Research on writing development has suggested that the difficulty of monitoring one's own thinking in this way seems to account for limited writing abilities. Children and beginning writers have difficulty writing because they have to take an objective point of view about their own thoughts and sentences (Daiute, 1981, 1982; Kroll, 1978). Taking an objective point of view, or "decentering" in Piagetian terms, develops relatively late for complex skills such as reading and writing (Brown, 1975, 1978; Flavell, Friedrichs, & Hoyt, 1970). Being able to make evaluations as one works also means knowing the rules of the writing game—what good texts look like and how they are created.

When readers, writers, and others involved in complex cognitive tasks consciously monitor their thought processes, they perform better on related tasks (Brown, 1978; Flavell et al., 1970). Some people benefit from explicit training on

* I thank the Spencer Foundation for funding my research reported in this chapter. I also thank my collaborators at Teacher's College, Columbia University and elsewhere: Thomas Bever, Robert Taylor, Sharon Liff, Pegeen Wright, Sandy Mazur, Sharon Moore, Steven Suckow, Victor Muslin, Robert Holzman, and Ursula Wolz. Special thanks to Thomas Bever and Lucy Calkins for their insightful comments and suggestions on drafts of this chapter.

these complex self-monitoring behaviors (Brown, 1978), but the overall effects of training on cognitive self-monitoring have not yet been clearly established.

Researchers and teachers have tried several approaches to guide children's self-monitoring and thereby help them revise more. Teachers have marked papers. They have written questions, comments, or corrections in margins and between lines. And they have underlined misspelled words and awkward sentences to focus children's attention on problems in their texts. Teacher and peer conferences have proved to be especially helpful in stimulating revising skills in children at much younger ages than we have ever seen before (Calkins, 1980; Freedman, 1981; Graves, 1982). Conferences help children identify weaknesses in their texts and sometimes to improve the texts as well.

These approaches to stimulate children's revising rely on oral or written conversational contexts—comments on papers, checklists, and conferences. What the approaches have in common is that they offer children models and strategies for looking at their writing objectively. These strategies, moreover, all involve a form of conversation as a foundation for writing. Results from this line of research suggest that explicit self-monitoring is important in writing development, but we need more specific information on the role of inner dialogues and the value of using them to solve specific problems.

The relationship between self-monitoring and revising is now an active subject of inquiry, in part, because the computer has offered a way to present writers with specific, albeit limited, comments on their texts under the writers' autonomous control. Writers can get help from on-line planning and revising programs that offer responses to their texts. Studying writing in this context has offered insights about the nature of inner diaglogues and the value of different ways of stimulating beginning writers to talk to themselves.

This chapter reviews the goals and findings of recent studies on conversational prompting to increase writers' conscious control over the writing process (Collins, Bruce, & Rubin, 1982; Daiute, 1981, 1982; Kiefer & Smith, 1984; Woodruff, Bereiter, & Scardamalia, 1981–2). The chapter includes (a) a discussion on the proposed value of self-monitoring in writing development, (b) a review of representative automatic analysis and prompting programs as stimulators of writers' self-monitoring; (c) a summary of recent research on the effects of automatic prompting on beginning writers, and (d) a discussion of the implications of human/computer interactions for writing development.

Writing Development

Research on the development of children's writing abilities indicates that children have difficulty revising because they have not developed strategies for critiquing, evaluating, and improving their texts. Young children do not spontaneously critique their plans and texts because they have difficulty taking alternative points of view (Kroll, 1978) or because they have not been taught how to revise (Bereiter, 1980).

The writer must act as a reader to identify parts of the text that are not clear, not supported, or that have other problems. Writers benefit from activities providing some of the supports of conversation such as feedback about the text (Calkins, 1983; Graves, 1982) and prompting on strategies for improving it (Bereiter & Scardamalia, 1981). Monitoring one's own thought processes can stimulate objectivity. This view that children can learn to consciously control their creative processes rather than wait for mysterious bursts of inspiration is a general thrust in developmental inquiries.

One current question in developmental inquiries is "Can we help children improve their thinking skills by teaching them to think about their own cognitive processes?" (Brown, 1975; Kuhn and Amsel, 1983; Markman, 1979; Waters, 1982). People monitor their thought processes as they identify problems in cognitive tasks, plan ways to solve the problems, and evaluate their success at solving them. This involves conscious decision-making about strategies for cognitive tasks, such as remembering information or understanding a text (Brown, 1978). A musician, for example, may think that a piece he or she has composed is fine until hearing it aloud. Upon noticing that something sounds bad, the musician might simply try new phrasings or might analyze the cacophonous sequence to identify the problem before deciding how to fix it. When addressing the problem directly and systematically, the musician is monitoring internal creative processes.

People are engaged in such cognitive self-monitoring all the time although it varies in explicitness and complexity. Brown, Bransford, Ferrara, and Campione (1983) have identified two types of self-reflective cognitive activities. The type that young children seem to acquire is a "regulation of cognitive activities." When encouraged, children can use strategies such as meaningfully categorizing pieces of information they have to learn, but they do not use such strategic learning aids spontaneously or consistently. The other type of metacognition is acquired relatively late, when children can discuss their knowledge about knowledge (Brown et al., 1983). At this point, they consciously decide to use cognitive strategies for achieving specific goals, rather than use a trial and error approach until they are successful at a particular task. These children can discuss their approaches to cognitive activities, and their performance bears out that they have used the strategies.

When children learn to monitor their cognitive behaviors, their performance improves, as does their ability to predict their own success (Flavell, 1979). For example, children who learn to monitor their own memory strategies do better on memory tasks (Brown, 1978; Flavell, 1979; Flavell et al., 1970; Kreuitzer, Leonard, & Flavell, 1975). As children mature, their assessment of their mental abilities becomes more accurate. Flavell et al. (1970) showed that younger children (kindergartners and second graders) predicted that they would be able to remember more items on a memory test than did older children (fourth), but the younger children remembered fewer items than the older children did.

Some people learn to evaluate their thinking and their performance spontaneously, while others require training or experience on specific tasks. In some cases, children's performance on complex cognitive tasks such as reading comprehension has improved after they have been trained to use specific strategies (Brown, 1975; Markman, 1979). Brown (1978) states that adults as well as children attempting complex tasks such as text comprehension may lack self-guiding strategies and the ability to predict and evaluate their performance: "one must proceed by initially training some skills before attempting to induce the monitoring and control of these strategic behaviors" (p. 134). This is especially true of slower students who lag in developing metacognitive control spontaneously (Brown, 1978; Kohlberg, Yaeger, & Hjertholm, 1968).

When studying writing, we can observe self-monitoring processes more directly than we can when studying memory and comprehension activities. In writing, the stimulus for self-monitoring—the text—and the result of self-monitoring—revising—are available for direct observation. The writer's thoughts are recorded on the page, and the reviser's actions result from decisions about the content and form of the ideas as they appear on the page. Moreover, revising involves several subprocesses that can be observed for indications about different types of self-monitoring and partial successes. Hayes & Flower (1980) have identified two subprocesses in revising: identifying a problem in a sentence and correcting the problem. Even adults with limited writing ability have been unable to remedy problems that they can identify in writing. Such information alerts us to the possible partial effects of self-monitoring and suggests that the writer may have successfully identified a problem after self-questioning but does not know the appropriate way to improve the text.

Setting writing within the context of conversation has been a way to show children how to control their own thought processes. Such self-monitoring often involves talking to oneself. In conversation, listeners stimulate speakers and guide them in expressing and clarifying ideas, while in writing they have to guide themselves. Mature writers learn to carry on their own inner dialogues about content, form, and the creative process. The process of internalizing monitoring strategies is often manifested in "private speech"—speech that is not directed to an interlocutor. Research suggests that such verbal mediation of difficult tasks may be important (Brown et al., 1983; Kohlberg et al., 1968). Children's use of audible private speech reflects a "pull to cognitive activity" (Kohlberg et al., 1968). Children first ask themselves questions, then make statements that seem to be answers to implied or internally posed questions. Verbalization eventually seems to disappear, but even adults are heard muttering to themselves when wrestling with particularly difficult problems. Prompting that guides writers to ask themselves questions rather than respond to questions by actual interlocutors may be most useful in stimulating autonomous self-monitoring. Prompting may show young children how to monitor their own thought processes, while it stimulates adults to focus their attention selectively on the task at hand.

Instructional strategies such as conferencing, corresponding, and prompting help young writers make the difficult transition from speaking to writing. Graves (1983),

Calkins (1983), and many classroom teachers have found that even first graders begin to make conscious decisions and comments about ways of improving their texts after they discuss first drafts with teachers and peers. The children seem to internalize the conversations they have with others about their writing. Similarly, Levin (this volume) has found that children find writing easier when they directly address their readers in letters. Levin's elementary school subjects in California used a computer mail system for writing to children in Alaska, so they had a specific reader in mind as they wrote. This reader gave direct and quick feedback in writing.

Other researchers have used verbal messages or prompts to test the value of conversational supports that are more under the child's autonomous control. Bereiter and Scardamalia (1981) have found that suggestions such as "Will my reader understand the relationship between these two points?" have stimulated revising in eight-year-olds. The researchers presented a set of similar questions on note cards the children could refer to when they felt they did not know what to do to improve their texts.

This research on the value of conversational stimulations for writing raises several issues. First, we need to distinguish the importance of dialogues in offering students self-monitoring strategies from the importance of the motivation provided by another person's interest in their writing. Second, we have to determine the nature of inner dialoguing and the related analysis of complex tasks. Researchers and teachers currently accept a holistic or global approach to viewing writing development. In its most extreme form, this approach assumes that children learn all they need to know about writing by writing and discussing their texts with readers. According to this theory, children learn to write well-developed, interesting texts with good sentence structure, spelling, and punctuation by discussing their texts. Presumably, even general questions from readers offer the writer sufficient information for learning the qualities of good texts and the steps in creating them. Conferencing has not been studied experimentally, so we do not know the specific developments that occur. But it seems that readers' comments offer beginning writers more information than copy-editing marks or than their own rereading.

Some important questions about the development of inner dialogues remain: What specific processes does the writer internalize from conferencing and conversational prompting? What are the differences between cognitive and social effects of conversational stimulations of writing behavior? Are the explicit analyses always a step in development, or are they only necessary when writers wrestle with specific problems? When does self-consciousness interfere with the creative process rather than enhance it?

Drawing on conversation to teach writers to carry on inner dialogues seems to demystify the writing process. If we learn that children write better and more easily because they talk themselves through their texts, we can help those who have writing blocks and other writing difficulties. Moreover, studying writers' autonomous control of their thought processes gives us insights about the value of self-monitoring compared to the social motivation of conversation. Finally, the study of younger writers' verbal self-monitoring may offer insights for understanding the difficulties that adults have when they begin to write. Just as many children build their written language skills on their oral language abilities in conferencing situations, older writers may benefit from learning to talk to themselves about their writing.

I am suggesting that writers internalize the social and conversational activities that enable them to create clear, independent texts that communicate to many readers. The hypothesis is that learning to write involves a complex mixture of talking to one's self and to others about the content, form, and creation of the text. Mature writers, in short, talk to themselves about their writing and their writing talks to them as well. Developing writers learn to do this by talking to others about their writing, by reading comments about their writing, and eventually role playing a reader who can make such comments. One step in studying the value of self-talk in writer's development is to study the differences in the learning strategies of writers who develop inner dialogues spontaneously and those who need some training. In short, I am studying the value of young writers' control over their thinking processes. Such an inquiry will help us decide if suggesting verbal self-monitoring strategies to beginning writers will help them express themselves clearly or will stifle them.

In summary, the recent research on writing and self-monitoring suggests that writers manage many cognitive and physical tasks as they compose and, especially, as they revise. Writers have to view their ideas objectively so they can experience their writing as a reader would. Being objective in this way requires some role playing, like that in conversation. In addition, writers have to use their mental capacities efficiently (Daiute, 1981; Flower & Hayes, 1981; Shaughnessy, 1977). They should not burden themselves with evaluation tasks at the same time they are composing (Elbow, 1975). Creating and critiquing ideas, text structures, and punctuation at the same time puts burdens on the writer's short-term memory capacities (Daiute, 1980, 1981). Such competing activities may cause an impasse. Beginning writers have to learn to choreograph the many processes and contents involved in writing. Because this is a cognitively demanding task, some writers need explicit instruction on managing their own writing processes.

Computer Prompting

The computer can suggest a link between conversation and composition. Computer programs can identify objective features of texts and present prepared statements in relation to these features (Daiute, 1985). Writers initiate and control these responses themselves. Computer prompting seems to be a useful tool for helping writers take an objective point of view and learn some strategies and rules about the writing process, but we do not yet know the results of this human computer interaction.

Computer programs typically include comments or prompts to people who use the programs. Often these prompts are instructions or error messages. Prompts can guide writers in routine tasks such as naming a file. "Name file to edit" is an example of a prompt that appears on the screen at the beginning of an editing session with one word-processing program. Prompts also inform computer users of certain errors they make as they interact with the program. Messages such as "illegal command" often appear, but they are not always decipherable because they tend to refer to the inner workings of the machine, which writers do not always understand. Understandable or not, prompts make the computer look as though it is talking to the user in writing.

ELIZA is a classic example of computer prompting. Joseph Weizenbaum, a computer scientist, wrote the ELIZA program to illustrate that rather simple programs can appear to ask questions and respond to the answers people write. A person interacts with the ELIZA program as though talking to a psychiatrist. ELIZA responds to the person using the program by identifying key words such as "mother," when they are spelled correctly, and then by presenting one in a set of related responses stored in the program. ELIZA's responses appear in upper case in this example from Weizenbaum (1976).

I need some help, that much seems certain

WHAT WOULD IT MEAN TO YOU IF YOU GOT SOME HELP

Perhaps I could learn to get along with my mother

TELL ME MORE ABOUT YOUR FAMILY

My mother takes care of me

WHO ELSE IN YOUR FAMILY TAKES CARE OF YOU

My father

YOUR FATHER

You are like my father in some ways

WHAT RESEMBLANCE DO YOU SEE

You are not very aggressive but I think you don't want

me to notice that

WHAT MAKES YOU THINK I AM NOT VERY AGGRESSIVE

You don't argue with me

WHY DO YOU THINK I DON'T ARGUE WITH YOU

You are afraid of me

DOES IT PLEASE YOU THAT I AM AFRAID OF YOU

Weizenbaum used this program to demonstrate the limits of the computer's apparent consciousness. His program presents prompts automatically in response to specific words and word patterns the writer types into the computer. It does not react to meanings or other abstractions that are not reducible to exact words or patterns of words. The prompts simply point to text features and leave the thinking up to the writer.

Researchers have used conversational computer prompting like Weizenbaum's to stimulate writers as they compose (Burns & Culp, 1980; Collins, Bruce, & Rubin, 1982; Woodruff, Bereiter, & Scardamalia, 1981–82). Researchers have also added computer analysis to stimulate writers as they revise (Daiute, 1983; Kiefer & Smith, 1984; Miller, Heidorn, & Jensen, 1981). The programs present conversational prompts such as "Write everything you know about the topic" or "Have you given your reader enough details about your point?" The words "the topic" and "the point" can be replaced by words or phrases that the writer has noted as the topic to the program.

Programs can do text analyses based on exact instructions. Writers can initiate the prompting, if the program includes commands they can use to request help. While reading silently or aloud, writers are presumably also posing questions to themselves and thus thinking about their writing critically. These prompts can appear one at a time within, under, or above the part of the text in question.

Burns and Culp (1980) developed a computer program that guides college students in forming ideas for an essay by providing instructions intended to help them collect information relevant to the topic. In the example, the program responses appear in capitals.

DURING THIS EXPLORATION PROCESS, YOU WILL BE ASKED TO CLARIFY THE PURPOSE OF YOUR PAPER ON FEAR OF DEATH.
SO HOW WOULD YOU BRIEFLY DESCRIBE THE PURPOSE OF YOUR PAPER BY COMPLETING THIS STATEMENT: THE PURPOSE OF THIS PAPER IS TO . . .
Examine the fear of death people have, where we get those fears, and how we may reduce those fears.
FINE, WALT, YOU AND WILL TALK ABOUT YOUR PURPOSE. RELAX NOW, WALT, AND ENJOY THIS BRAINSTORMING SESSION.
WHAT OBJECTS DO YOU ASSOCIATE WITH THE FEAR OF DEATH? HOW MIGHT THEY BE INCLUDED IN YOUR THEME?
Fear of the Unknown, cessation of life, fear of causing pain to our loved ones.
THAT'S THE IDEA, WALT. GIVE ME SOME MORE INFO NOW.
Pain is another fear causer, knowing we have to die does not relieve the pain/fear of dying.
SUPER, WALT!
ANYTHING ELSE? (YOU CAN ADD MORE INFO, ASK A QUESTION, OR GIVE A COMMAND—WHATEVER YOU WISH.) (Burns & Culp, 1980, p. 3)

Burns and Culp report that prewriting prompts on the computer stimulate writers' thinking and help them become aware of what they do and do not know about a topic. Walt's writing is hardly a composition or even a first draft, but this writer has begun to explore his topic, and he has made notes that he can use for additional planning and composing.

Woodruff, Scardamalia, and Bereiter have developed prompts to guide children in using basic discourse elements in their essays. One program offers writers suggestions after they have not typed for twenty seconds. If the child does not request help, the program waits 25 seconds the next time the child stops. This prompting is intended to encourage the child to write anything about the topic rather than suffer through silences. Writing down ideas that seem related to a topic has proved to be a more effective method for beginning writers than trying to work through the creation of a text in mind (Elbow, 1975).

If the child using the computer-aided composing programs developed by Woodruff et al. wants help, the program offers a list of nine statements about the structural elements of essays. For example, the list on the screen reads, "When you are writing an argument you can include: 1. a statement of belief, 2. an explanation of your belief." The child can press a button to get more information about any item on the list. The program also presents questions such as "Do you have an opinion on this topic?" and related expansions such as "Okay, let's tell the reader."

Woodruff et al. report that children liked using the computer-aided composing programs. Their young subjects said that the programs made writing more enjoyable and easier. The fact that the children consulted the various help features many times suggested to the researchers that the children found the interactive writing guide to be helpful. Nevertheless, the papers written on the computer were not rated as better. Nor did they include more words. The researchers also noted that the prompting seemed to stimulate a passive disposition to composing—what they referred to as a "what next" strategy of waiting for the computer to come up with idea stimulation.

The children in this study enjoyed the supports of conversational prompting, but they relied on them too much. This may have happened because writers need more than one session to become comfortable with computer writing tools and to adjust to new forms of composing (Daiute, 1983). Young writers may also follow writing guides too closely, if the suggestions represent discourse structures or writing strategies that they have not used and they are not developmentally ready to use.

While some prompting programs are designed as thought stimulators, others are designed as thought organizers. "The Publisher" developed at Bolt, Beranek, and Newman is an example of such a guide. The program sets up date, salutation, and body sections of letters. Programs based on the form of a document may stimulate writers' thinking because they can focus on the content rather than superficial aspects of the document form, which the computer program can provide. Programs can also prompt writers to think about their drafts. Other planning programs prompt writers to compose texts based on the sections they have to include in a specific document. For example, book reports often include brief summaries of the text, analyses of the plot conflict, character sketches, and the reader's interpretation and opinion of the book.

Such programs offer two types of cognitive support for beginning writers: The prompts are intended to (a) help writers guide the search for information, and (b) to help writers use their limited short-term memory capacities efficiently by encouraging them to focus on one aspect of writing at a time. The value of prewriting prompts is that they offer the natural conversational mode for beginning a writing task, and they seem to guide and stimulate the writer's search for information in long-term memory.

Researchers have also used the analytic capacities of the computer to stimulate writers' objectivity about their texts and thus stimulate revising. Computer programs that "mark papers" note specific words that may be mistakes or that may relate to problems in the content and form of the text. Unlike most teachers and editors, text analysis programs identify superficial text features such as spelling, punctuation problems, and words like transitionals, which are related to text organization. Programs cannot always indicate for sure that a particular word is "wrong," nor can they identify the logic, organization, or even grammatical problems that people can. Since the programs have to be told exactly what to do, they can identify "recieve," for example, as a misspelled word, but they cannot make notes like "the meaning of this sentence is not clear," in response to semantic or logical problems in the text. Computer programs cannot even identify spelling mistakes with 100% accuracy. Like the computer analyst ELIZA and Walt's computer composition guide, programs can present only general questions in relation to specific words and patterns.

The computer needs exact instructions, because it usually searches through the text character-by-character along the same path each time. It searches from left to right, letter-by-letter, line-by-line. So, if the writer asks it to search for the word "love," a program stops at every "l," if it is next to an "o" and then a "v," and an "e." And if the writer has not told the program to look for "love" surrounded by spaces, it identifies the "love" in "gloves."

Such imperfect recognition leaves a lot up to the writer. Researchers and teachers have observed that since the computer is not always "right," the child using text analysis programs maintains control over the text and the revising process (Daiute, 1982). This assumption is plausible, but it still has to be confirmed by research.

The Writer's Workbench (WWB) programs were originally developed at Bell Labs for writers of technical and scientific reports, and the programs have also been used extensively by students at Colorado State University. The STYLE and DICTION programs check for features such as repeated words, unnecessary words, usage errors, and readability. SUGGEST offers information for improvements. When the program has completed its analysis, it offers the writer a list of the occurrences of that error on a printout or on the screen.

Output from the STYLE program run on an essay entitled "Children," reported in Kiefer and Smith (1984).

Children
readability grades:

(Kincaid) 10.5 (auto) 11.7 (Coleman-Liau 9.7)
Flesch 8.8 (61.6)

sentence info:

no. sent 43 no. words 1009
av. sent leng 23.5 av word leng 4.54
no. questions 0 no. imperative 0
no. content words 574 56.9% av leng 5.85
short sent (<18) 40% (17) long sent (>33) 19% (8)
longest sent 48 wds at sent 21; shortest sent 11 wds at sent 5

sentence types:

simple 35% (15) complex 37% (16)
compound 7% (3) compound-complex 21% (9)

word usage:

verb types as % of total verbs
to be 18% (21) aux 25% (30) inf 28% (33)
passives as % of total
prep 10.8% (109) conj 3.2% (32) adv 5.3% (53)
noun 26.2% (264) adj 14.1% (142) pron 5.8% (59)
nominalizations 1% (12)

sentence beginnings:

subject opener: noun (4) pron (3) pos (0) adj (10)
    art (12) tot 67%
prep 14% (6) adv 2% (1)
verb 0% (0) subj-conj 16% (7) conj 0% (0)
expletives 0% (0)

This program offers detailed analyses but no prompting to integrate the analysis with a conversational strategy. Adults may not need the relationship of the analyses to writing strategies made explicit, but some of the results of research on the WWB programs suggest that even adults could use explicit prompting to stimulate revising of organization and meaning.

In one study (Gingrich, 1982), two groups of 14 adult writers each used the programs to analyze documents they wrote. After a one-week training session, the writers used the Workbench system for ten weeks. On-line data collected during writing and analyses, questionnaires, and interviews suggested to the researchers that the writers liked using the programs and found them helpful. The writers made changes in their documents but they made mostly changes in surface features rather than in organization.

The most frequently used programs were those that identified word and usage problems. The researchers found that although the writers reported that they needed help organizing their writing, they did not use the ''org'' program, intended to help with organization, as much as they used the word and phrase analysis programs. This may be because the ''org'' program requires that writers make several conceptual leaps. ''Org'' prints out the first and last sentences of each paragraph. Such an aid is less concrete than that in the other programs showing problems in specific words. To benefit from the "org" program, writers have to be aware of the relationship between overall text structure and the functions of different types of sentences in paragraphs. A writer can, for example, benefit from "org," when he or she has a relatively long text. If the writer has attempted to use such a structure, the "org" program shows the overall structure of the piece, and then by reading the reduced version of the text the writer can see any point that is out of order.

The difficulty of relating pattern analyses to features of good writing is compounded by the fact that most computer systems do not display the entire text at one time. Such a limit may make using a feature such as "org" difficult, because as writers evaluate the reduced version of the text, they need to consider the overall text as a whole. Developmental differences also account for use of specific features. Younger writers and beginning adult writers tend to revise single words and phrases rather than larger text units (Calkins, 1980). In research on junior high school students, Daiute (1983) found that ninth graders make more use of programs like "org" that involve thinking about more than one sentence at a time than do seventh graders. This suggests that developing writing abilities may involve processing words, phrases, and sentences before paragraph and text structures.

In a more recent study on the effects of the Workbench programs on the writing of college freshmen, Kiefer and Smith (1984) have found that "textual analysis with computers intrigues college writers and speeds learning of editing skills." Two groups of randomly selected students taking freshman composition courses used the Writer's Workbench, DICTION, SUGGEST, STYLE, and SPELL programs one hour a week for a 13-week semester. These students edited more thoroughly and learned to edit on their own. Kiefer and Smith gave a two-part editing task, pre- and post-treatment attitude surveys, and pre- and post-summary and response essays which were rated according to the holistic scoring measure. The experimental subjects improved more than the control subjects (15.03 compared to 10.50) on part two of the editing task—revision of errors for simplicity, directness, and clarity, which are taught by DICTION, SUGGEST, and STYLE. Experimental students did not score significantly higher than the control subjects on part one of the test, which covered material both groups had in class which was not included in the programs. Nor did the experimental group show more gain in writing fluency according to holistic scores on the summary and response essay. The attitude survey showed that the experimental students found the computer programs to be enjoyable, easy, and not frustrating. These results show that programs like the Writer's Workbench can help students learn editing skills, but these skills do not transfer to writing ability more than material covered in class transfers. This lack of transfer of specific editing feedback to writing fluency is not surprising since the computer feedback in the Workbench program is geared to local editing, whereas class discussions probably are more concerned with the style, organization, and effects of the texts.

These automatic analysis programs present relatively superficial feedback that draws writers' attention to the wording in their texts. Although such limited computer responses may have the value of leaving the decisions up to the writer, researchers have also found value in offering more substantive and complex computer feedback.

Complex programs on large computers can analyze or parse sentences, although the parses are not correct all the time. In order to parse sentences, the computer programs have to include detailed information about exact words. For example, a program could begin to parse a sequence of words if it knows the part of speech of each word. These part-of-speech assignments have to be made by a person who enters them into the program. Such programs require time and storage space and would not work well on texts created with a large number of words for which it does not have part-of-speech assignments. The program needs to know rules such as the likely orderings of words or specific parts of speech, so it can make guesses. "Dance," for example, can be a noun or a verb. If it follows an article such as "the" or "a," it is probably a noun. The computer can build and store such guesses as it considers each word in a sentence.

The Epistle program, developed at the T. J. Watson Research Center, does grammar and style checking of words and sentences in texts entered into the IBM 370 computer. The system is designed to offer office workers a computer package to help them improve their business letters. Epistle works from a general language-processing system called NLP, used as a parser to identify the syntactic structure of English sentences. Such complex analyses require large computers, extensive research, and development efforts.

Once writers have put a letter on the IBM system, they can select style, grammar checking, and spelling options. The problem sequences appear enclosed in blocks on the screen in the color coded for the particular problem. Above the color-highlighted problem section is an identification of the error: "Structure is not parallel. 'Neither Mr. Jones or Mr. Walters.' " Correction options and grammar rules related to the problem overlay the text on the screen if the writer requests further information. Errors appear in the context of the text, but writers cannot immediately switch to the word processing program to make changes without losing the Epistle notes from the screen. Thus, writers have to take notes from the screen, which is not the most efficient use of their time and thought power. The program offers writers information that can help them evaluate words and sentences more objectively, but the analyses are not related to larger text structures or to the writing process. Miller and his colleagues are now further developing and testing Epistle to extend its interactions with the writer to prewriting and units larger than the sentence.

A program with grammatical parsing capacities can offer more reliable feedback on sentence structures than systems that base their feedback on identification of individual words, word patterns, and statistics rather than parsing rules. When the Epistle spelling-checking program is working, for example, it will more accurately identify the misuse of "to" for "too" than existing systems do because it will not only compare words in a text to words in a dictionary, but it will also back up this list-checking with grammatical analyses showing that "too" meaning "also" rather than "to" in the verb infinitive is probably required. In this way, the computer program that the writer interacts with is more sensitive than text analysis programs based on word lists and patterns.

Writers have to learn about the features of good and bad writing in a way that helps them improve their own sentences. Seeing the first sentence of each paragraph together is useful to a writer who is aware that first sentences are often topic sentences, are salient, and suggest overall organization of the text, even if they are not topic sentences. While pointing out such features can help mature writers focus on text structure, young writers need more explicit relating of text analysis features to qualities of good writing and strategies for creating it. Prompting and analysis programs can stimulate writers to think about their writing, but the comments should be integrated into the complete writing process, with considerations about efficient use of the writer's mental-processing space and relating analyses and prompts to the writing process. Young writers also need help in focusing their cognitive and physical efforts as they write, so they do not overburden working memory or have conflicting agendas about the activities involved in writing. With these points in mind, we did a study on the value of computer word processing, text analysis, and prompting tools for helping children take more control of their writing processes. We wanted to learn about the negative as well as the positive effects of computer-guided revising. We expected that as children learned to talk to themselves about the writing process, they would enjoy writing more, revise more, and write better.

In a study on the role of children's verbal self-monitoring stimulated by the computer, we developed a prompting program with limited text analyses. We designed the prompting program (Catch) for the Spencer Foundation study "The Effects of Automatic Prompting on Young Writers" (Daiute, 1983). The text analysis program works within a computer word-processing program and presents prompts that relate to the writing process. Catch does similar types of analyses to the Workbench, but it guides student writers in relating the analyses to their texts and the writing process. The Catch analyses and prompts are intended (a) to stimulate children's internal discussions about their writing, and (b) to limit physical and information processing burdens so that the child has sufficient time and cognitive space for pondering and improving the text.

At any time during or after composing a text, the writer can give a command to see the list of Catch features. The program presents comments and questions about the completeness, clarity, organization, sentence structure, conciseness, and punctuation of the text that the writer is working on. Some of the features present questions such as "Does this paragraph include a sentence that states its point?" Other features identify words and phrases that may include problems. If the writer, for example, selects the "empty word" option, the program identifies unnecessary words such as "sort of" and "well." As these words are highlighted on the computer screen, a prompt appears at the bottom of the screen. The prompt that appears with "empty words" is "The highlighted words may not be necessary. Do you need to make changes?" The writer can immediately make changes if he or she wishes. Writers using Catch are in control of all evaluations and changes. They are aware that the program may identify words that are "empty" in some contexts such as "well" in "Well, I will begin with my childhood," but not in others, such as "My first memories are of throwing pennies into a well."

The prompts vary in form, function, scope, and relation to the writing process. Some focus on aspects of the purpose and content of the piece, others on form. While some of the features present questions about important text qualities writers tend to look for as they revise, others offer specific information about words, phrases, and sentences. For example, the "point" option presents the writer with the prompt "Does this paragraph have a clear focus?" Such prompts are intended to stimulate the writer to focus on the organizational, semantic, and logical aspects of text that state-of-the-art computer consciousness cannot understand. Moreover, the writer, researchers, and teacher can easily change the prompts to make them more clear, more personal, or more elaborate.

Unlike the Writer's Workbench or Epistle, Catch also works within the word processing program the writer uses to create the text. When designing Catch, we assumed that writers could benefit from prompting, if they did not have excessive physical and information processing burdens to control at the same time as they were evaluating a text. For this reason, we integrated the analysis, prompting, and word processing, so writers could easily make changes in their texts as they viewed the analyses on the screen. When writers have to refer to printouts of analyses or switch from one program to another, they may take more time to consider the appropriateness of the computer analyses and suggestions.

The prompts appear one at a time in the context of a first draft. In this way, the writer's attention is more likely to be focused on one specific problem at a time, which may reduce information processing burdens that could compete with self-monitoring activities (Brown et al., 1983; Daiute, 1983; Markman, 1979). Note cards, check lists, or comments in margins have to be processed simultaneously, and the writer has to know how to select from among a large list of questions. Reading, selecting, integrating, and acting on suggestions for text critiquing may be too much for writers to do at once.

Finally, once the writer decides to make a change on the computer, it is easy to do. Word processing programs offer writers the capacity to make changes by giving commands, and the program does the recopying and reformatting for them. These commands could remove one possible cause of limited revising—the physical chore of recopying, which many children report as difficult (Calkins, 1980; Collins et al., 1982; Daiute, 1982).

The computer does some tedious checking and draws the writer's attention to these features, but the writer makes all the decisions about the text. Ideally, writers who use automatic analysis and prompting programs know generally how they work. They should be aware that the programs are noting specific features that may be associated with text problems, but the programs are not making informed judgments about the text quality and meaning.

Effects of computer prompting like the ones described caution us to take a closer look at developmental differences in benefits from externally prompted self-monitoring. The questions are "Do automatic analyses and prompting, even when superficial, stimulate writers' development of self-monitoring abilities?" "Is there evidence of increased self-monitoring in increased revising?"

The purpose of the study "The Effects of Automatic Prompting on Young Writers" (Daiute, 1983) was to identify the value of conversational prompts presented by the computer rather than by another person. Computer prompting is more efficient than prompts on note cards or checklists but is also more limited than the prompting in human conferences. In addition, the writer initiates and controls computer prompting more autonomously than when discussing texts with others. We studied the value of computer prompting to begin to identify the cognitive value compared to the social value of conversational prompting. We also wanted to find out whether limited computer feedback would stimulate or limit the child's control over the text.

We found preliminary evidence that conversational prompts directly under young writers' control can help writers revise more, suggesting that such prompting stimulates them to think more about their writing. Results from this study show that after using the word processor and Catch revision guide for one month, children made a higher mean number of revisions. Nevertheless, some children changed more words when they were not prompted by the computer, while others changed more words when they referred to the computer prompts.

Method

Eight 12 year old subjects wrote with a word processing program and Catch for fifteen hours over a five-week period. The subjects wrote drafts and revisions on nine autobiographical topics. They wrote pre- and post-treatment writing samples and a short story with pen. Using the word processing program and Catch, the children wrote 5 part autobiographies, 2 short stories, and a piece on a topic of their choice. The subjects were trained to touch-type and to use the computer programs. The subjects used Catch to stimulate revising after they said that they had improved the piece as much as they possibly could without any help. We compared the subjects' writing on the computer before and after they used the Catch prompting to their writing in pen and with no prompting.

Analyses

Comments by two of our subjects reflect different predispositions to prompting. One young writer made a comment suggesting that he was sensitive to the computer prompting: "The 'long sentences' feature helps me find run-ons and even some other problems, because it makes me read my sentences. But, some of the others like 'guide words' don't." Like the fourth graders in Flavell's study cited earlier who were aware of the approximate number of items they would and would not be able to remember in a memory task, this student was aware of the program aids and limitations in relation to his writing. In contrast, this comment by a younger writer suggests that she was not ready to evaluate her texts on her own, even though she expresses the value we intended for Catch. "When you don't want to really look hard at your work you can just use Catch to review it with you. I'd rather have someone correct my work. It just says 'Do you need to make changes?' I'm not supposed to know."

Our analyses of the subjects' writing in pen before they used Catch and after they had used it for five weeks suggest that the program stimulated changes in revising behavior. All writing samples were analyzed for number of words, sentence complexity, revisions, errors, and quality. These analyses offered information for profiles on characteristic revising strategies of children who benefit from prompting and those who do not.

The amount and nature of change between drafts and completed texts was the main measure of self-monitoring in this study. We predicted that the more revising the subject did, the more self-monitoring he or she had done to lead to critical evaluation and change in the text. We have adapted Faigley and Witte's (1980) revision taxonomy for our analyses. This taxonomy provides categories for the types of changes made in a draft, such as a substitution of one word for another, or the addition of a paragraph, and a distinction between meaningful versus superficial changes. The taxonomy also provides separate categories for revisions that significantly alter the overall meaning and purpose of the text and those that do not. For example, if subjects make more changes in response to prompting, but the changes are superficial this may be an indication of a response to prompting but not evidence of self-monitoring assimilated to their knowledge about the purposes and effects of writing. In addition, Faigley and Witte suggested noting the number of words and punctuation marks (units) involved in each revision. Appendix A is a example of a piece coded for revisions.

We followed Daiute's error taxonomy (1980, 1981) for categorizations of typical anomalous sentence structures and usage problems in first drafts. Recording sentence and word problems and the rates at which children revised them provided additional information on the relationship between prompting and revising.

Results

Catch seems to have stimulated closer revising of first drafts and less rewriting. After using Catch for one month, most of the children made changes more places in their texts, but these changes involved fewer words. They made more revisions per word and slightly more types of revisions on the posttest than on the pretest, but the post-test revisions involved fewer words (297) than the pre-test revisions (417). The analysis of the types of changes made showed a higher percent of deletions on the posttest (12.7% of all revisions) than on the pretest (6.7%). They made more substitutions and consolidations on the posttest (16.4% and 2.2%, respectively) than on the pretest (15.7% substitutions and no consolidations). On the other hand, they made fewer additions on the posttest (5.2%) than on the pretest (8.2%).

The number of errors per word (error rates) in the pre- and posttests illustrate revising that is increasingly efficient. The children's error rates (number of word and sentence errors per word) were roughly equivalent on the pre- and posttests (.37 and .39 per word, respectively). But, in the posttest the children corrected more errors (43.4% compared to 31.9%) and made fewer new ones (19.5% compared to 34%). Finally, the error rates were lower on the posttest revisions (.26) than on the pretest revisions (.35). These results differ from those reported by Levin, Riel, Rowe, and Boruta (this volume), who found that children using only a word processing program made more and corrected more errors when they used the computer.

After using Catch, most subjects made more types of changes in their texts and corrected more errors, but increasing revising activity and efficiency did not lead to overall improvements in quality ratings.

The results reported above are based on mean scores that apply to most of the subjects. Two case studies from the project indicated that there may be different stages of readiness for self-monitoring stimulation in writing. Janie and Randy are two young writers who responded differently to computer prompting. Janie was 11½-years-old at the time of the experiment, and Randy was 12½. Although Randy was ranked as a better writer (the best of 8) than Janie (sixth of 8), they performed equally well on a sentence memory task, indicating equal overall language-processing ability.

Analyses of revisions stimulated by prompting and without it show that Janie revised more when Catch guided her, but Randy revised much more when he did not have prompting. In addition, Janie made more meaningful (addition of clarifying information) versus superficial (punctuation) revisions when she used Catch. On the other hand, Randy revised more and more meaningfully without external prompting. Table 1 is a chart noting the differences between Janie's and Randy's pretests, posttests, and midtests.

The subjects wrote the pre- and posttests and one sample on the midtest in pen. The subjects had no prompting when they used pen. The subjects used the word processing program with Catch on one midtest sample and 7 samples they wrote throughout the experimental period. As Table 1 illustrates, Janie and Randy differed in almost every feature we analyzed. Janie's sentences on the computer were more complex than Randy's, but Randy's were more complex in pen, and he increased his sentence complexity more from pre- to post-treatment writing. Janie revised more with computer prompting but less in the no prompting posttest, while Randy revised more on the posttest: His number of revisions dropped on the computer sample in the midtest but then raised on the posttest. Janie made more meaningful revisions on the computer; however, Randy made more meaningful revisions in pen, when he had no prompting.

Table 1. Janie and Randy Summary Statistics

Measures	Pretest (No prompts)	Posttest (No prompts)	Midtest	
			(Pen)	(Computer)
Complexity words/unit				
Janie	10.6	10.2	9.5	11.3
Randy	8.5	9.4	11.9	9.9
Revision types				
Janie	17	10	8	11
Randy	16	20	18	7
N of words and punctuation marks in revisions				
Janie	43	15	13	37
Randy	21	157	164	21
% meaningful revisions made				
Janie	13.7	0	25.5	0
Randy	9	40	0	68.5
Errors made				
Janie	9	11	15	8
Randy	8	8	5	7
% errors corrected				
Janie	22	54	60	8
Randy	25	25	100	0
Quality				
Janie	3−/3−	2/1	/3	2/2
Randy	5/5	7/5+	4	2

Janie Computer Draft

Janie opened her mailbox, and she found an airplane ticket to "anywhere in the world". Janie was so exited and ready to pack, but she wonderd were the ticket came from, who pad for it, and all that stuff.

For hours she thought and thougt butshe couldnt think of why someone would send that ticket. Than her mother came home and said anxiously "did the tickets come yet?", with that Janie ran outside, went to the mailbox and found another ticket.

Janie Computer Revision

Janie opened her mailbox, and she found an airplane ticket to "anywhere in the world" Miami, Florida. Janie was exited and dy to pack. But she wonderd were the ticket came from and who paid for it. For hours Janie thought and thought, but she couldnt think of why someone would send the ticket. Than her mother came home and said anxiously "did the tickets come yet?!", with that Janie ran outside, went to the mailbox and found another ticket. From that she knew were the ticktes had come from. Now, without saying anything to her mother she started to pack.

Randy Computer Draft

Randy was walking to his friend's house one sunny day. A man came over to him and handed him 100.00. Randy said "are you sure you didn't just lose this?"
The man responded"no! I've been watching you to see if you're the lucky one to win this 100.00 for doing good deeds. You helped the old lady on Tuesday; you fixed the woman's carborater on Wed-nesday; and you picked he nickle the man had dropped on Tuesday and handded it back to him, and that wrapped the award up for you. I'm proud of you, son!!!!"
"Well thankyou!! I always do those things but I'm glad someonefinally noticed it!"

Randy Computer Revision

Randy was walking to his friend's house one sunny day. A man came over to him and handed him 100.00. Randy said "Are you sure you didn't just lose this?"
The man responded"no! I've been watching you. To see if you're the lucky one to win this 100.00. for doing good deeds. You helped the old lady on Tuesday. You fixed the woman's carborater on Wednesday. And you picked up the nickle and handed it back to the man on Tuesday. That wrapped the award up for you. I'm proud of you, son!!!!" "Well thankyou!! I always do those things. But I'm glad someone finally noticed it!"

Interpretation

There are several possible reasons why overall the subjects' revisions involved fewer words, even though they made more changes in texts when they worked on the computer and when they worked in pen after using the computer for one month. One reason why the children changed fewer words may be that they were not yet comfortable using all the computer commands. When first working with a word processing program, children tend to use the commands that apply to smaller units such as moving the cursor backward and forward character by character rather than by word or sentence. Similarly, even though the program provides commands for erasing sentences, children tend to erase single characters as they move the cursor across the screen. This cautious editing required learning fewer commands. And, moving slowly and locally may help the novice computer user maintain a sense of control over the text. Our editing system works with labeled command keys, so remembering commands should not have been a problem. Similarly, the system prompts and maneuverability are very easy to use and to understand. The program does not require mode switching or multiple keystroke commands. Since most novice adult word-processing writers use the complex commands, such as erasing by words and sentences, children's use of low level commands seems to parallel their general concern for the smaller units of text such as letters and words.

Children were extremely concerned with the text appearance on the screen, so they may have avoided making changes that spanned across lines or screensful of text, because such changes often leave uneven lines of text on the screen. Fixing uneven lines, then, requires reformatting the text. Our program had only rudimentary formatting commands, and although this made the program easy to use, it did not provide sufficient tools for easily manipulating words on the screen. For this reason, our subjects may have avoided making big changes, even though they recognized the need for changes as evidenced in the increased number they made. We also noted that children need several sessions to practice moving sections of text with the word-processing program. This extra practice on "block moves" might have made them more comfortable making changes involving many words. Nevertheless, results from other studies of children's revising (Calkins, 1980) and children's text-editing behavior (Levin et al.) suggest that young children tend to make changes in individual words and phrases rather than in larger textual units involving many words.

Changing fewer words may also have related to the Catch features. Although prompts focus on all levels of discourse, an interview with the subjects and their use patterns suggested that they preferred the Catch features on word, sentence, and punctuation units rather than on paragraphs and text organization. The older the writer, the more he or she finds the higher-level features useful. Young writers' tendency to work on small sections of text does not mean that discussion about organization, writing goals, and strategies for achieving the goals are not useful. But, when left on their own or when encouraged by concrete heuristics, children tend to work with smaller units. The Catch features related to words and sentences were more concrete than the text-level features because individual words and sentences are highlighted on the screen.

In spite of the overall decrease in the number of words involved in revisions in the posttest, most of the children made more revisions that were coded as meaningful rather than superficial. The possible explanation that subjects changed fewer words in the posttest than in the pretest because they became lazy about recopying after discovering the joys of the computer automatic-recopy feature can be refuted by the fact that several subjects changed many more words on the posttest than on the pretest or on the computer.

Our results also suggest that recopying is not an empty task. Calkins's (1980) findings that children edited closely or rewrote texts almost from memory are consistent with our findings that when children had to recopy they changed more words. Analyses of the differences in meaningfulness of the changes and the types of changes suggest that when revising with an instrument that requires recopying, children tend to change the piece mostly by adding and deleting large sections.

Prompting stimulates self-monitoring if it relates to emerging skills. The different patterns illustrated by analyses of Janie's and Randy's texts suggest that there are developmental periods at which children can benefit from a prompting program. Janie was obviously ready to learn more about how to revise. She needed to be shown the self-questioning strategy and the features to look for, but then she became dependent on them, at least for a short time. On the other hand, Randy—a stronger writer—revised more when he used his own strategies, which may have been better or more relevant to each text than those on the computer. Randy learned new strategies from Catch, but then needed to work without his computer guide because something about it limited him. Randy is a more mature writer than Janie, so he learned something from the program but did not need it all the time. As a matter of fact, after responding to prompting, his autonomous self-monitoring surpassed the computer prompting. Like Randy, Janie may have eventually transferred the conferencing strategies suggested by the computer to her spontaneous revising. Randy may have, in turn, become dependent on the programs as guides for a period when he began to make changes of the next level of complexity such as organizational changes. As noted earlier, Randy felt that the "guide words" feature was not helpful. It may be that his next step in writing development would have been to use transitionals consciously to guide his reader through the discourse structure of his text. At that point, he may find the "guide words" feature useful and may even be dependent on it until working on text structure is something he does spontaneously. Older writers like those in the Kiefer and Smith study may use text analyses to learn about writing, but they probably benefit from computer guides more as reading and memory aids as they revise long texts than as developmental aids. For adults, the attention-getting aspects of identifications such as "empty word" features may be helpful to draw the writers' attention to local features. In summary, one's development as a writer, which usually but not always goes along with one's age, determines the usefulness of prompting.

The research on the effects of automatic prompting on young writers supports the studies suggesting that children have transition periods when they are sensitive to prompted self-monitoring. Studies suggesting that there are sensitive periods for transfer of prompting strategies to self-monitoring are consistent with theories that cognitive capacities do not develop in a smooth incremental progression. Rather, sometimes younger subjects seem to do better on certain tasks than do older ones (Bever, 1975; Goldstein, 1965). Such surprising lags in older subjects are presumably due to the development of new cognitive strategies of organizing stimuli in the world (Carey & Diamond, 1977; Langer, 1969). During a transition stage in development, cognitive capacities and strategies are reorganized (Carey et al., 1980; Carey & Diamond, 1977; Carey, Diamond, & Woods, 1980; Langer, 1969). New cognitive structures may develop at certain points in development to help with a transition from relatively immature to more mature cognitive strategies (Bever, 1975; Langer, 1969). Prompting for self-monitoring may help specifically at these transition times when children need a new "pull to cognitive activity" (Kohlberg et al., 1968). Our study on the effects of computer prompting raised the issue that the ability to benefit from analyses and prompts increases with writing ability. We will further explore this question by working with a wider ability range and comparing the subjective and objective effects of Catch according to writing ability.

Although researchers have found that revising activity is related to better writing (Bridwell, 1980; Sommers, 1980), we do not have clear evidence that stimulating students' revising with computer prompts leads to improvements in writing quality ratings. The quality ratings of posttest samples written in pen by 5 of the 8 subjects were better than the pretest samples in pen, but the quality ratings of the midtest samples written on the computer were lower than those of midtest pieces written in pen. Since we did not have a control group, we do not know whether the increase in writing quality was attributable to Catch, the computer, or extensive writing for five weeks during summer vacation. The lower scores on the computer texts in contrast to the mean improvement in writing with pen suggest that as children get used to using a new writing instrument, the quality of their writing may suffer for a time when they use that instrument. Fortunately, however, their writing scores improve when they return to the instrument with which they had most experience even though they did not use that familiar instrument during the experimental period.

Together with the recent work by Woodruff, Bereiter, and Scardamalia (1981), this study shows that the interactive capacities of the computer can be used in studies of self-monitoring. This study suggests that self-monitoring strategies may transfer across writing media when they occur in relation to a specific skill. The changes occurred in pen while the children did 85% of their writing on the computer, and the only guided revising was on the computer. Similarly, the Kiefer and Smith study showed a transfer of specific editing skills when the subjects referred to the computer supports as well as when they did not.

These preliminary studies suggest, however, that some children revise more when the computer talks to them, but others do better on their own. Like Randy, some children learn additional revising strategies from the computer, but they use these best when they talk to themselves.

Researchers and teachers have said that the word processor even without added features like Catch stimulate revising, so we have to compare the writing and revising strategies of children who use the word processor and Catch to those of children who use only the word processor. In Daiute and Kruidenier (1984), results from a large study with control groups will be reported.

Conclusion

The studies described earlier suggest that the computer analyses and prompts affect writers' performance. This inquiry into the role of explicit self-questioning suggests that the development of complex cognitive skills like writing may require a stage of explicit self-monitoring during which writers are able to transfer guided monitoring to autonomous self-monitoring. As Brown (1978) noted, some children develop metacognitive strategies spontaneously, while other children need training in using explicit strategies. Applebee and Langer (1983) have also noted that explicit training on writing strategies may serve as "scaffolding" that is useful during growth stages but can be taken away later because it is no longer needed. The current Daiute study also suggests that self-monitoring is a central factor in writing development.

This chapter has discussed the role of specific self-monitoring in helping children control and organize their thoughts about complex tasks. The study raises questions about what we teach children to do when we teach them to write. Recent writing research has shown that we should guide children through the processes writers use rather than simply focus on the end product. Our research suggests that this process may involve an internal dialogue. Revising has been a useful and revealing measure of inner dialogue in the current study. This inquiry has not yet addressed planning processing in writing when old information combines in new ways to create novel ideas, organizations, or wording. Planning processes are more difficult to observe, so we will guide the study of inner dialogues during planning by results of studies on revision.

After years of focusing on the differences between writing and speaking, the prompting studies encourage researchers to consider the language production activities—talking and writing—as related; this relationship will be clearer, if we know more specifically the ways in which writing draws on conversational supports. The studies comparing writing on the computer and in pen will also give us more information about the effects of the writing instrument, which in a process theory of writing must be considered as one of the participants, especially when the writing instrument talks to the writer as the computer does. Similarly, with the increase in computer text analyses, we should know about the effects of the language the computer uses and the effects of its limited consciousness on the child's emerging consciousness. If the computer talks mostly about word counts, it may draw the children's attention to specific features in the text when they may otherwise just skim over the text, and it frees children to explore the deeper meanings and expression. Or the limited consciousness of the computer interlocutor may draw children to its own low-level concerns. Continued research and listening should tell us more about whether writers talk to themselves.

Appendix A

Sample Revision Analysis

Janie

Draft of Chapter 4

This may sound pretty weird and sad but sometimes I dream that the whole world would blow up. Another person and I would be the only survivors and we together would start the world all over again. The other person and me would rule the world. We would learn all the technology we need to know, how to fly and airplanes, and all that stuff. We would also learn to care for eachother. I think I would rule the world better than the president rules the United States of America. I hate to say it but its what I think.

Revision

[1]This may sound weird/[2]but I dream that the whole world would blow up/[3]Another person and I would be the only survivors/[4]We would start the world over again/[5]We would rule the world together/[6]We would also care for eachother a great deal.

[7]We would learn the technology we need to know, how to fly airplanes, and all that stuff./

[8]I think I would rule the world better than President Regan rules the United States/[9]I hate to say it, but its what I feel.

T-unit	Types of revisions		Units involved
1	22		2
2	12		1
3	04		1
	12		1
5	16	5 →	1
6	14		1
8	11		3
	13	8 →	1
9	13		1

References

Anderson, R. C. (1977). The notion of schemata and the educational enterprise. In R. C. Anderson, R. J. Shapiro, & W. E. Montague (Eds.), *Schooling and the acquisition of knowledge*. Hillsdale, NJ: Lawrence Erlbaum.

Applebee, A. N., & Langer, J. A. (1983). Instructional scaffolding: Reading and writing as natural language activities. *Language Arts, 60*(2), 168–175.

Bereiter, C., & Scardamalia, M. (1982). From conversation to composition: The role of instruction in a developmental process. In R. Glaser (Ed.), *Advances in instructional psychology* (Vol. 2). Hillsdale, NJ: Lawrence Erlbaum.

Bereiter, C. (1980). Development in writing. In L. Gregg & E. Steinberg (Eds.), *Cognitive processes in writing*. Hillsdale, NJ: Erlbaum.

Bever, T. G. (1975). Psychologically real grammar emerges because of its role in language acquisition. In D. P. Dato (Ed.), *Georgetown University roundtable on language and linguistics*. Washington, DC: Georgetown University Press.

Bridwell, L. S. (1980). Revising strategies of twelfth grade students' transactional writing. *Research in the Teaching of English, 14,* 197–222.

Bridwell, L. S., Nancarrow, P. R., & Ross, D. (1984). The writing process and the writing machine: Current research on word processors relevant to the teaching of composition. In R. Beach & L. S. Bridwell (Eds.), *New directions in composing research*. New York: Guilford.

Brown, A. L. (1975). The development of memory: Knowing, knowing about knowing, and knowing how to know. In H. W. Reese (Ed.), *Advances in child development* (Vol. 10). New York: Academic.

Brown, A. L. (1978). Knowing when, where, and how to remember. In R. Glaser (Ed.), *Advances in instructional psychology*. Hillsdale, NJ: Lawrence Erlbaum.

Brown, A. L., Bransford, J. D., Ferrara, R. A., & Campione, J. C. (1983). Learning, remembering, and understanding. In J. H. Flavell & E. M. Markman (Eds.), *Cognitive Development* (vol. 5, 77–150). New York: Wiley.

Brown, A., & Smiley, S. (1977). *The development of strategies for studying prose passages* (Technical Report No. 66). Urbana-Champaign, IL: University of Illinois Center for the Study of Reading.

Bruner, J., & Olson, D. (in press). Symbols and texts as tools of intellect. In G. Steiner (Ed.), *The psychology of the 20th century: Piaget's developmental and cognitive psychology within an extended context* (vol. 7). Zurich: Kindler.

Burns, H., & Culp, G. (1980). Stimulating invention in English composition through computer assisted instruction. *Educational Technology, 20,* 5–10.

Calkins, L. (1980). Children's rewriting strategies. *Research in the Teaching of English, 14,* 331–341.

Calkins, L. (1983). *Lessons from a child on the teaching of writing*. Exeter, NH: Heineman.

Carey, S. (1982). Face, perception—anomalies of development. In S. Straus (Ed.), *U-Shaped behavioral growth*. New York: Academic Press.

Carey, S., & Diamond, R. (1977). From piecemeal to configurational representation of faces. *Science, 195*, 312–314.

Carey, S., Diamond, R., & Woods, B. (1980). Development of face recognition—a maturational component? *Developmental Psychology, 4*(7), 257–269.

Collins, A. (1982). *Teaching reading and writing with personal computers*. For National Institute of Education's Reading Synthesis Project. Unpublished manuscript.

Collins, A., Bruce, B. C., & Rubin, A. (1982). Microcomputer-based writing activities for the upper elementary grades. In *Proceedings of the Fourth International Congress and Exposition of the Society for Applied Learning Technology*, Orlando, FL.

Daiute, C. (1980). *A psycholinguistic study of writing*. Unpublished doctoral dissertation, Columbia University Teachers College.

Daiute, C. (1981). Psycholinguistic foundations of the writing process. *Research in the Teaching of English, 15*(1), 5–22.

Daiute, C. (1981, 1982). *The effects of automatic prompting on young writers*. Interim reports to the Spencer Foundation. Chicago, IL.

Daiute, C. (1983). *The effects of automatic prompting on young writers*. Paper presented at the annual meeting of the American Educational Research Association, Montreal.

Daiute, C. (1985). *Writing and computers*. Reading, MA: Addison Wesley.

Daiute, C., & Kruidenier, J. (in press). *Applied Psycholinguistics*.

Damon, W. (1981). Patterns of change in children's social reasoning: A two-year longitudinal study. *Child Development*.

Elbow, P. (1975). *Writing without teachers*. New York: Oxford University Press.

Faigley, L., & Witte, S. (1980). *Measuring the effect of revision changes on text structure*. Paper presented at the annual meeting of the National Council of Teachers of English, Cincinnati, OH.

Flavell, J. (1979). Metacognition and cognitive monitoring. *American Psychologist, 34*, 906–911.

Flavell, J., Friedrichs, A., & Hoyt, J. (1970). Developmental changes in memorization processes. *Cognitive Psychology, 1*, 324–340.

Flower, L., & Hayes, J. R. (1981). A cognitive process theory of writing. *College Composition and Communication, 32*(4), 365–388.

Freedman, S. (1981). Influences on evaluators of expository essays: Beyond the text. *Research in the Teaching of English, 15*, 245–255.

Gingrich, P. (1982). Writer's workbench: Studies of users. *29th International Technical Communications Conference Proceedings*. Piscataway, NJ: Bell Laboratories.

Goldstein, A. (1965). Learning of inverted and normally oriented faces in children and adults. *Psychonomic Science, 3*, 447.

Graves, D. (1983). *Writing: Teachers and children at work*. Exeter, NH: Heinemann.

Hayes, J., & Flower, L. (1980). Identifying the organization of writing processes. In C. Gregg & E. Steinberg (Eds.), *Cognitive processes in writing*. Hillsdale, NJ: Lawrence Erlbaum.

Heidorn, G. E., Jensen, K., Miller, L. A., Byrd, R., & Chodorow, N. S. (1982). The epistle text-critiquing system. *IBM Systems Journal, 21*(3), 305–326.

Hunt, K. (1965). *Grammatical structures written at three grade levels*. Urbana, IL: National Council of Teachers of English.

Kiefer, K., & Smith, C. (1984). Improving students' revising and editing: The Writer's Workbench System at Colorado State University. In W. Wresch (Ed.), *A writer's tool: The computer in composition instruction* (pp.65–82). Urbana, IL: National Council of Teachers of English.

Kobasigawa, A., & Middleton, D. B. (1972). Free recall of categorized items by children at three grade levels. *Child Development, 43*, 1067–1072.

Kohlberg, L., Yaeger, J., & Hjertholm, E. (1968). Private speech: Four studies and a review of theories. *Child Development, 39*, 691–736.

Kreuitzer, M., Leonard, C., & Flavell, J. (1975). An interview study of children's knowledge about memory. *Monographs of the Society for Research in Child Development, 40*.

Kroll, B. M. (1978). Cognitive egocentrism and the problem of audience awareness in written discourse. *Research in the Teaching of English, 12*(3), 269–281.

Kuhn, D. (1977). Conditional reasoning in children. *Developmental Psychology, 13*, 342–353.

Kuhn, D., & Amsel, E. (1983). *Causal inference in multivariable contexts.* Unpublished manuscript.

Langer, J. (1969). Disequilibrium as a source of development. In P. H. Mussen, J. Langer, & Carrington (Eds.), *Trends and issues in developmental psychology*, New York: Holt.

Lawlor, J. (Ed.) (1982). *Computers in composition instruction.* Los Alamitos, CA: SWRL Educational Research and Development.

Markman, E. M. (1979). Realizing that you don't understand: Elementary school children's awareness of inconsistencies. *Child Development, 50*, 643–655.

Matsuhashi, A. (1980). *What composition teachers can learn from pause research on speech.* Paper presented at the annual meeting of the National Council of Teachers of English, Cincinnati, OH.

Miller, L., Heidorn, G., & Jensen, K. (1981). *Text-critiquing with the EPISTLE system: An author's aid to better syntax.* Paper presented at the National Computer Conference, Chicago, IL.

Papert, S. (1980). *Mindstorms.* New York: Basic Books.

Piaget, J. (1954). *The origins of intelligence in the child* (M. Cook, Trans.). New York: Basic Books.

Rohwer, W., Jr., Raines, J., Eoff, J., & Wagner, M. (1977). The development of elaborative propensity during adolescence. *Journal of Experimental Child Psychology, 23*, 472–492.

Salatas, H., & Flavell, J. (1976). Behavioral and metamnemonic indicators of strategic behaviors under remember instructions in first grade. *Child Development, 47*, 81–89.

Schwartz, H. J. (1982). Monsters and metaphors: Computer applications for humanistic education. *College English, 44*(2), 141–152.

Scribner, S. (1977). Modes of thinking and ways of speaking: Culture and logic reconsidered. In R. O. Freedle (Ed.), *Discourse production and comprehension.* Norwood, NJ: Ablex.

Shaughnessy, M. (1977). *Errors and expectations.* New York: Oxford University Press.

Siegler, R. S. (1976). Three aspects of cognitive development. *Cognitive Psychology, 8*, 481–520.

Sommers, N. (1980). Revision strategies of student writers and experienced writers. *College Composition and Communication, 31*, 378–388.

Taylor, R. P. (1980). *The computer in the school: Tutor, tool, tutee.* New York: Teachers College Press.

Vygotsky, L. (1965). *Thought and language.* Cambridge, MA: MIT Press.

Waters, H. S. (1982). Memory development in adolescence: Relationships between metamemory, strategy use, and performance. *Journal of Experimental Child Psychology, 33*, 183–195.

Weizenbaum, J. (1976). *Computer power and human reason: From judgment to calculation.* San Francisco: Freeman.

Woodruff, E., Bereiter, C., & Scardamalia, M. (1981–1982). On the road to computer-assisted compositions. *Journal of Educational Technology Systems, 10*(2), 133–148.

8

Muktuk Meets Jacuzzi: Computer Networks and Elementary School Writers

James A. Levin
Margaret M. Riel
Robert D. Rowe
Marcia J. Boruta
University of California, San Diego

Introduction

Computer word processing systems are now coming into widespread use by adults. For the past several years, we have been conducting research on how such systems can be used to help elementary school students write and learn to write.

Many people who use word processing systems view them as just a better tool for accomplishing the same old tasks. We started with a similar viewpoint: Initially we viewed a computer word processing system as just a better tool for collecting data on the processes of writing. However, it soon became apparent that the use of word processing in conjunction with electronic message systems forms a new communication medium with distinct properties from the conventional medium of paper-and-pencil and with important implications for the ways children can learn to write. With this in mind, we framed our research with a number of basic questions:

- Can young children learn to use computer word processing systems for writing?
- Will students *want* to use a word processing system instead of paper and pencils?
- How will the use of word processing systems affect student writing?
- In what instructional settings can word processing systems be effectively used?

To answer the first two questions, we developed a word processing system called The Writer's Assistant for use by school children. Children from a variety of different settings have demonstrated that such a system can be used with positive results. We have observed students varying in age from 4 to 14 effectively using this word processor in regular classrooms (Levin, Boruta, & Vasconcellos, 1983; Miller-Souviney, 1984; Rowe, 1983), in resource room settings (Riel, 1985), in after-school clubs (Laboratory of Comparative Human Cognition, 1982; Levin & Kareev, 1980), and in homes (Levin & Kareev, 1980).

In this study, students in two classes used The Writer's Assistant for a full school year and were interviewed at the end of the year. One of the questions was "Which do you like better: writing with the computer or writing by hand with pencil and paper?'' Of 30 students interviewed, 26 preferred the computer, 2 preferred writing by hand, and 2 were uncertain.

The students were then asked why they preferred one medium over the other. The answers given by the students were fairly insightful and somewhat surprising. Although we had gone to considerable effort to provide them with tools for high-level planning and revision of their writing, the students' answers almost entirely focused at a much lower level. The most common reason given for preferring to use the computer was some variant of ''It doesn't hurt your hand.'' While ''writer's cramp'' is not likely to be a major problem for elementary school students, the problem of fine motor control for many students *is* significant.

Reading and writing are complementary skills, yet children usually develop the eye coordination necessary for reading prior to the development of fine motor skills necessary for printing or cursive writing. Improvements in writing technologies in the past such as typewriters did not change this asymmetry. The keys of typewriters jam under the fingers of very young children. The computer keyboard, however, is easy for small hands to use, and the text is displayed as well-formed text on a display screen, which makes monitoring what is being written easier. We have observed young children in a kindergarten–first-grade classroom work productively with computer keyboards (Black, 1983). These differences in the medium of writing may allow students to begin writing at the same time they begin reading.

The next most common reason for preferring to use a word processor was some variant of ''When you erase, you don't rip your paper.'' Students valued the ability to revise more easily and to produce neat, professional-looking text. The Writer's Assistant, like most current word processors, is a ''screen editor'' so that when you erase text, it disappears from the screen.

A sixth-grade teacher (Rowe) observed that his students were correcting their text with the computer with greater enthusiasm than he had seen in their previous paper-and-pencil editing. To further explore this phenomenon, he conducted a small experiment on editing in the two different writing media.

A Cross-Media Experiment on Editing

In a class of 29 sixth-grade students at an elementary school in San Diego County, a writing assignment was given, based on a story about the way in which glass is made. The students were given this story starter: ''Think about what it would be like to be a grain of sand. Write a story about you being a grain of sand and going through the process of becoming a piece of glass. Start it like this: One day I was sitting on the beach, minding my own business when suddenly. . . .''

A few weeks later, the teacher passed the stories back to the class with no marks or comments on them. The teacher announced that he read the stories and felt that they were very good. He went on to explain that he wanted them to edit their own papers and rewrite them in their best handwriting. Almost all the students had done editing before and knew what to do without any further instructions.

Later, a similar assignment was arranged, but with the use of an Apple computer and the Writer's Assistant word processing system. The students used a computer-based story starter for newspaper articles to generate a story. Then the students were shown how to use the editing capabilities of the word processing system. When they finished writing their original drafts on a computer printout, they were asked to use the system to edit their stories so we could send them off to other classes.

The data from the 10 students who completed all four writing tasks were selected by the teacher for analysis. The paper-and-pencil drafts were longer (average length of 101.9 words) than the computer texts (58.8 words), so we will report both average numbers of errors and average error rates. Errors are defined here as only incorrect spelling of words, incorrect capitalization or punctuation, and incorrect syntactic structures.

In the paper-and-pencil first drafts, there were 14.2 errors or 0.14 errors/word; in the computer first drafts there were 7.3 errors or 0.12 errors/word. In their rewritten versions, the students corrected 43.7% (6.2) of the paper-draft errors and they corrected 78% (5.7) of the computer-draft errors.

More importantly, the students made 5.5 *new* errors when recopying on paper with pencils. Nine of the 10 rewritten copies contained one or more new errors. Using the computer, students introduced only 0.4 new errors (more than a factor of ten less). Only 3 of the 10 computer-revised papers contained new errors.

The final drafts recopied on paper still contained a large number of errors (10.6 or 0.10 errors/word), since corrected errors were balanced out by new errors. The final drafts edited on the computer contained a much smaller number (2.0 or 0.03 errors/word).

To verify that this finding was not related to the difference of topic, the teacher analyzed a second paper-and-pencil writing exercise in which the students were prompted to write on the same topic as the previously described computer writing exercise, a newspaper article. Ten of these compositions were selected at random. The first drafts averaged 86.1 words; the "corrected" versions were about the same (79.2). The students made 8.5 errors (0.10 errors/word) on the first drafts; on the corrected versions they made *more* errors (9.2 errors; 0.12 errors/word)! While they fixed an average of 3.3 of the errors that they made in the first draft, they introduced 4.0 new errors in rewriting their compositions. Nine of the 10 students introduced new errors.

When the class was told about these results they responded by saying that it made sense, because when they edited on the computer all they had to deal with was the mistakes and the computer would print out what was already correct. In contrast, when they had to edit and write their stories over with paper and pencil they not only had to correct their errors, but also had to redo everything that was originally correct. They went on to say that with paper and pencil they had to think not only about what was wrong, but also about what was right and redo it. With the computer, they could concentrate solely on the problems and the computer would take care of the part that did not need corrections.

The conclusion suggested by this experiment is that editing with paper and pencil is difficult for elementary school students to adopt as a working strategy because it has a small (in some cases *negative*) value for improving a piece of text, since new errors are introduced in the new version at about the same rate as old errors are corrected. On the other hand, editing with the computer has a much more positive value, since inadvertent new errors are introduced at a much lower rate.

The Blank Screen Problem: Writer's Block and Dynamic Support

Even though computers make editing easier, their use does not guarantee that interesting writing and revision will occur. The use of computers alone does not solve the problem of teaching students how to write. The blank screen is just as intimidating as the blank page. In fact, some people find a blinking cursor more intimidating than a newly sharpened pencil and yellow pad.

However, the computer can provide for three types of interactions that can be important support for the novice writer. First, computers enable collaborative writing among pairs of children that is difficult to create in the pencil-and-paper medium. The presence of another peer writer during the writing process provides for problem-solving help in idea generation and immediate response to the written text. Second, computers are interactive media. This means that they can be used to provide the student with a great deal of prewriting or idea formation help (Collins, Bruce, & Rubin, 1982; Daiute, this volume; Levin, 1982). Finally, computers can be used to create "functional" writing environments which provide students with an audience for their work. When students realize that people will be reading their work not merely to evaluate it but for real communicative purposes, they take a very different approach to writing and actively engage in the revision and editing of their own writing and the writing of their peers (Collins, 1982; Levin et al., 1983; Riel, 1985).

Cooperative Peer Writing and Revision

Most approaches to computer use and writing presume a lone individual, working in at least temporary isolation. We have uncovered many reasons for challenging this presumption. Many people have suggested the value of collaborative writing, but it is difficult to share a pencil or to write a text collaboratively on a piece of paper. It is much easier to divide up the work of writing on a word processing system. The display is more public and legible, the keyboard extends in space more than a pencil, and in fact some writing actions require simultaneous multiple keypresses (capitalized letters, special punctuation marks). Elementary school students spontaneously come up with many different ways of dividing up the work of writing collaboratively (Levin & Boruta, 1983).

One of the values of cooperative peer writing is that it provides social resources to confront the blank screen. Even when neither student begins with an idea of what to write, the discussion of the problem often presents solutions. In the process of entering the text, one partner often takes prime responsibility for typing, and the other takes more of a monitoring role, pointing out local typing errors but also maintaining the global context for newly inserted text. Thus, when the new text piece is entered, the pair can continue on, while an individual novice writer could have lost the global view and become blocked at that point. In this social system the task of writing can be distributed across the cooperative peers.

An equally important function of cooperative peer writing is the immediate audience (the partner) who can respond to the text as it is being written. A partner's response of "That doesn't make sense!" can be far more effective for encouraging revision than red marks on a paper a week later.

Interactive Text Prompters

Another approach we have developed to the "blank screen" problem is based on "interactive text," text which explicitly shares the initiative for interaction between the original writer of the text and the "readers" (Levin, 1982). Using a system which we have called the Interactive Text Interpreter (ITI), we have provided students with a dynamic range of support for writing. For example, we have used a newspaper prompter which helps students write different kinds of newspaper articles. The prompter starts by asking the "reader" (the student writer) what kind of article is to be written, presenting a list of possibilities: news, sports, weather, fun, life, sharing, or something else. Once the writer chooses a topic area, for example, news, the prompter then asks whether the writer knows how to write a headline. If the student says "no," advice is given. Then the prompter accepts any headline the writer types in, saving it with the accumulated article. This process of offering help, prompting for sequencing, providing alternatives, and uncritically accepting and saving input continues, until the writer specifies that the article is finished.

This kind of prompting is useful for overcoming the initial blank screen, but does not produce finished text. The responses to prompts and suggestions that a writer types in have the quality of rough notes. So at the end of this "prewriting" process, the writer can take the saved text and revise it, using the Writer's Assistant word processing system.

We have developed prompted writing activities in the domains of descriptive, narrative, and expository writing as well as poetry, letter writing, and story writing. The ITI system is simple enough to use that people with no programming experience (but with expertise in writing instruction) can produce sophisticated branching prompter texts in a short time (Levin, 1982).

Functional Writing Environments

Functional writing environments are those in which one is writing for real communicative purposes rather than just as an exercise (Heath & Branscombe, this volume). Most school writing is performed as an exercise, with the teacher as the sole audience. With the aid of word processing systems, it is possible to create "functional" writing environments in classrooms in which the writer is focusing on communicating with someone else. In these environments, concern with the mechanics of writing is secondary to, but instrumental for, communicating clearly. The most interesting writing we have seen in our research has occurred when, working closely with teachers, we have been able to jointly construct such functional writing settings.

For example, one successful functional writing environment has been a classroom newspaper. Students in several classrooms we have worked with have used the prompting and editing systems described earlier to create and revise articles that are put together and printed out as a class newspaper. Although the notion of a class newspaper is not new, computer word processing systems make it plausible for elementary school students to revise text and the newspaper setting makes revision a sensible and desirable activity.

Computer Networks and Extended Audiences

As an extension of the functional writing environment of a class newspaper, we have been exploring the ways that computer text-message networks can be used to help children learn to write. In the fall of 1982, we interconnected two classrooms in San Diego County with four classrooms in Alaska, including two rural Eskimo villages.

Our first guess on how to organize this network was to model it on pen-pal letters. So we set up a "computer pals" network. This communication network provided the kind of audience we were looking for. Children found themselves writing to other children from quite diverse backgrounds. For example, here is one electronic message from a child in one of the Eskimo villages to a child in San Diego.

DEAR COMPUTER PAL:

I AM IN MR. VANCIL'S 5TH GRADE CLASS HERE IN WAINWRIGHT. IT IS VERY COLD OUTSIDE TODAY. OUR TEMPERATURE IS 14 DEGREES BELOW ZERO. WHAT IS IT LIKE IN YOUR TOWN ? THE SUN WENT DOWN ON NOVEMBER 18 AND WILL NOT BE BACK UNTIL JANUARY 24. IT IS LIKE NIGHT ALL DAY LONG. TO DAY OUR JANITOR SHOT A RABID WHITE FOX ON OUR BACK STEPS. I'M GLAD WE WERE NOT OUT AT RECESS.

WE LIKE TO EAT MUKTUK AND FROZEN FISH. WE ALSO LIKE WARMED CARIBOU BLOOD TO DRINK. MUKTUK IS WHALE SKIN . TO US IT TASTES GOOD. WE HAD A FEAST AT THE HIGH SCHOOL ON THANKSGIVING. WE HAD DUCK SOUP, CARIBOU SOUP, FROZEN FISH AND MUKTUK. WHAT DID YOU EAT?

WELL I DON'T HAVE ANYTHING ELSE TO SAY. WRITE TO ME ON THIS COMPUTER. MR. VANCIL SAYS HE WILL HELP ME READ YOUR LETTER.

GOODBYE
FRITZ

In contrast, here is a computer pal message from one of the San Diego students to an Alaskan student:

MY NAME IS MICAH.I LIKE TO PLAY FOOTBALL. I PLAY OFFENSIVE TACKLE AND DEFENSIVE END. WHATS YOUR SPORT? MY HOUSE ADDRESS IS ⟨his home address⟩. I DO NOT LIVE IN A TWO-STORY HOUSE. I HAVE A JACUZZI BUT NOT A POOL.DO YOU LIVE IN A TWO-STORY HOUSE?DO YOU HAVE A JACUZZI OR A POOL? WE HAVE SIX PEOPLE IN MY FAMILY. HOW MANY PEOPLE DO YOU HAVE?WELL I HAVE TO GO NOW BY. YOUR FRIEND MICAH

While there are many benefits from this form of communication, it lacked some crucial features of the social writing environment that we sought to create. The computer pal network depended on a one-to-one matching of students. When students were matched, responses to letters needed to appear regularly enough so that students did not lose interest, something difficult to ensure for all students. The writing of personal letters was only one of many forms of writing in which we wanted the students to gain expertise. Finally, and most importantly, letter writing did little to encourage students to revise and edit their own work. Since revision was an important goal of ours, we continued to search for a different form of a computer network.

The computer pal network was transformed in January of 1983 into a student "news-wire" service known as The Computer Chronicles. Within this framework we were able to explore more fully the influence of "audience" on students' writing and revision.

The Computer Chronicles Newswire

The Computer Chronicles Newswire is a computer supported functional writing system, which encourages children to work together on a school newspaper project. It is a larger network of communication between children who know little about each other personally, but who are sharing conceptions of their life styles and worlds. This news network is explicitly modeled on the international news wire services that are important to adults. Whenever possible, we help students see the parallels between their work and the work of newspaper reporters and editors.

The Computer Chronicles News Wire began with students from two San Diego schools and from two Alaskan schools exchanging news articles. Each classroom generated and edited articles on their own computers, which were sent to all the other classrooms. Then each classroom chose the articles they wanted for their own local version of the Computer Chronicles Newspaper, which they assembled and edited on their class computer.

The students from one of the schools in San Diego were participating in one of our research projects called the Mental Gym (Riel, 1985). In this project we have been investigating the effectiveness of computer-supported social environments for helping students who trail behind grade level in their academic studies. The children who came to the Mental Gym to work on reading and writing difficulties were made reporters and editors responsible for the production of the Mental-Gym version of the Computer Chronicles. These children began working on the computer with some vague notions of a newspaper and of sending stories to kids in Alaska, New York, and other places. Their understanding and interest grew as they became more aware of what it meant to participate in such a network. To describe how this social support system for writing operated, we will begin with the computer and then widen the frame of reference.

Computer Chronicles Prompter. We have already briefly described the development of the Interactive Text Interpreter system and its use in the writing process. The Computer Chronicles Prompter (CCP) is an Interactive text designed to help students write newspaper articles. Students select a section of the newspaper and are given guidelines and suggestions for the type of writing they have selected. The power of interactive texts is that they can be easily modified. The different sections of the CCP differ in terms of how much support is provided in the writing activity. For example, in the beginning, students coming to the Mental Gym did not know how to respond to a prompt calling for a description. It was easy to modify the file so that students could, at this junction, indicate that they needed more help. A series of questions then suggested some of the relevant dimensions of a description of the topic they were working with. As the students became more skilled, they relied less on these prompts for organizing their ideas. The teacher's ability to tailor the prompter to meet the specific needs of the students is what makes it such a valuable aid in the writing process (Riel, Levin, & Miller-Souviney, 1984).

Team Work on Computer Chronicles. Students in the Mental Gym always work on the computer in pairs. As already mentioned, we feel that this teamwork is helpful in the writing process. Students' discussions of the computer prompts help to organize their thoughts to begin the writing process. Their immediate reaction to the prose of their partner can have an immediate impact on the quality of their writing. Often, incomplete idea fragments produced by one student were completed by the student's partner.

Students themselves are aware of the influence of cooperative work on their writing. In a posttest interview, Daemon, one of the students working at the writing center at the Mental gym, said that what he liked least about school was language and writing. Later, when asked which activities he liked most in the Mental Gym, he said writing and editing stories for the Computer Chronicles. When the contradiction in these statements was pointed out, his response was to give a good description of the social dimensions of learning: "Me and Juan are a team, we get to do it together. In the class we don't get to discuss anything. Juan gives me ideas."

In a later interview, Daemon was able to identify skills that his partner had learned from him. For example, when asked what Juan had learned from him, he said, "How to spell words, because when he came to the Mental Gym he had trouble spelling. I just helped him and now he is a good speller." The pretests on these students indicated that Juan and Daemon began with different strengths and weaknesses. The posttests suggest that these students were able to improve their writing skills by learning from one another. We are currently doing a detailed analysis of the process of these changes in writing and editing done by these pairs of students over the 12-week period.

Computer Coaches. In addition to computer and peer support in the Mental Gym, the students had the help of "computer coaches." The coaches at the gym were university undergraduates who knew little about computers but who could provide encouragement and serve as "adaptive experts" when problems arose. As the students in the Mental Gym became more skilled, they became less dependent on help from coaches. We are currently analyzing the form and frequency of the help provided by the computer coaches.

Sending and Receiving Articles. Students used the Computer Chronicles Prompter to generate the articles, then would immediately edit their text with the Writer's Assistant. Their editing at this point mainly consisted of making sure there were complete sentences and correct punctuation. In general, there was not much content revision at this point. These articles were then sent out on the Newswire. At the same time, the students received stories written at each of the other locations participating in the network. Students who came to the Mental Gym to work on reading would read and edit some of the incoming stories. They were eager to read the stories that were received, taking copies home to review and evaluate these potential newspaper articles. Since they frequently disagreed, a vital component was added to the writing system: editorial board meetings.

Editorial Board Meetings. Students were invited to come to the Mental Gym as soon after lunch as they wished to take part in these meetings. All the students *willingly* gave up part of their recess to participate in editorial board meetings to read and evaluate stories. Each story from the news service, including their own, was read by one of the students. Then the group made a decision either to reject the article or to accept it with or without revisions. A decision was based on a majority vote and the formulation of a "good" reason for its acceptance or rejection. The role of the adult participant was only to record the results and to judge whether or not the given reason was acceptable.

The students began with simple reasons such as "too short" but soon found a short article that was acceptable because it had "good details." The students quickly determined whether they liked or disliked a story, but they were less aware of why they made these evaluations. Having to find a reason helped them understand their evaluations. When one of the articles that was written by a pair from the Mental Gym was about to be read, the authors withdrew the article and said that they would fix it. They saw their own writing in the context of the evaluative framework that they had helped create. It was not acceptable and they knew it. But more importantly, they knew how to fix it. It needed more details. They took the typed copy of the story and used the Writer's Assistant to write a new version of the story. When the story was finished it was much improved, but contained one unclear sentence. When this problem was identified in a subsequent board meeting, they went back to the Writer's Assistant and dropped the unclear sentence. They were pleased when the story was accepted.

The students were also proud of their ability to locate errors and fix problems in the articles written by other students. When a story was found to need editing, all the students wanted to be the ones to edit it. Contributions of stories written by children in Alaska (for whom English was a second language) gave the students practice in correcting a variety of grammar errors. Students felt a real sense of accomplishment when they could improve on articles written by other students. While they were well aware that their own writing skills needed improvement, editing of these articles helped them see that they had skills that other children found difficult.

The editing and revision done at this stage was more likely to deal with larger units of text. For example, a sentence at the end of a story was deleted because it duplicated a sentence in the middle of the text. The major concern of the editorial board was that an article "make sense" as well as be well written. When students were satisfied with an article, it was accepted. Since students saw this as *their* newspaper, they accepted the responsibility for locating errors and collectively worked to improve the articles.

While evaluation and editing were an important outcome of the editorial board, there was another important kind of learning taking place. Students were learning about life styles and customs that were different from their own. They were beginning to understand the role that newspapers play in a society and how such communication networks function. Students were forming their ideas about what makes a story "newsworthy," they were dealing with issues of what is appropriate and inappropriate for this medium, and they were beginning to understand what things about their own environment were special or different.

The editorial board meetings then served a number of important functions. They set new standards for stories that students would write in the future as well as guides for how old stories might be rewritten. They provided motivation and suggestions for the editing of stories. And they provided a learning environment in which students learned about themselves, others, and communication.

The writing that takes place in the Computer Chronicles Newswire activity can be summarized in Table 1. Each level is important, but the total system provides an exceptionally rich learning environment for literacy skills.

Summary

Writing with microcomputers and in message networks is definitely different from writing with pencil and paper for a teacher in a classroom. One important way in which writing with a word processor is different from writing with pencil and paper is that revision is much more productive with a word processor. The vast majority of the elementary school students we worked with preferred using a word processor, and their most common reasons were the ease of text input and editing. The power of a text editor is that it makes revision a real option for beginning writers.

Even with a powerful word processing system, novice writers still face the blank-screen problem. We have examined two approaches to helping writers deal with this problem. In the first approach, we have designed and studied the use of "dynamic support" systems of writing prompters. In these systems, the dynamic properties of the new computer media are used to supply a range of reading/writing experience, spanning the gap to help a novice writer become an expert.

In a second approach, we have created "functional" environments for writing, those in which the main goal of the writing process is to communicate with some other rather than to accomplish some classroom exercise. We have used computer networks to allow students in different schools to communicate with each other, organized as a news network. Students in each school composed and edited newspaper articles which were sent over the Computer Chronicles Network to other schools. Each classroom then organized an editorial process by which some of the articles coming in from the Network were selected and edited for their own newspaper.

There are ways in which this new communication medium offers unique, new opportunities for writing instruction and for writing research. However, to take advantage of the medium, we have to examine carefully not just the properties of the software and hardware but also the social and instructional contexts for learning.

Table 1. The Computer Chronicle Newswire

Activity	Purpose
Cooperative use of the Computer Chronicles Prompter (CCP)	Prewriting ideas, writing the articles with immediate response
Cooperative use of the Writer's Assistant following CCP	Revision and editing of articles
Completed articles are sent out and received on the CC newswire	Postwriting
Editorial board meetings	Evaluation of articles
Cooperative use of the Writer's Assistant on accepted articles	Revision and editing of selected articles
Editorial board meetings	Reevaluation
Local editions of the Computer Chronicles are produced and exchanged with other schools using the CC newswire	Postwriting
Whole class	Evaluation of newspapers of other schools

References

Black, S. (1983). *Computers in the classroom: The development of computer use.* La Jolla, CA: The Interactive Technology Laboratory.

Collins, A. (1982). *Teaching reading and writing with personal computers.* For National Institute of Education's Reading Synthesis Project. Unpublished manuscript.

Collins, A., Bruce, B. C., & Rubin, A. (1982). Microcomputer-based writing activities for the upper elementary grades. In *Proceedings of the Fourth International Congress and Exposition of the Society for Applied Learning Technology,* Orlando, FL.

Laboratory of Comparative Human Cognition. (1982). A model system for the study of learning difficulties. *The Quarterly Newsletter of the Laboratory of Comparative Human Cognition, 4,* 39–66.

Levin, J. A. (1982). Microcomputers as interactive communication media: An interactive text interpreter. *The Quarterly Newsletter of the Laboratory of Comparative Human Cognition, 4,* 34–36.

Levin, J. A., Boruta, M. J., & Vasconcellos, M. T. (1983). Microcomputer-based environments for writing: A Writer's Assistant. In A. C. Wilkinson (Ed.), *Classroom computers and cognitive science.* New York: Academic Press.

Levin, J. A., & Boruta, M. J. (1983). Writing with computers in classrooms: "You get EXACTLY the right amount of space!" *Theory into Practice, 22,* 291–295.

Levin, J. A., & Kareev, Y. (1980). *Personal computers and education: The challenge to schools.* La Jolla, CA: Center for Human Information Processing.

Miller-Souviney, B. (1984). *Computer-supported tools for expository writing: A study of classroom practices.* Unpublished master's thesis, University of California, San Diego.

Riel, M. M. (1985). The Computer Chronicles Newswire: A functional learning environment for acquiring literacy skills. *Journal of Educational Computing Research, 1* (3), 1985.

Riel, M. M., Levin, J. A., & Miller-Souviney, B. (1984). Dynamic support and educational software development. (Report # 4). La Jolla, CA: Interactive Technology Laboratory.

Rowe, R. D. (1983). *A computer in the classroom: The education of a teacher.* La Jolla, CA: Laboratory of Comparative Human Cognition.

9

Revising and Computing: Case Studies of Student Writers*

Lillian Bridwell
Geoffrey Sirc
Robert Brooke

University of Minnesota

In July 1982, when James Fallows wrote in the *Atlantic* that working with a word processor is "satisfying to the soul," we and our colleagues had just launched a major project to determine how computers could be used in a writing program. He explained that he liked writing with a computer because "each maimed and misconceived passage can be made to vanish instantly, by the word or by the paragraph, leaving a pristine green field on which to make the next attempt" (p. 84). We thought then what we think now: Making revision easier for our students might be a major contribution to their progress as writers. In an update (March 1983), he wrote, "My liaison with the computer has moved into comfortable middle age. I am looking for a warm meal on the table, for a dependable friend" (p. 107). We, too, have overcome our initial zeal enough to take a critical look at what the computer has done for our students. We want to keep our perspective about what it can do and what it can't do, what we should buy, and what we should build to help them learn to write well.

When we tried to learn from others, we discovered that no one else had studied the effects of using word processors on writing (see Bridwell, Nancarrow, & Ross, 1984; Bridwell & Ross, 1984; and Nancarrow, Ross, & Bridwell, 1984, for the results of our search) and that few studies of computer-assisted instruction in writing were relevant to our students' needs. Since then, there have been a few studies of writing on computers (e.g., Collier, 1983; Daiute, 1983), but the work to understand how this new writing tool will affect both developing and experienced writers has just begun.

This study represents our second in a series of projects that should begin to answer some of our questions. In the first study (Bridwell, Johnson, & Brehe, in

* This work was sponsored in part by a grant from the Fund for the Improvement of Postsecondary Education, "Integrating Computer Technology to Serve the Needs of Students and Teachers in Writing Courses," Lillian Bridwell and Donald Ross, coprincipal investigators. The information and interpretations in this report are those of the authors and do not necessarily represent those of the funding agency. The authors also wish to thank the Microcomputer Group at the University of Minnesota's Computer Center for their support.

press), we wanted to know whether learning to compose with a word processing system would affect either the products or the processes of experienced writers. We found that their own styles of composing—the successful rituals they had evolved over their careers as writers—were more significant predictors of how they accommodated to the computer (or forced the computer to adjust to them!) than any influence of the computer itself.

In this study, we direct our attention to revision but ask more general questions as well. Do students, who may not have a long history of successful rituals, do things differently as they write with a computer? Does the computer change the kinds of texts they produce? How useful is the computer to them as a revising tool? Does the computer do any harm? What do we need to provide in a "computer-composing" environment to teach writing? As we designed our project, we benefited from earlier surveys of our students, reported in the next section, but we continue to seek a better synthesis of techniques for teaching writing with the technology available for writing.

Surveys of Students in Word-Processor Sections

Having studied students in 3 to 4 word-processor sections per quarter for two years, we knew that some students have a tendency to balk when they feel they are being forced to learn about the computer. Far more often than we wanted, we received evidence of a bitter introduction to the new writing technology: "I like the word processor, but as a student with a job and other classes and the rest, it's too much to ask to *have* to learn it. It should be optional." An unfortunate reality, which might have prompted such frustration, was that our lab at that time was limited to only four terminals and one printer; hence, we could only guarantee limited time on the terminals in our lab. Even when a few classes were allowed access to the lab, students found it difficult to share four machines. When students are allowed to determine how they will use computers, it is not unusual for them to do more and more of their composing on-screen for their writing classes as well as more and more of their written work for other courses. Our end-of-quarter surveys were filled with cries for a lab with more hardware open 24 hours, demands we have begun to meet.

As one part of the current study, we again surveyed our students to see if we had solved any of these problems and if they were successfully taking advantage of the word processing software for revision. Seventy-five percent of the students described in the 3 classes responded to our questions, and we report these findings. The surveys help to describe the environment within which our student writers worked. We then turn to case studies of 5 students who wrote in this environment.

Students in 3 upper-level writing courses which are discipline-specific participated in the survey we report here. The 3 courses were "Writing About Engineering, "Writing About Science," and "Preprofessional Writing for the Business Major." These sections had been earmarked as "word processor sections," which means that an instructor familiar with computers and word processing teaches the course, and the students participate in a two-week introduction to the word processor. In this introduction, an experienced staff member showed them how to use basic commands (adding, deleting, and rearranging text; cursor movement, and scrolling) and gave them a step-by-step handout explaining the machine's operations and capabilities. The students then did exercises designed to familiarize them with the basic commands, and were free to use the machines as often as they could reserve time (generally a minimum of 2 hours per week). They completed assignments designated by the instructor to be done either totally or in part with the computers; in this study, the writers used microcomputers and MicroPro International Corporation's "WordStar," a widely used word-processing package.

The 48 surveys completed by students in 3 sections of upper-division writing left no doubt that the students saw the value of the computer as a writing, revising, and editing tool. Table 1, which contains both the text of the survey and the findings, shows that despite severe time constraints, 83% of the students found a way to use the computers "regularly for more than one" of their assignments. Furthermore, when we asked them if they thought using word processing improved their writing, nearly one fourth of them thought the quality of their writing was "significantly better" because of the computer, and over half gave it credit for making their writing "somewhat better." None thought it did any damage. When asked specifically whether it interfered with their composing processes, most thought that it did not, but those who thought it did had problems we could address and solve in our new lab: poor typing ability for one student (although most "hunt and peck" typists reported that they saved time and that the computer was helpful), access time for four students, learning the computer keyboard initially, automatic footnote numbering, moving columns, noise in the room, etc.

Only one student thought the computer substantially interfered with his or her composing: "It interfered with my creative processes because of the quickness of editing, etc. It didn't allow enough time to 'mull' things over." We suspect, however, that even more students were lured to produce polished texts too quickly, a criticism we had heard from experienced writers in an earlier study (Bridwell, Johnson, & Brehe, in press).

The ability to edit quickly and easily may be a mixed blessing, but it is one that does not escape most new computer users. One of the experienced writers in the earlier study said that while he was "tinkering" with the text he could think about more substantive textual and rhetorical problems. We read this kind of comment in many student surveys. Even if they did not claim to concentrate on larger problems *while* they were editing, they were almost all aware of the time savings: "I could use the time I saved [by] using the word processor to improve my compositions even more."

For some students, the polished look of their texts, even in early stages, may provide a kind of positive reinforcement and evoke the desire to continue to revise their papers. One student wrote, "[I could] see the results of my writing quickly so that corrections could be made; also the spelling/style checker made for easy correc-

Table 1. Student Responses to Using Computers in Writing Courses, Expressed as Percentages to Each Item ($N = 48$)

Item: How often did you use the word processors?

Never	2.1
Exercises only	2.1
Some for one writing assignment	2.1
Regularly for one	8.3
Some for more than one	2.1
Regularly for more than one	83.3

Item: What did you use the computer for?

Preparing final manuscript only	8.3
Editing final manuscript	14.6
Editing and revising drafts	29.2
Composing from start to finish	47.9

Item: Did the computer interfere with what you were doing?

Yes	31.3
No	43.7
No response	25.0

Item: What value do you place upon word processing?

A great advantage	62.5
A useful tool	35.4
Just a fancy typewriter	2.0
A disadvantage	0

Item: Do you think the word processors made a difference in the quality of your writing?

Significantly better	22.9
Somewhat better	56.3
About the same	20.8
A little worse	0
Much worse	0

Item: How helpful to you was using a computer for your writing in this course?

Very	64.6
Somewhat	33.3
Not very	2.0

Item: How helpful to you will using a computer for your writing be in your career?

Very	60.4
Somewhat	37.5
Not very	2.0

Item: Did you use any other tools?

Spelling checker	43.8
Style checker	20.8

tions. . . . I didn't feel the pressure of having to fight with a typewriter [over whether to revise]." A similar advantage is echoed in another comment: "Once I got used to the machine, I could concentrate on style and content without worrying about the time [it would take] to rewrite papers."

Another student used a verb too rare in student evaluations of writing tasks: "I *enjoyed* them because I could get the typing done, error-free in one sitting." Repeatedly in the surveys, we found words like, "fun," "made editing a game," "easier"—and even "I loved the machines." Another pattern in the language students used to describe revising and editing picks up video-game jargon. We heard about "zapping hunks of writing," for example.

One surprise, given the number of students who reported access difficulties, was the percentage of students who claimed to compose everything, from start to finish, on the computer screen. Nearly half claimed to do this for at least one assignment, and one of the primary reasons given was the freedom they felt to write down their ideas, knowing that if they could salvage anything from their early attempts, they would not have to retype it. This freedom, we believe, contributed to their sense that their writing was better. Students often thought they used their time for things more important than preparing manuscripts. One student who composed early drafts on paper described his composing process this way: "[I] typed in rough drafts and modified them until [the] final [was] found." This notion of writing to discover what one has to say has been standard fare in our writing program, but often with the computer we see evidence that revision really means "reseeing" and discovering. Perhaps most importantly, however, much of this revising is self-initiated to improve a draft before anyone else ever responds to it. But, as we shall demonstrate in the case studies, there are some prices to pay.

Case Studies of Five Students

Beyond surveying all students in the three classes, we studied 5 students, examining their composing processes in detail to see what happened to their revision strategies when they moved to the computer for their writing.

We chose the business writing section for the case studies because the instructor had decided that he would require all, except the first, of his eight weekly assignments to be handed in in the form of word-processed printouts. He believed that his students could learn enough in their two-week training session to allow them to open a file and transcribe a written draft on the computer. This would, he hoped, defuse any anxiety that might be induced if students thought they had to learn the machine well enough to transfer their entire composing process to the screen. In addition, the assignments in the course were typically short—business letters, memos, etc.—so writing with a computer for the first time involved a smaller risk for the students. Rather than saturating the students with the machine's technology, he allowed them to determine for themselves the kind of "computer-composing" they would do. His requirement for a word-processed printout did not prevent students from using the computer as much as they wanted for each assignment. The case study subjects were guaranteed as much time as they needed with the microcomputers.

The instructor of the business writing course asked his class on the first day of the quarter if any students would be willing to participate in a study to observe how students adapt to the word processor in their composition class. As recompense, they were excused from an oral report due at the end of the quarter. Five students volunteered, and those were the students we observed. Possibly, this method of selecting subjects yielded a biased sample, but the instructor described them as "typical." We have been careful not to suggest that they characterize the entire range of students in the classes.

The five, 3 males and 2 females, ranged in age from 21 to 23. None had ever used a computer for writing before, although one student had taken an introductory programming course in computer science. The 5 students were all business majors, specializing in either accounting (Jerry, Don, and Debbie) or marketing (John and Melinda). There was nothing extraordinary about their writing backgrounds, except that Debbie had had some experience working on the school newspaper of the community college from which she had transferred.

Rather than give our subjects writing tasks just for this study, which might introduce variables unrelated to a study of computers in writing classes, we decided instead to study writing samples produced for their course. Assignments in the business course were designed to meet the stated goal of "Preprofessional Writing for the Business Major" which is a pragmatic one, developing the skills necessary for effective business writing. By discussing various communication strategies and practicing them in a variety of common business forms—letters, memos, proposals, and formal reports—the students in the class learn to analyze and meet the needs of an audience in the marketplace. For our primary objects of study, we chose two sets of letters—one done early in the quarter, and the other toward the end. We chose the business letter, with its explicit concerns with voice, tone, and audience analysis, because it was targeted by the instructor as the assignment that required the students to apply most of the concepts he stressed in business communication. Also, we felt that while the letters were long enough to get a valid sample of our subjects' composing skills, their relative brevity allowed for in-depth analyses.

The texts we solicited as data, then, are samples of utilitarian writing. Marder (1982) offers a caution on this type of writing, arguing that "writers [in this genre] tend to report and explain what they already know. . . . The piece has been worked out—the relationships made, the graphs drawn, the conclusions reached—before the writer begins to report or explain or argue" (p. 4). We feel, however, that our subjects, as nonprofessionals, were inexperienced enough in the genres of business writing so that these texts involved genuine discoveries for them; writers' first struggles with rhetorical problems, however conventional these problems have become for experienced writers, make their composing processes worth studying.

For their first assignment, our subjects used "traditional" methods: a handwritten draft which was then revised and typed. The subjects wrote two types of business communication: a letter of inquiry in which the sender poses a question or a number of questions to someone in business; and a letter of response, which takes the point of view of the person addressed in the previous letter and answers that letter. These two texts were composed by our subjects during the third week of the quarter. For the second set of letters, the students worked in front of the computers. They were permitted to bring notes with them to the sessions, but only one subject, Jerry, did so. They wrote a series of three "collection letters" in which they took the point of view of a credit manager who has to decide on three progressive strategies for obtaining payment from a delinquent account. These were completed—in as many sessions as the students felt they needed to finish the assignment during the eighth week of the quarter—after they had been using the word processor regularly for about seven weeks.

In a more traditional research design, we would have been careful not to confound tasks, i.e., writing done early versus late in a course, and treatments, i.e., using handwriting versus computers. However, as stated earlier, we were not testing for significant differences in an experimental design but *describing* differences observed in a given context. We also knew that it would be important to allow students to gain some facility with the computer before studying how it might affect their writing processes. In our discussion of the findings, we attempt as often as possible to link causes and effects, but we do not claim that we have specifically "isolated" the effects of using a computer for writing. Instruction undoubtedly influenced our findings, mingling with the effects of the computer.

For the in-depth case studies, we used two computer programs developed in cooperation with the University of Minnesota Computer Center. The first program stores and prints out a complete record of every keystroke made by our subjects on the computer. It records the keystrokes, both the regular letters the writer types and the word-processing commands the writer gives the computer, and links these data to the computer's internal clock so that the operations have a time reference. These keystrokes are automatically stored in the computer's memory, but the procedures are invisible to the writer. The program then arranges this information to produce a printed record of the composing process. All the keystrokes appear on a wide computer printout, with each line representing a 15-second interval. With this literal record of composing, we can determine when each word was typed, how long the writer paused between each unit of language, and what revising operations were performed on existing texts. We recorded the composing sessions of all 5 subjects for our case studies.

The second program uses the time record of keystrokes to recreate the composing session on the computer's screen. We can replay the sessions just as they occurred in "real time," or we can replay them in "slow motion" to study how the language was composed, in "fast forward" to find specific episodes, or in "freeze frames." We used the replays in this study as stimuli for interviewing two of our case study subjects, asking them to describe in detail what they were doing as they composed.

For the case study subjects, we also coded the revisions we encountered in the "traditional" sample (both within the handwritten draft and those made in the process of typing that draft) and those made during the word-processor sessions, comparing them to see what differences there were which might be attributed to the composing tools they used. To do this coding, we adapted Bridwell's (1980) revision classification scheme. The primary change we made was based on her view that "phrase level" and "clause level" changes were sometimes difficult to code accurately, so we collapsed these categories into an "intrasentence level."

The codings for the "traditional" letters were derived from the drafts of each letter; following Bridwell's methods, we coded every change made at any time. With the "computer-composed" letters on floppy disks, we could not rely on paper copies to preserve a complete record of all changes made, so we analyzed the keystroke record and watched the "playback" of each session, coding changes as they appeared on the screen. When subjects made changes on paper copies of their writing, they were coded using the same procedures as for traditional writing.

We have tried in these case studies to weave a chronological record of each of the students' composing processes with the evidence we gathered from studying their paper-and-pencil methods, their computer keystroke files, the replays of their writing sessions, and their interviews as they talked to us about what they often did and what was changing. We often use the word "traditional" to mean their "old" ways of composing before the computer, both what they told us about them and what we could observe from the two samples we had them write without the computers. We cannot assume that what they told us is completely accurate, and in a few cases we have found conflicting evidence. Neither can we assume that these "traditional" processes apply beyond the context of this particular writing course and these writing tasks. We use "computer composing" to mean whatever they did while they were working with the word processing systems, even though several of them continued to use paper for planning and some drafting.

All the numbers we have reported represent frequencies of changes per 50 words of final text. Often we cite a number in parentheses after a statement about revision at a certain level; in every case, these are changes per 50 words. Other researchers have used other constants (e.g., Bridwell, 1980, used changes per 100 words; Faigley & Witte, 1981, used changes per 1,000 words), but since our texts were shorter than those in these studies (between 100 and 200 words), we thought 50 words represented the right unit to describe properly the amount of revision in the letters our students composed. Table 2 contains the summary of the findings. Anyone who cares to do so can, with a little multiplication, compare our data with other studies, but any comparisons would be highly speculative because of the differences in writers, writing tasks, and contexts.

In our descriptions of each of the 5 students, we report the interviews and the results of our revision analyses. We report our interviews with the students first, because they provide a context for interpreting the work each student did. Initial interviews, in which we asked students about their writing backgrounds, composing processes, and attitudes concerning the word processor, were obtained from the 5 students at the time of the first writing sample. We also interviewed them after each of their word processor sessions. Interviews lasted about 20 minutes and elicited

Table 2. Mean Frequencies of Revisions per 50 Words[a] in "Traditional" and "Computer" Composing

Student	Surface	Word	Intrasent	Sent	Multisent	Total
Don						
T	1.44	3.48	2.32	0.11	0.00	7.35
C	5.42	0.82	0.74	0.09	0.00	7.07
Jerry						
T	1.52	3.87	1.74	0.00	1.12	8.25
C	5.43	3.05	0.69	0.14	2.69	12.00
John						
T	1.02	3.09	0.65	0.00	0.00	4.76
C	6.19	0.94	0.00	0.00	2.86	9.99
Melinda						
T	2.14	4.99	4.06	0.72	1.18	13.09
C	11.33	3.04	1.79	4.00	7.09	27.25
Debbie						
T	2.52	3.93	2.42	0.30	1.11	10.28
C	7.58	2.44	2.04	0.26	1.71	14.03

[a]Based on numbers of changes at any time during composing, per 50 words of final draft. Means based upon changes made on 2 letters written with "traditional" paper and pencil and on 3 letters composed with computers with one exception, Melinda, for whom only 2 computer letters were available.

information about how the students felt about the work they did on the computers. Finally, we conducted "playback" interviews with two of the students, asking them to comment on their intentions as they watched the record of their composing unfold on the screen.

Don

Interviews. Don is less than enthusiastic about writing, especially revising. During his initial interview, he told us that he was glad he took a freshman-level communications course instead of the composition course because he enjoyed not having to revise assignments, something which was required of his friends in composition classes. Don did admit that he enjoyed one type of writing task, and that was research-based writing, perhaps because he saw it as the manipulation of texts rather than the creation of them. Most of the writing he says he does for his courses is of a problem-solving nature, involving source-gathering to back up claims.

He described his typical process as beginning with a brief outline, done only if he is familiar with the topic; otherwise, he just proceeds to "write it all out." After his draft is finished, he admits to doing some revision, but nothing major, he stresses— "mostly rephrasing, no extensive revising, just certain parts." Then he will simply type up that final version, doing little or no editing as he types. His typing speed is approximately 40 words per minute.

Don's initial attitude upon being told that he would be using word processors in his composition class was mainly one of delight; he looked at the microcomputer as a "toy, something to mess around with." He took to the machine slowly but steadily, gradually building up to doing all his written course work on the screen. He identified himself as a computer "drafter/transcriber," not quite ready to shift his entire composing process to the screen, still needing a "very rough draft" to enter the lab with, then composing a more polished draft on the word processor, together with editing it as well. Although he did not bring a draft into his sessions for us, he said he had to do all his planning for tone before he started typing on the machine so that the words could then flow as he composed.

Many students tell us they like the word processor because it allows them to revise more, but Don, who admitted to us at the start that he hated revising, identified the word processor's major feature as its ability to *cut down* on the need for revision: "You don't have to recopy all the good stuff . . . [and] can turn a rough draft into a final easier." He guessed that most of the revising he did on the word processor was surface-level correcting of spelling and punctuation errors. Hence, he saw the machine, besides being fun, as a "cosmetic aid," both in fixing his surface errors and in making his writing more legible to work on because he does not like to see his "chicken scratching" when he writes.

Revision Analysis. Don's actual record of revision bears out his descriptions and attitudes toward revision. In his "traditional" sample, he focuses on changes at the word (3.48/50 words) and intrasentence (2.32) levels, with a marked preference for deleting (1.44) and substituting (1.88) over adding (.28) words. He makes a few surface corrections, one sentence change, and no multisentence changes.

In keeping with the pleasure he felt because he thought the computer allowed him to cut down on revision, the keystroke record shows that he does, in fact, decrease—from 7.35 to 7.08 changes per 50 words. This comparison becomes more significant when the number of spelling or typographical changes (4.80) is subtracted; Don makes almost half the number of revisions on the word processor as he makes typically. Word-level changes decrease from 3.48 to .82; intrasentence level changes decrease from 2.32 to .74.

In one sense, Don appears to find an advantage because the word processor meshes with his goals for writing—to cut down on what he has to do. However, this may not contribute to his growth as a writer. Don is a "pass/fail" student, opting to "make it or break it" without having a writing grade spoil his grade-point average. His letters received low B's and high C's from a relatively "positive" teacher. He averages about 15 minutes of computer time per letter. If his goal is merely to obtain a passing mark, these results show a highly successful adaptation to the word processor: Using the computer and doing almost no revision, he can crank out a passing document in less than an hour (far less time than direct typing with correction would take). He is the only writer of the five *not* to increase significantly the number of formatting changes. This lends support, we think, to the notion that Don may simply not now care about the quality of his writing, a factor that may say more about his revision processes than whether he uses pen and paper or a computer.

Jerry

Interviews. Jerry's professional interests lie in the stock market; he is "indifferent" to almost any composing concerns, except those he deems "practical." For example, when asked how he felt about the four composition classes he has taken, the only one he felt was valuable to him was an advanced composition course which stressed matters of format. He also said the only writing on which he would expend any effort was a text which had importance in the real world: a resume or letter of application or a letter to graduate school.

Otherwise, Jerry's initial description of his composing process made it sound as though he is unwilling to do much more than produce a minimal draft. He begins each writing assignment, he says, by writing the first paragraph as if it were for the final draft. Then, as he told us, "I always get sick of doing that after a while, so I start typing." He simply types slowly through to the end of the text. He claimed he will occasionally change something if it is not the way he wants it, but more often, due to time pressures, he will simply leave it. Jerry types at a speed of 25 words per minute.

Jerry told us during the "playback" session we did with him that we were watching a very atypical composing session for him: "I spent longer on these letters than I ever would have normally." Indeed, he completely revised his first letter, which was certainly not his style as he earlier described to us. The reason for that extensive revision came, we found out in that replay session, when he went back after the first letter was finished to write in the addressee's full name; this "concretized," he said, the mental image of his audience and convinced him he had problems with the tone of that first letter. He directly attributed the word processor's capacity for easy revision to his rewriting of that first letter to capture his newly discovered voice. He said he probably would not have changed his tone in this major way, if he had been required to go back and rewrite everything. In fact, Jerry saw this as the only possible *disadvantage* to composing on-screen, that the writer feels "compelled" to revise.

Another capability of the word processor that increased Jerry's revisions, besides ease, was that he could revise from a "clean" copy. When he first described his process to us, he told us he would write for a while, get sick of that, and just proceed to type up the whole paper. Later we found out why: "It becomes such a mess, . . . I just think, 'Enough is enough, I'm just gonna write the final draft.' " This idea corresponds to Don's comment on the same subject and others who have told us that they do not bother inserting changes or making corrections on a handwritten draft because the resultant physical text would be too hard to decipher.

As a writer for whom format, the "look" of the final text, was a paramount concern, it made sense that Jerry would respond well to the formatting capabilities of the word processing package. During his session on the machine, he was continually playing with the spacing between lines in his letters, centering headings, boldfacing, and subscripting for just the right "look." In his playback session, he told us how important this "professional" look was to his writing: "You want to get results, be taken seriously. You don't want it to be taken as a joke." We watched him punch in commands to justify the right margin like clockwork every time he began a new letter. Once he broke a large paragraph into two smaller ones; when asked in the replay for his reasoning behind the move, he replied, "It looks better." Even in his programming class, he told us, he would spend many extra hours putting all the proper margins and spacing into his program "so it looked nice" when he printed it. So for Jerry, the word processor permitted the development of a concern (revision) that would not have been there otherwise, and allowed for the full enhancement of a concern (formatting) that was of chief importance to him.

Revision Analysis. When we analyzed his revisions, we found that Jerry had indeed emphasized the *looks* of his texts. A self-proclaimed "nonreviser," his traditional process showed two particular points of focus: the word level and the format. With pen and pencil, Jerry made 3.87 changes per 50 words at the word level, the greatest percentage being deletions of words he found redundant (1.61). This kind of revising extended to the phrase level to a lesser degree (1.74). But of all the subjects, Jerry showed the greatest interest in formatting in his traditional process. He made extensive notes to himself about the precise positioning of text on the page, about one note per major section of his letters. Thus, the "nonreviser's" traditional process shows him to be a reviser of sorts, attending to both the "looks" of the finished page and to the levels below the sentence.

On the computer, Jerry's revisions show an overall jump from 8.25 per 50 words to 12.00 as well as a change in the level of focus. As with the other writers, the use of the keyboard caused an increase in spelling and punctuation changes (1.52 to 5.43), but Jerry also shows a *decrease* in word and intrasentence level revisions and an *increase* in formatting revisions. Both the word and intrasentence level decrease can be largely attributed to fewer deletions.

Jerry seems to pay less homage to redundancies on the word processor than to where and how to display the text he has. His formatting changes double (1.12 to 2.26), and include deciding to boldface *and* underline a phrase, spending several minutes with different variations on placing "Sincerely," and alternating between a memo heading and a letter heading.

Like Don, Jerry's process changes qualitatively as he moves to the word processor, but, as with other writers, his changes are consistent with patterns in his traditional method. As a pen-and-pencil composer, Jerry shows a concern for formatting; as a computer composer, formatting expands as a concern, seemingly at the expense of his usual search for things that need deleting. The way the text looks appears to become as important to Jerry as what it says.

John

Interviews. John told us that he has begun to like writing in the last couple of years, but he also stated flatly that he has no taste for "the creative stuff." John's relatively positive disposition toward writing may be a result of his more involved composing process, a process he delineated carefully when we asked—and which, we might add, appears "creative" in the energy he gives to initial problem solving. His first step is mental organization. Then he composes a general outline, with no details; afterward, he will go back and flesh out that outline. He will next proceed to write an initial draft, which would then be revised twice: first, for grammar and spelling, next for stylistic and organizational changes. Then he will type up his final draft. John informed us he would only revise a lot if his text were written for a composition class; with assignments for his business courses, "it's just a question of getting the information across." His typing speed is 25 words per minute.

John took to the word processor well. Early in the quarter, he transcribed rough drafts, but midway through, he "almost always composed on it." He also began to do much of his written work for other courses on the machine. The features of the word processor which John used most were its ability to move things around easily to see how they read (it would be easier to see than just crossing it out, he added) and its ability to free up his composing process: He liked not having to worry about margins and carriage returns. A need for fluidity in composing seems important to John; he identified his "flow" of tone between letters as the major strength of the collection letters he composed with the computer. And in that regard, he liked the machine's capacity for visualizing combinations for his inspection: "[I] had to see it on the screen before I knew how it would sound." He feels he makes "more major revisions . . . in terms of changing sentences" on the word processor. John is yet another person who attributes any increased revision to the screen's neat appearance: "Once you start scribbling out, things get so confusing on a piece of paper that you can't really tell what you did or how it reads or anything." John also represents another phenomenon we discovered among student-users of the word processor: He told us he was unable to compose on a typewriter but can easily compose directly on a microcomputer. It may be that the fluid nature of word-processor composing allows him to transfer a paper-and-pen writing style to the screen. The only disadvantage he found was that "constant button pushing" made it a little tedious.

Revision Analysis. The revision record shows that John revised very little with pen and paper, and, save for formatting and spelling changes, revised even less on the word processor. In the first set of letters, he showed a concern with getting the entire text done in one draft. He began with the full letterhead and opening address, as if this written version *were* the final copy, and made very few changes save for an occasional word or phrase level revision. In his traditional letters (of average length and slightly better-than-average quality, judging by the instructor's grades), John made only 4.76 changes per 50 words, with most of these coming at the word level (3.09). With pen and paper, John seemed to be able to say what he wanted to say in one great rush through the text.

With the computer, John's patterns were similar to Jerry's—a drop in traditional word revisions and an increase in spelling and formatting changes. While his total revisions appeared to jump—from 4.76 to 9.99 on the word processor, the major changes were spelling and typographical corrections (1.02 to 6.19) and rearrangements of what he had written (0 to 2.86). Changes at the word, intrasentence, and sentence levels occurred less frequently (3.74 to .94).

On the surface, the word processor *appears* to have caused John's revisions to regress, particularly in the light of Sommers's (1980) findings that experienced, professional writers attend to larger units of discourse than do student writers. But, if the instructor's grades are any indication, John is a good writer. He classifies himself as a "B+" writer in his initial interview, and his grades bear this out.

Several things could account for his lack of revision. First of all, he may not need to revise much if his initial planning process, what he calls "mental organization," is successful. Second, by the end of the quarter he had probably internalized the teacher's expectations to the degree that he had no need for the "trial, error, revision" method of discovery in composing. Finally, the business letter with its well-defined purpose, audience, and format may not demand extensive revision of a capable writer. In his particular case, the magnitude of revision—on or off the computer—may not be an indicator of successful composing processes at all. That he was pleased with word processing suggests that he had no trouble in transferring his effective strategies to it.

Melinda

Interviews. Melinda actively dislikes writing. Her freshman composition courses, she felt, were "merely a repeat of high school comp." She hates to write, she said; it takes too long for her "to get everything together." She also worries about how her writing is going to sound. She feels she is just an average writer, in contrast with our other subjects who gave themselves above-average self-evaluations.

Melinda relayed a brief, blunt outline of her composing process. First, she said, it was important for us to know that she *had* to leave a writing assignment to the last minute. To begin, she reads over the assignment 2 or 3 times. Then she writes only one draft (she was emphatic about this point as well) which she will type and revise at the same time. She never changes this process, she assured us. Melinda has a part-time secretarial job and a high typing speed of 65 words per minute.

Melinda, with a full course load and a part-time job, found the word processor inconvenient, simply because it entailed having to be on campus more often than she would have preferred. Time was also an indirect factor in her word-processor composing in that she admitted she felt pressured when she wrote in the computer lab; she could not stop thinking about the other students waiting to get on the machines. Yet she admitted the machines were "handy" and "impressive," especially for revision.

Her usual composing process on the word processor was to come in with a draft and then simply transcribe and revise on screen, but later she began to expand the kind of revisions she made. Given her initial assessment of her "traditional" process, particularly her reluctance to write because of a worry over the "sound" of her writing, it is no wonder she subsequently gravitated to the word processor's capacity to allow a writer to experiment with various syntactic combinations: "Sometimes I took the whole thing out and started over." Fairly typical, then, of her methods is the following sequence taken from one of her sessions:

I am disappointed to learn of

[line deleted]

We are surprised t

[line deleted]

We are dismayed

[line deleted]

Your account for $_____ is _____ days overdue. Frankly, we're disappointed in you. So fork over the dough or Vito will come over to collect in another manner.

[last line deleted, then pause,
then previous two lines deleted
as well]

Frankly,

[word deleted]

Your account for $_____ is now _____ days overdue. Frankly, we don't know what to say anymore. We've given you every opportunity to clear this matter and you have not responded to our inquiries.

When asked what determined her revisions, she claimed it was an attempt to improve the "sound" of her letters; she wanted to rid her writing of an "unprofessional" sound "like someone in junior high wrote it." She too claimed she would not revise as much without the word processor, but that she "would probably try to keep it all inside my head instead of putting it on the screen in front of me," a process easily noted in the sample, especially in the line about "Vito," which was perhaps her way of joking with herself until she could capture the tone and "sound" she was after. With traditional methods, she claims, she hates to have to write it out, then scratch it out (a tendency quite evident in the handwritten sample we received from her); on the screen she can type lines in, play around with various combinations, and study them before they become permanent. Even with her quick typing skills, she claimed she would never retype a draft in order to make a few changes.

Revision Analysis. The record of Melinda's revisions shows that she had the most "balanced" traditional revision process of the five writers. She made changes in all five levels of our category system, with a clear preference for word (4.99) and intrasentence (4.06) changes. Of these, the most common were word substitution and intrasentence deletion. Her pattern is clear: posing an initial phrasing for an idea, then rubbing it out and trying another. The following is an example of her "paper" revision process and is later entirely rewritten when typing the final draft.

In response to your inquiry, it seems evident that the machines are being used too frequently

   [sentence deleted]

Due to the heavy use of the word proc, it

   ["it" deleted] [clause deleted]

When the machines are overworked,

   ["overworked" deleted]

used heavily, they will become overheated and consequently malfunction.

In her traditional process, Melinda made relatively few spelling changes (.83) and relatively few comments or changes involving formatting (.59). Her attention remains at the phrase, clause, or word levels, constantly staging and substituting different ways of expressing the same underlying semantic content.

With the computer, Melinda's revising process undergoes an extensive change, the most dramatic of all the writers. Her total number of changes skyrockets from 13.09 to 27.25 per 50 words. Some of this jump can be attributed to an increase in typographical and spelling changes due to the computer's "quick" keyboard. But two other, far-reaching changes in her process seem more important.

The first is an extension of her "tinkering" procedures to larger units of text. Where in the traditional samples, she attends to words and phrases, with the computer she revises sentences and multisentence chunks. She makes more than 6 times the number of multisentence changes and more than 4 times the number of sentence level changes with the word processor.

The second major change is the beginning of a concern with formatting. She made a very few notes to herself about how to type the final draft, but when she moved to the computer, she began to spend greater time experimenting with various spatial configurations. She *made* 4.61 formatting changes per 50 words, either by writing in "dummy" formats of blank lines to be filled in later, or by using carriage returns and line deletes to alter the space between chunks of written text.

Both of these changes seem rather remarkable in the light of her difficulty with the keyboard (11.33 changes per 50 words), not to mention the time pressure she was under because of her work schedule and the distractions she said she felt, knowing that someone might be waiting for her to relinquish the computer. In addition, the changes represented are probably more significant than the numbers might indicate, since the probability for making a multisentence change is much lower than the probability for making a surface level change.

Despite her descriptions to the contrary, Melinda clearly started out as an "extensive reviser" as compared to the other writers and increased her revision when she used the computer for what it does best for writers—adding and deleting text in the blink of an electrical impulse.

Debbie

Interviews. When asked how she felt about writing in general, Debbie thought for a moment and answered, "I don't *dread* it." This seems to sum up her anxious attitude about composing: She does not hate it as much as she worries about it. While the other four students were excused from doing an oral report as recompense for participating in our study, Debbie made arrangements with her instructor to do the oral report and instead be excused from turning in a revised assignment. Although she liked her previous writing courses, she preferred to take literature-related courses. She gladly volunteered the information that she preferred doing business writing "to something more creative." But, then again, she was the only student in our study who had writing experience beyond required course work.

Her composing process, as she described it to us, may be a reflection of her anxiety since she claims to revise quite often. First, she will review her material, and then write out a list of major ideas. Her rought draft follows, but she assured us that she revises as she writes the draft: "Maybe I shouldn't use this word" is the kind of thing she asks herself while she's drafting. After that draft is completed, she will revise again, writing a final handwritten copy. That copy is then revised again as she types. Debbie's typing speed is approximately 50 words per minute.

Debbie did not learn the word processor as quickly as the other students in our study. Even eight weeks into the quarter she was continually forgetting to use the control key. No surprise, then, that she identified the word processor's greatest disadvantage as the difficulties she had in learning it. Hence, she did not adapt enough to compose on the computer screen; in fact, she began her session for us by writing, with pen and paper, for approximately five minutes, jotting down notes, addresses, and a first sentence.

Debbie rereads constantly on the screen. Her session is filled with pauses in which one can almost see her reading through her text (though we did not have to guess, she told us in her replay session): The cursor stops in the middle of the second or third paragraph of a letter, there will be a pause of over a minute, and the next thing seen on screen is the cursor jumping up to the first paragraph to add a line.

In her initial interview, Debbie described her traditional process as incorporating many revisions. What was amazing, given her poor command of the word processor, was that she seemed to revise almost as much on the screen. She knew virtually none of the easy revision commands and instead added or deleted a character at a time. It was a tedious process, and messy, too, since so much of her old text would remain on the screen while she was generating something new. But she fought through the interference, by her ignorance of most functions, to preserve her old process. And despite that interference, she still claimed in her postsession interview that revising on the word processor was "easier."

During her replay session, Debbie continually attributed the cause of her many revisions to "sound." At one point we watched her delete a sentence, character by character. When asked why she got rid of it, she replied, "It didn't sound right." We were then rather puzzled to see, character by character, the exact sentence reappear on the screen. When challenged for a reason, Debbie mused, "I guess it sounded pretty good. . . . When writing things, sometimes something doesn't sound good, then you go back and it does." The point of view of her first collection letter was changed midway through from "we" to "I," because, as Debbie said, it "sounded more personal; it sounded too phony to say 'we'—there was only one person writing the letter." She, like Melinda, appreciated the machine's capacity for experimentation with working out the right sound combination.

Cooper and Odell (1976) also report the importance of sound considerations in writers' composing; our study made us aware of how inextricably linked visual appearance is to sound as perceived by students. Debbie also enjoyed the fluidity of composing on-screen: At one point in her last letter, her rate of production was noticeably faster than at any other time. When she saw it, Debbie smiled at how fast she was composing. "I'm really going on a going streak," she said, and attributed it to not wanting to forget what she wanted to say.

Revision Analysis. Debbie's experience with composing on the computer can best be described as a determined fight to remain the same. Her traditional process showed a wide range of revisions at all levels, primarily on word and intrasentence changes. She showed at these levels a kind of tinkering similar to Melinda's— deleting a word here, a phrase there, adding substitutes, until she found an expression that satisfied her. She made goal-directed notes to herself as reminders in the margins (e.g., "setting," "problems," "urgency"), something none of the other five students did. In traditional revision, she went through three drafts: first, a sketch of the major points she will make, loosely formed into a rough draft; second, a rough draft in which word and intrasentence substitutions prevail; lastly, a typed draft with a few word changes and some surface revisions.

Debbie's revisions increase on the computer, but this is largely due to surface changes, an artifact of the sensitive computer keyboard our students used. Like three others, she makes more format changes (.40 to 1.26), but her word and intrasentence changes show a slight decrease. Behind all the numbers lies very much the same process, reorganized to a great extent because Debbie, in this study, had failed to gain control over the word processing system.

She shared with the other subjects a new concern with the looks of her text as it emerged, but every time she made a change, the system consequently disturbed the nice neat lines and margins of the original, and Debbie faced a problem. Whereas the other students mastered a "reforming command" which automatically tidied the text, Debbie did her reforming by hand, carefully typing over the rest of the paragraph below her change, then deleting (using the character delete key repeatedly, rather than the word- or line-delete command) the "old" version of the lines she had just retyped. This method of reforming text proved incredibly time-consuming, and clearly discouraged, to some degree, her traditional process of word and intrasentence revision. In fact, considering how difficult she had made the word processor for herself, it was surprising that she made any other changes at all. What we saw, however, was a dogged determination to revise in her usual ways.

Summary of the Findings

Our study of these five writers partially confirms and partially rejects one of our original hypotheses, that using the microcomputer for word processing would affect the students' composing—specifically revising—processes.

Surface Errors

The most immediately obvious change was the tremendous increase in the number of surface level, typographical changes. None of these students was a poor typist, so the increase in typographical errors was new and caused by problems in adjusting to the electronic keyboard. However, none of the writers complained significantly about this increase in errors; almost all the "errors" were caught and easily corrected immediately (within one word), and so they were not necessarily a problem. Other students in our courses who were not touch-typists had reported that it was still faster to produce a text on the computer than by hand, due to the savings in retyping time from draft to draft. Those who used the spelling and style programs to check their essays also reported that they could find any "typos" they missed automatically, another reason why this might not have been a significant problem.

Even so, in our purchases for our expanded computer lab, we have ordered a different kind of keyboard, one which "clicks" like a conventional typewriter, to cut down on these typing problems. Some word processing packages allow the writer to turn the clicking on or off. As with so many other features of microcomputers, those who know them well do not always agree on what is an advantage and what is a disadvantage. Although experts might prefer the "quick" electronic keyboard, novices might find the slower, mechanical ones easier to use. We also provide an on-screen typing tutorial for students who want to learn touch-typing skills.

Formatting

Using the computer generally increases a concern with the visual appearance of one's writing (true for 4 of our 5 students, and for many others we have interviewed and surveyed). Even in early stages, what appears on the screen can have a polished quality because of the ease of formatting. This appearance may be a mixed blessing. Many researchers who have studied revision (Bridwell, 1980; Sommers, 1980) have found that inexperienced writers often equate revision with "cleaning up" their writing, often ignoring more important features. In our study, however, we often encountered students who said that seeing their writing in a polished form allowed them to pay *more* attention to larger rhetorical and textual problems.

The motivation to revise may be linked with writers' notions about what good writing should be, criteria which develop at least partially as they read polished texts. As inexperienced writers' first efforts approach the visual quality of written texts, they may be better able to judge them against "print" standards as opposed to viewing their own handwriting in highly idiosyncratic ways. We do not have sufficient evidence in this study to determine the effects of the "looks" of one's writing on improvements in writing, but it is a central question to explore as we watch more and more writers move to word processing.

Certainly for the subjects of our case studies, the appearances of a business letter and its format are, and should be, important. All of the writers were aware of the pragmatic consequences of the letter upon their readers—a central theme in the course they were taking. In future studies, we will have to determine whether writers composing other kinds of written texts are equally as conscious of the visual quality of their writing as these writers were. We have limited evidence from students that they *are* aware of visual criteria no matter what they are writing, and we have a hunch that these criteria may develop after years of experiences with printed texts, with television, and, to a lesser extent, with video games—experiences they bring to the highly visual medium of computer composing.

Expanding Revision Units

In some cases, the machine allows the *extension* of revision strategies already present in the traditional processes of our students. How much this increase in revision is due to the task or to the effects of the instruction in the class is open to question. Melinda, for example, moved to larger units of discourse for revision, and Jerry was able to focus on his concern with the looks of his documents. But, at the same time, other subjects reacted differently. Debbie, who had a traditional process similar to Melinda's, failed to extend her tinkering because, we believe, she failed to master the word processing system—she had to fight to stay the same. John and Don both *decreased* their revisions, restricting rather than expanding their processes—but, as we have already mentioned, they may have *tried* to use the computer to limit their revising.

Conclusions from Case Studies

The way the machine is used is not a function of the computer by itself, the writer by herself, or the task by itself—all three interrelate. Melinda's extensive tinkering, for example, makes great sense against her overall response to the class. She became fascinated with the ideas of "voice," "tone," and "subtext"—bringing in examples of "bad" and "good" letters from her job as a secretary, and thanked the instructor after the course for helping her become aware of the *affective* side of business prose. Against such a background, her toying with the reexpression of the same semantic content in different tones is understandable (as, for example, her sentence about Vito, the collection man, which shows a humorous awareness of the threat concealed in her deleted sentences).

On the other extreme, writers like John and Don seem to show different degrees of detachment from their writing, and what we see as lack of revision may be lack of interest on different levels: John, disinterested because the task is too easy; Don, because the task is too hard. Both writers' ability to complete assignments in 15 minutes, in contrast to Melinda's hour-and-a-half sessions, denotes levels of commitment to the task that need to be kept in mind—especially when John's final letters, for example, receive the same marks as Melinda's. There are different returns for the time involved here.

To explore fully the ways the word processor changes revision processes, therefore, we need more than just five subjects and one task. By looking at these students' processes in detail, however, we have found interesting questions which we can now ask in large-scale studies. The technology works for us as researchers, in that we already have the capability to gather minute information effortlessly in the computer's memory for many writers. What it can't do for us, however, is tell us what to look for. That we still have to discover by studying real people in dynamic contexts—not by analyzing keystrokes.

Written Language Production

One long-range goal of behavioral studies of the composing process, beyond studies of what is effective in teaching writing or what the consequences are of using computers, is to contribute to a model of written language production. Assuming that all current models, from transformational syntax to artificial intelligence, "cognitive process" models, and pragmatic studies of context, are inadequate to predict how an individual will produce a given text in a particular context, it seems only appropriate to describe what actually occurs during composing. To make meaning of the results, one is forced to speculate, and this path is fraught with peril. One clear example of how descriptive data have been misused is sentence-combining. The early work was purely descriptive, but in the decade which has followed it, teachers, researchers, and developmental theorists have used many findings as "normative," even as benchmarks against which "writing ability" or "writing development" could be measured. The critics of such interpretations (Kleine, 1983, among others) are right to conclude that such applications are superficial, indeed even misleading as evidence of writing growth. But the point remains that knowing how syntactic variation is manifested in various types of writing by writers at different ages, etc., is valuable information when interpreted carefully, descriptively, and *speculatively* as to what it says about language production and growth.

With this caveat clearly before us, then, we think it might be important to consider what the data about frequencies of revision and conditions under which they occur might mean to a theory of written language production. First, if one could assume that researchers gathered such data over an infinite number of writers, over an infinite number of writing contexts, and over an infinite number of writing tasks, one might find that the frequencies for certain types of changes take on a certain shape, with means that suggest patterns of behavior as language is produced. Take word level changes, for example. Examining age-level differences, one might find that the shape of this frequency distribution is bimodal, with relatively high frequencies at, say age 15 when writers are struggling to describe the world around them, and again at age 18 among college writers who make a giant leap into academic discourse. Before, in between, and after, when the world seems more apparent, the ability to express a certain concept might be more stable. But this is only one variable, and it is important to consider an array of causal factors before one speculates about *how* humans produce written language. If one examined frequency variations in more or less demanding contexts, one might find that familiarity with the reader or the information being expressed was really more powerful as a predictor. The list of contributing variables—anxiety, psychomotor skill, rate of production, "style" of planning or problem solving—would have to be carefully examined before the numbers could be accurately interpreted. But the quest seems worth pursuing for two reasons: (a) we know our current models of language production are inadequate, and we would hope that inductive studies of "performance" could lead to more adequate models of "competence"; and (b) to use the data for any practical purposes, we must have a better idea of what they mean *and what they don't mean*. To attribute quick value judgments to a gain in revision changes per se is a superficial interpretation. We do not yet know what all our numbers "mean," but we hope that in our attempts to describe them, we have been careful to suggest a rich range of possibilities.

References

Bridwell, L. S. (1980). Revising strategies in twelfth grade students' transactional writing. *Research in the Teaching of English, 14,* 197–222.

Bridwell, L. S., Johnson, P., & Brehe, S. (in press). Computers and composing: Case studies of experienced writers. In A. Matsuhashi (Ed.), *Writing in real time: Modelling production processes.* New York: Longman.

Bridwell, L. S., Nancarrow, P. R., & Ross, D. (1984). The writing process and the writing machine: Current research on word processors relevant to the teaching of composition. In R. Beach & L. S. Bridwell (Eds.), *New directions in composition research.* New York: Guilford Press.

Bridwell, L. S., & Ross, D. (1984). Integrating computers into a writing curriculum; or, buying, begging, and building. In W. Wresch (Ed.), *A writer's tool: The computer in composition instruction* (pp. 107–119). Urbana IL: National Council of Teachers of English.

Collier, R. M. (1983). The word processor and revision strategies. *College Composition and Communication, 34,* 149–155.

Cooper, C. R,, & Odell, L. (1976). Considerations of sound in the composing process of published writers. *Research in the Teaching of English, 10,* 103–115.

Daiute, C. A. (1983). The computer as stylus and audience. *College Composition and Communication, 34,* 134–145.

Faigley, L., & Witte, S. (1981). Analyzing revision. *College Composition and Communication, 32,* 400–414.

Fallows, J. (1982, July). Toys: Living with a computer. *The Atlantic,* pp. 84–91.

Fallows, J. (1983, March). Computer romance, Part II. *The Atlantic,* pp. 107–109.

Kleine, M. (1983). *Syntactic choice and a theory of discourse: Rethinking sentence-combining.* Unpublished doctoral dissertation, The University of Minnesota.

Marder, D. (1982). Revision as discovery and the reduction of entropy. In R. A. Sudol (Ed.), *Revising: New essays for teachers of writing.* Urbana, IL: National Council of Teachers of English.

Nancarrow, P. R., Ross, D., & Bridwell, L. S. (1984). *Word processors and the writing process: An annotated bibliography.* Westport, CT: Greenwood Press.

Sommers, N. (1980). Revision strategies of student writers and experienced adult writers. *College Composition and Communication, 31,* 378–388.

10

Theory and Practice in Computer-Aided Composition*

Lawrence T. Frase
AT&T Bell Laboratories

Kathleen E. Kiefer
Charles R. Smith
Colorado State University

Mary L. Fox
AT&T Bell Laboratories

This chapter reflects two perspectives on computer-aided composition—a psychological perspective and an instructional perspective. The psychological perspective focuses on how computers can support cognitive processes: to develop automated aids for tasks people frequently do and to conduct research on how well such aids work, including their effects on human attitudes and performance. The instructional perspective focuses on teaching with automated aids, that is, on installing hardware and software to support classroom activities and to speed learning.

Psychological and instructional perspectives are entwined throughout this chapter which aims, broadly, to highlight the potential for computing in the humanities. Indeed, though computer programs we describe were developed in an industrial context, they were put into instructional use primarily by faculty engaged in teaching English. We see in this an important trend. Where yesterday computing tools were almost exclusively the domain of engineering, mathematics, and computer science, today they begin to touch all aspects of the humanities, as well. It is this connection between technology and human activities, especially teaching and learning, that we pursue in this paper. We first provide some background on the content of the UNIX WRITER'S WORKBENCH[1] software (a set of automated editorial aids) and then go on to describe tests of the system, including effects on students and teachers of college composition.

Multidisciplinary Contributions

Knowing our limitations can help us design tools to overcome them, but to do the job right takes the combined efforts of people with varying backgrounds. Recent work in two related fields helps us understand ways in which we can use computer technology to overcome, or at least compensate for, limitations in human information processing. First, psychological and linguistic research on what makes text

---

* We thank Nina Macdonald for comments on an early draft of this chapter.

[1] UNIX is a trademark of AT&T Bell Laboratories; WRITER'S WORKBENCH is a trademark of AT&T Technologies, Inc.

easy or hard to understand and what makes writing easy or hard to do, gives us useful empirical data on text formatting, wording, and graphic displays (Hartley, 1981). Work in cognitive psychology also identifies areas of information design amenable to automated aids. Specifically, work on writing (Mosenthal, Tamor, & Walmsley, 1983) and stages of documentation (Frase, Keenan, & Dever, 1980) reveal the subskills of composition (such as planning) and elements of the broad process of writing (such as gathering source information) that are candidates for automated support. Along with this research on text design and cognitive science, rhetorical traditions (Kinneavy, 1971; Lanham, 1979) have had substantial effects on the teaching of composition, thus balancing knowledge derived from empirical study with knowledge derived from rationalistic methods.

But knowledge alone cannot solve problems; we need tools to put that knowledge to work efficiently, and this is where computers come in. Computer language analysis has already stimulated applications of cognitive science and principles of text design. McMahon, Cherry, and Morris (1978) showed how language analysis, for example, vocabulary or part-of-speech analysis (tasks human beings find tedious and difficult) can be done easily and accurately by computers. Furthermore, if we have models of how human experts solve complex tasks, programs can often be written to reproduce those human activities. As an example, rules for text design have been incorporated into computer programs that recommend specific page layouts—for instance, the most suitable column width for a particular text (Frase, Macdonald, & Keenan, in press). Knowledge-based expert systems (Duda & Shortliffe, 1983) in other areas, such as surveying and medical diagnosis, are additional examples of computer applications based on the analysis of human expertise.

Although computer-assisted instruction has been available for years, computing resources have only recently started to become accessible to the educational community. Availability of well-articulated computing environments, not just isolated bits of software and hardware, will have far-reaching consequences for education; so this is yet another theme behind our discussion. Just as rhetorical or cognitive theories and document design reflect the contrast between theoretical and practical aspects of writing, computer science and system development reflect theoretical and practical aspects of implementation. Having theories or new tools and knowing how to use them does not necessarily change the world. One also needs an environment (like the early Ford factories) in which to develop and extend their reach. The development and wide availability of office and educational computing environments will greatly encourage the rapid creation, testing, and exchange of new educational tools.

The UNIX operating system provided us just such a development environment for automated writing aids; the portability of its tools encouraged extensions into the classroom. The UNIX system has been a major resource for text processing and other applications, including software development and networking. Furthermore, the system is widely used in education, government, and industry, so developments can be shared rapidly and widely. The system emphasizes portability of tools, including those that were the basis for development of the WRITER'S WORK-

BENCH system. And so, although this chapter focuses on computer aids for writing, those aids appear as only part of a larger story, which includes establishing conditions for the development and delivery of those aids.

To summarize, cognitive science has given us a systematic account of reading and writing skills; rhetorical standards and principles for writing and text design have given us rules for translating this knowledge into design decisions; computer science provided tools for converting these decisions into automated aids for writing; and the UNIX system software development environment provided the glue binding these elements together. Cooperation among theoretical and applied domains, such as rhetoric, computer science, cognitive psychology and the teaching of composition, encouraged by a congenial computing environment, resulted in the work reported in this chapter. We expect similar developments in other areas of the arts and humanities.

WRITER'S WORKBENCH Software: Program Structure

In this section, we briefly summarize the WRITER'S WORKBENCH programs and then review research and applications of the programs. Table 1 lists the WRITER'S WORKBENCH programs and shows their overall structure. The programs are described elsewhere at length (Cherry, 1982; Cherry, Fox, Frase, Gingrich, Keenan, & Macdonald, 1983; Cherry & Macdonald, 1983; Frase, 1983; Frase, Macdonald, Gingrich, Keenan, & Collymore, 1981; Frase, Macdonald, & Keenan, in press; Gingrich, 1983; Macdonald, 1983; Macdonald, Frase, Gingrich, & Keenan, 1982; Smith & Kiefer, 1983).

The programs shown in Table 1 are quite diverse; however, they concentrate on stylistic measures. The programs thus focus on a subset of the skills that make up the art of writing. Notably, the programs rely on advice (or prescriptions) of experts on writing and psychological research on linguistic and text design problems (Macdonald, 1983). Thus, the programs are a source of knowledge, to be used or not, depending on the student, teacher, or writer.

The *parts* and *style* programs (Cherry, 1980, 1982) are the basis for several assessments provided by the WRITER'S WORKBENCH programs. *Parts* assigns a grammatical part of speech to each word in a text and *style* converts this information into a table of text variables. Among other things, *style* reports four different readability calculations, tabulates parts of speech, and reports the percentage of complex sentences. Given this information, and information about the intended audience, *prose,* another program, offers a commentary on an author's style. Another program, *proofr,* suggests spelling and punctuation corrections as well as wording changes. With this feedback, the author can then make changes or go to information files for help with various aspects of writing (see *punctrules* and *worduse* commands in Table 1).

In addition, programs can be altered in various ways, for instance, by including a flag (a letter appended to a command) to restrict or expand the output. For example,

Table 1. Selected Writer's Workbench Programs

Commands

abst	evaluates text abstractness
match	collates styles of different texts
parts	assigns grammatical parts of speech
sexist	finds sexist phrases and suggests changes
style	summarizes stylistic features
syl	prints words of selected syllable length
topic	suggests topics, keywords
parts	assigns grammatical parts of speech
wwb	runs proofreading and stylistic analysis
proofr	gives proofreading comments
diction	finds awkward phrases and suggests changes
double	detects repeated typings of words
punct	checks punctuation
spellwwb	checks spelling, using spelldict
prose	gives extended editorial comments
style	summarizes stylistic features
parts	assigns grammatical parts of speech

Explanations

prosestand	prints standards used to evaluate text
punctrules	explains punctuation rules
worduse	explains frequently misused words
wwbaid	describes programs and how to use them
wwbhelp	gives information about commands and functions

Environmental tailoring

dictadd	adds phrases to user specified dictionaries
spelladd	adds words to spelldict dictionary
mkstand	builds standards for prose from user documents

User-specified dictionaries

ddict	personal list of awkward phrases
sexdict	personal list of sexist terms
spelldict	personal list of correct spellings

Note. Indented commands are automatically run by the less indented commands that immediately precede them.

the output of the *prose* program can be reduced to a few summary lines by requesting a short version using the "−s" flag. Hence, the style of feedback is placed under the author's control.

An author can request other analyses and print sentences that have certain characteristics, for instance, sentences exceeding a certain length, or sentences in the passive voice, or sentences above a selected readability level. In addition, an author using *prose* or *match* can compare features of a text with statistics derived from texts supplied by the program developers or created from a set of documents supplied by the author.

In short, the WRITER'S WORKBENCH programs are generic in the sense that they permit many applications for different texts and purposes. Next we review studies to determine whether program analyses correspond to what humans do and whether the programs are limited in the type of texts that they can analyze. Other studies were conducted, but the two reported here seem representative.

Program Validity

In this section we give examples of evaluative activities that went along with development of the WRITER'S WORKBENCH programs. Like any other educational tool, perhaps more so, software needs to be evaluated against relevant standards of performance.

Some WRITER'S WORKBENCH programs use easily defined standards for evaluating features of text such as punctuation rules (e.g., placement of commas inside double quotation marks). In other cases, however, program measures are complex enough that information is needed on how well program outputs agree with human judgments. For these complex cases we conducted studies to determine whether the programs provided valid and reliable data. Not all our original programs survived such trials and hence do not appear in the current WRITER'S WORKBENCH system. Furthermore, contexts for using the programs vary, and a valid and reliable program for one purpose might be useless or misleading for another, so one needs to be cautious about how individual programs are used (Frase, 1981). We next review two studies of program validity.

Text Abstractness[2]

Here we first describe the *abst* program, and then we review a study that was done to determine if its output agrees with human judgments.

Rationale and Design. The *abst* program evaluates the abstractness of text based on the proportion of highly abstract words it contains. The program was developed as follows. Imagery and concreteness norms were obtained for nouns (Paivio, Yuille, & Madigan, 1968), verbs (Klee & Legge, 1976) and adjectives (Berrian, Metzler, Kroll, & Clark-Meyers, 1979). Three hundred and fourteen words, falling at least one standard deviation below the mean on concreteness or imagery ratings, were selected to measure abstractness. The *abst* program searches passages for those abstract words, prints the percentage of total words that are abstract, and lists them for inspection.

Program measures of abstractness were compared to human judgments of ab-

---

[2] Patricia Gingrich collected data for this study.

stractness. A two-way analysis of variance, using passages and subjects as random variables, was conducted on subjects' ratings of abstractness. The two factors were readability level (medium, difficult) and abstractness (low, high).

Procedures. Each of 40 short passages (about 150 words) used in previous research (Coke, 1974), of medium and difficult readability, was scored for abstractness by the computer program. The passages covered a variety of subjects. Mean reading grade levels for the passages of medium difficulty was 9.94, and for those of high difficulty, 18.33. We then selected, for human judgment, the 5 most abstract and 5 least abstract passages from each of the two readability groups. The passages of medium readability contained .42% abstract words in the low abstract passages, and 3.22% in the high abstract passages ($M = 1.82\%$). The difficult passages contained .69% abstract words in the low abstract passages, and 5.17% in the high abstract passages ($M = 2.93\%$).

Twenty-three AT&T Bell Laboratories technical employees (employees with M.A. and Ph.D. degrees) served as subjects.

Each subject received a booklet containing the experimental passages, printed one per page with instructions defining the concept of abstractness and describing how to rate passages on a five-point scale of abstractness (5 was highest).

Results. The mean abstractness rating for the low abstract passages was 2.77; for the high abstract passages 3.37; $F(1,198) = 46.16$, $p<.001$. The mean abstractness rating was 2.71 for the medium readability passages and 3.42 for the difficult passages; $F(1,198) = 60.05$, $p<.001$. In addition, there was an interaction between passage readability and abstractness; $F(1,330) = 4.33$, $p<.05$. The reliability of a single judge, estimating the intraclass correlation, was $r_1 = .43$, which is moderate. The magnitude of the abstractness effect represents an eta coefficient of .45, indicating that 69% of the passages classified as abstract by computer were so classified by human readers.

In short, passages rated relatively abstract by the computer were also rated abstract by humans, and the computer and human ratings agreed moderately well. There was also an interaction between readability and abstractness: Subjects rated the difficult passages relatively high in abstractness even if the computer rating was low. This interaction suggests that some dimension of text difficulty, not related to the program measure of abstractness, influenced subjects' judgments about abstractness in the difficult passages. (A more complete description of this study is in Frase, Gingrich, & Keenan, 1981.)

Parts of Speech

Parts is a program that assigns parts of speech to words in sentences. When first released, *parts* proved to be about 95% accurate in its assignments (Cherry, 1980). The texts used in that study ranged from first- to sixth-grade level in readability and were free from grammatical and spelling errors. We wanted to test the performance of *parts* on text with higher readability levels (more complex) and less predictably correct grammar and spelling. Therefore, we tested *parts* on freshman placement tests. These student texts represent a broad range of readability levels, and they contain errors of grammar and spelling. *Parts* uses grammatical and lexical features to make its assignments; hence poor writing could affect not only *parts,* but how the *style* program (which depends on *parts*) assigns sentence type and voice. This study was intended to determine the accuracy of the *parts* program with texts of varying quality.

Design and Procedures. Entering college freshmen at Colorado State University (CSU) take a written placement test. Each student reads a one-page, single-spaced article on a topic chosen to provoke controversy. The students have one hour to read the article and to write an essay in response.

The essays are then holistically scored by English department faculty and sorted into three categories: high, medium, and low quality. For this study, essays were selected from tests given in 1981 to yield about 6,000 words of student text in each quality group. Thus, there were 11 essays in the high group, 15 in the medium group, and 21 in the low group.

Working independently, two graduate students at CSU assigned a part of speech to each word in the essays. They were instructed to use the same word classes used by the final pass of the *parts* program: noun, verb, adjective, adverb, conjunction, preposition, interjection, auxiliary verb, pronoun, subordinate conjunction, article, be, and possessive. Next, the experts classified each sentence as either simple or complex, and active or passive voice.

In all the agreement analyses (parts of speech, sentence types, and voice) the sample was first reduced to only those words or sentences about which the two graduate students agreed on the assignment. Thus we arrived at an ''expert consensus'' with which to compare *parts*'s assignments. These data represent 92% of the original total sample. (The final sample comprised 18,923 words.)

Results. The overall agreement between *parts* and the graduate students was 90%. This compares well with the 95% agreement reported in Cherry's[3] (1981) validation study. This level of agreement, in the face of grammar and spelling errors, shows the robustness of *parts.*

The slight decrease in agreement with the experts from high- to low-quality student text was significant ($p<.01$); 91.8%, 90.5%, and 88.8% agreement, respectively. For the graduate students, there was a nonsignificant decrease in agreement from high- to low-quality student text (92.7%, 93.0%, 91.5%). From this we conclude that *parts* agrees with expert judges slightly less on poor-quality texts than on good-quality texts, but the difference in agreement is quite small.

In addition, *parts* showed high agreement with experts in assigning sentence types. It agreed with them on 92% of the simple sentences and 88% of the complex

---

[3] We thank Lorinda Cherry for comments on this study.

sentences. Voice assignments were also accurate. Computers and humans agreed on 96% of the active-voice assignments and on 91% of the passive-voice assignments.

In summary, data from our experiments show that the programs are valid and reliable under a variety of text conditions. User response, next discussed, shows that they are also useful.

Studies of Users

The following section reviews studies to determine the response of users to WRITER'S WORKBENCH programs. While early tests were going on at AT&T Bell Laboratories, an opportunity arose to try the programs in college composition courses. This resulted in trials of the programs in English courses at CSU, which we also review.

Technical Users

We have explored user response to the programs since they first became available within AT&T Bell Laboratories. Table 2 shows the results of a survey of 63 randomly selected users (Frase, Macdonald, Gingrich, Keenan, & Collymore, 1981). The data show that most users think that the documentation and program output are clear, that the programs do not miss much, and that the programs are likely to find things the writer would miss. In addition, users believe that the programs do not adversely affect the time they spend on documents, and a significant number believe the programs improve their writing skills.

Gingrich (1983) reported trials of the programs in two company locations. Results show that technical writers are more likely to detect editorial problems after exposure to the programs than before, and users generally have the same positive response to the programs as staff at AT&T Bell Laboratories. From these field trials of the programs it appears that automated editorial feedback seems to influence editing skills and user attitudes; however, detailed experimental studies are still needed.

Table 2. Proportion Agreement with Statements Evaluating Characteristics of Writer's Workbench Programs

Opinion statement	Proportion(N)	Probability
1. Program explanations are clear	.84(63)	<.001
2. Supporting documentation is clear	.92(53)	<.001
3. Programs improve writing skills	.56(54)	<.02
4. Programs do not miss problems	.64(47)	<.05
5. Programs detect problem writers miss	.70(50)	<.01
6. Programs useful for technical and nontechnical material	.80(35)	<.001

Note. Probabilities determined by binomial test. Expected proportion was .50, except statement 3 for which expected proportion was .60.

College Students

Shortly after the WRITER'S WORKBENCH programs became available at AT&T Bell Laboratories, CSU began a project to use editing programs to help composition students revise and edit their papers before turning them in for marking (Kiefer & Smith, 1983; Smith & Kiefer, 1982). Since programs for textual analysis might help students edit surface errors as well as revise content and organization, CSU had begun to use such programs when the WRITER'S WORKBENCH system appeared. The *style, diction,* and *suggest* programs were available to CSU from AT&T Bell Laboratories at the time, and CSU began further discussions with AT&T Bell Laboratories to test the entire WRITER'S WORKBENCH system.

CSU began testing *diction, suggest,* and *style* in a pilot project in September, 1981, with 38 students in college composition. With the signing of a research exchange between AT&T Bell Laboratories and CSU in November, parts of the WRITER'S WORKBENCH system useful for composition students were selected[4] and organized. In spring, the pilot project grew to 140 students using 17 programs from the WRITER'S WORKBENCH system. After successful tests, described later in this chapter, CSU expanded the project to include nearly the entire composition program in the fall of 1982. During the fall and spring of 1982–83, 37 faculty members and 28 graduate teaching assistants instructed 2,800 students who used the WRITER'S WORKBENCH programs for all writing assignments. Currently, about 4,000 students at CSU use the programs each year.

Implementing the Programs. The CSU project began with parts of the WRITER'S WORKBENCH system, hence the new additions extended the line of thinking begun earlier. Designed to be used by technical writers, however, the WRITER'S WORKBENCH system needed to be altered for specific classroom needs. The first semester pilot study, for example, showed that young writers with limited time at a few terminals needed paper copy to make thoughtful use of program analyses. *Style,* for instance, notes overreliance on subject openers, but students in the first pilot study—if they had time for stylistic revisions at all—made little use of this advice in their revisions. Much as *style* piqued students' interest, on-line revision in response to all its analyses was impossible. Furthermore, students do not need the entire set of WRITER'S WORKBENCH programs. Some programs, for example, are not relevant to student writing. The *acronym* program, useful for technical writers in finding undefined acronyms, rarely speaks to the problems of students. The *sexist* program, similarly, includes job titles CSU students never use in their writing.

To solve problems caused by limited terminal time and constraints of some programs, CSU[5] altered program dictionaries, selected and organized programs and program parts, and put the resulting tailored programs under one name so that they would all run with a single command. (The architecture of the UNIX operating

---

4 We thank Thomas McCall, CSU Computer Center, for his help.

5 The work of Blake Stewart, analyst at the CSU Computer Center, is greatly appreciated.

system and the WRITER'S WORKBENCH software were designed to facilitate such modifications.) As a result of these changes, students receive printed copies of their essays with output from a revised version of the programs. Hard copy, of course, permits economical use of terminal time, encourages complete and thoughtful revision, and offers a view of the entire text, not merely the 21 lines visible on a standard video display screen. To help students apply program advice to their papers and to replace the WRITER'S WORKBENCH system's on-line informational programs, a user manual was prepared and distributed to all students in computer-assisted composition classes (Smith & Kiefer, 1983). Thus, a major contribution of the staff at CSU was to tailor the system for local use. For this purpose, educational software must allow users to easily add and subtract new system components such as dictionaries.

One new program, two new dictionaries, and several other changes completed the current CSU version of the WRITER'S WORKBENCH programs. These changes included regrouping and renaming commands so that only certain facilities were used by students. These changes to the original programs are based on our professional biases about what a composition course should include. A review of the changes is given in Smith and Kiefer (1983). An important feature of the WRITER'S WORKBENCH software, and the UNIX system within which it operates, is that such local changes are easily done.

Students in the computer project at CSU continue to do little composing and revising at the keyboard. Rather, they bring handwritten rough drafts to the computer room, type them into the computer (with whatever revising they might ordinarily do when recopying a paper), run the *spell* program on-line to remove obvious typographical and spelling errors, and then call for the programs to run. Students collect hard copy, work on revisions in class, in conference, or at home, return to the computer to make changes in the text, and print out a clean copy. After instructors grade papers, instructors may ask students to revise again. Computer records of papers are available for about three weeks so that students may revise the computer file rather than retype the entire paper.

CSU's implementation of the WRITER'S WORKBENCH system in its writing programs does not necessarily change the composition classroom. Teachers can, if they choose, teach their classes just as they have in the past. Two years' experience has shown, however, that students heed the computer suggestions more if they have specific guidance from an instructor or a well-informed peer editor. Some teachers, thus, incorporate peer review, long encouraged by the recommended syllabus for college composition at CSU. Others, using the WRITER'S WORKBENCH system as an adjunct to their classes, rely mainly on exercises to help students understand the suggestions offered by the programs. Still others discuss program output in weekly conferences rather than in the classroom itself.

Design. CSU tested the WRITER'S WORKBENCH in college composition classes in two pilot projects during the first year of installation (Kiefer & Smith,

1983). The control groups were run in the fall semester and the experimental groups in the spring semester, when students in college composition had access to the revised programs. Thus, students who used the WRITER'S WORKBENCH programs were all in the spring semester, whereas those not using the programs were in the fall semester; hence the experimental data must be interpreted cautiously.

We measured changes in students' attitudes and in their writing and editing skills. Tests used in this study were identical to those reported in Kiefer and Smith (1983). (Later, we summarize data from that study for comparison with the present one.) Four experienced teachers of college composition (CC)—two regular faculty and two graduate students—had taught sections in the fall semester and had collected data to use for comparison with their experimental sections in the spring semester. All instruments were administered as pre- and posttests both semesters. Teachers followed the same syllabus, used the same textbook, and gave the same assignments in both the fall and the spring semesters. These teachers did not discuss computer suggestions with students in the spring semester so that changes, if any, could be attributed to use of the WRITER'S WORKBENCH programs.

Subjects. In the control groups in the fall, 99 students completed the course taught by the teachers picked for the yearlong experiment. Of these, 39 were freshmen, 57 sophomores, and 3 juniors; half were female, half male. In the spring semester, the experimental group included 83 students: 61 freshmen, 21 sophomores, 1 junior; 64% were female.

Procedures. Students registering for CC in the spring semester knew that they would be using a computer as part of the course but did not know that they would be involved in a test of its effectiveness. Before students heard any details about the computer, all teachers with experimental sections administered the attitude survey and the editing quizzes (one of two parallel forms). The editing tests included a section on mechanics (spelling and punctuation, for instance), and another section that required students to make editorial changes. The attitude test included 33 short statements about various topics. Students rated their agreement with these statements on a 5-point scale. Teachers then explained how the computer would assist students in preparing papers. In the second class meeting, teachers asked students for an impromptu writing sample—an original short essay summarizing and responding to a selected essay.

Students were then assigned to use the computer at times fitting into their class schedules. Throughout the semester, students had one hour to transcribe a written rough draft into the computer, check spelling, and call for output from the programs. Just before the paper was submitted for grading, students returned to the computer for a second half-hour to revise as they wished, based on computer suggestions.

In the fifth and tenth weeks of the semester, students in the experimental groups completed short surveys of their attitudes toward the computer. During the final exam period, students wrote a second writing sample—again an impromptu summary-and-response essay.

Results

Student and teacher attitudes. In the pre- and posttest attitude survey, only one of eight questions about computer-assisted instruction showed a significant difference for control and experimental groups. Students in control groups were unsure in response to "Computer-assisted instruction damages student-teacher relationships." Students in experimental groups were unsure at the beginning of the semester but disagreed at the end of the semester (change $p<.01$).

Surveys of users' attitudes toward the computer text editor and the WRITER'S WORKBENCH programs showed that 85% of the students easily learned to use the computer and that over 75% found the course more enjoyable because of the computer. Over 60% felt they were learning more about style and diction with the WRITER'S WORKBENCH programs. Finally, to our pleasant surprise, 65% said they would look forward to another composition class if it used computers.

On an attitude survey, instructors participating in the experiment all agreed that uniform formatting and typing make grading papers easier, that the programs sensitize students to language more quickly than grading does, and that the feedback students get from the programs helps in grading when students see the computer flagging the same items instructors mark. Other points on which the instructors teaching experimental sections agreed include the more positive student attitude in CC, more rapid student progress in the course, and an increased instructional emphasis on style. Instructors agreed that CC students should learn style and diction as emphasized by the WRITER'S WORKBENCH programs, that the computer programs have a positive effect on students' papers and editing skills, and that, although they grade papers no more quickly, they now have more time for substantive comments.

Performance. Two-way analyses of variance, using groups (control and experimental) and tests (pre- and posttests) as independent variables, were conducted. Comparison of pre- and posttests showed that the programs had positive effects on writing skills under some conditions, but in most cases effects were comparable to those with the control subjects. Analysis of the pre- and postwriting samples, too, suggested that the programs may improve writing in general (composition holistic ratings) beyond that achieved by the control subjects, but intriguing interactions, between treatment and pre- and posttest, did not reach beyond the .10 level of significance. We forego discussion of such interesting "tendencies" in favor of a cautious interpretation of the obvious effects. Semester gains on all variables were significant for the holistic and editing tests for both control and experimental groups. Thus, all students learned, and they learned a great deal. Table 3 summarizes the findings, and it also reports data from the earlier study (Kiefer & Smith, 1983). (Study 1 in Table 3 is the Kiefer and Smith study; Study 2 is the present study.) Scores reported in Table 3 are gain scores. Strongest gains came from changes in scores on the revision tests, where posttest scores were usually twice that of the original scores. All gains, from pre- to posttest, were significant.

Students were asked in both semesters to record the time they spent composing, typing, and revising texts on two essays. A few generalizations: Some students

Table 3. Gains on Editing and Holistic Tests from Two Studies

Tests	Study 1		Study 2	
	Control	Experimental	Control	Experimental
Holistic	1.9	1.1	1.1	1.5
Editing				
Mechanics	2.3	4.9	3.0	2.5
Revision	6.2	10.6	4.6	5.6

Note: The *N*s in Study 1 for control and experimental groups were 46 and 38, respectively. In Study 2, *N*s were approximately 99 and 78 (not all students were available for all tests).

spend many hours composing their essays and some as little time as possible; typical students spend between 6 and 8 hours preparing papers, whether they use the computer and the WRITER'S WORKBENCH programs or not; teachers demand and get about the same commitment from term to term—one teacher's students, in fact, spending the same amount of time (7.5 hours) on a comparison/contrast topic in both fall and spring; students spend about the same time typing their essays whether they use the computer or not. Students spend very little or very much time revising—one student, for example, spending 11 hours revising a paper his classmates spent less than an hour on.

Using the WRITER'S WORKBENCH programs, then, appears to require no more time than preparing papers in the standard way, but students using the computer did one more revision before handing in their papers than students in the control sections.

Conclusions

Data collected on the validity of programs suggest that the most critical ones work well even with poor quality writing. For instance, the *parts* program, the basis for many judgments in the WRITER'S WORKBENCH programs, is quite robust in the face of poor quality English. This means that the programs could be used at lower grades than we had expected, or perhaps to help with English as a second language.

The WRITER'S WORKBENCH programs clearly provide important supports for composition: The *spell* program alone saves poor spellers much editing time and encourages average spellers to look up questionable spellings. But beyond mechanical aids that improve the look of the typed page, as teachers of English we feel that the programs are important teaching aids. Because of the programs, instructors had more time available in class to teach other than mechanics. While computers and the WRITER'S WORKBENCH programs may not reduce total composition time, they stimulate teachers and students to more thoughtful use of that time. In fact, students using the WRITER'S WORKBENCH programs averaged one more revision of their papers, compared to other students, before handing them in. Furthermore, according to attitude tests, instructors believe the programs have a significant effect on student writing. Industrial employees share the view that the programs help improve writing skills.

Our research data do not reveal massive differences between control and experimental groups, although two thirds of our experimental comparisons favored groups using computers in composition. There is also the question of whether computer use itself, independent of the software, encourages positive changes in writing. In short, there are many questions about writing with computers that should be explored, yet experiments to date have been mainly field trials that rely on intact classrooms. Finer experimental designs are needed to determine the subtle effects of such programs and to explore important theoretical questions.

We have seen students whose attention is often drawn to a surface weakness revise beyond simple editing for the error, particularly with programs that suggest patterns of vagueness or stylistic weakness. Some students attend only to the specific point the computer notes, but more students find themselves recasting entire paragraphs because they can, with computer help, see their texts objectively. Even if the computer suggestion is inappropriate, students look at the word, sentence, or paragraph in a way they did not before. In fact, indirect consequences of computer aids for writing may be as important as the direct ones (Frase, 1984; Hayes, 1984); we suggest this as an important area for further research.

Finally, many students prefer to receive critical feedback from an impartial machine. Too often students reject teachers' marginal comments because they see teachers as unfairly biased against "their style." Students rarely accuse the computer of such bias.

Summary

This paper has a few simple themes. The first is the potential for really interesting computer applications when people from different domains work together. Quite simply, the combined effect of people from computer science, English composition, and psychology, has led to automated writing aids (and ours are not the only ones) that may very well help writers improve their texts and learn more about their craft. We believe that computer applications will increasingly encourage such interdisciplinary cooperation.

Another theme has been the role of computers in translating rules and exhortations into stable public educational artifacts. The WRITER'S WORKBENCH programs embody the theories and biases of teachers of English. Having these as programs makes them available for all to use and for all to criticize. A related theme here is the importance of a congenial computing environment to ease creation and transfer of these educational resources.

Yet another goal of the chapter was to review data on program validity and instructional consequences. We saw evidence of program validity and were encouraged, but certainly not convinced, by experimental data showing that program users do as well, and frequently better, than students who do not use the programs. Users, almost without exception, are highly positive about the potential consequences of the programs; however, definitive studies have yet to be done.

A most important point is the ease with which we can now move instructional ideas and tools from one classroom to another. Important advances have and will come, not just from developing programs to do small jobs, but rather from carefully laying the groundwork for the exchange of tools within academic domains. To a large extent, the work we described is an example of such an exchange.

References

Berrian, R. W., Metzler, D. P., Kroll, N. E. A., & Clark-Meyers, G. M. (1979). Estimates of imagery, ease of definition, and animateness for 328 adjectives. *Journal of Experimental Psychology: Human Learning and Memory, 5,* 435–447.

Cherry, L. L. (1980). PARTS—A system for assigning word classes to English text. Computing Science Technical Report No. 81. Murray Hill, NJ: Bell Laboratories.

Cherry, L. L. Writing tools. (1982). *IEEE Transactions on Communication, VOL. COM-30,* (1) 100–105.

Cherry, L. L., Fox, M. L., Frase, L. T., Gingrich, P. S., Keenan, S. A., & Macdonald, N. H. (1983). Computer aids for text analysis. *Bell Laboratories Record,* May/June, 10–16.

Cherry, L. L., & Macdonald, N. H. (1983). The UNIX WRITER'S WORKBENCH Software. *Byte, 8* (10), 241–246.

Coke, E. U. (1974). The effects of readability on oral and silent reading rates. *Journal of Educational Psychology, 66,* 406–409.

Duda, R. O., & Shortliffe, E. H. (1983). Expert systems research. *Science, 220,* 261–268.

Frase, L. T. (1981). Ethics of imperfect measures. *IEEE Transactions on Technical Communications, PC-24,* 48–50.

Frase, L. T. (1983). The UNIX Writer's Workbench Software: Philosophy. *Bell System Technical Journal, 62* (No. 6, Part 3), 1883–1890.

Frase, L. T. (1984). Knowledge, information, and action: Requirements for automated writing instruction. *Journal of Computer-Based Instruction, 11,* 55–59.

Frase, L. T., Gingrich, P. S., & Keenan, S. A. (1981, April). *Computer content analysis and writing instruction.* Paper presented at the annual meeting of the American Educational Research Association, Los Angeles.

Frase, L. T., Keenan, S. A., & Dever, J. J. (1980). Human performance in computer-aided writing and documentation. In P. A. Kolers, M. E. Wrolstad, & H. Bouma (Eds.), *Processing of visual language, II.* New York: Plenum.

Frase, L. T., Macdonald, N. H., Gingrich, P. S., Keenan, S. A., & Collymore, J. L. (1981). Computer aids for text assessment and writing instruction. *Performance & Instruction Journal,* November, 21–24.

Frase, L. T., Macdonald, N. H., & Keenan, S. A. (in press). Intuitions, algorithms, and a science of text design. In T. Duffy & R. Waller (Eds.), *Designing usable test.* New York: Academic Press.

Gingrich, P. S. (1983). The UNIX Writer's Workbench Software: Results of a field study. *Bell System Technical Journal, 62* (No. 6, Part 3), 1909–1921.

Hartley, J. Eighty ways of improving instructional text. (1981). *IEEE Transactions on Professional Communication, PC-24,* 17–27.

Hayes, J. R. (1984, April). *Detecting text problems.* Paper presented at the annual meeting of the American Educational Research Association, New Orleans.

Kiefer, K. E., & Smith, C. R. (1983). Textual analysis with computers: Tests of Bell Laboratories' computer software. *Research in the Teaching of English, 17,* 201–214.

Kinneavy, J. J. (1971). *A theory of discourse.* New York: Norton.

Klee, H., & Legge, D. (1976). Estimates of concreteness and other indices for 200 transitive verbs. *Journal of Experimental Psychology: Human Learning and Memory, 2,* 497–507.

Lanham, R. A. (1979). *Revising prose.* New York: Scribner.

Macdonald, N. H. (1983). The UNIX Writer's Workbench Software: Rationale and design. *Bell System Technical Journal, 62* (No. 6, Part 3), 1891–1908.

Macdonald, N. H., Frase, L. T., Gingrich, P. S., & Keenan, S. A. (1982). The Writer's Workbench: Computer aids for text analysis. *IEEE Transactions on Communication (Special issue on communication in the automated office), COM-30*(1), 105–110. Also in L. T. Frase (Ed.), Special issue: The psychology of writing. *Educational Psychologist,* 1982, *17,* 172–179.

McMahon, L. E., Cherry, L. L., & Morris, R. (1978). UNIX time-sharing system: Statistical text processing. *Bell System Technical Journal, 6,* 2137–2154.

Mosenthal, P., Tamor, L., & Walmsley, S. A. (1983). *Research on writing.* New York: Longman.

Paivio, A., Yuille, J. C., & Madigan, S. (1968). Concreteness, imagery, and meaningfulness values for 925 nouns. *Journal of Experimental Psychology Monograph, 76* (1, Pt.2).

Smith, C. R., & Kiefer, K. E. (1982). Computer-assisted editing in expository writing. *Proceedings of the Second Annual Micro Ideas Conference,* 87–90.

Smith, C. R., & Kiefer, K. E. (1983). Using the Writer's Workbench programs at Colorado State University. In S. K. Burton & D. D. Short (Eds.), *Sixth International Conference on Computers and the Humanities.* Rockville, MD: Computer Science Press.

Wainer, H., & Thissen, D. (1981). Graphical data analysis. *Annual Review of Psychology, 32,* 191–241.

PART III

Theories of and Research on Revision

11

How "Normal" Speaking Leads to "Erroneous" Punctuating

Jane Danielewicz
Wallace Chafe
University of California, Berkeley

In this chapter we extend Mina Shaughnessy's (1977) discussion of punctuation errors by considering some of the ways in which the punctuation habits of inexperienced writers reflect the considerable prior experience which all of them have had as speakers. The writers we will be looking at are freshman college students. They have had at least a decade and a half of experience in speaking and listening, with almost constant practice and reinforcement in these skills in their daily lives. In contrast, their familiarity with reading, and even more with writing, is based on scant and spotty experience at best. It is no wonder that so many students are speaking experts and writing novices. And it is no wonder, as we will illustrate, that they carry over into their writing various practices which are less at home there, even though as spoken practices they may be quite normal and unremarkable.

Shaughnessy made several points about the punctuation habits of inexperienced writers. One was that their punctuation repertoire consists of little more than commas, periods, and capitalization. Such writers make only infrequent use of question marks, exclamation points, and quotation marks; less use of semicolons; almost no use of parentheses, hyphens, and dashes; and absolutely no use of dots (for ellipsis), brackets, or underlining (Shaughnessy, 1977, p. 17). Another point was that a basic writer has problems with punctuation "not because he has no competence with sentences at all but because the writing down of sentences introduces new competencies that he has not been taught, including not only a knowledge of the names and functions of the various marks but also an ability to manage the structure that writers depend upon to overcome the redundancy, fragmentation, and loose sequencing that are natural in speech" (Shaughnessy, 1977, p. 27).

Our plan here is to compare some of the ways basic writers use commas and periods with analogous uses of intonation and pauses by educated speakers. We will show that writers at this stage do not, in fact, suffer from a lack of knowledge of what commas and periods are for. If they suffer from anything, it is from a lack of knowledge of the special kinds of structures that are characteristic of writing but not of speaking, as Shaughnessy suggested. Their use of commas and periods reflects in many cases an accurate appreciation of how these marks may be used to capture prosodic features of normal speech. Their ''errors'' come from assuming that the uses of spoken language can be transferred to writing without change.

Because spoken and written language have special purposes and special constraints on their production, the two differ also in form. Written language is not simply speech written down, nor, of course, is spoken language a faulty rendition of writing. We thus find different characteristics which are typical of each mode, even though spoken language often contains some written-like features and vice versa.

The processes of speaking and writing differ in various ways. Speakers typically produce language spontaneously and rapidly in a socially interactive environment. Writers typically produce language deliberately and slowly, in isolation from others (Ong, 1982). Since speech is primary in order of acquisition, experience with writing develops inevitably out of an existing experience with speaking. This priority is particularly evident in the creations of inexperienced writers, for whom the transition from speaking to writing skill has not fully materialized. Inexperienced writers often create prose whose form is neither wholly spoken nor wholly written. Our purpose here will be to identify some features of spoken language intonation and pausing which such writers carry over to written punctuation. In so doing we hope to go some way toward clarifying the kind of influence that spoken language may have on the composing process.

We have found that punctuation errors can be a valuable source of information on how speaking influences writing. In writing, punctuation is a device for dividing texts into units, or to signal semantic and syntactic relationships. In speaking, such functions are performed by prosody, above all by intonation and pausing. Written punctuation reflects to some degree the intonational and pause boundaries of speech. One might, therefore, expect that writers could learn to punctuate well by relying on their intuitive knowledge of spoken language prosody. Unfortunately, the relation between spoken prosody and written punctuation is not a simple one, and this fact creates problems for inexperienced writers who have not yet become familiar with the complexity of the relation.

Our written punctuation "error" data come from writing which was produced by students in a remedial freshman writing program at Berkeley. Our spoken language data come from a project to investigate differences between speaking and writing, sponsored by the National Institute of Education, Grant G-80-0125 (Chafe, 1982; Chafe, in press; Chafe & Danielewicz, in press). The speakers were university people (professors and graduate students) engaged in dinnertable conversations, or (in a few cases) in talking informally to a class.

Intonation Units and Sentences

Most of our discussion will be based on the interplay between two kinds of spoken language units and their analogues in written language. The spoken language units we will call "intonation units" and "sentences." Both require some discussion.

Recent research on spoken language has converged on the identification of a prosodic unit which appears to be the minimal unit of spoken language production (compare, for example, the "information units" of Halliday, 1967; the "tone

units" of Crystal, 1975; and the "idea units" of Chafe, 1980). This unit is characterized above all by a single, coherent intonation contour. Usually it contains a
single intonation peak, and usually it is preceded and followed by a pause. In the
following illustrative sequence of intonation units the pauses are indicated with
three dots. A comma indicates a phrase-final intonation (typically a rising pitch),
while a period indicates a sentence-final intonation (a falling pitch). Henceforth the
pitch patterns transcribed in these two ways will be referred to as "comma intonations" and "period intonations," respectively.

Example 1 (spoken)

(a) ... It's possible,
(b) ... isn't it,
(c) ... that since emotions are so murky,
(d) ... and so hard to understand,
(e) ... that even when you do understand them,
(f) ... you seldom understand them in the way you could explain to someone else.
(g) ... That there's very little that you could say to someone.
(h) ... Who's young.
(i) ... That could in any sense educate them.

We have hypothesized (Chafe, 1980) that these intonation units are the linguistic
expressions of single focuses of attention on the part of the speaker. They appear to
represent the amount of information which a speaker can focus on and verbalize at
one time. The mean number of words in an intonation unit in English is about six,
and its mean duration, including pauses, is about two seconds.

Sentences in spoken language are more problematic (Chafe, 1980, pp. 20–29).
Whereas the majority of intonation units end with a comma intonation, some end
with a period intonation. The period intonation gives an impression of closure or
finality to the preceding sequence of intonation units. Sometimes this period intonation coincides with grammatical or syntactic closure, and in that case we feel
satisfied in concluding that it signals the boundary of a sentence. Such is the case at
the end of intonation unit (f). At other times the period intonation marks off a unit
which is not grammatically a sentence, for example intonation units (g), (h), and (i).
In cases like these we have the impression that the speaker has added a series of
afterthoughts to the coherent sentence which preceded them.

We can look now at several types of cases in which a speaker has produced a
prosodic structure which is quite natural in speaking, but which, when produced
analogously in written language yields a punctuation structure that is nonstandard.
From these examples we will see that inexperienced writers have learned quite well
to represent what we are calling a comma intonation with a written comma, and
what we are calling a period intonation with a written period. Their mistakes stem
from their facility in doing this, combined with their failure to realize that there are
certain conventions of writing which disallow such direct representations of speak-

ing. We will discuss first certain nonstandard uses of commas, the most prevalent type of "error," and then certain nonstandard uses of periods which result from a similar carryover of spoken habits.

Nonstandard Uses of Commas

There is a style of speaking in which a relatively long sequence of intonation units occurs with comma intonation at the end of each unit, and in which many of these intonation units are syntactically complete sentences. Only after many such comma intonations have been produced does the speaker finally come to rest with a period intonation:

Example 2 (spoken)

(a) ... Everybody comes,
(b) ... they hire a band,
(c) ... they have it at one of the halls,
(d) the Moose Hall,
(e) the— knights of Columbus Hall,
(f) ... everybody comes and gets drunk,
(g) ... lo—ng tables,
(h) everybody dresses up,
(i) it's terrific though,
(j) cause everybody of every age comes,
(k) ... and they're dressed,
(l) ... it's just fantastic you know.

Here there are a number of syntactically complete sentences that fail to end with the period intonation usually associated with the ends of sentences. When this speaker finally arrived at a period intonation, it signaled something which might more appropriately be regarded as a paragraph boundary than the ending of a sentence.

A similar style may surface among inexperienced writers, who use commas effectively to represent the comma intonation of speech, and periods to represent the period intonation, according to a similar pattern:

Example 3 (written)

(a) Now I am so confused that I don't know that to call them because their moods change so much,
(b) they want to be called something different every hour,
(c) I think the easiest thing to call them is ruthless animals that know how to pick the soft spots in males.

Although the written punctuation units here are longer than the intonation units in the spoken example (as is typical in writing), this writer similarly failed to use periods where they would have been appropriate. Just as the speaker of Example 2 kept her sentence alive with comma intonations, seemingly for a longer period than necessary, so the writer of Example 3 used commas in an analogous way.

Although we cannot answer this question at the moment, it would be interesting to know whether some speakers are more prone than others to use the kind of comma intonation pattern illustrated in Example 2, and whether it is just those speakers who, as beginning writers, are most apt to write in the style of Example 3. If that should turn out to be true, then instruction in the avoidance of that style in writing could be especially aimed at such individuals.

Note the lack of sentence final pitches in the following example from spoken language (a sequence of two dots indicates an especially short pause):

Example 4 (spoken)

(a) ... It's funny though,
(b) ... I do think that makes a difference but,
(c) ... I can recall ... uh ... a big undergraduate class that I had,
(d) ... where ... everybody loved the instructor,
(e) ... and he was a ... real .. um .. old world ... Swiss guy,
(f) ... this was a biology course,
(g) ... a—nd he ... left all of the .. sort of .. uh ... real contact with students .. up to .. his assistants.

Again, by the time this speaker had come to the sentence-final intonation, he had created something resembling a paragraph.

Notice, now, how the following writer used a similar strategy at the end of the first independent clause, marking it with a comma rather than a period:

Example 5 (written)

(a) Take for example the people of the Tiv tribe,
(b) because their culture had instilled in them certain morals and values,
(c) their thought and ideas could only reflect those traditions.

It is interesting that the initial clauses in both Examples 4 and 5 functioned to provide an introductory orientation for the sentence to follow. By failing to signal the end of a sentence at the end of the first clause, both the speaker and the writer emphasized the semantic link between that clause and the material to follow.

In the following example, on the other hand, the first intonation unit is something more like a topic sentence:

Example 6 (written)

(a) Language has played a major role in the survival of mankind,
(b) without such a precise means of communication I doubt that humans would have progressed as quickly as they did.

Inexperienced writers are thus likely in various ways to exhibit a lack of strict correspondence between syntactic closure and sentence-final intonation, a lack which they are quite accustomed to in ordinary speaking.

By far the most common form for a spoken intonation unit to take is that of the clause. A clause is composed of a subject and a predicate, and normally both are verbalized together in a single unit. Not infrequently, however, a speaker will devote one intonation unit to the subject and another to the predicate:

Example 7 (spoken)

(a) ... You see human relationships,
(b) ... are the things,
(c) ... that are the most subtle,
(d) ... and the most difficult to understand.

We are concerned for now with the break at the end of (a), the subject of the sentence. (The kind of break which occurs at the end of (b) will be discussed later.) There is evidence that speakers are unable to verbalize within a single intonation unit more than one concept that has been recalled from long-term memory (Chafe, in press). If that is true, it explains why the subject of a sentence sometimes appears as a separate intonation unit. The speaker's cognitive capacity in an example like this one was insufficient to verbalize subject and predicate together in a single intonation unit. As a result, the subject noun phrase was produced with its own separate intonation contour, with the predicate following after a pause. This pattern is particularly frequent when the subject is a long one:

Example 8 (spoken)

(a) ... Like almost anyone .. Cindy ... meets when we're like at the beach or in the park,
(b) ... will ... uh—ask how old he is.

Evidently inexperienced writers who do the same are reflecting an awareness of this quite familiar spoken pattern. Here are some examples, with increasingly long and complex subjects:

Example 9 (written)

(a) Changing the meaning of all our words,
(b) would be like creating a new language.

Example 10 (written)

(a) Something that must be understood when attempting to clarify the reason for a lack of universal communication,
(b) is that language has very little to do with misinterpretation.

Example 11 (written)

(a)   If it is true that people of different cultures but of the same language background cannot interpret situations in the same fashion then the theory that culture and not language is what forms and creates thought,

(b)   is true and correct.

Sometimes this style of punctuating can create a temporary ambiguity for the reader:

Example 12 (written)

(a)   But if you wanted to use language as a tool of communication or self expression,

(b)   the constant change which Humpty Dumpty talks about,

(c)   is neither practical nor responsible.

The phrase enclosed by commas—"the constant change which Humpty Dumpty talks about"—seems at first to be in apposition to "a tool of communication or self expression," even though that interpretation makes little sense. The reader is then surprised to find in (c) that (b) was actually the subject of the sentence. We use this example to emphasize the point that normal spoken strategies, when transferred to writing, can lead to problems in understanding for a reader.

Speakers will sometimes produce a comma intonation at the end of a clause which is then followed either by a restrictive relative clause, as in Example 13 (see also Example 7) or by a complement clause, as in Example 14:

Example 13 (spoken)

(a)   And the letters are supposed to represent the noise,

(b)   that the informant made.

Example 14 (spoken)

(a)   ...   There's always the possibility,

(b)   ..   that one reason why there's no education along those lines,

(c)   ...   is that .. nobody can think of anything to say about it.

In such cases the speaker seems to have thought of, and to have presented, the first clause as a separate item of information—"the letters are supposed to represent the noise,"—"there's always the possibility,"—with the following relative clause or complement clause then expressing a second idea. Such examples show, at least, that speakers may focus their attention separately, first on a main clause, and then on a relative or complement clause dependent on it.

Similar examples appeared in our writing samples. Example 15 shows a comma before a restrictive relative clause, and Example 16 shows a comma before a complement clause introduced by "that":

Example 15 (written)

(a) One of these other categories,
(b) that I can be classified in is that of an only child.

Example 16 (written)

(a) It is true,
(b) that it is not necessary to state this entire phrase in order to simply say that it is against the law to lie in court.

Here the writers, like the speakers in Examples 13 and 14, focused separately on the first element—"one of these other categories,"—"it is true,"—before shifting their attention to the information in the dependent clause.

In general, speakers often use a comma intonation to end an intonation unit after one item has been recalled from long-term memory, pausing before the next item, regardless of the effect this procedure may have on the overall syntax. They may do so in less obviously motivated places than those illustrated above. For example, in 17 there is a pause between a numeral and the complex noun phrase to which it is logically attached. Evidently the numeral was costly enough of cognitive effort to merit its own intonation boundary:

Example 17 (spoken)

(a) There were a good six,
(b) ... different .. problems and resolutions in that story.

Inexperienced writers do similar things. For example, here is a written comma boundary after the quantifier "whole," which contrasts markedly with the commaless sequence after it:

Example 18 (written)

(a) Lucy never was able to form whole,
(b) and completely new sentences whereas Helen was able to start conversations and express her ideas.

In Example 19 there are commas, first between a preposition and its object, then before a prepositional phrase:

Example 19 (written)

(a) This is why many only children will have things like,
(b) expensive cars and clothes that other children,
(c) from large families don't have.

The following speaker stopped temporarily after an adjective ("nasty"), where there might have been a valid clause boundary, but then added a prepositional phrase:

Example 20 (spoken)

(a) ... Because he was nasty,
(b) ... to someone and therefore they wouldn't lend him ... their notes for a particular class the next week.

This writer did something similar:

Example 21 (written)

(a) It is much more effective to extend the meaning of truth,
(b) into a sentence,
(c) rather than to simply define it.

Speakers tend to chain intonation units together by using coordinating or subordinating conjunctions like "and" or "because." Sometimes, after such a conjunction, they will add an adverbial phrase which sets a framework for whatever follows. In such cases it is typically true that the conjunction plus the adverbial phrase will form one intonation unit, separate from what follows:

Example 22 (spoken)

(a) ... And ... it seems like a ... f—airly fruitless debate,
(b) ..   because lots of times,
(c) ... things that have the same function have the same shape you know.

Of interest here is the intonation unit "because lots of times," composed of a conjunction plus an adverbial phrase. If this were written language, the standard rules of punctuation would set off "lots of times" with commas on both sides. Evidently there is a tradition of writing to the effect that an adverbial phrase like this one breaks up the integrity of a sequence like "because things that have the same function, etc." It would seem, however, that speakers have a different logic. As they proceed in thought and speech toward the last main idea, they produce a conjunction and an adverbial clause together as a unitary introduction to that idea. The break is between all this introductory material as a whole and all the material which follows.

Inexperienced writers may do just the same. In the following example, line 23(b) is analogous to line 22(b). Proper written punctuation would have required a comma after the "and," but this writer followed the different, spoken strategy:

Example 23 (written)

(a) Language is responsible for describing and communicating ideas,

(b)   and with proper usage,
(c)   they can be the most important link we can have with our society in the past, present,
       and future.

Nonstandard Uses of Periods

Although inexperienced writers "err" more frequently in the use of commas, they
are by no means free of spoken-language–induced "errors" involving periods as
well. We saw in Example 2 that there is a style of speaking where there are few
period intonations: The comma intonation is used at the ends of many sentence-like
constructions. There also exists an inverse of that style in which the period intonation is used in place of many comma intonations. Here speakers use a falling pitch at
the end of every intonation unit. The following example is typical:

Example 24 (spoken)

(a)   It was in the summer.
(b)   And .. my room was small.
(c)   ... It was like ... nine by twelve or something.
(d)   It seemed spacious at the time.

       This is a style which represents an extreme degree of the kind of "fragmenta-
tion" to which spoken language is prone (Chafe, 1982). Not only intonation units
but sentences as well are produced as separate small chunks of speech which contain
an average of not more than six words each. Children often talk this way, but adults
sometimes do too, as the above example shows (Chafe, 1980, pp. 20–22).
       Inexperienced writers may produce the same kind of language:

Example 25 (written)

(a)   The night came when we landed at the airport.
(b)   To my amazement there was fog.
(c)   I thought that only San Francisco had a fog.
(d)   The airport was full of people and noisy.

Whereas someone listening to spoken language like that illustrated in 24 is not
likely to notice anything unusual, a reader, used to sentences of more varied length
and complexity, may find a passage like 25 choppy and uninteresting.
       Spoken language typically contains a number of intonation units which function
as afterthoughts, as noted in connection with Example 1 earlier. These are cases in
which the speaker produced a sentence-final syntactic and intonational closure but
then decided to add an additional phrase or clause. Such an added intonation unit, in
retrospect, would have belonged syntactically to the sentence which preceded it.
But it was by now too late for the speaker to delete the earlier period intonation.

For example, in the following sequence the speaker had finished a sentence at the end of the line (a), as was evident from both the syntax and the period intonation. At that point, however, she paused and then uttered (b). The latter functioned syntactically as a modifier of "the waste paper basket," and not, of course, as an additional sentence, but the speaker could not at this point retrace her steps to erase the period intonation she had already produced at the end of (a):

Example 26 (spoken)

(a) ... And I was sort of ... en .. disentangling my hair .. from the waste paper basket.
(b) ... Which is under there.

Often the "which" in such cases refers to the entire preceding sentence, as in the following example:

Example 27 (spoken)

(a) ... I just this year have ... dropped down to teaching halftime.
(b) .. Which is what I've always wanted.

Here are some analogous examples by inexperienced writers, who in a sense "erred" only in not realizing the nonstandard nature of this usage in written language:

Example 28 (written)

(a) Language limits the concepts of a culture to its own culture.
(b) Which means that there is much outside our own little world which we do not understand.

Example 29 (written)

(a) For this quality of work she receives much praise from her bosses.
(b) Which is the reason why fall is her favorite season.

Finally, we can take notice of those cases in which an afterthought consists of nothing more than a noun phrase, usually one which serves to amplify or substitute for the sentence-final noun phrase produced immediately before:

Example 30 (spoken)

(a) ... A—nd ... let's see Steve built a .. small .. kayak.
(b) .. One man sized kayak.

Quite parallel are the following written examples, where conventional punctuating would dictate either a comma or a colon in place of the first period:

Example 31 (written)

(a)   My father had taken pictures in Algeria.
(b)   Photographs of sand dunes, oases, lone automobiles on miles of crumbling asphalt
      roads.

Example 32 (written)

(a)   Anne Sullivan opened a new light in which Helen could begin to see.
(b)   The light of language,
(c)   and with this light Helen's soul did awaken.

Summary

We have seen that the way inexperienced writers use punctuation often reproduces
patterns found in spoken language, a fact which suggests that these writers are at
least adept at using commas and periods to capture the intonation and pauses of
speech. But, whereas the prosody of speech reflects the process of creating language spontaneously and rapidly in an interactive, social environment, the punctuation of writing only indirectly mimics and is often at odds with the spoken model.
The deliberateness, slowness, and solitariness of writing have led writers to evolve
their own literate structures, and their own rules for punctuating them. The result is
that carrying over spoken prosodic habits into the punctuation of writing often leads
to nonstandard, and sometimes infelicitous results. We do not, of course, mean to
say that all punctuation "errors" derive from familiar speech habits, but only that a
significant proportion of them do. There may well be other "errors" which can
only be regarded as the result of the under- or overlearning of punctuation rules.
   Among the nonstandard devices we have considered have been the following:

1.   the use of rising rather than falling pitch in speaking, and of commas in writing,
     at the ends of grammatical sentences (Examples 2–6)
2.   the introduction of an intonational boundary in speaking, or of a comma in
     writing, between the subject and the predicate of a clause (Examples 7–12)
3.   the introduction of an intonational boundary in speaking, or of a comma in
     writing, before a restrictive relative clause or a complement clause (Examples
     13–16)
4.   the introduction of an intonational boundary in speaking, or of a comma in
     writing, after significant pieces of information of other kinds (Examples 17–
     21)
5.   the failure to set off the beginning of an adverbial phrase with an intonational
     boundary in speaking, or with a comma in writing (Examples 22–23)
6.   the fragmentation of language into a series of brief units bounded with falling
     pitches in speaking, or with periods in writing (Examples 24–25)
7.   the addition of supplementary, "afterthought-like" material after a falling
     pitch boundary in speaking, or after a period in writing (Examples 26–32)

What are the implications for the teaching of writing? We believe that it is salutary for teachers to be aware that inexperienced writers may actually be doing a good job of representing in writing the already extensive knowledge they have of speaking. If their nonstandard punctuations can be seen as inappropriate extensions of spoken language into a different medium, not as random errors, then teachers can concentrate on pointing out specific ways in which the requirements of writing differ from those of speaking. Shaughnessy was right in suggesting that students need primarily an ability to manage the structures which are peculiar to writing and which differentiate it from speech.

To end with a bolder stance, we hazard the suggestion that carrying over speaking habits into writing may not in every instance be a bad thing. Perhaps punctuating as one speaks can in some cases lead to greater readability and greater impact, if only students can learn to do it with the judiciousness that writing allows and fosters.

References

Chafe, W. (1980). The deployment of consciousness in the production of a narrative. In W. Chafe (Ed.), *The pear stories: Cognitive cultural, and linguistic aspects of narrative production.* Norwood, NJ: Ablex.

Chafe, W. (1982). Integration and involvement in speaking, writing, and oral literature. In D. Tannen (Ed.), *Spoken and and written language: Exploring orality and literacy.* Norwood, NJ: Ablex.

Chafe, W. (in press). Cognitive constraints on information flow. R. Tomlin (Ed.), *Coherence and grounding in discourse.* Amsterdam: John Benjamin.

Chafe, W., & Danielewicz, J. (in press). Properties of spoken and written language. In R. Horowitz & S. J. Samuels (Eds.), *Comprehending oral and written language.* New York: Academic Press.

Crystal, D. (1975). *The English tone of voice.* London: St. Martin.

Halliday, M. A. K. (1967). Notes on transitivity and theme in English. Part 2. *Journal of Linguistics 3,* 199–244.

Ong, W. (1982). *Orality and literacy: The technologizing of the word.* London & New York: Methuen.

Shaughnessy, M. P. (1977). *Errors and expectations. A guide for the teacher of basic writing.* New York: Oxford University Press.

12

Revision, Addition, and the Power of the Unseen Text

Ann Matsuhashi
Eleanor Gordon
University of Illinois at Chicago

The concepts of *knowing that* and *knowing how* (Ryle, 1949) seem particularly well-suited to studies of writing. For while writers often regard their craft as a competence process, a *knowing how,* instruction is often centered on the *knowing that,* the principles that can be derived from the study of competence. Traditional instruction has usually recommended that the less skilled be made aware of these competence principles and urged to follow them.

Donald Murray (1984), in the introduction to his new "knowing how" writing text, poses the problem this way: "Our students do not learn to write, then write. . . . Few students can listen to a lecture on writing or read a textbook on writing in advance of writing and understand the lessons they may need to learn. We are asking them to imagine and understand an experience they have not yet had . . . . The challenge is to combine experience with instruction" (p. xiii). Ryle's comments are in accord with Murray's: "We learn *how* by practice, schooled indeed by criticism and example, but often quite unaided by any lessons in the theory" (Ryle, 1949, p. 41).

Ryle's prime example, fittingly, was Aristotle's rules of correct reasoning and argument. He pointed out that everyone "knew" these rules already, maintaining that no one "plans arguments before constructing them," and that "Efficient practice precedes the theory of it" (Ryle, 1949, p. 30). And while exercises of *knowing how* can be seen as observances of principles (usually tacit), "they are not tandem operations of theoretically avowing maxims and then putting them into practice" (Ryle, 1949, p. 46). In other words, a principle drawn from competent performance is meaningless to a learner if he or she has not somehow understood it already, in his or her own doing of the task.

The learner of *knowing how* is in continual training, training which necessarily consists of a task of some kind. This leads many to decide that the best way to "teach" writing is to simply set the students at it, on their own. But there is a real and effective role for the teacher—to increase opportunities for the most productive type of practice and to set up writing situations in such a way that student skills are expanded upon.

In what follows we will approach the study of revision from a *knowing how* point of view. First, we review several studies of revision which point to the limited revising competencies of beginning writers and to egocentrism as the cause for these limitations. We then review studies which explore the tacit knowledge students have for writing and revising. Finally, we describe our study: an attempt to learn what students can do when placed in revising situations which elicit the best that they *know how* to do. This leads us to examine student writers in their *knowing how* process and practice, and to text writing tasks in which, it is hypothesized, further *knowing how* skills are released, discovered, and developed.

Revision Research

Research Evidence of Limited Student Revision

The results of several key studies on revising converge on the following three points:

1. When asked to revise, inexperienced writers typically make only low-level mechanical and word-level changes (Bridwell, 1980; Emig, 1971; Faigley & Witte, 1981; Perl, 1979; Sommers, 1980; Stallard, 1974).
2. When asked about revising, these inexperienced writers define revising as rewording, error-hunting, and scratching out (Sommers, 1980).
3. Experienced writers exhibit a more sophisticated repertoire of revision strategies than do inexperienced writers (Faigley & Witte, 1981; Sommers, 1980).

These conclusions come from taxonomic descriptions of revisions and from interviews. Of particular interest for this study is the descriptive scheme developed by Faigley and Witte. Their scheme differed from the taxonomies of Bridwell and Sommers which identified only the linguistic level (e.g., word, clause, sentence) or the operation (e.g., addition, deletion, substitution) entailed by the revision. Instead, Faigley and Witte sought to identify revisions that affected the *meaning* of the text.

To this end they set up a taxonomy of revisions based on two distinctions: those that affect meaning (text-base changes) and those that do not (surface changes). Meaning-affecting changes introduce new information or remove old information. Surface changes simply paraphrase the content without altering the substance of the information. Faigley and Witte's study replicated the results summarized earlier; inexperienced writers' revisions were largely (88%) surface changes, whereas 24% of the advanced student revisions and 34% of expert adult revisions were text-base changes. An expert writer given a student text to revise produced a high percentage (65%) of text-base changes by concentrating on the three processes of addition, consolidation, and distribution. Faigley and Witte were thus able to demonstrate through text analysis what Sommers had concluded from interviews: Skilled writers go about revising in very different ways from unskilled writers. Our goal in the present study was to construct situations in which inexperienced writers might exhibit revising behaviors more like experienced writers'. The revisions made were to be studied as units of meaning, using Faigley and Witte's scheme.

Egocentrism as the Cause of Limited Revision Skills

Speculation on the reasons for students' writing difficulties abounds, much of it centering around an informal interpretation of the Piagetian concept of egocentrism: "a cognitive state in which a person fails to perceive others' perspectives" (Barritt & Kroll, 1978, p. 54). Also referred to as role-taking skill, this necessary ability requires that the writer recognize a need for effective communication, evaluate the nature of the task, and take the necessary steps to fulfill the task (Brown, 1980; Flavell, 1976).

Attempts to measure these dual communicative aspects of writing—audience awareness and role-taking ability—suggest that, in some cases, children increase syntactic complexity and use more abstract nouns for adult rather than peer audiences (Crowhurst & Piche, 1979; Martlew, 1983). But these results are by no means definitive. Walter Ong (1975) questions the extent to which writers actually consider audience. Furthermore, this somewhat casual interpretation of egocentrism (see Bruner, 1966, p. 78, for a critique) has been adopted wholesale by several researchers to explain limited revision skills, citing their students' inability to adopt the appropriate role-taking skills and to view their writing with detachment.

Beach's study (1976) compared extensive revisers and nonrevisers among college juniors and seniors and noted the ability of the revisers not only to see the text holistically, but also to detach themselves from their texts, to criticize them objectively. Nonrevisers were more egocentric, less able to view their writing with detachment. Noting that teacher evaluation produced improved revision whereas self-evaluation did not, Beach (1979) called for cooperation between student and teacher in evaluation, so that the teacher might foster an "outside perspective" in the student's view of his or her own writing.

Similarly, Lunsford (1980), who examined the content of basic writers' essays, found that basic writers focused on the self in their writing, that they had trouble decentering. A check of grammatical subjects of clauses revealed that preoccupations with self dominated their work. Both Beach and Lunsford call for "helping" less skilled writers: in Lunsford's (1980) words, to "become more proficient at abstracting and conceptualizing" (p. 287) and in Beach's (1976) words, to get away from "textbook conceptions" of revision as error-picking and "to provide alternative, helpful models of the revision process" (p. 164).

The complementary notions of writer-based prose and reader-based prose (Flower, 1981) also depend on the concept of egocentrism. Writer-based prose, "the record and the working of [the writer's] own verbal thought" (Flower, 1981, p. 19), is contrasted to reader-based prose, that which is autonomous and shares language and context between writer and reader. Flower (1981) advises instructors to concentrate on "teaching writers to recognize their own writer-based writing and transform it" (p. 37). She then offers techniques designed to change writer-based prose into reader-based prose: Select a focus of mutual interest to the writer and the reader, move from scenarios to concepts, and move from a narrative structure to a rhetorically appropriate structure.

All these insights based on the concept of egocentrism and its effect upon student writing seem too general to be valuable for observers' and teachers' understanding of where and how it is that unskilled writers fall short in revising techniques. As pedagogical advice they seem out of reach: Knowing *that* does not insure knowing *how*. Substitute analytic thinking for narration? Develop concepts, not facts? How can we be certain that a young writer can even understand these terms, let alone find it possible, cognitively and behaviorally, actually to do these things?

Research that Explores Students' Tacit Knowledge

While communicative awareness undoubtedly plays an important role in writing ability, at present we simply do not know much about how it contributes to revision processes (Nold, 1982). Further, to assume that the ability to take the audience's role when writing is equivalent to what a writer does when revising stretches our current knowledge further than it can reasonably be stretched. What we are left with, then, is a depressingly poor prognosis for our basic writers. When asked to revise, they focus on low-level mechanical and lexical changes, ignoring the organizational and rhetorical aspects of the text. But these remarkably stable research results may tell us more about the nature of the research task than about the tacit or hidden abilities of our students: What we really have learned is how students respond to the directive: "Revise!" Isn't it possible that students have an ability to revise that remains untapped by the research designs described earlier?

To explore this possibility we discuss the work of other researchers who have manipulated the writing or revising situation in an attempt to study the tacit knowledge of beginning writers. Most of these studies, it is important to note, are informed to some degree by a cognitive process theory which shapes the research design as well as the interpretation of the results. Such theories focus on the *how* of writing, positing underlying processes to explain the behaviors observed during writing.

One way to think about revision is to imagine a writer, thoroughly involved in the writing process—leaning forward over a desk or peering at a display terminal as the text accumulates. The writer is "on a roll," composing from sense to grapheme with little conscious awareness of the process. But then the writer, aware of some dissonance, stops, puts the pen down or saves the text in memory, and begins to reread, noting several problems with the text. The writer has shifted, we might say, to a "debugging mode." The changes that ensue, if any, we classify as revision. They may be as limited as a typographical correction or as complex as the sort of massive "re-vision" (Murray, 1978) that constitutes a new beginning.

The "debugging" analogy is useful, because it focuses our attention on the processes of revision rather than solely on descriptions of the size or type of linguistic units involved. Debugging and revising are both specialized problem-solving activities carried out in the intellectually demanding contexts of writing computer programs and writing texts. Anyone who writes software must be a debugger because, unless the program works the first time, changes must be made. (Obviously, the analogy breaks down: Unlike writing, a program either works or it does not.) And even though computer science students learn general guidelines for writing "error-free code," the debugging activity which necessarily follows is often referred to as an "art," reflecting a keen intuitive ability to locate and eliminate the problem.

Both problem-solving tasks, revising and debugging, share constraints on attention and memory. Whatever the task, writers or debuggers must function within the limited capacity of short term memory for conceptual bits of information. Fortunately, though, memory and planning operate strategically, chunking related bits of information together (Simon, 1969/1981; Hayes-Roth & Hayes-Roth, 1979) in response to intentions and goals. For the study of writing this means that even though one has limited focal attention to devote to any particular aspect of the writing task, one can *choose* the appropriate level at which to focus one's attention (Cooper & Matsuhashi, 1983; de Beaugrande, 1982, in press). As we demonstrate later in this chapter, even inexperienced writers can, during revising, choose to focus their attention on either low-level mechanical changes or high-level meaning changes.

Bartlett's (1982) research on revision strategies illustrates that children even as young as ten can direct focal attention to correct certain kinds of errors. Significantly, she found that children were better at detecting problems of referential ambiguity in *others'* texts than in their own. The fact that these children could apply these detection processes in one situation but not in another suggests that the skill is not controlled by a generalized egocentric inability to take the audience's point of view. Rather, these children had used different cognitive strategies adapted for the task.

Bartlett (1982) hypothesized that the ability to detect and correct certain kinds of errors depends on "the ease with which relevant knowledge can be recollected or represented" (p. 349). The fact that the young writers could not do the special sort of "rereading" required to detect such surface problems as referential ambiguity in their *own* texts suggests that the writers' attention was focused on a high-level meaning representation of the text. Apparently, quite the opposite occurred for the high school and college writers in Bridwell's, Sommers's, and Faigley and Witte's studies; these writers could not release themselves from an almost exclusive focal attention to surface error in their own texts.

Scardamalia, Bereiter, and Goelman (1982), like Bartlett, studied the attentional capacities of young children (grades 4 and 6). Of particular interest to our study is their examination of how young writers make the transition from the oral to written mode. By manipulating composing situations to simulate this transition, they were able to report some tentative conclusions about the cognitive processes at work during writing.

To overcome the usually low quantity of writing produced by children, Scardamalia et al. provided a social but contentless "cue" to spur production during writing and dictation. By asking the child to say more about the recently completed persuasive task, they hoped to replicate the kind of cues that keep a conversation rolling. They analyzed the persuasive tasks using a scheme based on Toulmin (1958) that suggested coherence ratings for the written and dictated texts. Before production cuing, the written texts ranked lowest in both quality and quantity. The cuing, it was found, led to improvement in the written texts but not the dictated ones. What this means for cognitive processes is that additional work on the written texts depended on the complexity of the mental representation of the preceding text. The dictated texts may have offered a less coherent framework for adding to the text. For college-level writers, the notion of adding material suggests interesting questions since several researchers have remarked on the paucity of additions during revision (Faigley & Skinner, 1982).

Questions for Research

The most productive area for further research in revision, we believe, concerns the effect of situation on writing. One sort of situation, a metacognitive one, occurs when we cue the writer to revise. This directive elicits a schooled response, a *knowing that* revision involves a limited range of surface structure manipulations. Another sort of situation, a cognitive one, elicits the writer's ability to orchestrate the myriad processes involved in writing and revising. This kind of knowledge, only intermittently conscious, represents a *knowing how,* a tacit ability to traverse the full range of revisions. Cuing the writer to add, we believed, would enable the writer to move beyond an exclusive concern with the text's surface. We also asked, how might we further enable writers to free themselves from surface constraints? Perhaps by removing the text, itself a seductive surface.

This perspective suggested that we study revision processes by designing three revising situations (described more fully in the Methods section) distinguished by three cues. The first of the three situations simply replicates the cue to revise. We were interested in establishing that our beginning college writers would produce the same sort of limited revision produced in the previously cited studies. The other two situations would illustrate, we hoped, a much broader range of revision for beginning college writers. For both of these revising situations we issued the cue to *add;* we thought *add* might be free of the strong metacognitive connotations that the word revise usually has for students. Further, use of the cue *add* responds to the single most common complaint about student revision: its failure to produce substantial, meaning additions to a typically spare text.

The second revising situation allowed the writer to add after rereading, while still looking at the text. In the third revising situation the writer added without looking at the text. A crucial question for us was, if, after rereading, students listed their planned additions based on a mental representation of the unseen text, would they then produce more high-level, text-base revisions?

Because these three situations seemed to offer progressively richer revising situations we hypothesized an increase in the mean proportion of text-base revisions in each of the two addition situations.

Method

Subjects

Subjects were enrolled in the basic composition course (101) at the University of Illinois at Chicago (UIC). Composition 101 is the first of two required writing courses; assignment to the 101 level is based on ACT scores and performance on a mandatory, objective placement test. Most students were freshmen, but a few were upperclassmen who had been unable to fit composition into their previous years' schedules. We relied on the randomness of computer assignment to determine that the six classes used for the study were typical. UIC is an urban commuter school with a high proportion of first generation, American-born students and nonnative speakers of English, both groups representing a wide range of racial and ethnic backgrounds. The majority attended Chicago public and parochial high schools, with the remainder from nearby systems. Most students in the study were between 17 and 19 years old.

Procedure

The six classes placed into three groups of two classes each. Group 1 was composed of 35 students, Group 2 of 35 students, and Group 3 of 40 students, for a total of 110 subjects in the study. During the first week of school of the fall quarter (for the majority their first quarter in college) before any instruction had begun, the three groups were asked to write an argumentative essay during one 50-minute class session. We asked them to write on every other line and to leave wide margins. The assignment was as follows:

Write an essay answering the following question. Be sure to make it clear which side you support. Imagine that parents and students will be reading your essay. Try to convince them that your point of view is right.

Who has (had) it harder—your generation or your parents' generation?

Essays were collected at the end of the first session and returned unmarked during the next class meeting. During this second 50-minute session, all three groups received identical first instructions: "Read your essay over carefully." After they had finished reading, all students were given red pens and asked to use them for the task to be assigned. Each group was assigned a different task:

- *Group one* was told: "Revise your essay to improve it."

- *Group two* was told: "Add five things to your essay to improve it." (These additions were made while the students looked at the text.)
- *Group three* was told to turn the essay over to the blank back page, and then to "List and number five things you want to add to improve your essay." When the lists were complete they were told, "Turn back to your essay and write in the number of each addition, placing it wherever you think is appropriate." This done, the student was instructed to "Write out the added material next to its number as you'd like it to appear in the finished version of the text."

The term "things" was used in these instructions so as to avoid suggesting any particular types of changes. We encouraged students to supply their own preferred revisions/additions. When questioned by students, we responded with some version of, "Whatever things you think will improve the essay are fine." As an incentive, all groups were told that if the task resulted in an improved paper, the original grade would be raised.

Data Analysis of Argument Structure

Since our aim was to compare the three revising situations and not to devise elaborate descriptions of every kind of revision, we developed a simple 6-item taxonomy that would accomodate all of the revisions. The basic distinction for this study is between surface revisions—those that do not affect meaning—and text-base revisions—those that affect meaning (Faigley & Witte, 1981). Each revision was coded as a surface revision or as one of the five types of text-base revisions. Working independently, we found a high level of agreement in our coding for the two major categories; the few differences were resolved through discussion. In preparation for further analysis, the percentage of text-base changes for each writer was computed.

The single category of surface revisions included addition, deletion, substitution, syntax, and correctness. We restricted ourselves to counting instances of revision without considering length: For example, whether the writer added a single word or an entire sentence, if that addition did not affect the meaning it was counted as a single surface change. Addition and deletion are self-explanatory; substitutions combined a deletion and an addition. Syntax revisions included changing sentence boundaries, changing active/passive sentence constructions, and changing main/subordinate clause relationships. Correctness included changes in punctuation, spelling, and paragraph markers.

Text-base revisions were categorized according to changes in the argument structure (Toulmin, 1958). Faigley and Witte's taxonomy distinguishes between the two types on the basis of meaning, but because we wanted to analyze student revisions for their function in argument, we needed a discourse-specific taxonomy (Cooper, 1983). Toulmin's scheme worked well for this purpose. Even though it conceptualizes arguments in terms of single sentences, it handles the common-sense questions posed in arguments of any length: What have you got to go on? How did you get there? By what authority do you say that? Most importantly, it enabled us to identify a writer's purpose in making a specific change.

The components of an argument can be categorized as follows (adapted from Rieke & Sillars, 1975, pp. 77–78):

> *Claim:* the conclusion to the argument. The statement that is advanced for the adherence of others. May be actually stated or implied.
>
> *Data:* statements about persons, conditions, evidence, or events that data offered in support of a claim.
>
> *Warrant:* a statement of general principle that establishes the validity of the claim on the basis of its relationship to the data.
>
> *Backing:* any material that is provided (specific instance, statistics, testimony, values or credibility) by the arguer to make the data or warrant more believable to the audience.
>
> *Qualifier:* a reservation or restriction placed on the universal applicability of some claims.

The way the components function in argument will be illustrated in the following paragraph from Andrew Hacker's (1983) article on the feasibility of "full employment" in the United States.

> During 1981, 117.2 million persons held paying jobs at some point this year.[1] This is a fairly impressive figure.[2] If we take the ages between eighteen and sixty-five as the approximate employment span, it would appear that almost 85% of us had jobs at one time or another.[3] However, appearances can be deceiving.[4] In effect, we have a two-tier employment force as Table 1 shows.[5] The lower segment largely consists of the 52 million persons who either held part-time jobs or worked only part of the year.[6] Their wages averaged $5,795, which suggests that in most cases they were largely supplemental: women comprised a majority of the group.[7] Most of the unemployed also fell in this stratum.[8] Their number averaged 8.3 million in 1981, but the total of those who were out of work during particular months was actually higher.[9] Thus there were full-time breadwinners who lost their jobs during the year and settled later for part-time work.[10] In most cases, then, the second tier consists of people who fill in when extra hands are needed, taking available work at modest pay.[11] (p. 27)

Hacker's first claim is implied. He leads the reader to expect that it will be his central claim, but in fact it turns out to be a false claim. It is supported by data [1]; stated, it would be something like "A significant number of people are employed these days in this country." The warrant [2] "fairly impressive figure" forms a bridge from data to claim by calling on the reader to affirm that this is a large number, saying in effect, "Don't you agree?" and answering the anticipated question, "How did you get there?" (from data to claim).

To further support the warrant [2], "fairly impressive figure," sentence [3] furnishes backing, which, in this case delimits characteristics of the group under discussion. The subordinate clause, "If we take the ages between eighteen and sixty-five as the approximate employment span," establishes certain parameters under which the warrant operates. This statement demonstrates that the warrant can still operate under new, more restrictive conditions to establish the relationship between the data and the claim. The independent clause in sentence [3] offers a new piece of data: another sort of "impressive figure"—85%.

Next, Hacker brings in a new warrant [4] as the basis for his central claim that employment cannot be defined as one global number; rather, it should be seen as a two-tier system [5]. This new warrant, like all warrants, offers a general, common-sense principle readily agreed upon by many. It is difficult to argue with the statement "appearances can be deceiving." The last five sentences muster up data that serve as evidence for the "two-tier" claim.

Not all arguments use the same kinds of data, warrants, and backing in support of claims as Hacker's does. His arsenal of definitional/statistical tactics is simply not available to students such as the writers in our study, writing impromptu essays, albeit arguments, based largely on personal experience. However, the categories of argument functions are the same for all types of argument—hence, their usefulness in our study of student writing.

Results

The results of this study confirmed our hypothesis: Beginning college writers moved beyond a concern with surface structure to increase the mean percentage of text-base revisions when cued to add. They increased the mean percentage further still when cued to add to the unseen text. The mean proportion of text-base revisions for each group increased from .16 to .40 and finally to .65 across the three revising situations. Figure 1 graphically illustrates the increasing proportion of text-base revisions across the three revising situations.

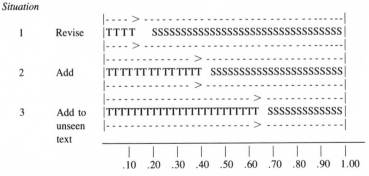

Figure 1. Mean proportion of text-base (T) and surface (S) revisions in three revising situations.

Table 1. *T*-Tests and Analysis of Variance for Three Revising Situations

Situation	Proportion		Text-base				
	M	*SD*	*M*	*SD*	*df*	*T*	*P*
Revise vs. add (1 vs. 2)	.16	.21	.40	.27	68	4.21	*p* <.0001
Revise vs. unseen text (1 vs. 3)	.16	.21	.65	.35	73	7.25	*p* <.0001
Add vs. unseen text (2 vs. 3)	.40	.27	.65	.35	73	3.41	*p* =.001

Note. One-way analysis of variance. $F(2) = 27.75$, $p<.0001$.

A total of 1,307 revisions—812 surface and 495 text-base—taken from 110 argumentative essays were included in the analysis. Strong significant differences emerged for the model when tested by a one-way analysis of variance. Further *t*-tests indicated significant differences between all pairs of groups (see Table 1).

The three revising situations can also be viewed from a worst-case/best-case point of view by examining the percentage of writers who made either zero or all text-base revisions (see Table 2). In the first situation, cued by the *revise* signal, 40% of the students made zero text-base revisions and none of the students made all text-base revisions. The influence of the cues *to add* and *add to the unseen text* reduced the percentage of students making zero text-based revisions to 14.3% and 7.5%, respectively. Conversely, the percentage of students who made all text-base revisions increased from 0% in response to the *revise* cue to 5.7% and 34.5%, respectively.

Discussion

We had hypothesized that using the cue *add* instead of *revise* would increase the proportion of text-base revisions over surface revisions. We have included in the appendix sample essays from each of the three revising situations to illustrate the shift in revising practices. The extent of the increase, particularly in situation 3— add to the unseen text—suggests some intriguing speculations about cognitive processes in writing.

Table 2. Percentage of Writers Making Zero Text-Base Revisions or All Text-Base Revisions

Revising situation	Zero text-base revisions (%)	All text-base revisions (%)
1 Revise (*N* = 35)	40	0
2 Add (*N* = 35)	14.3	5.7
3 Add to unseen text (*N* = 40)	7.5	34.5

This revising/adding situation enabled beginning writers to behave, in at least one way, like skilled writers. By avoiding the usual instruction to revise, we circumvented the expected response so often found in research on revision and replicated here: the tendency of beginning writers to fasten on surface structure correctness and word-level changes. This tendency reflects a metacognitive awareness of their experience which connects revision with correction. It appears that, cognitively, this connection all but consumes the limited cognitive resources a writer has for revising. The crucial issue is whether or not these writers can revise on any other level. Previous studies have explained these low-level revising limitations as a generalized egocentric inability to view the text as an entity outside themselves. Our study demonstrates otherwise.

How can we account for the increased proportion of text-base revisions in both the *add* and the *add to the unseen* text situations? Evidently, in these new situations the writer is freed from the overwhelming *knowing that* and allowed to move towards a *knowing how*. In cognitive terms, the writer adopts a high-level mental representation of the text, seeing it more as a whole in order to add to it.

When the writer adds to a text while looking at it, to some extent he has been freed by the instruction to add. But the presence of the text (exhibiting as it does unfortunate word choice, missing commas, and all the other surface wrongs) can interfere with attempts to focus on meaning-additions.

When the writer plans additions to an unseen text, something different happens. Recent research on reading comprehension tells us that after reading, verbatim memory for prose fades quickly. As time passes, the reader remembers the central ideas, or in other words, the gist (Kintsch, 1974; Meyer, 1975). After rereading, when the writer adds to an unseen text, his plans are based on a mental representation of the text. The opportunity to plan—free from both the presence of text and the efforts of prose production—offers an incentive to work exclusively with the idea structure of the text.

It has been suggested that skilled writers' ability to move fluently from low-level to high-level representations of the text depends on their having made the low-level operations routine. One unfortunate pedagogical implication of this view is the treatment of writing as a series of component skills taught in building-block fashion. The alternative is to provide situations which enable students to traverse the various layers of cognition during writing and revision. In this view, writing would be taught holistically, as a competence process.

Yet practiced writers point to writing's complexity and individuals' varied processes and ask how we can justify singling out one operation, addition, as a crucial strategy for revising. Not every writer adds when revising or even necessarily engages in extensive revision (Halpern & Liggett, 1984). Besides the simple justification that one must find somewhere to begin with the study of revising, the best justification comes from the students themselves. The oft-heard cry, "How long does it have to be?" tells us that they *know that* their writing is too sparse but don't *know how* to do something about it.

**Table 3. Percentage of Text-Base Revisions
in Five Argument Categories Across Three
Revising Situations**

Category	%	N
Claim/subclaim	28	139
Data	61	301
Warrant	8	39
Backing	0	2
Qualifier	3	14
Total N of text-base revisions		495

Types of Additions

As might be expected, additions to the argument structure of essays in all three
revising situations concentrated on data and claims. Revising situations 2 and 3
simply elicited more of the same kinds of additions that situation 1 had brought
forth. The few text-base revisions in situation 1 held the same distribution of types
of argumentative statements—claim/subclaim, data, warrant, backing, and
qualifier—as in situations 2 and 3 (see Table 3).

Most often when students added a claim, they added a paragraph to support it.
Here is an example:

Religion has undergone several changes over the years. [CLAIM] It has become much less
strict. [SUBCLAIM] We are not forced to go to services like our parents were, and many do
not fear the wrath of God or the devil like our parents did as small children. [DATA] Our
lifestyle causes us to disbelieve many things that we cannot comprehend.[WARRANT]

Nearly two thirds of all additions were data. Whether the instruction is to revise
or to add, the first choice of beginning writers is to add information. In this essay
question which invites students to compare and contrast their generation with that of
their parents, data usually served to fill out the contrast between the two generations. Often, when the first version contained details of one generation's difficulties
and the contrast was implied, the writer added the details about the other generation,
making the contrast explicit. Apparently, students have a learned schema for com-
parison/contrast essays, but under the pressure of first-draft production, they are
unable to devote the time to fill out the data in the way they *know how* to do before
pushing on to the next point. The *add* situation gives them time to recapture the
schema. Here's the way one student fills out the contrast between the generations
(additions are in uppercase):

Most of our dads fought in World War II, and some in the Vietnam War, therefore our
parents were forced to take time out to serve. THE TIME CONSUMED AND THE INJU-
RIES, MENTAL AND PHYSICAL, ARE A SIGNIFICANT FACTOR TO THE CHAIN OF

EVENTS OF THE LIVES OF OUR PARENTS. [DATA] WHILE WE ON THE OTHER HAND, AS OF YET, ARE NOT FIGHTING A WAR AND THEREFORE HAVE THE TIME TO DEVOTE TO OUR "GOALS' IN LIFE.[DATA] WHILE, AS FOR OUR PARENTS, that valuable amount of time could have been used more fruitfully than killing our fellow man. (*Placing politics aside*) Or they, our parents could have had a meaningful job and have had a more suitable life.

Beyond the general inclination to add claims and data, a few students saw the need to bring into play other components of the argument structure. In this example the student added a qualifier in the form of a definition to the first paragraph. This addition served to narrow and focus her thesis:

I think our generation has it harder. Jobs are very hard to find these days. THE FIELD OPEN MOST IS IN COMPUTERS. [DATA] You have to be very skilled. SKILLED MEANING ABLE TO OPERATE NEW TECHNOLOGICAL DEVICES. NO OBSOLETE MACHINERY LABOR. [QUALIFIER] That's why we go to college to get such skills. People around my parent's age didn't have to go to college to find a new job. Unskilled workers worked on the production lines, coal mines, auto industries and etc. They got paid enough to support a family.

Only two students out of 110 added single statements of backing. Backing, in Toulmin's scheme, offers verifiable and specific support for a warrant. Even though backing can look like data, it functions to support the warrant rather than the claim. Here is an example:

The previous generation of people were easier going. A good time consisted of going to get a shake at the shop because drugs and drink were not so heavily emphasized as they are now. THE PEER PRESSURE ON SMOKING AND DRINKING WERE NOT PRESENT AS THEY ARE NOW. [WARRANT] SIMPLE STATISTICS ARE PROOF OF THIS; THE TEENAGE ALCOHOLIC RATE HAS DOUBLED OR TRIPLED SINCE THE GENERATION BEFORE US.[BACKING]

The use of warrants by student writers presents some interesting complications. The essence of the problem is not the number of warrants (every claim necessarily has a warrant) so much as it is whether the warrant should remain implicit or be made explicit. Students have a very difficult time perceiving the need for explicit warrants. For instance, to take two examples from student papers, one student appropriately left unstated the warrant to support the claim that his parents had it hard because they, as teenagers, were forced to leave their homes and live in the forest when the Germans invaded Russia in World War II. There is no need, certainly, to provide a warrant, a general principle connecting the data to the claim. Few people would question that the claim, "hard," is warranted by the difficult facts of his parents' existence. No one need ask this student, how did you get from your data to your claim?

However, another student failed to make explicit a necessary warrant to establish a relationship between her claim that her parents had a "free and easy" life and her data that in her parents' generation, "usually only the man of the house had a job," and "the Lady of the house stayed home." She filled out the contrast by stating that today, young women of her generation must work (see Appendix, situation 2). The implied warrant that working at a job is harder than working at home is neither obvious nor generally accepted.

In the following example, the writer added a warrant at the conclusion of the essay offering a general principle with which to justify his claim:

My parents' generation had enough jobs. My generation will have enough jobs if there is another war or maybe a miracle. Although I am not really familiar with my parents' generation's hardships, I honestly believe neither generation has the right to take top billing in the self-pity department. EVERYTHING IS HARD UNTIL IT BECOMES ROUTINE. [WARRANT]

Location of Revisions

Beyond analyzing the proportion of text-base revisions we wondered about differences in the locations chosen for additions. To categorize the additions' locations we divided each text into thirds and counted the sentence additions in each section (see Table 4).

In contrast to Scardamalia et al.'s (1982) request to add at the end of the text, our request that situation-3 revisers list additions on the back of their papers and then insert them "wherever it seem(ed) appropriate" encouraged the student writers to add throughout the text as skilled writers do. Additionally, we expected that in situation 2 (add) students would have been influenced by the recency effect, so that the end portion of the text would remain salient during the addition process, providing the most expedient location for addition. However, this proved not to be the case because writers in situation 3 also made virtually the same percentage of additions in the last third as writers in situation 2.

The slightly higher percentage of additions in the middle of the texts for situation 3 represents several students' additions of entirely new paragraphs to the text. Also, it should be noted that writers in both situations 2 and 3 most often made their last-

Table 4. Percentage of Sentence-Length Revisions in Three Locations

Situation	First third of text		Second third of text		Third third of text	
	%	N	%	N	%	N
Add	21	28	15	21	64	136
Add to unseen text	15	54	23	82	62	217

third additions just prior to the conclusion, a likely spot for adding new points to an argumentative essay.

Planning for Addition

Revising situation 3—add to the unseen text—provided students an opportunity to plan by listing their additions on the back of their essays. An examination of these lists suggested that students applied at least two different conceptual approaches to planning. We noticed that about one third of the students listed all content plans, another third made no reference to content at all, and the last third made mixed references (see Table 5). The content plans ranged from a brief mention of a topic to detailed notes. In the noncontent lists students noted general metacognitive directions that could, in fact, have been applied to any essay. We have listed below examples from the content (see also revising situation 3 in Appendix) and the noncontent lists:

Content List
1. More peer pressure on students in today's society.
2. Lack of discipline and training to be independent.
3. Growing and popular exploitation of sex with little emphasis on love (sexual abuse).
4. The popularity of nihilism, children today are seeing that so many people don't care—or don't want to care—the growth in violence.
5. The corruption in government and politics—ever more present today—in the people this country are supposed to look up to.

Noncontent List
1. A more descriptive choice of words would help the essay. Work on the diction.
2. The conclusion should be stronger.
3. Spelling checked over.
4. Title of essay added.
5. Overall "clean-up" of entire essay, checking sentences, putting the paper in better order, getting rid of redundancies, etc., grammar probably checked.

Seeing the marked difference between these lists, we wondered about the additions generated by the content and contentless plans. Interestingly, we found a sharp

Table 5. Characteristics of Lists for Adding to Unseen Text

List	No content	Mixed	All content
Number of writers	14	13	13
Average % of text-base additions	41	67	90

increase in the percentage of text-base revisions for those students who had listed content plans reflecting consideration of the idea structure of the essay (see Table 5). Students who planned to add content made more than twice as many text-base additions as students who planned without considering content. Seven students in the content group made all text-base additions, compared to 4 students in the mixed group and 2 in the contentless group. Furthermore, of the 3 students who made zero text-base additions (see Table 2), 2 listed contentless plans and the third student listed only one content addition and four noncontent additions.

These results raise some interesting questions: Do these different planning styles reflect individual's planning and writing styles, or are they an artifact of the research task? In other words, would some students have planned with contentless lists no matter what the instruction?

Had we directed the students to add "information" instead of "things" more of their lists might have included content plans, but this new direction might have contributed to even more data being added. This "data-concentrated" perception of the task might, in turn, interfere with their ability to focus on other components of the argument such as warrants. Or do some writers think in terms of data no matter what the instruction? Could this be a reason why making warrants explicit when needed is so often neglected?

These questions all deal with the ways in which students see text. To conclude, students see the text most often as a surface problem area to be corrected and adjusted. What seems most difficult for students is overcoming the inertia which keeps them responding at this low level. Our situations provided a way for students to adopt a higher-level representation of the text. This move helps to focus their limited attention on the crucial aspect of writing—the making of meaning. Our *add* and *add to the unseen text* situations offer a starting point for thinking about the layout of an argument and how to revise it. Teachers may go on to develop other, more specific, tasks designed to address the various components of arguments.

The final assessment of any revision, of course, depends on whether or not the change improved the essay. The very fact that student writers—noted for their paucity of idea content—were able to produce more text-base material suggests that their essays have improved. The student-written examples above bear this out. This improvement was brought about without any instruction. Imagine what planned, focused instruction could accomplish. As we begin to recognize the range of students' *knowing how,* we can move beyond the dead center of their *knowing that* revising means correcting surface errors. Now, the possibilities for revision are unlimited.

Appendix: Three Revising Situations

```
Task: Who had (has) it harder, your generation or your parents'
      generation?
```

SITUATION 1: Revise

                    My Difficult Generation

    In my opinion, my generation has it harder in a sense that

                            [when my parents were my age]
our country is more technical than [~~in my parents' generation~~]. My

                                          [a higher
generation is faced with increasing technical jobs and [~~almost~~

educational requirement.]
~~force to go college or a vocational school~~.]

    First of all, the jobs that didn't require technical skills

are decreasing greatly. This causes young people to be jobless

if they don't have any technical skills. In my parent's

generation, many unskilled jobs were available but nobody didn't

want them because they were very hard. Many people [then] had to

        [those]
take [~~them hard~~] jobs because they needed them, but my parents'

                                [in my generation]
generation still had jobs. For a [~~younger~~] person [~~today~~] to find a

    [and]   [,]
job1 // if they are unskilled // [it] is very difficult.

                                [technical]
        Although many of the jobs today require[s̸] a // skill, some of those

                            [background]
jobs also require[s] a higher educational [~~requirement~~] than in my

parents' generation. Many young people are practically forced to

obtain some higher educational abilities. Since the cost of

        [and]
college [~~or~~] vocational schools are rising, it is very difficult for

a young person to get those educational requirements for those

technical jobs. In conclusion, some jobs are available[,] in my

                            [a]
generation[,̸] that doesn't require some type of // technical skill[s̸]

                    [background]
and a higher educational [~~requirement~~], but these type of jobs are

                                      [that]
decreasing. Many of the jobs // are available requires either a year

                                                          [a]
or two of college or vocation school and maybe some type of //

technical skill[s].

SITUATION 2: Add 5 Things

     It is much more difficult for today's young generation to

survive then it was for the parents of today. Today's young

generation faces greater hardships. Young people have a very hard

time finding and keeping a job and also surviving in today's

economic crisis.

     The parents of today grew up in a free and easy environment.
[Usually only the man of the house had a job.]
[Both of their parents hardly ever worked. Usually only the man

of the house had a job.] The Lady of the house stayed home, had

children and maintained a home environment for her family to

return to. The children went to school as usual, and girls of

that day and age just worried about finding a responsible husband

                              [She usually got
                  married right after high school. Today's young
                  lady gets a degree and becomes a professional.
                  She gets her career first and then gets married.
                  People of today support each other.]
to support her for the rest of her life. // Sure men had to

                              [For a man of today, it's
                  hard to get a job but once he gets the job, he
                  has to be able to keep it.]
work but not as hard as today's man. // Today's parents didn't

have to worry about a nuclear war, another depression, a national

disaster, as far as the economy goes, or Russia's satellites

falling to Earth and dumping radioactive Uranium in your

backyard. Sure, men of those days had to worry about the draft

[Today's younger generation not only has to worry about
                   but has]
but // to worry about if the Earth is going to exist tomorrow or,

                              [Women of
               the older generation never even thought of being
               drafted, for today's young woman it's very
               possible.]
if it does, will we or anything else on this planet. //

Today's young generation may be free to express feelings

about sex and drugs, and other controversial items more openly but they

also get to worry about venereal disease, PCP, and whether violence on

television is going to harm their children for the rest of their

lives. Young people of today have to worry about whether the

people working at the nuclear plant down the block are cabable to

work there and make it safe for the community, not to

accidentally cause a Radioactive leak to deform the generations

to come.

The older generation lived in a time of peace and flowers.
**[The crime rate and murder rate is much worse now then it was
was then. Less convictions are made per crime now also.]**
// Not too many things could change the life of a family then as

much as now. Young people of today know life is going to end

soon. Maybe not in their generation but possibly the next to

come. The end will be due to human stupidity, selfishness, and
                              [, and gas]
greed for power, money, [~~and~~] people //. To know the end of life

could be tomorrow is harder to live with or imagine then all the

hardships that today's older generation had to face.

This is just an opinion but to me, the facts show that

today's younger generation has it harder then today's parents'
            [But I also think that as generations go on, we learn

and become tougher. I'm sure that the next generation will
have it much harder thAn the young generation of today, if
we're still around.]
had it. //

SITUATION 3:   List, Then Add 5 Things to the Unseen Text

My parents' generation had it harder. When I was younger my

mother use to tell me of the life she had when she lived in

Puerto Rico. She told me that in her days she had to walk it to

school, at least fifteen to eighteen miles a day. Today, kids

have public transportation to take them to and from school.

Todays kids are also able to go to work and be able to have an

education. But my mother only got as far as the ninth grade,

because she hd to find a job to help my grandmother support the

other eleven kids since my grandfather passed away.//[3 & 5] The
work was pretty hard for they had to pick the beans by
hand and climb the banana trees which is about fifteen
feet high to get the ripe bananas so as to sell them at
the market. Today you have machines with special equipment made to do that work for you, like tractors with
plows attached to them. Today we can work in comfort
with air-conditioned buildings with luxury seats, 2-hour
lunches with extra benefits. Before alal work was done
with no music, no air condition, and when you finished
eating it was back to work.

Today people can get anything they want, they can get four

brand new suits or two brand new car and still people complain

that they don't have enough to keep themselves happy.

Once I complained about a pair of shoes my mother bought me;

didn't like the style or the color. She took me aside and said,

"Look, I paid hard earned money so that you can have a decent pair

of shoes!" When she was younger she remembered having to wear

                              [1],one might have been a
black colored shoe and the other was a navy blue.
Also, they might have worn the same cloth's for
weeks at a time changing once every two weeks.

shoes that weren't even the same style //. They were bought at a flee

market store since it was the cheapest store around.

Before money was hard to earn being that the majority of the

people were farmers. Always depend[ing] on a good harvest so [as

to] the necessities for the family and farm.

Working hours in my parents generation started before

sunrise till sundown, at times putting in 12 to 14 hours a day

while today people usually put in eight hours a day, get into

their Cadillacs or Mercedes and go home, put something to eat in

the microwave oven and enjoy the rest of the evening. // [2] When
my mother got home from work she and her brothers
and sisters had to gather fire wood in order to
have a meal. My grandparents home was small, they
had two bedrooms and a kitchen and a living room
to accommodate fourteen people--2 adults and 12
kids. While today the average kid has his own
room with a TV and telephone. Talk about luxury
compared from the past generation.

Today's world is so computerized and full of technology

that people don't even have to do any physical work at all, since

everything is programmed and made easy for them. In yesterday's

generation you were lucky to get any leisure time if any at

all.// [4]Today's generation have a lot of time for recreation.
They spend around 4-6 hours at the movies or 17-20 hours
or more watching TV. While yesterday's generation couldn't
even afford top take a stroll along a park for fear of lost
time.

ADDITIONS

1. I would add more about the type of clothes my parents had to
wear by adding more description to the material.

2. I would have talked about the type of house they lived in like
a 4-room house to accomodate 14 people.

3. I would talk about the types of equipment used while working
on the farm compared to today's equipment.

4. I would have mentioned all the recreation today's generation
has to yesterday's generation.

5. I would have also mentioned something about the working
condition then, compared to today's air condition, and 1-2 hour
lunch breaks.

References

Bartlett, E. J. (1982). Learning to revise: Some component processes. In M. Nystrand (Ed.), *What writers know: The language, process, and structure of written discourse.* New York: Academic Press.

Barritt, L., & Kroll, B. (1978). Some implications of cognitive-developmental psychology for research in composing. In C. R. Cooper & L. Odell (Eds.), *Research on composing: Points of departure.* Urbana, IL: National Council of Teachers of English.

Beach, R. (1976). Self-evaluation strategies of extensive revisers and nonrevisers. *College Composition and Communication, 27,* 160–164.

Beach. R. (1979). The effects of between-draft teacher evaluation versus student self-evaluation on high school students' revising of rough drafts. *Research in the Teaching of English, 13,* 111–119.

Bridwell, L. (1980). Revising strategies in twelfth grade students' transactional writing. *Research in the Teaching of English, 14,* 197–222.

Brown, A. (1980). Metacognitive development and reading. In R. J. Spiro, B. Bruce, & W. F. Brewer (Eds.), *Theoretical issues in reading comprehension.* Hillsdale, NJ: Lawrence Erlbaum.

Bruner, J. S. (1966). *Toward a theory of instruction.* Cambridge, MA: Harvard University Press.

Cooper, C. R. (1983). Procedures for describing written texts. In P. Mosenthal, L. Tamor, & S. Walmsley (Eds.), *Research in writing: Principles and methods.* New York: Longman.

Cooper, C. R., & Matsuhashi, A. (1983). A theory of the writing process. In M. Martlew (Ed.), *The psychology of written language: A developmental approach.* Sussex, England: Wiley.

Crowhurst, M., & Piche, G. (1979). Audience and mode of discourse effects on syntactic complexity in writing at two grade levels. *Research in the Teaching of English, 13*(2), 101–109.

de Beaugrande, R. (1982). Psychology and composition: Past, present, and future. In M. Nystrand (Ed.), *What writers know: The language, process, and structure of written discourse.* New York: Academic Press.

de Beaugrande, R. (in press). Writing and meaning: Contexts of research. In A. Matsuhashi (Ed.), *Writing in real time: Modelling production processes.* New York: Longman.

Emig, J. (1971). *The composing processes of twelfth graders.* (Research Report No. 13). Urbana, IL: National Council of Teachers of English.

Faigley, L., & Skinner, A. (1982). *Writers' processes and writers' knowledge: A review of research* (Tech. Rep. No. 6). Austin, TX: University of Texas English Department. FIPSE Grant No. G008005896.

Faigley, L., & Witte, S. (1981). Analyzing revision. *College Composition and Communication, 32,* 400–414.

Flavell, J. H. (1976). Metacognitive aspects of problem solving. In L. B. Resnick (Ed.), *The nature of intelligence.* Hillsdale, NJ: Lawrence Erlbaum.

Flower, L. (1981). Writer-based prose: A cognitive basis for problems in writing. *College English, 41,* 19–37.

Hacker, A. (1983, June 30). Where have the jobs gone? *New York Review of Books,* 27–32.

Halpern, J., & Liggett, S. (1984). *Computers & composing: How the new technologies are changing writing.* Carbondale, IL: Southern Illinois University Press.

Hayes-Roth, B., & Hayes-Roth, F. (1979). A cognitive model of planning. *Cognitive Science, 3,* 275–310.

Kintsch, W. (1974). *The representation of meaning in memory.* Hillsdale, NJ: Lawrence Erlbaum.

Lunsford, A. (1980). The content of basic writers' essays. *College Composition and Communication, 31,* 278–290.

Martlew, M. (1983). Problems and difficulties: Cognitive and communicative aspects of writing development. In M. Martlew (Ed.), *The psychology of written language.* London: Wiley.

Meyer, B. (1975). *The organization of prose and its effects on memory.* Amsterdam: North-Holland.

Murray, D. (1978). Internal revision: A process of discovery. In C. R. Cooper & L. Odell (Eds.), *Research on composing: Points of departure.* Urbana, IL: National Council of Teachers of English.

Murray, D. (1984). *Write to learn.* New York: Holt, Rinehart, & Winston.

Nold, E. (1982). Revising: Intentions and conventions. In R. Sudol (Ed.), *Revising.* Urbana, IL: National Council of Teachers of English.

Ong, W. (1975). The writer's audience is always a fiction. *Publication of the Modern Language Association, 90,* 9–21.

Perl, S. (1979). The composing processes of unskilled college writers. *Research in the Teaching of English, 13*(4), 317–336.

Rieke, R., & Sillars, M. (1975). *Argumentation and the decision making process.* New York: Wiley.

Ryle, G. (1949). *The concept of mind.* London: Hutchinson.

Scardamalia, M., Bereiter, C., & Goelman, H. (1982). The role of production factors in writing ability. In M. Nystrand (Ed.), *What writers know: The language, process, and structure of written discourse.* New York: Academic Press.

Simon, H. (1969/1981). The psychology of thinking. In H. Simon, *The sciences of the artificial* (2nd ed.). Cambridge, MA: MIT Press.

Sommers, N. (1980). Revision strategies of student writers and experienced adult writers. *College Composition and Communication, 31,* 378–388.

Stallard, C. (1974). An analysis of the writing behavior of good student writers. *Research in the Teaching of English, 8,* 206–218.

Toulmin, S. (1958). *The uses of argument.* Cambridge, England: Cambridge University Press.

13

Revising, Composing Theory, And Research Design*

Stephen P. Witte
University of Texas at Austin

The past five years of composition research might be characterized as a quest for an adequate theory of composing, one powerful enough to explain what Flower and Hayes (1981b) have described as "among the most complex of human mental activities" (p. 39). This quest has not been unproductive, in part because it has drawn substantially on theoretical and applied work in text-linguistics and discourse analysis, problem solving, reading, cognitive psychology, literary criticism, and artificial intelligence. Although knowledge of composing is now much more sophisticated than it was a decade ago, many riddles of the universe of composing remain unsolved. A case in point is revising. While recent revision studies seem to have enlarged our understanding of revising, that knowledge is no doubt incomplete and still evolving.

Our knowledge of revising has been framed and in some ways limited by circumstances of history that have shaped research questions and methodologies. Humes (1983) and Witte (1983c) have recently noted that revision research has focused primarily on three questions: (1) At what points during the drafting of texts do writers revise? (2) What kinds of revisions do writers make in their written texts? and (3) What differences in kinds of revisions of written texts occur across writers of different abilities? These three questions, while interesting in themselves, all take as their point of reference the products of composing, whether "in progress" or "completed" texts. All three questions suggest a primary interest in the *effects* of revising on written texts, and this interest in revising as retranscription has diverted attention away from what may be more interesting questions: What *causes* or prompts writers of different abilities to revise written texts as they do (cf. Witte, 1983b, 1983c, 1984)? What features of written texts prompt writers of different ages and abilities to revise as they do? To what extent may the differences among groups of writers in the amounts and kinds of retranscriptions be the result of

* Many of the ideas expressed in the present chapter grew out of discussions I have had with Jane Witte, Bob Bracewell, Roger Cherry, John Daly, Linda Flower, Sarah Freedman, Paul Meyer, Anna Skinner, Roland Sodowsky, Nancy Spivey, and Keith Walters about the nature of composing generally and revising particularly. I would like to express my gratitude to Roger Cherry, Linda Flower, Sarah Freedman, Paul Meyer, Anna Skinner, and Keith Walters for the many helpful comments they made on earlier versions of the present essay.

differences in planning? In what ways may revising as retranscription be a function of the writer's ability to create a mental representation of a "projected" text or a "pre-text"?

In most studies of revising, causes have been addressed only indirectly if at all, on the basis of inferences about revising on the basis of retrospective interviews with writers (e.g., Faigley & Witte, 1981; Sommers, 1980) or on the basis of evidence gleaned from the effects of revising on written products (e.g., Bridwell, 1980; Faigley & Witte, 1981, 1984; Hildick, 1965; NAEP, 1977; Sommers, 1980; Stallard, 1974). The interest in effects, or outcomes, of revising has limited the range of important research questions in yet another way: It has excluded from study revisions that might have occurred before the writer committed words to paper. Except for what can be inferred from Flower and Hayes's (1980, 1981a, 1981b, 1984) work on "planning," little is known about "pre-textual" revisions and why they occur.

The Evolution of Current Knowledge of Revising

It is worthwhile to try to understand why research on revising has largely ignored the causes of revising and the question of "pre-textual" revising. Research on composing, like research in any discipline, is conditioned by the ways in which and the extent to which a current intellectual climate assimilates, accommodates, or reflects a larger intellectual tradition it has both inherited and become a part of. Three often overlapping aspects of this tradition seem especially salient in explaining the kinds of revision questions that researchers have chosen to investigate: (a) instructional and assessment practices that have emphasized the products of composing at the expense of underlying composing processes, (b) the high value that practicing writers have ascribed to revising written products, and (c) the absence—until recently—of theoretical models that would enable researchers to think about underlying causes of revising, defined as alteration of both text and pre-text. The following paragraphs offer a thumbnail sketch of these contextual influences.

The Tradition of Writing Instruction

Although complex historical forces can easily be oversimplified, research is certain to have been influenced by writing instruction. The teaching of writing in this country shows the marked influence of teachers trained in departments of English. For the most part, the training of teachers of writing is centered on the analysis of written texts, primarily *belles lettres* and primarily fiction and poetry. These departments, as Parker (1967) has shown, evolved because of a curious combination of historical circumstances and paradoxes. According to Parker, the English department was the offspring of an uneasy marriage between oratory and philology (rhetoric and linguistics). Following the formation of the Modern Language Association in 1883, the English department eventually forgot its parents and embraced the study and teaching of modern literature. Paradoxically, it was, however, "the teaching of freshman composition that quickly entrenched English departments in the college and university structure" (Parker, 1967, p. 347); as English departments became "entrenched" in the institutional "structure," graduate programs in English offered the prospective teacher "training [that] had almost nothing to do with what he found himself doing in the classroom" (Parker, 1967, p. 349), namely, teaching composition—a situation that has led, from time to time, to calls for the abolishment of freshman composition in colleges (e.g., Beckett, 1974; Bullard, 1964; Rice, 1960).

Although there is some evidence that graduate students in English departments are beginning to receive more training in the teaching of writing (cf. Witte, Meyer, Miller, & Faigley, 1981), historically the disjunction between what teachers are prepared to do in the classroom and what circumstances demand that they do has been perpetuated through each subsequent generation of graduate students, suggesting that the "union of literature and composition" in departments of English is "merely a marriage of convenience" (Parker, 1967, p. 350). As Parker (1967) points out, the teaching of composition has at least "made possible the frugal subsidizing of countless graduate students who cannot wait to escape it" (p. 350). These graduate students' principal training and interests are often focused on understanding and analyzing literary texts, not on understanding the processes of composing or on teaching students how to control those processes. And it is still students enrolled in graduate literature programs who do most of the teaching of composition in major American universities (cf. Witte et al., 1981). Traditional literature training has undoubtedly taught teachers how to analyze and to appreciate literary texts, both admirable educational goals in their own right; but when this training is applied to writing instruction and research, it results in a dominating concern for written products. When the product of composing is a dominant focus of writing instruction, the representation of revising as a final step in composing a draft is likely to be the consequence.

Reflecting most writing teachers' concern for the products of composing are writing curricula and the textbooks employed in their service. Too often writing curricula become bogged down in the smaller units of discourse by assuming that if students cannot produce "correct" sentences, they cannot produce longer texts. Echoing this assumption is the widespread and traditional use of handbooks, exercise books, and (to a lesser extent) sentence-combining books which emphasize style at the sentence level. Often reflecting the "correctness" assumption and the assumption that good writing consists primarily of well-styled sentences, stylebooks focus primarily on features of texts within the boundaries of sentences, and thereby suggest to their users that writing is a matter of producing well-formed sentences, of choosing apt words and expressions. Not surprisingly, stylebooks usually advocate a paraliterary style, a style associated with writers such as E. B. White or George Orwell or Joan Didion, modern writers of nonfiction prose who are part of the belletristic tradition that has been such a pervasive influence in the training provided writing teachers by departments of English.

Equally important, handbooklike texts and stylebooks—by treating revising as something that occurs only after a draft of a text is in hand—have contributed to the view of composing as a series of discrete stages, the last of which involves editing or revising an extant text. It is quite likely that such textbooks, which are widely used at the college level (cf. Witte et al., 1981), both influence and reflect grading practices and thereby shape students' notions about appropriate composing strategies, strategies that are directed toward local, sentence-level concerns during both the production and the revision of written products.

Much writing instruction at the college level also assumes that the proper way to teach students to write is to supply them with professional models to imitate. This assumption accounts, in large part, for the many "readers" or "anthologies" published each year for use in college writing courses and their subsequent adoption in freshmen writing courses (cf. Witte et al., 1981). Typically, such professional models are offered for study in hopes that by exposing students to them and by having students analyze those models, students' prose will take on some of the characteristics of the prose of, say, an E. B. White, a Wallace Stegner, or a Joan Didion. However, I suspect that teachers often fail to recognize that their students' limited experiences and knowledge and their lack of control over their own writing processes and strategies frequently not only preclude their producing similar texts but also limit their understanding of the professional models, matters quite inadvertently demonstrated in a recent article by Carton (1983). Heavy reliance on professional models, while entirely consistent with the training of most teachers of writing, may in some ways be counterproductive in the teaching of writing. The "models approach" calls attention primarily to features of written products while ignoring both composing processes and the conditions that separate the professional writer from the amateur—a wider range of experiences to draw upon in writing, a larger storehouse of world knowledge to use in developing ideas, a larger number of writing strategies to access during composing, a more finely developed sense of when to call on them, and a greater degree of control over the processes themselves.

The de facto segmentation of composing by most composition textbooks—what Rose (1981) has described as the "dismantling of process"—is not inconsistent with the training most writing teachers have received in analyzing literary texts and has, I would argue, conditioned the way teachers of writing, writing researchers, and writing students have come to think of revising. The three principal questions that revision research has addressed are byproducts of the conceptualization of composing in part caused by and in part reflected in the curricular and instructional practices I have described. Perhaps just as important is how such practices may have affected the results of studies of "poor," "inexperienced," and "novice" writers. Such writers are rather consistently reported to revise their texts primarily at the level of the word or sentence (e.g., Bridwell, 1980; Crowley, 1977; Faigley & Witte, 1981; Mischel, 1974; Perl, 1979; Sommers, 1978, 1980). That such writers are, in fact, incapable cognitively of doing otherwise is the implication of most revision studies. They may, however, simply be performing as they have been taught (cf. Matsuhashi & Gordon, this volume).

The Tradition of Writing Assessment

More than likely reflecting the pedagogical tradition described earlier but also in some sense shaping it, "indirect" and "direct" assessments of writing[1] have probably influenced the direction and the results of revision research as well, because they take as their point of reference the products of composing. Two developments in the history of large-scale testing of writing were particularly critical in focusing attention on the products of composing. The first was the conflation of literature and composition in college entrance examinations. This conflation followed from an earlier one, the 1892 decision of the National Education Association's "Committee of Ten" to link composition and literature in the high schools. The second critical development in the history of testing was the emergence, during the early decades of the twentieth century, of what was then known as "the new-type examination"—the objective test—that when applied to the assessment of writing places great value on the student writer's ability to make editorial changes, usually within sentences taken out of the context of whole discourse. As the frequency of large-scale assessments increased (in proportion to the ever-growing "social need" to sort, place, and certify increasingly larger numbers of students) and as large-scale assessments became increasingly dependent on "objective" or "indirect" measures of writing, sentence-level skills probably came more and more to be regarded as a central focus of writing instruction. In short, writing instruction often became tied to what testers claimed could be reliably measured (cf. Witte, Trachsel, & Walters, in press).

Not all large-scale assessments of writing have, of course, been of the "indirect" variety. In fact, one widely used "direct" method of assessment, holistic evaluation, emerged in its present forms as a reaction against the use of "indirect" methods (cf. Cooper, 1977; Odell, 1981; Witte, Meyer, Cherry, & Trachsel, in press; Witte, Walters, Trachsel, Cherry, & Meyer, forthcoming. Although holistic evaluation of writing and other "direct" methods of assessment presumably place less emphasis on sentence-level "correctness" and more on the quality of the whole text, "direct" methods of assessment are no less product-oriented than "indirect" methods and would seem, therefore, to encourage the view of revision as editing features of written texts, thereby reinforcing a linear-stage conception of writing that makes revising the final stage in a temporal sequence.

The "Professional" View of Revising

One of the pervasive influences on how writing is understood seems to be what practicing writers either say or imply about it, an influence that has probably

---

[1] For those not already familiar with the distinction between "indirect" and "direct" assessments, see, for example, Stiggins (1982); Spandel & Stiggins (1981); Hogan & Mischler (1980); Breland & Gaynor (1979). For treatments of the history of writing assessments, see Witte, Meyer, Cherry, & Trachsel (in press) and Witte, Walters, Trachsel, Cherry, & Meyer (forthcoming).

reinforced the way most writing teachers are trained. Many professional writers who have spoken of or written about revising see it as an important and necessary process of composing. For the most part, these professional writers depict revising as something writers do *after producing some written product*. This depiction reinforces a "traditional" view of composing that implies a linear sequence—that may be repeated—of discrete stages, the last of which is revising. Such a view is suggested by several of the writers represented in the *Paris Review* interviews (Cowley, 1958; Plimpton, 1963, 1967, 1976), by writers included in Hildick's (1965) study, by writers with whom Murray (1978) has spoken, and by writers whom Sommers (1980, esp. pp. 380–381) has interviewed.

Because his work has frequently appeared in forums accessible to writing teachers, Murray, a Pulitzer Prize winner, has been influential in calling attention to and articulating what might be called the professional view of revising. Murray's how-to-teach textbook (1968) and his essays on composing (e.g., 1978, 1980) suggest to teachers and researchers alike this "professional" model of revising, one that Murray contrasts with what might be called the "amateur" model:

> All effective writers know writing is rewriting. The inexperienced writer feels a revision is a failure. The amateur believes the writer is the person who can sit down and rip off an essay or a report. The professional writer knows better. Rewriting is what you do when you are a writer, for it is an essential part of the process of writing. It is the way in which you fit ideas into language. (Murray, 1968, p. 11)

In addition to the professional/amateur distinction, embedded in Murray's statement are three assumptions that inform much of the research on revision. The first assumption is that revising as a process of composing operates exclusively on extant texts. That is to say, revision is seen as retranscription. The second assumption is that "good" writers revise more than "poor" writers. The third assumption, more implicit than the other two, is that to understand revising—and to help students become "better" revisers and, therefore, "better" writers—research must compare the textual revisions of professional, effective writers with those of amateur, inexperienced (and, presumably, ineffective) ones. Ten years later, Murray (1978) reiterated his belief in the efficacy of the "professional model" of revising with equal force, beginning his much-cited essay on revising with the assertion that "Writing is rewriting" (p. 85) and thereafter treating revising as "the most exciting, satisfying, and significant part of the writing process" (p. 86). Berkenkotter's (1983) study of Murray's own composing processes, of course, indicates that contrary to what he claims, Murray does an enormous amount of planning and limited revising. However, Berkenkotter's findings have not to date affected the influence that Murray's statements have had on conceptions of revising.

The contrast between "professional" and "amateur" views of revising and the assumptions implied by it have influenced the direction of much revision research and have limited the kinds of questions that researchers have sought to answer. Researchers have operationalized this contrastive model primarily by designing studies that either call for or make explicit comparisons of the revisions, or re-transcriptions, of groups of writers of different abilities—as in the research of Stallard (1974), Beach (1976), Sommers (1978, 1980), Bridwell (1980), and Faigley and Witte (1981)—and by developing and applying taxonomies for classifying the revisions of writers of different abilities (e.g., Bridwell 1980; Faigley & Witte, 1981, 1984; Hildick, 1965; NAEP, 1977; Sommers, 1978, 1980).

If the theoretical motivations and assumptions of such research were appropriate, then we should not only expect that the various classes of "better" writers would do more revising but also that those writers who revised the most would produce the best written products, the best final drafts. These expectations have not, however, been borne out by the research. Rather, some research has shown almost exactly the opposite. A number of studies (e.g., Bridwell, 1980; Faigley & Witte, 1981; Hansen, 1978; NAEP, 1977; Perl, 1978, 1979) suggest that the amount of re-transcription often bears little relation to the overall quality of the completed text or to the group status of the writers studied. Although Sommers (1980) reports that, unlike her inexperienced writers, her experienced writers were capable of making global revisions in their texts, subsequent research (e.g., Faigley & Witte, 1981) indicates that the kinds of textual revisions do not adequately distinguish among writers of different abilities. In their study, Faigley and Witte (1981) found that the group that revised most, regardless of type of revision, was not the "experienced adult" writers, but the "advanced student" writers. This latter finding represents an anomaly that cannot be explained by the model of revision Murray advocates.

Traditional Models of Composing

I would argue that during at least the last forty years it is only the anomalous student whose knowledge of composing and whose composing practices have not been conditioned by product-oriented instruction and assessment in writing and by the "professional view" of revising. If my hypotheses about historical conditioning are tenable ones, then it is also only the anomalous writing researcher who has remained untouched by the historical context I have described. Recognizing the pervasive nature of these influences makes it easier to understand how and why twentieth-century conceptualizations of writing as a process evolved as they did.

Until recently, composing was represented as a series of discrete stages with revising as the last stage. A case in point is Rohman and Wlecke's (1964; Rohman, 1965) work on composing during the 1960s. Although it is now regarded, quite rightly, as extremely important for calling attention to writing as a process, Rohman and Wlecke's model specifies a linear sequence of three stages—"prewriting," "writing," and "rewriting." In light of the training that most teachers of writing traditionally receive (see earlier section), it is worth noting that Rohman and Wlecke's linear-stage conception of writing was much influenced by Abrams's (1953) plant analogy, which he used to explain "organic unity" in poetry (cf. Spivey, 1983). The view of composing as a series of three steps or stages may have seemed to some teachers and theorists comfortably similar to classical rhetoric's emphasis (as adapted to writing) on invention, arrangement, and style (cf. Nystrand, 1982; Sommers, 1980), but it was more likely seen as altogether compatible with the complementary traditions of product-oriented writing instruction and assessment. I suspect that for most teachers of writing and most researchers, the Rohman and Wlecke model, rather than delineating a "new" conception of composing, merely codified an extant, though perhaps not well articulated, theory of composing, thereby allowing both teachers and researchers to continue thinking of writing in fairly traditional ways.

A view of composing, and revising, similar to Rohman and Wlecke's is found in the work of Britton, Burgess, Martin, McLeod, and Rosen (1975) at the University of London Institute of Education. The Britton et al. model specifies a sequence of "conception, incubation and production" (Britton et al., 1975, p. 22), with revising depicted as something of a final substage of "production." According to Britton and his colleagues (1975), revision refers to "the final stage of the process by which the writer presents himself: every piece of writing can be, to some extent, a declaration, a tacit agreement with the reader that the writer accepts responsibility for his own creation" (p. 47). According to the Britton et al. (1975) model of composing, a writer moves sequentially and linearly from one stage to the next, even though "the distinction between them" cannot "always be sharply maintained" (p. 22). The Britton et al. and the Rohman and Wlecke views of composing as a linear process are similar to other formulations, such as those of Collins and Gentner (1980), King (1978), and Murray (1978).

From a theoretical and historical point of view, Murray's view of revising is consonant with the traditional linear-stage model of composing. In place of Rohman and Wlecke's traditional terms, however, Murray (1978) proposes "new terms for consideration, terms which may emphasize the essential process of discovery through writing: *prevision, vision,* and *revision*" (p. 86; Murray's emphasis). The importance that Murray ascribes to "discovery" might initially suggest something other than a linear-stage conception of composing, but his definitions of "internal" and "external" revision indicate otherwise. Murray (1978) sees "internal revision" as including "everything writers do to discover and develop what they have to say, *beginning with* the reading of the *completed first draft.* They read to discover where their content, form, language, and voice have led them. They use language, structure, and information to find out what they have to say or hope to say" (p. 91; emphasis mine). "Internal revision" is exclusively writer orietned, and it apparently occurs only as a response to a "completed first draft." Although a "completed first draft" is not a requirement for it to occur, Perl and Egendorf's (1979) "retrospective structuring" (p. 125) is a construct quite similar to Murray's "internal revision." "External revision," in contrast, occurs in response to the need "to communicate what [writers] . . . have found they have written to another audience" (Murray, 1978, p. 91), an "external" one. Limited as it is to retranscription, Murray's distinction between "internal" and "external" revision is, for the most part, compatible with Flower's (1979) distinction between "writer-based" and "reader-based" prose, with Sommers's (1980) description of the revising of her experienced writers as ''a series of different levels or cycles'' (p. 387), and with Bereiter and Scardamalia's (1983) distinction between ''low-road'' and ''high-road'' writing strategies. By itself, Murray's notion of ''external revision'' is consistent with Britton et al.'s (1975) view of revision as ''the final stage of the process by which a writer presents himself'' (p. 47) to an audience. Whether revising is viewed as ''internal'' or ''external,'' the focus of study seems always to be on the effects of revising on some written version of the product.

I do not wish to imply that stage conceptions of composing have singularly limited recent revision research. To the contrary, I discussed such conceptions at some length because, first, they have been so influential in calling the attention of researchers and teachers alike to composing as a process and because, second, what those models imply about revising in particular and about composing in general strike me as not altogether unexpected links in a historical chain. Stage conceptions of composing, as well as the view of revising as retranscription which they imply, reflect and have helped to shape what Hairston (1982) and Young (1978) have referred to as the traditional paradigm of composition. This paradigm, as the preceding thumbnail sketch of historical influences suggests, restricts revision research to examining retranscriptions of written products. Such a restriction limits both the ''what'' and the ''when'' that can be the focus of research on revising. In the following section, I explore the theoretical implications of and alternatives to the traditional paradigm.

Composing and Revising: Theoretical Considerations

Revising as Retranscription

Research on composing and revising has not entirely separated itself from the historical context described in the preceding section, although alternatives to conceptions of composing as a fixed series of linear stages now commonly appear in the literature on composing (e.g., de Beaugrande, 1982, 1984; Flower & Hayes, 1981a; Hayes & Flower, 1980; Nold, 1979, 1981; Sommers, 1978, 1979, 1980; Tierney & Pearson, 1983). From a historical point of view, it is worth noting that most published research on revising was planned and executed within a context much influenced by the fixed linear-stage model. Even Sommers's (1978) seminal dissertation on revising, which in some ways forcefully challenges linear-stage models of composing, was completed largely without the benefit of alternative models and in the face of what I have suggested is a powerful tradition of writing instruction and assessment. Despite the claims of some researchers to the contrary, most research on revising, by focusing primarily on retranscriptions, presupposes something like a stage conception of composing. That is to say, research on revising has largely limited the phenomenon—even when seen as a recurrent process—to the final stage in a sequence of stages and has narrowly defined revising as the manipulation and alteration of features in written texts.

Nevertheless, much of the recent work on composing and revising has developed as a reaction against the simplistic view of composing represented by the traditional linear-stage model. For the most part, the traditional model has been challenged for two reasons. First, the view of composing as consisting of fixed stages taken up in a linear sequence has been challenged on the grounds that it does not allow for the various processes of composing to function recursively (e.g., Emig, 1971; Flower & Hayes, 1981a; Hayes & Flower, 1980; Nold, 1979, 1981; Perl, 1980; Sommers, 1978, 1979, 1980). Second, the traditional model has been challenged because it represents composing as a linear rather than a hierarchical process (e.g., Flower & Hayes, 1981a; Gould, 1980; Hayes & Flower, 1980; Sommers, 1979, 1980).

Both concepts, recursion and hierarchy, represent significant theoretical advances over the traditional fixed-stage model of composing, even though revising is usually seen as a text-directed process. Although Sommers (1979) recognizes "that any observable behavior such as composing must unfold linearly over time" (p. 47), she criticizes stage models of composing because they fail to recognize that writing often comprises subprocesses that can function both simultaneously and recursively. For Sommers (1979), stage models better describe "the written product than the process," because they identify "stages of the product and not the process" (p. 47). Sommers (1979) argues that, "according to systems theory" (p. 47), if composing were

> only such a linear activity, then we should be able to construct a behavioral checklist in which we predict that at a given point a writer should be in the thinking stage of the process, then he/she will gather information, then he/she will write, and then he/she will rewrite. And then if these stages were reliable and valid junctures, then we should have completion criteria for each stage so that we could tell when one stage is terminated and another begins. Each stage must be mutually exclusive, or else it becomes trivial and counter-productive to refer to these junctures as stages. (p. 47)

On the basis of her studies of experienced and inexperienced writers, Sommers (1980) "redefined" revising as "*a sequence of changes in a composition—changes which are initiated by cues and occur continually throughout the writing of a work*" (p. 380, Sommers's emphasis). As Sommers (1979) has argued, conceptualizing revising as a recursive process largely unfixed in time allows revising to be understood, first, as a process that can interrupt other composing processes at any given time rather than as a process that writers activate after composing in order to "clean up" a rough draft and, second, as a process that cannot be dissociated from a more general review process. Sommers (1980) later described this review process as "the process by which writers recognize and resolve the dissonance they sense in their writing," dissonance that is caused by detecting "incongruities between intention and execution" (p. 385). To conceptualize revision as a recursive process is to assert that revising is potentially a more complex process than merely polishing a rough draft.

Like Sommers (1979, 1980), Nold (1979, 1981) limits revising to "the *re-transcribing* of text already produced" (Nold, 1981, p. 68), and she stresses the importance of conceptualizing revision as a recursive process. Nold (1981) also sees revising as a subprocess of "reviewing." Reviewing is a process during which writers respond to a complex set of cues, only some of which have to do with "tidying up" the text; but reviewing is not a "one-time" process as fixed linear-stage models of composing would indicate. Indeed, according to Nold (1981), all of the processes of composing are recursive: "As their texts grow and change, writers plan, transcribe and review in irregular patterns" (p. 68). In part because revising for Nold (1981) refers to *retranscribing* text, it "is not a subprocess in the same way as planning, transcribing and reviewing are" (p. 68), and it is motivated or caused by "dissonance." According to Nold (1981),

> Writers retranscribe because they have decided, after reviewing text or their plans, that portions of the text are not what they had intended or not what their readers need. But in order to retranscribe, writers must be able to generate a more acceptable solution. If they cannot, they will not change their text. This analysis of revising shows that revising strategies cannot be inferred from the text alone: writers indeed may want to revise, but not be able to because they lack more promising solutions. (p. 68)

In addition, implicit in Nold's view of revising as retranscription is the possibility that revising can result in poorer texts. Nold (1981) continues: "To judge a text against intended meaning . . . requires that writers must conceive their *text's* meaning (for an audience) separately from their *intentions*" (p. 74). It would seem, therefore, that ideally much of the writer's attention during retranscription or revising is given over to converting what Flower (1979) calls "writer-based prose" to "reader-based prose."

With respect to revising and the superordinate process of reviewing, recursion for both Nold and Sommers refers primarily to altering extant text after transcription. This view of recursion is largely consistent with Murray's (1978) description of revising and with that of Perl (1978, 1979); and it is this view of recursion in revising assumed in studies that have examined within- and between-draft revisions of texts (e.g., Bridwell, 1980; Faigley & Witte, 1981, 1984). Conceptualizing revision as recursive retranscription, while consistent with the historical context described previously, has limited our understanding of revising by narrowly limiting the focal points of study. This recursive retranscription model of revising, while seemingly advancing knowledge of revising, has resulted in at least one research anomaly (cf. Schwartz, 1983; Wall, 1983) that remains unaccounted for by the model, namely, that experienced adult writers may do less revising within and between drafts than less-skilled writers but still produce texts superior in quality to those of their less-skilled counterparts (cf. Faigley & Witte, 1981).

According to this retranscription model, before revising can occur, the writer must, first, identify a problem in an extant text and then, and only then, solve the problem, the solution to which manifests itself in an altered text. If, as probably happened with Faigley and Witte's (1981) "experienced adult" writers, problems were either anticipated and then avoided before committing text to page or solved through revising something like a pre-text, then there would result little observable retranscription, of any kind. Similarly, it seems reasonable to assume that as texts grow longer and more complex, reviewing in order to retranscribe text becomes an increasingly more demanding cognitive task. It follows, then, that if novice or inexperienced writers in revision studies are given writing tasks that elicit texts requiring more reviewing or a different kind of reviewing than these writers are accustomed to doing, then the review process may be greatly overtaxed, resulting in fewer revisions except at local levels of text or in fewer appropriate or worthwhile revisions at any level. Conversely, if experienced adult writers or expert writers are given writing tasks that place relatively small demands on their writing processes generally, little recursive retranscription may result, perhaps because all required planning occurred prior to transcription or perhaps because the writer's projected text or pre-text was appropriately altered before transcription.

The point is that the amount of retranscription is altogether dependent on at least two factors that are commonly ignored in revision research—the nature and complexity of the writing task itself (cf. Nold, 1981) and its relationship to the quality and kind of planning and pretextual revision that occurs. That is to say, if a projected text, a pre-text, is one result of the planning writers do prior to transcribing, then it follows that revising, as a subprocess of composing, can function recursively to alter plans and goals and to alter the nature of the pre-text, and it follows that revising plans and pre-texts can affect the amount and kinds of retranscriptions once a pre-text is translated into text. Because revision research has ignored these variables and because reported results only focus on the effects of retranscribing, it becomes well-nigh impossible to draw confidently many conclusions about revising "patterns" from the extant literature.

The Implications of Hierarchy for Revising Theory

The concept of hierarchy is crucial to the expanded notion of revising that I am advocating. Sommers (1979) asserts that "it is possible to view the composing process . . . as a hierarchi[c]al set of subprocesses" (p. 47). According to Sommers (1979), conceptualizing composing as a hierarchical "set of sub-processes" permits the "conception of the writer moving in a series of non-linear movements from one sub-process to another while he/she constantly moves the force of his/her attention among matters of content, style, and structure, solving continuous sets and subsets of complex cognitive, lexical, syntactical, and rhetorical problems" (p. 47). Indeed, Sommers's notion of revising as a subprocess of reviewing and as a process capable of interrupting composing at any point implies that revising can be embedded in other processes. This notion of processes embedded in other processes is more consistent with hierarchical models than with linear ones (cf. Flower & Hayes, 1981a). Similarly, Nold's (1981) conceptualization of revising as a subprocess of reviewing, which itself can both interrupt other processes and affect those processes, is consistent with the notion of a hierarchical system.

In its recognition of the concepts of hierarchy and recursion, the work of Sommers and Nold represents a major break with the historical context described earlier.

Although Sommers and Nold make the concept of hierarchy a part of their theories, its implications are not elaborated extensively; and the emphasis in their work on revising as retranscription links their work directly to that context. It is the "cognitive process theory" of Flower and Hayes (1981a, 1984; Hayes & Flower, 1980) that allows revision research to move beyond its moorings in "traditional" conceptualizations of composing. In the Flower and Hayes theory of composing, the concept of hierarchy as well as the concept of recursion receives considerable attention. Flower and Hayes (1981a) describe the principal strengths of their theory:

> A cognitive process theory of writing . . . represents a major departure from the traditional paradigm of stages in this way: in a stage model the major units of analysis are *stages* of completion which reflect the growth of the written product, and these stages are organized in a *linear* sequence or structure. In a process model, the major units of analysis are elementary mental *processes,* such as the process of generating ideas. And these processes have a *hierarchical* structure . . . such that idea generation, for example, is a sub-process of Planning. Furthermore, each of these mental acts may occur at any time in the composing process. One advantage of identifying these basic cognitive processes or thinking skills writers use is that we can then compare the composing strategies of good and poor writers. And we can look at writing in a much more detailed way. (pp. 367–368)

Figure 1 depicts Flower and Hayes's model which includes three major components, with the two-directional arrows suggesting the possible interactions among those components.

In the Flower and Hayes model, both the "writer's long-term memory"—which includes "knowledge of topic, audience, and writing plans"—and the "task environment"—which includes two components, the "rhetorical problem" (consisting of "topic," "audience," and "exigency") and the "text produced so far"—

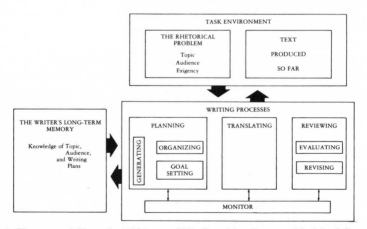

Figure 1. Flower and Hayes's (1981a, p. 370) Cognitive Process Model of Composing.

place constraints on "writing processes" themselves. Flower and Hayes's studies (1980, 1981a, 1981b, 1984) of thinking-aloud protocols suggest that good writers accommodate these constraints during "planning." Planning, according to Flower and Hayes, consists of three subprocesses—"goal setting," "generating," and "organizing." Planning in the Flower and Hayes model refers, in effect, to the process by which writers construct mental representations of "procedural" and "substantive" goals for their intended texts. Although writers may frequently evaluate goals and sometimes alter them, some goals are, in turn, "translated" into written text—the "text produced so far." When the "text produced so far" is found, through "evaluating," a subprocess of "reviewing," to be incongruous with the writer's mental representation of goals or text, "revising" can result.

The Flower and Hayes model of composing clearly represents a more robust theory of composing than its predecessor, the linear-stage model, and it seems consistent in many ways with the views of composing offered by Sommers (1980) and Nold (1981). The Flower and Hayes model appears to depict all of the major components of composing—both the internal processes of the mind working and the external and internal cues that may affect the decisions writers make during composing. Scardamalia and Bereiter's (in press) assessment of the Flower and Hayes model is probably accurate: The model "appears to do what it is supposed to do, which is to serve as a frame for working out more detailed and possibly more controversial accounts of how the mind copes with writing tasks" (ms. p. 5), and "The strength of the model lies in its claim to account for the amazing diversity of mental events during composition on the basis of a relatively small number of . . . subprocesses" (ms. p. 11). If Scardamalia and Bereiter's assessment of the Flower and Hayes model is apropos, then three questions need to be addressed:

1. What does the Flower and Hayes model predict about revising that differs from product-oriented stage conceptions of composing and from what I have described as product-oriented research on revising?
2. What elements of composing are either absent from the model or need to be included or expanded upon in order to make it a "more detailed" account than it currently is "of how the mind copes with writing tasks"?
3. How would these additional or expanded elements affect our understanding of "revising"?

For an answer to the first question, we must examine the relationships among the processes of composing that Flower and Hayes identify. Partial, although "possibly controversial," answers to the second and third questions must be sought in the extant literature on discourse production. Complete, definitive answers to the second and third questions—if possible at all—must await the findings of much subsequent research.

As Sommers (1979, 1980) does explicitly and as Nold (1981) does implicitly, Flower and Hayes (1981a) see composing as consisting of "elementary mental *processes*" that have a "*hierarchical structure*" (p. 367); that is to say, the processes of composing are part of a "hierarchical system" (p. 375). According to Flower and Hayes (1981a),

> a hierarchical system is one in which a large working system such as composing can subsume other less inclusive systems, such as generating ideas, which in turn contain still other systems, and so on. Unlike those in a linear organization, the events in a hierarchical process are not fixed in a rigid order. A given process may be called upon at any time and embedded within another process or even within another instance of itself, in much the same way we embed a subject clause within a larger clause or a picture within a picture. (p. 375)

If we assume that writing occurs in order for a writer to communicate something to an audience and that composing is a hierarchical rather than a linear process and if we grant saliency to processes and subprocesses depicted in the Flower and Hayes model, then—as the Flower and Hayes model suggests—reviewing and the subprocesses of evaluating or revising can be embedded in planning or in the subprocesses of generating, organizing, or goal setting. If revising can thus become a subprocess of, say, generating, then—as Scardamalia and Bereiter (in press) assert—"it makes little psychological sense to treat changing a sentence after it is written down as a different process from changing it before it is written" (ms. p. 15).

To insist from a cognitive psychological point of view that revising a written text is the same process as revising a pre-text is to insist (a) that a writer's plans and goals can be "instantiated" mentally as a pre-text that may or may not be translated into a written text, (b) that both revising a pre-text and retranscribing a written text may be similarly motivated, and (c) that both can have similar effects on the written text itself. To the extent that the Flower and Hayes model represents the major processes that figure in composing, both retranscribing and pretextual revising are affected by the writer's ability to manipulate through the "monitor" the "processes" themselves, by the writer's perception of the "task environment," by the writer's "long-term memory," and by the interactions among all these components. Accordingly, any theory of revising and any study of revising must in some way accommodate the writing task, composing and its subprocesses, the pre-text, the text produced, and the interactions among them.

Dissonance and Pretextual Revising

One way to account for these aspects of composing is to recognize the role that dissonance can play prior to transcription, as the writer's planning processes define and shape the mental representation that I call a pre-text, which can take multiple forms—from sensory images, to concepts, to metaphors, to feelings (cf. Flower & Hayes, 1984). However, to understand the role that dissonance can play during pretextual revision, it is necessary to understand its influence on retranscription.

Both theoretical and empirical research on textual revision suggests that the amount and kind of retranscribing is affected to a significant degree by the dissonance or disjunction writers perceive between intentions (i.e., goals) and execution (i.e., written text). If no dissonance or disjunction is perceived or if the writer cannot resolve this dissonance, little or no retranscription (cf. Nold, 1981) or little or no "retrospective structuring" (Perl & Edgendorf, 1979, p. 125) can occur. The perception of dissonance, then, must be regarded as a necessary cause of retranscription. However, dissonance cannot be regarded as a sufficient cause of revising a written text: That writers recognize disjunction or dissonance does not necessarily mean that they can resolve it (cf. Nold, 1981) or that their attempts to resolve the dissonance will be satisfactory. Furthermore, writers of different abilities appear capable of detecting different kinds of dissonance (cf. Sommers, 1980; Witte, 1983c) or disjunction between their intentions and their written texts. Skilled writers appear capable of evaluating written texts against demands for both "global" and "local" coherence (Witte, 1983c; cf. Agar & Hobbes, 1982; Hobbes & Evans, 1979) but less-skilled writers appear capable of evaluating written texts principally against demands for within-sentence "correctness" (cf. Faigley & Witte, 1981; Perl, 1979; Sommers, 1980; Witte, 1983c). In addition, if detecting dissonance between intentions and written texts were both a necessary *and* sufficient cause of revising those texts, then writers of like ability (e.g., the "experienced adult" writers in the Faigley & Witte, 1981, study) would alter or revise written texts in similar ways—unless, of course, no dissonance were detected. This suggests that some combination of four conditions must be present before retranscribing to resolve dissonance between intentions and written texts can occur: The writer (a) constructs an inappropriate representation of the rhetorical or communication problem; (b) generates less-than-adequate "procedural" and "substantive" goals and plans (cf. Flower & Hayes, 1981b) for solving the rhetorical problem; (c) inaccurately translates or instantiates "procedural" and "substantive" goals and plans; and/or (d) projects a text that is incongruous with either the rhetorical problem or the writer's plans for solving that problem.

The importance of accommodating the pre-text in revising theory and research derives from the fact that these four conditions for revising (i.e., retranscribing) the written text to resolve dissonance between intention and execution can each be eliminated by embedding the subprocess of revising into another process or subprocess of composing. Indeed, this is what is meant by composing as a hierarchical process; because composing is a hierarchical process, writers—as Scardamalia and Bereiter remind us—are just as capable of revising a sentence before it is written down (that is, a pre-text) as after. I would argue that there is no reason to limit our thinking about such pre-texts to single sentences; the pre-text, I suspect, can be any of a number of different mental representations of projected meaning (cf. Flower & Hayes, 1984) and can change in extensiveness and kind during the course of planning or production.

Changing or revising a pre-text presupposes evaluation of it in light of variations on two questions: "Is this really what I want to communicate?" "Is this really how I want to communicate my message to my audience?" If the answer to either question is "no," dissonance results. Such dissonance can be (but not necessarily "will be") resolved by revising either "substantive" or "procedural" goals and plans, the result of which will be a revised pre-text. Revising ineffectively or not revising at all something like a pre-text thus becomes a necessary condition for revising or not revising a written text: If the writer fails to resolve dissonance at the level of pre-text, that dissonance is likely to persist following the production of a written text and will likely result in textual revising to eliminate the dissonance providing that the writer has a strategy for resolving it; if the dissonance is resolved prior to transcription, little or no retranscription may be necessary. To limit the study of the causes of revising to perceived dissonance between intentions and transcribed text is either to deny that composing itself is a hierarchical process or that its subprocesses are integral parts of that hierarchical process. Accordingly, revising research that limits itself to examining changes in written texts or drafts espouses a reductionist view of revising as a stage in a linear sequence of stages. Research predicated on such a reductionist view of revising can, therefore, only describe either irrelevant or incomplete patterns of revising for writers of different abilities. That is to say, the patterns described can be no more complete than the comprehensiveness of the methodology used to identify them or the comprehensiveness of the operational definition of revising adopted.

Discovery, Planning, and Revising

Expanding the concept of revising to include not only retranscribing but also revising a pre-text necessitates our rethinking the role of "discovery" during composing. Characterizations of composing as "discovery" (e.g., Coles, 1974, 1978; Dowst, 1980: Elbow, 1973; Murray, 1968, 1978, 1980; Perl, 1979; Perl & Egendorf, 1979; Sommers, 1980) fairly consistently limit "discovery" to an outcome of transcription. Thus, to paraphrase Shakespeare, by indirection writers presumably find directions out.[2] Discovery during transcription is, I suspect, directly tied to the quality and amount of planning that occurs before transcription and, accordingly, to the nature of the writer's pre-text. The discovery model of composing is similar in many important respects to what Flower and Hayes (1981b) call "the *generate and test* strategy (e.g., pick a puzzle piece and see if it fits)" (p. 40) or a "trial and error strategy [that] reflects our inveterate tendency as problem solvers to jump to a quick

---

[2]It is my opinion that to base a pedagogy on the discovery model of composing is to teach what in many cases must be a terribly inefficient, albeit somewhat romantic and inspirational, method of composing. To teach according to the discovery model alone is to encourage writers to become less rather than more efficient by advocating and reinforcing inefficient, time-consuming behaviors. This is not to say that the discovery model of transcribing is wrong; indeed, for some good writers, writing may always well be a process of discovery. It is only to say that representing transcribing only as, or primarily as, discovery is both to disallow alternative, and more efficient, means to an end and to misrepresent composing practices.

solution, often before we understand the problem'' (p. 40). The "generate and test strategy," according to Flower and Hayes (1981b), "turns out to be a remarkably inefficient procedure, though not an entirely uncommon one" (p. 40). The inefficiency of the discovery-through-transcription model of composing is, I suspect, directly related to the quality of a writer's planning and the effects of that planning on the writer's mental representations and revisions of pre-texts.

Consider portions of the first and third drafts of one recent student of mine who reports that he always starts writing before having "a very good sense of what I'm going to say." The drafts were written during an hour-and-fifteen-minute class period in response to an assigned topic that asked students to assume the role of the editor of the local college newspaper and to answer charges from readers that the newspaper had violated its policy against "sexist advertising." What follows is the opening paragraph of the student's initial draft.

(1a) It has come to my attention that many of you have been upset by an advertisement which recently appeared in our newspaper concerning the Ford Motor Co. (1b) I have also received many letters from the academic community charging that we have flagrantly violated our own policy of vowing to oppose sexism in advertising. (1c) Therefore it is my responsibility as head editor and representative of *The Daily Texan* to clear up this controversy so that we maintain our policies and reputation as a quality newspaper.

Compare this sample with the first paragraph of the same student's third draft:

(2a) A Mustang advertisement which recently appeared in *The Daily Texan* has apparently upset some of our faithful readers. (2b) Several recent letters have charged *The Texan* with flagrantly violating its own policy of opposing sexism in advertising. (2c) As editor of *The Texan*, I wish to answer this charge.

Some striking differences occur between these two opening paragraphs. Perhaps the most startling difference is in focus. The first is abstruse, as though the writer had only a vague sense of where he wanted his text to go and what he wanted his readers to take from it. This lack of focus is reflected both in the text's structure and in the content of individual sentences. Expressions such as "It has come to my attention that" in (1a) prevent the text from taking deliberate aim at the issue at hand, as does the writer's heavy reliance on first- and second-person pronouns. The misplaced modifier—"concerning the Ford Motor Co." in (1a)—suggests that the writer is discovering relationships among propositions as he translates content into prose. Imprecise wording as in "policy of vowing to oppose" in (1b) to mean "policy of opposing" suggests imprecise and hurried thinking. Many of these infelicities that prevent clear focus in the student's first draft are eliminated by the writer's third draft.

The writer's third draft focuses immediately in (2a) on the "Mustang advertisement," a key ingredient of the rhetorical situation that demands a response from the newspaper. The awkward combination of "It has come to my attention that many of you have been upset" in (1a) and "I have also received many letters from the academic community" in (1b) is replaced by the simpler and more direct "Several recent letters" in (2b); and the long third sentence, (1c), that attempts to make explicit what most readers of such a response would infer, is replaced in the writer's third draft by a sentence which is one third the length of the original and which is focused on the writer's immediate purpose. Collectively, the first and second paragraphs illustrate, I believe, what Flower and Hayes (1981b) call "the generate-and-test strategy," which is necessitated either by inadequate planning or by the writer's inability or unwillingness to revise pre-textually. For the writer of the first and second paragraphs, translating or transcribing may be largely a process of "discovery."

Compare these two beginning paragraphs with the opening paragraph of the only draft of a second student, one who claims to "spend more of my time thinking than writing when I do an assignment. I think a lot about the assignment and what I need to do with it and once I start writing, I think very carefully about what I'm going to write down."

(3a) A Ford Mustang advertisement that recently appeared in *The Texan* has generated an intense public controversy. (3b) During the past week, *The Texan* has received a torrent of letters, charging that the Mustang ad is blatantly sexist and that this newspaper has violated its own policy of opposing sexism in advertising. (3c) These charges deserve an answer.

This opening paragraph, written as part of the second student's only draft, differs in important ways from the first draft of the first student's initial paragraph, and it differs in subtle ways from the first student's third draft. The differences between the first student's third draft and the second student's first draft are not merely differences in style, although many readers would undoubtedly prefer "generated an intense public controversy" in (3a) to "apparently upset some of our faithful readers" in (2a) or "*The Texan* has received a torrent of letters" in (3b) to "Several recent letters have charged *The Texan*" in (2b).

Two other differences between the second and third paragraph strike me as much more telling. First, in writing her first and only draft, the writer of the third paragraph seems to have made more explicit use of knowledge of the rhetorical situation. For example, the patronizing tone suggested by "our faithful readers" in (2a) and the almost personal confrontation between editor and reader suggested by (2c) is nowhere evident in the third paragraph. In its place, the writer of the third paragraph has adopted a "rhetorical stance" (cf. Booth, 1963) that allows her to focus attention not on personalities but on the issue at hand. In addition, the writer of paragraph two apparently sees a need to identify himself explicitly with "editor," an identification that would have been obvious to readers of any newspaper in which such a statement might have appeared. Second, by adopting her particular stance, the writer of the third paragraph focuses in successive sentences on everything that the reader needs in order to understand the issue at hand and on nothing that is not crucial to that understanding.

This focusing is achieved primarily through what might be called an interlacing of topics across the boundaries of sentences (or, more properly, t-units) (cf. Witte, 1983c, 1983d; Witte, Cherry, Meyer, & Trachsel, 1984; Witte, Meyer, Cherry, & Trachsel, in press; Witte & Sodowsky, 1984). The first sentence, (3a), calls attention quite clearly to what lies at the heart of the issue, namely, the "Ford Mustang advertisement," not merely the "Mustang advertisement" as in (2a) of the first student's third draft or "an advertisement" as in (1a) of the first student's first draft. The second sentence, (3b), is interlaced with "recently," "*The Texan*," and "intense public controversy" of (3a) through the use of "During the past week," "*The Texan*," and "torrent of letters" while adding what is essentially new information about the controversy. The ordering of this information in (3b) is important, with the temporal connector appearing first, followed by "*The Texan*" as the subject of the main clause and the receiver of the "torrent of letters," which is itself modified by two parallel participial phrases. The ordering of many of these same content items differs from that in (2a) where "letters" is the subject of the main clause with "have charged" the verb. This difference between the ways the content items are ordered in (3b) and (2b), together with a similar difference between the ordering of content items in (3c) and (2c), affects the amount of work the reader must do in order to construct meaning for the text. With the focus of (2c) on "editor" and "I"—which detract from the issue at hand—and the relegation of "charge" to the last word of (2c), the reader must make the connection between "letters have charged" in (2b) and "charge" in (2c) over a much longer span of text than between "charging" in (3b) and "charges" in (3c).

These examples of two students' writing are not atypical, at least not of the students who enroll in classes I teach. What the three paragraphs can tell us about the two students' composing processes is not, of course, altogether clear, because their texts are the results of those processes and not the processes themselves. Coupled, however, with the students' statements about their composing processes, these three texts suggest that the two students compose in very different ways. The first student, in order to produce an acceptable response to the assigned task, had to revise his written text extensively. The first student seems to have relied on the "generate-and-test" strategy and the "discovery" model of composing it implies. The second writer, on the other hand, did not revise her text at all, except for two changes in spelling and one conversion of a dependent clause to a participial phrase, changes that were marked on the only draft she wrote. But revising is, I suspect, no less a critical part of her composing process than it is for the other student writer. My guess is that revising simply occurred before she committed words to the page. She apparently planned carefully and deliberately, spending "more time thinking than writing"; and her planning resulted in "discoveries" that made up her pretext, a mental representation or projection of "what I'm going to write down." I suspect that the student's plans, like the plans of the writers included in Flower and Hayes's studies, were revised considerably between the time she encountered the rhetorical problem and the time she put pen to paper, as she seemingly systematically "discovered" not only what she wanted to communicate but also how her content should be framed to meet the demands of the rhetorical situation; and I suspect that when she revised those plans, she also revised her pre-text, "what" she intended "to write down" and how she intended to frame it.

Like the texts and composing processes of these two students, the ways my own texts evolve and my own composing processes point to differences in when discovery occurs and in what representation of "meaning" is affected by discovery. For me, these differences affect both the amount and kind of pretextual revising I do and the amount and kind of retranscription I do.

When I make a list of items to be purchased at the neighborhood grocery, I typically have already discovered what I want to put on that list prior to my writing it. When I write a note requesting that our daughter be excused from classes in order to keep an appointment with her orthodondist, I do not discover what I want to communicate as I write the note; although I may not know the exact words or the exact form of individual sentences, I know exactly what topics I need to cover and the general framework of the projected text well in advance of transcription. When I write to an oil company about a payment that has not been credited to my account, I know exactly what I want to communicate when I sit down at the typewriter. Even rather complex writing tasks often involve very little "discovery" during the process of transcribing text and require very little "internal revision" or "retrospective structuring." For example, at least four of my recent articles (Witte, 1983a, 1983c, 1983d; Witte, Daly, Faigley, & Koch, 1983) involved little "discovery" once transcribing began, although all required at least some "external revision" to convert to "reader-based prose" what was in draft too close to "writer-based prose." This is not to say that transcribing during composing never involves "discovery" for me, that "internal revision" and "retrospective structuring" never occur when I write. To the contrary, several essays and a book I have written (e.g., Witte, 1980; Witte & Davis, 1980; Witte & Faigley, 1981, 1983), as well as the present essay, entailed a great deal of "discovery" during transcription and, as a consequence, a great deal of "internal revision" and "retrospective structuring." These latter pieces also took proportionally much longer to write than the former ones. But the point is that writers are fully capable of completing writing tasks, some of them quite complex, with most substantive "discovery" occuring well before transcription.

Pre-Textual Revising and Pre-Text

"Retrospective structuring" in light of discovery, or recursive revising of written text in light of discovery, requires a complementary process in order to account for at least two anomalies in the research on revising—that fewer textual revisions (i.e., retranscriptions) do not necessarily result in poorer written texts and that skilled writers do not necessarily retranscribe more than less-skilled writers. This complementary process might be called "projective restructuring." Such a complementary process accounts for the two anomalies by allowing "reviewing"—and its subprocesses of "evaluating" and "revising"—to be embedded in other processes and subprocesses, as Flower and Hayes's model and their examinations of thinking-aloud protocols suggests it is. Any theory of composing that fails to recognize that many writers can know what they want to write and how to frame it before they write it and that writers are fully capable of revising pretextually strikes me as singularly inadequate.

If, as I am suggesting, revising a pre-text is as important as revising a written text, what is the nature of the pre-text and the nature of the revising process? Because composing has a hierarchical structure, its subprocesses operate on pre-texts as well as texts. When I prepare to write a grocery list, I might think "cough syrup" but pretextually revise "syrup" to read "medicine" because I have to worry with spelling *syrup* in a way I do not in spelling *medicine*. Because both terms refer, for my wife and me, to a particular cough formula recommended by our family physician for allergy-prone patients, either term communicates my intended message to its audience equally well. Similarly, when I write to request that our daughter be excused from class for an appointment with her orthodontist, I pretextually revise "2 p.m." to specify additionally "Mrs. Costello's fifth-period science class in Room 34" in order to increase the probability of my not having to wait for the school secretary to locate our daughter and then page her. When I write to the oil company, I may initially think "my account" but write "account # 196 3045 896A," because I have anticipated that my audience, in order to verify my payment, will need that information. Just as important, the pre-texts I construct are framed to meet the demands of particular rhetorical situations: The pre-text for my grocery list reflects the sequence of aisles that its user will encounter in gathering the items for purchase; the note to the school secretary is pretextually framed to reflect the order in which the secretary will need the information to execute the task I want her to perform; and my pre-text of the letter to the oil company frames or organizes content so that the letter's unknown audience can efficiently grasp the nature and the source of the problem and the solution that I want him/her to implement. With the exception of pre-texts like the pretextual grocery list, the frame of which I use regularly, my pre-texts often undergo extensive revision before I ever commit words to paper; and these revisions most frequently represent responses to the question, "How should this material be shaped to accomplish my purpose?"

Although revising a pre-text can be accommodated in the Flower and Hayes model of composing, the model itself is not specific enough to suggest the nature of that process or the nature of the pre-text itself. Research on discourse comprehension helps provide some of the needed specificity. Particularly important is the research within the "constructivist tradition" (cf. Spivey, 1983)[3] and the extension of that research to composing by Bracewell, Frederiksen, and Frederiksen (1982).

---

[3] For a detailed examination of the tenets of the "constructivist tradition" as well as a systematic review of the literature on comprehension within that tradition, see Spivey (1983). A fair amount of my own thinking about how writers construct meaning has been influenced by Spivey's dissertation and by the conversations she and I have had about the matter.

The "constructivist tradition" in comprehension research assumes, principally, that when readers read a text, they engage in an active process of meaning construction (cf. Goodman, 1967; Kintsch, 1974; Rosenblatt, 1978; Rumelhart, 1977; Tierney & Pearson, 1983), a process that is dependent both on what readers bring to the text (cf. Mandler & Johnson, 1977; Rumelhart & Ortony, 1977; Stein & Glenn, 1978; Thorndyke, 1977) and on features of the text itself, such as propositional structure (cf. Frederiksen, 1975; Kintsch, 1974; Meyer, 1975), anaphoric cohesion (cf. Carpenter & Just, 1977; Clark, 1977), and topical structure and staging (cf. Clements, 1979; Grimes, 1975; Marshall & Glock, 1978; Vande Kopple, 1982, 1983).

According to much of the research on comprehension, this active construction process results in a mental representation of the meaning. This mental representation of meaning is often characterized as a semantic or text base made up of a set of propositions (e.g., Frederiksen, 1975; Kintsch, 1974, 1977; Kintsch & van Dijk, 1978; Kintsch & Vipond, 1979; Meyer, 1975; Miller & Kintsch, 1980). These propositions are said to consist of "word concepts, one serving as a predicator and the others as arguments" (Kintsch, 1974, p. 5). The semantic or text base that readers are said to construct mentally is not identical to the surface text that they read. Kintsch (1974) claims that

> when subjects read a text, they store in memory a propositional representation of that text which is not necessarily a precise copy of the text base from which the text had been generated in the first place. Specifically, if there were some propositions in the original text base that were not represented explicitly in the [surface] text itself, the reader will infer these propositions and store them in memory in the same way as other propositions that were represented explicitly in the [surface] text. (pp. 153–154)

The Kintschian view of how data are acquired from reading and represented in memory may not be a wholly adequate one, because it seems possible that those data can be stored in multiple forms, only one of which is a propositional text base. In addition to being stored as a propositional text base, data acquired from a text can be stored, for example, as sensory images, feelings, and metaphors. Whatever form these data take in memory, they are probably not stored in random order. Even research within the "constructivist tradition"—most of which assumes that data acquired from texts is stored as a propositional text base—seems divided on the issue of how they are ordered.

According to one view, acquired information is represented hierarchically in memory (cf. Meyer, 1975; Thorndyke, 1977) such that less important propositions are embedded in or subsumed under more important ones. This top–down organization of meaning in memory allows readers, according to Kintsch and van Dijk (1975, 1978; van Dijk, 1980), to construct a "macrostructure" or "gist" (in effect, a summary or abstract) of the text read through a series of "macrorules" (discussed most fully in van Dijk, 1980). This hierarchical organization of information in memory according to importance allows for some propositions represented in the surface level of a text being read not to be remembered at all and for others to be forgotten quickly. However, it seems unlikely that meaning can be constructed or information from a text hierarchically organized in memory independent of knowledge and knowledge structures already possessed by the reader. Thus according to a second view, readers, rather than constructing in memory a macrostructure for the text read, comprehend a text by attaching the acquired information to existing knowledge structures such as "schemata" (cf. Anderson, 1977, 1978; Bartlett, 1932; Rumelhart, 1975, 1980; Rumelhart & Ortony, 1977; Schallert, 1982; Spiro, 1977, 1980; Thorndyke, 1977), "frames" (cf. Minsky, 1975; Tannen, 1979; Winograd, 1977), and "plans" or "scripts" (cf. Anderson, Spiro, & Anderson, 1978; Schank, 1973; Schank & Abelson, 1977; Spiro & Tirre, 1980). Given this second view, the meaning a reader constructs for a text must represent a synthesis of newly acquired information with extant knowledge and knowledge structures, or it must represent a synthesis of acquired information and newly constructed frames (cf. Bracewell, Frederiksen, & Frederiksen, 1982; Bruce, 1980; Collins, Brown, & Larkin, 1980) when the text read contains information completely new to the reader.

Comprehending written texts and producing them are not, of course, isomorphic processes, as some (e.g., Kline & Huff, 1983) seem to claim. Indeed, as Bracewell (1980) has shown, to insist on or to assert a fundamental identity between the two processes is to ignore their essential differences and the different cognitive demands they make on language users. Differences between the cognitive demands made on language users by comprehension and production can be attributed primarily to the necessity of accommodating an audience during composing, an audience that is often both physically and psychologically distant from the writer. Writers, in short, must deal in substantially different ways than readers with the four elements of context described by Campbell and Holland (1982)—the context of sentences linked to form a coherent text, the context of graphic layout, the context of use or functions, and the context of users. Furthermore, if the processes of producing and comprehending written texts are not clearly differentiated, then it becomes impossible to account for the fact that comprehension skills always develop prior to production skills (cf. Bracewell, 1980: Bracewell, Frederiksen, & Frederiksen, 1982). Nevertheless, comprehension and production subsume processes of meaning construction. As Bracewell, Frederiksen, and Frederiksen (1982) argue, comprehension and production both depend on "framing" and "regulating" processes, but they do so in significantly different ways.

These processes, framing and regulating, are perhaps most readily illustrated with reference to research on conversational discourse. Bracewell, Frederiksen, and Frederiksen (1982) explain:

> The language of conversations should be viewed not only as content (that is, talk about things), but also as reflecting two important processes: (a) those that regulate the flow of conversational exchanges among participants, and (b) those that negotiate and establish a *framework* within which participants' utterances can be interpreted and understood.

In conversations, successful communication requires both the establishment of a common frame or structure (Frake, 1977) and the smooth regulation of the flow of turn-taking, side sequences, openings, closings, and topic shifts (Sacks, Schegloff & Jefferson, 1974). Regulating processes are characteristic of adult conversations and are learned as children acquire principles for turn-taking and producing speech that is topically and conversationally related to their own and others' speech acts.

In addition to these regulative aspects, conversations typically are structured in terms of larger topically related units such as scenes, events, and entire speech activities (such as might occur in a lesson or a task-oriented dialogue). The term *frame* has been used to refer to the structure of such units that provide a context within which individual speech acts are coherent parts. To account for variability and change in contextual frames over the course of a conversation, the concept of frame had to be extended from a fixed notion to one of frame as *constructed* by participants through their interactions.

The cognitive processes that underlie such framing processes involve both frame knowledge (that is, knowledge of particular substantive or discourse structures such as how to order a meal at a restaurant) and an ability to make the inferences necessary to construct an appropriate frame. The latter has been referred to by Gumperz (1977) as conversational inference, while the former is referred to as frame knowledge (i.e., knowledge of types of discourse units such as genres, speech events, and task contexts). (p. 148)

According to Bracewell, Frederiksen, and Frederiksen (1982), framing and regulating processes that govern the structure, content, and direction of conversations also figure importantly in discourse comprehension and production:

Research on discourse comprehension has tended to focus both on the structure of discourse and on the processes that underlie discourse comprehension. The nature and complexity of discourse structure is fundamental to both the comprehension and production of extended spoken or written text. In comprehension of written text, it is principally the text structure that has to support the reader's comprehension, and in writing, the text structure is the principal means for expressing a conceptual structure or frame. Viewed somewhat more deeply, the reader must use the text structure to infer a writer's conceptual structure, and a writer must produce a text that is able to sustain a reader's inferences about the underlying conceptual structure. (pp. 148–149)

However important framing and regulating processes are in comprehending and producing written texts, the processes function differently during reading than they do during writing. As Bracewell, Frederiksen, and Frederiksen (1982) explain,

The discourse features, propositional structure, and underlying frame structures identified as important to comprehension are central to a description of discourse production. A writer must acquire a capacity (a) to generate conceptual frame structures and propositions to represent them, and (b) to select and manipulate language features using them to encode propositions and signal underlying conceptual frames. Processes of frame construction are likely to occur both in production and comprehension; the principal difference between them is the degree of constraint on frame construction. In reading, the text constrains frame construction; in writing, frame construction is constrained . . . by the writer's knowledge and the text he or she has previously written (Frederiksen & Dominic, 1981). Regulating processes in comprehension involve text-based control of comprehension; in writing they involve the writer's use of language features and text structure to control the reader's processing. (p. 150)

Given Bracewell, Frederiksen, and Frederiksen's (1982) account of framing and regulating processes that figure importantly in the production of written texts, the elements of context (cf. Campbell & Holland, 1982) that influence those processes, and the possibility that data acquired from texts can be stored in a number of different forms, it is possible (a) to suggest some needed specificity for Flower and Hayes's (1981a) cognitive process model, and (b) to indicate somewhat more precisely the processes involved in text production and their relationship to what I have called a pre-text and to the process I have called pretextual revising.

Contrary to what is sometimes suggested by those who would view transcribing written texts solely or primarily as a process of discovery, writers do not undertake composing tasks as though each were a task distinct from all others. Both experienced and novice writers have access to knowledge of a variety of schemata, frames, scripts, and prose genres (cf. Bereiter & Scardamalia, 1984; Bracewell, Frederiksen, & Frederiksen, 1982) that they have acquired as part of their normal development as users of oral and written language, structures that can be used either as organizing principles in memory or as organizing principles during text production and comprehension. To be sure, experienced writers' knowledge of such structures may differ in both kind and degree from that of inexperienced writers; to assert otherwise would be to deny obvious differences, for example, between the discourse production and comprehension abilities of children and adults. Likewise, not all experienced writers have equivalent knowledge of or access to such structures; if they did, all experienced writers—if they had access to equivalent subject matter knowledge—would be equally proficient in producing and comprehending any given text.

Consider again the texts and composing processes of the two students discussed previously. Because the writing assignment (that is, the rhetorical task or problem presented) was controlled, both writers had equivalent "subject matter" or "substantive" knowledge. That is to say, the content stored in memory had to be either identical or nearly identical in both cases. Yet the processes that produced those texts seem to differ in important ways, as do the texts themselves, particularly the first and the third, the former a first draft produced by a student who anticipates retranscribing extensively and the latter produced by a student who retranscribes very little. To the extent that pre-texts consist of "propositional" content, the pre-texts of the two students could not have differed substantively. Given what can be reasonably inferred about the two writers' composing processes, together with the resulting texts, I would hypothesize differences between the two students' respective pre-texts, and I would speculate that those differences have to do less with substance or content and more to do with the organization of substance or content in memory. That is to say, the two writers differ in their respective "abilities" to frame, prior to transcription, the propositional content of their messages. For the writer who apparently had little need to revise the text she produced, the content seems to have been adequately "framed" prior to transcription; for the writer who revised extensively, the content seems not to have been.

The consequence of inadequate or inappropriate framing of the content—in whatever form it is stored—of a pre-text is, I would hypothesize, extensive re-transcription, if the writer is sensitive to the four elements of context specified by Campbell and Holland (1982) and if the writer is capable of acting in response to those elements during revision of a written text. If a writer inadequately "frames" the pre-text and cannot revise the pre-text or the frame, and if a writer is incapable of altering the frame in response to contextual demands or situational constraints during revision of a written text, little revision as retranscription will be evident. Similarly, if a writer is capable of revising a pre-text that he/she evaluates as inappropriate for the particular rhetorical problem, little revision as retranscription may result. Conversely, if a writer cannot revise a pre-text judged inappropriate but can either "discover" an appropriate text during transcription or revise an inap-propriate transcription, a great deal of retranscription may very well result. In the former case, the retranscription will likely be of the within-draft variety, and in the latter case, it will likely be of the between-draft variety. In short, the nature of the writer's pre-text and the writer's ability to revise it can affect the amount and kind of retranscription.

Given the concept of pre-text and the process of pretextual framing, it is possible to hypothesize some fairly specific differences in the decision-making processes that writers of different abilities employ during composing. Pretextual framing is, as I have suggested, dependent on and reflective of the availability in a writer's working memory of structures for organizing information both conceptually and rhetorically. In the case of the two student writers discussed earlier, I would specu-late that the second writer had access to a "framework" (what might be called a "response from a newspaper editor" schema or frame) for organizing the proposi-tional content of her pre-text that simply was not available during planning to the first writer. In other words, the second writer's prior knowledge of this frame and her ability to apply that knowledge to a novel production task, resulted in different composing strategies and in decidedly different patterns of revision as retranscrip-tion. However, the production task was also a novel task for the first writer, but it appears to have been novel in a significantly different way than it was for the second writer. The second writer seems to have been able to access and apply what Brace-well, Frederiksen, and Frederiksen (1982) refer to as a "frame." The first writer seems to have had access to a much less complex frame as he transcribed his initial draft, a frame that seemed to operate primarily at the level of the sentence and that resulted in such hackneyed expressions as "It has come to my attention. . . ." The first writer's evaluation of his initial draft seems to have led to the discovery of a frame by which to organize the content of his text, a frame similar to the one employed in the only draft written by the second student writer; this discovery led to multiple between-draft retranscriptions.

The availability or unavailability of a framework for organizing the content—whatever its form—of a pre-text and the ability to apply that framework to a pre-text affects the processes that "regulate" discourse production. If the content of a pre-text can be adequately and appropriately framed according to contextual demands and situational constraints prior to transcription, then the decisions that writers must make during transcription and retranscription differ from those made when the pre-text is not adequately framed. That is to say, decisions regarding message content, topicality or staging, coherence relations, and cohesion can be made at different points during the composing process, depending on the writer's ability to construct and revise a pre-text. This difference with respect to what is revised and when revision occurs seems to have been a critical one in the cases of the writers of the texts discussed earlier. And it seems to be the case when I confront composing tasks of varying difficulty for me as a writer.

The nature of the pre-text that writers construct is probably a function of the quality, kind, and extent of planning that occurs prior to transcription. This planning results, I believe, in mental representations of intended meaning, or pre-texts, that can take a variety of forms and that can vary considerably in their approximation to prose (cf. Flower & Hayes, 1984). However, the relationship between planning and the pre-text that I believe writers construct and between the pre-text and the written text is, at present, unclear. Bracewell, Frederiksen, and Frederiksen (1982) point out that "While research on the writing process has described planning and some transcribing processes in detail, generally . . . processes at all levels have not been related to the text structure and features the writer produces" (p. 151). As the present essay suggests, one hypothesis worth investigating is that the amount, kind, and quality of planning is likely to affect the nature of the writer's pre-text as well as revisions of it and, in turn, the nature of the processes by which texts are transcribed and retranscribed. A second hypothesis suggested by the present essay is that knowledge of "frames" and the ability to adapt them to "novel" composing tasks prior to transcription will likely affect the amounts and kinds of retranscription. A third hypothesis is that the process of "framing" itself will likely affect planning, the nature of the pre-text and pretextual revising, and the nature of the written text and revision as retranscription. But whatever the relationships among planning, the pre-text, pretextual revising, and textual revising, it is clear that defining revision exclusively as retranscription, as mandated by the historical context that has shaped revision research, and that employing extant methods for investigating revising will not solve the riddle that is revising.

Some Concluding Remarks

In the preceding paragraphs, I examined diachronically and synchronically some of the underlying assumptions that have come to inform theories of composing in general, theories of revising in particular, and revision research. In the course of this examination, I argued that certain of these assumptions should be abandoned or modified because results of revising research suggest that those assumptions are invalid and because many of these assumptions have not allowed theory and research to deal adequately with the causes of revision. I also argued that the implications of the concept of hierarchy have not been fully worked out either in theory or in empirical research.

As correctives to or modifications of composing and revising theory, I made a number of claims, posited a number of alternative explanations that might feasibly be investigated, although which of the available research methodologies would be most suited for such investigations remains uncertain. These alternative explanations and claims center around two not unrelated questions: When does revising occur? And what can be the focus of the revising process? I argued, partly on theoretical grounds and partly on empirical grounds, that if composing is a hierarchical process, then the subprocess of revising can be embedded into the subprocess of planning, the result of which is a pre-text that can take a number of forms and that can be revised in much the same way and for many of the same reasons that a writer would revise a written text. Two consequences of embedding the subprocess of revising into the planning process are that revising cannot be defined only as retranscription, as it has been in virtually all revision studies, and that the writer's pre-text must be seen as a causal influence on retranscription. In addition, I argued that the failure of revision research and theory to acknowledge the importance of pretextual revising has led to suggestions about revising patterns that can be considered neither reliable nor valid.

Whether my present speculations will lead to a "more detailed" account "of how the mind copes with writing tasks" is itself a matter of some speculation. However, given the results of studies that have examined revision as retranscription and given the current state of composing theory, the claims I made about composing and revising and the alternative explanations I have articulated seem reasonable ones. Yet I fully expect that even if these claims and assumptions, these speculations, prove useful in moving revision research and theory beyond its moorings in retranscription, they should still be regarded as tentative. Like the pre-text that is so central to my speculations, the universe of composing and our perceptions of it can be characterized by only one constant—change.

References

Abrams, M. (1953). *The mirror and the lamp*. New York: Oxford University Press.

Agar, M., & Hobbs, J. R. (1982). Interpreting discourse: Coherence and the analysis of ethnographic interviews. *Discourse Processes, 5,* 1–32.

Anderson, R. C. (1977). The notion of schemata and the educational enterprise. In R. C. Anderson, R. J. Spiro, & W. E. Montague (Eds.), *Schooling and the acquisition of knowledge.* Hillsdale, NJ: Lawrence Erlbaum.

Anderson, R. C. (1978). Schema directed processes in language comprehension. In A. Lesgold, J. Peligrino, S. Fokhema, & R. Glaser (Eds.), *Cognitive psychology and instruction.* New York: Plenum.

Anderson, R. C., Spiro, R. J., & Anderson, M. C. (1978). Schemata as scaffolding for the representation of information in connected discourse. *American Educational Research Journal, 15,* 433–440.

Bartlett, F. C. (1982). *Remembering: A study in experimental and social psychology.* Cambridge, England: Cambridge University Press.

Beach, R. (1976). Self-evaluation strategies of extensive revisers and non-revisers. *College Composition and Communication, 27,* 160–164.

Beckett, F. E. (1974). *College composition: The course where a student doesn't learn to write.* Bruce, MS: Calcon.

Bereiter, C., & Scardamalia, M. (1983). Does learning to write have to be so difficult? In A. Freedman, I. Pringle, & J. Yalden (Eds.), *Learning to write: First language/second language.* Applied Linguistics and Language Studies Series. London: Longman.

Bereiter, C., & Scardamalia, M. (1984). Learning about writing from reading. *Written Communication, 1,* 163–188.

Berkenkotter, C. (1983). Decisions and revisions: The planning strategies of a publishing writer. *College Composition and Communication, 34,* 156–169.

Booth, W. C. (1963). The rhetorical stance. *College Composition and Communication, 14,* 139–145.

Bracewell, R. J. (1980). Writing as cognitive activity. *Visible Language, 14,* 400–422.

Bracewell, R. J., Frederiksen, C. H., & Frederiksen, J. D. (1982). Cognitive processes in composing and comprehending discourse. *Educational Psychologist, 17,* 146–164.

Breland, H. M., & Gaynor, J. L. (1979). A comparison of direct and indirect assessments of writing skills. *Journal of Educational Measurement, 16,* 119–128.

Bridwell, L. S. (1980). Revising strategies in twelfth grade students' transactional writing. *Research in the Teaching of English, 14,* 197–222.

Britton, J., Burgess, T., Martin, N., McLeod, A., & Rosen, H. (1975). *The development of writing abilities (11–18).* Schools Research Council Studies. London: Macmillan Education.

Bruce, B. C. (1980). Plans and social actions. In R. Spiro, B. C. Bruce, & W. Brewer (Eds.), *Theoretical issues in reading comprehension.* Hillsdale, NJ: Lawrence Erlbaum.

Bullard, K. (1964). Academic boondoggle. *College English, 25,* 373–375.

Campbell, L. J., & Holland, V. M. (1982). Understanding the language of public documents because readability formulas don't. In R. J. Di Pietro (Ed.), *Linguistics and the professions: Proceedings of the second annual Delaware symposium on language studies.* Norwood, NJ: Ablex.

Carpenter, P. A., & Just, M. A. (1977). Reading comprehension as the eyes see it. In M. A. Just & P. A. Carpenter (Eds.), *Cognitive processes in comprehension.* Hillsdale, NJ: Lawrence Erlbaum.

Carton, E. (1983). On going home: Selfhood in composition. *College English, 45,* 340–347.

Clark, H. H. (1977). Inferences in comprehension. In D. LaBerge & S. J. Samuels (Eds.), *Basic processes in reading: Perception and comprehension.* Hillsdale, NJ: Lawrence Erlbaum.

Clements, P. (1979). The effects of staging on recall from prose. In R. O. Freedle (Ed.), *New directions in discourse processing.* Norwood, NJ: Ablex.

Coles, W. E., Jr. (1974). *Teaching composing.* Rochelle Park, NJ: Hayden.

Coles, W. E., Jr. (1978). *The plural I: The teaching of writing.* New York: Holt, Rinehart, & Winston.

Collins, A., Brown, J. S., & Larkin, K. M. (1980). Inference in text understanding. In R. Spiro, B. C. Bruce, & W. Brewer (Eds.), *Theoretical issues in reading comprehension.* Hillsdale, NJ: Lawrence Erlbaum.

Collins, A., & Gentner, D. (1980). A framework for a cognitive theory of writing. In L. W. Gregg & E. Steinberg (Eds.), *Cognitive processes in writing.* Hillsdale, NJ: Lawrence Erlbaum.

Cooper, C. R. (1977). Holistic evaluation of writing. In C. R. Cooper & L. Odell (Eds.), *Evaluating writing: Describing, measuring, judging.* Urbana, IL: National Council of Teachers of English.

Cowley, M. (Ed.). (1958). *Writers at work: The "Paris Review" interviews.* New York: Viking.

Crowley, S. (1977). Components of the composing process. *College Composition and Communication, 28,* 166–169.

de Beaugrande, R. (1982). Psychology and composition: Past, present, and future. In M. Nystrand (Ed.), *What writers know: The language, process, and structure of written discourse.* New York: Academic Press.

de Beaugrande, R. (1984). *Text production: Toward a science of composition.* Norwood, NJ: Ablex.

Dowst, K. (1980). The epistemic approach: Writing, knowing, and learning. In T. R. Donovan & B. W.

McClelland (Eds.), *Eight approaches to teaching composition*. Urbana, IL: National Council of Teachers of English.

Elbow, P. (1973). *Writing without teachers*. New York: Oxford University Press.

Emig, J. (1971). *The composing process of twelfth graders*. (Research Report No. 13). Urbana, IL: National Council of Teachers of English.

Faigley, L., & Witte, S. P. (1981). Analyzing revsions. *College Composition and Communication, 32*, 400–414.

Faigley, L., & Witte, S. P. (1984). Measuring the effects of revisions on text structure. In R. Beach & L. S. Bridwell (Eds.), *New directions in composition research*. New York: Guilford Press.

Flower, L. (1979). Writer-based prose: A cognitive basis for problems in writing. *College English, 41*, 19–37.

Flower, L., & Hayes, J. R. (1980). The cognition of discovery: Defining a rhetorical problem. *College Composition and Communication, 31*, 21–32.

Flower, L., & Hayes, J. R. (1981a). A cognitive process theory of writing. *College Composition and Communication, 32*, 365–387.

Flower, L., & Hayes, J. R. (1981b). Plans that guide the composing process. In C. H. Frederiksen & J. F. Dominic (Eds.), *Writing: The nature, development and teaching of written communication*. Hillsdale, NJ: Lawrence Erlbaum.

Flower, L., & Hayes, J. R. (1984). Images, plans, and prose: The representation of meaning in writing. *Written Communication, 1*, 120–160.

Frake, C. O. (1977). Plying frames can be dangerous: Some reflections on methodology in cognitive anthropology. *Quarterly Newsletter of the Institute for Comparative Human Development, 1*, 1–7.

Frederiksen, C. H. (1975). Representing logical and semantic structure of knowledge acquired from discourse. *Cognitive Psychology, 7*, 317–348.

Frederiksen, C. H., & Dominic, J. F. (1981). Introduction: Perspectives on the activity of writing. In C. H. Frederiksen & J. F. Dominic (Eds.), *Writing: Process, development, and communication*. Hillsdale, NJ: Lawrence Erlbaum.

Goodman, K. S. (1967). Reading: A psycholinguistic, guessing game. *Journal of the Reading Specialist, 4*, 126–135.

Gould, J. D. (1980). Experiments on composing letters: Some facts, some myths, and some observations. In L. W. Gregg & E. W. Steinberg (Eds.), *Cognitive processes in writing*. Hillsdale, NJ: Lawrence Erlbaum.

Grimes, J. (1975). *The thread of discourse*. The Hague: Mouton.

Gumperz, J. J. (1977). Sociocultural knowledge in conversational inference. In *28th annual roundtable, Monograph series on language and linguistics*. Washington, DC: Georgetown University.

Hairston, M. (1982). The winds of change: Thomas Kuhn and the revolution in the teaching of writing. *College Composition and Communication, 33*, 76–88.

Hansen, B. (1978). Rewriting is a waste of time. *College English, 39*, 956–960.

Hayes, J. R., & Flower, L. (1980). Identifying the organization of writing processes. In L. Gregg & E. Steinberg (Eds.), *Cognitive processes in writing*. Hillsdale, NJ: Lawrence Erlbaum.

Hildick, W. (1965). *Word for word: The rewriting of fiction*. London: Faber & Faber.

Hobbs, J. R., & Evans, D. (1979). *Conversation as planned behavior*. (Tech. Note No. 203). Menlo Park, CA: SRI International.

Hogan, T. P., & Mischler, C. (1980). Relationships between essay tests and objective tests of language skills for elementary school students. *Journal of Educational Measurement, 17*, 219–227.

Humes, A. (1983). Research on the composing process. *Review of Educational Research, 53*, 201–216.

King, M. L. (1978). Research in composition: A need for theory. *Research in the Teaching of English, 12*, 193–202.

Kintsch, W. (1974). *The representation of meaning in memory*. Hillsdale, NJ: Lawrence Erlbaum.

Kintsch, W. (1977). Reading comprehension as a function of text structure. In A. S. Reber & D. L. Scarborough (Eds.), *Toward a psychology of reading: The proceedings of the CUNY conference*. Hillsdale, NJ: Lawrence Erlbaum.

Kintsch, W., & van Dijk, T. A. (1975). Comment on se repelle et on resúme des histoires. *Languages, 40,* 98–116.

Kintsch, W., & van Dijk, T. A. (1978). Toward a model of text comprehension and production. *Psychological Review, 85,* 363–394.

Kintsch, W., & Vipond, D. (1979). Reading comprehension and readability in educational practice and psychological theory. In L. G. Nilsson (Ed.), *Perspectives in memory research: Essays in honor of Uppsala University's 500th anniversary.* Hillsdale, NJ: Lawrence Erlbaum.

Kline, C. R., Jr., & Huff, R. H. (1983). Reading, writing: Radix. *Visible Language, 17,* 163–176.

Mandler, J. M., & Johnson, N. S. (1977). Remembrance of things parsed: Story structure and recall. *Cognitive Psychology, 9,* 111–151.

Marshall, N., & Glock, M.D. (1978). Comprehension of connected discourse: A study into the relationships between structure of text and information recalled. *Reading Research Quarterly, 14,* 10–56.

Meyer, B. J. F. (1975). *The organization of prose and its effects on memory.* Amsterdam: North-Holland.

Miller, J. R., & Kintsch, W. (1980). Readability and recall of short prose passages: A theoretical analysis. *Journal of Experimental Psychology: Human Learning and Memory, 7,* 335–354.

Minsky, M. (1975). A framework for representing knowledge. In P. Winston (Ed.), *The psychology of computer vision.* New York: McGraw-Hill.

Mischel, T. (1974). A case study of a twelfth-grade writer. *Research in the Teaching of English, 8,* 303–314.

Murray, D. M. (1968). *A writer teaches writing: A practical method of teaching composition.* Boston: Houghton Mifflin.

Murray, D. M. (1978). Internal revision: A process of discovery. In C. R. Cooper & L. Odell (Eds.), *Research on composing: Points of departure.* Urbana, IL: National Council of Teachers of English.

Murray, D. M. (1980). Writing as process: How writing finds its own meaning. In T. R. Donovan & B. W. McClelland (Eds.), *Eight approaches to teaching composition.* Urbana, IL: National Council of Teachers of English.

NAEP (National Assessment of Educational Progress). (1977). *Write/rewrite: An assessment of revision skills.* (Writing Report No. 05-W-04). Denver, CO: National Assessment of Educational Progress.

Nold, E. W. (1979). *Revising: Toward a theory.* Unpublished manuscript. (ERIC Document Reproduction Service No. 172 212)

Nold, E. W. (1981). Revising. In C. H. Frederiksen & J. F. Dominic (Eds.), *Writing: Process, development, and communication.* Hillsdale, NJ: Lawrence Erlbaum.

Nystrand, M. (1982). Rhetoric's "audience" and linguistics' "speech community": Implications for understanding writing, reading, and text. In M. Nystrand Ed., *What writers know: The language, process, and structure of written discourse.* New York: Academic Press.

Odell, L. (1981). Defining and assessing competency in writing. In C. R. Cooper (Ed.), *The nature and measurement of competency in writing.* Urbana, IL: National Council of Teachers of English.

Parker, W. R. (1967). Where do English departments come from? *College English, 28,* 339–351.

Perl, S. (1978). *Five writers writing: Case studies of the composing process of unskilled college writers.* Unpublished doctoral dissertation, New York University.

Perl, S. (1979). The composing processes of unskilled college writers. *Research in the Teaching of English, 13,* 317–336.

Perl, S. (1980). Understanding composing. *College Composition and Communication, 31,* 363–369.

Perl, S., & Egendorf, A. (1979). The process of creative discovery: Theory, research, and implications for teaching. In D. McQuade (Ed.), *Linguistics, stylistics, and the teaching of composition.* Akron, OH: University of Akron, L & S Books.

Plimpton, G. (Ed.). (1963, 1967, 1976). *Writers at work: The "Paris Review" interviews* (Series 2–4). New York: Viking.

Rice, W. (1960). A proposal for the abolition of freshman English, as it is now commonly taught, from the college curriculum. *College English, 21,* 361–367.

Rohman, D. G. (1965). Pre-writing: The stage of discovery in the writing process. *College Composition and Communication, 16,* 106–112.

Rohman, D. G., & Wlecke, A. O. (1964). *Pre-writing: The construction and application of models for concept formation in writing.* (U.S. Office of Education, Cooperative Research Project No. 2174). East Lansing: Michigan State University.

Rose, M. (1981). Sophistical, ineffective books—The dismantling of process in composition texts. *College Composition and Communication, 32,* 65–74.

Rosenblatt, L. (1978). *The reader, the text, the poem: The transactional theory of the literary work.* Carbondale: Southern Illinois University Press.

Rumelhart, D. E. (1975). Notes on a schema for stories. In D. G. Bobrow & A. Collins (Eds.), *Representation and understanding: Studies in cognitive science.* New York: Academic Press.

Rumelhart, D. E. (1977). Toward an interactive model of reading. In S. Dorniv (Ed.), *Attention and performance IV.* Hillsdale, NJ: Lawrence Erlbaum.

Rumelhart, D. E. (1980). Schemata: The building blocks of cognition. In R. J. Spiro, B. C. Bruce, & W. F. Brewer (Eds.), *Theoretical issues in reading comprehension.* Hillsdale, NJ: Lawrence Erlbaum.

Rumelhart, D. E., & Ortony, A. (1977). The representation of knowledge in memory. In R. C. Anderson, R. J. Spiro, & W. F. Montague (Eds.), *Schooling and the acquisition of knowledge.* Hillsdale, NJ: Lawrence Erlbaum.

Sacks, S., Schegloff, E. A., & Jefferson, G. (1974). A simplest systematics for the organization of turn taking in conversation. *Language, 50,* 696–735.

Scardamalia, M., & Bereiter, C. (in press). Written composition. In M. Wittrock (Ed.), *Handbook of research on teaching* (3rd ed.). New York: Macmillan Education.

Schallert, D. L. (1982). The significance of knowledge: A synthesis of research related to schema theory. In W. Otto & S. White (Eds.), *Reading expository material.* New York: Academic Press.

Schank, R. (1973). Identification of conceptualizations underlying natural language. In R. Schank & K. Colby (Eds.), *Computer models of thought and language.* San Francisco: Freeman.

Schank, R., & Abelson, R. P. (1977). *Scripts, plans, goals, and understanding: An inquiry into human knowledge structures.* Hillsadale, NJ: Lawrence Erlbaum.

Schwartz, M. (1983). Revision profiles: Patterns and implications. *College English, 45,* 549–558.

Sommers, N. I. (1978). *Revision in the composing process: A case study of experienced and student writers.* Unpublished doctoral dissertation, Boston University.

Sommers, N. I. (1979). The need for theory in composition research. *College Composition and Communication, 30,* 46–49.

Sommers, N. I. (1980). Revision strategies of student writers and experienced adult writers. *College Composition and Communication, 31,* 378–388.

Spandel, V., & Stiggins, R. J. (1981). *Direct measures of writing skills: Issues and applications* (rev. ed.). Portland, OR: Northwest Regional Educational Laboratory.

Spiro, R. J. (1977). Remembering information from text: The "state of schema" approach. In R. C. Anderson, R. J. Spiro, & W. E. Montague (Eds.), *Schooling and the acquisition of knowledge.* Hillsdale, NJ: Lawrence Erlbaum.

Spiro, R. J. (1980). Constructive processes in prose comprehension and recall. In R. J. Spiro, B. C. Bruce, & W. F. Brewer (Eds.), *Theoretical issues in reading comprehension.* Hillsdale, NJ: Lawrence Erlbaum.

Spiro, R. J., & Tirre, W. C. (1980). Individual differences in schema utilization during discourse processing. *Journal of Educational Psychology, 72,* 204–208.

Spivey, N. N. (1983). *Discourse synthesis: Constructing texts in reading and writing.* Unpublished doctoral dissertation, University of Texas at Austin.

Stallard, C. K. (1974). An analysis of the writing behavior of good student writers. *Research in the Teaching of English, 8,* 206–218.

Stein, N.J., & Glenn, C. G. (1978). An analysis of story comprehension in elementary school chil-children. In R. O. Freedle (Ed.), *New directions in discourse processing*. Norwood, NJ: Ablex.

Stiggins, R. J. (1982). A comparison of direct and indirect writing assessment methods. *Research in the Teaching of English, 16*, 101–114.

Tannen, D. (1979). What's in a frame? Surface evidence for underlying expectations. In R. O. Freedle Ed., *Discourse production and comprehension*. Norwood, NJ: Ablex.

Thorndyke, P. W. (1977). Cognitive structures in comprehension and memory of narrative discourse, *Cognitive Psychology, 9*, 77–110.

Tierney, R., & Pearson, P. D. (1983). Toward a composing model of reading. *Language Arts, 60*, 568–580.

Turner, A., & Greene, E. (1978). The construction and use of a propositional text base. *JSAS Catalog of Selected Documents in Psychology, 3*, 38 (ms no. 1713).

Vande Kopple, W. J. (1982). Functional sentence perspective, composition, and reading. *College Composition and Communication, 33*, 50–63.

Vande Kopple, W. J. (1983). Something old, something new: Functional sentence perspective. *Research in the Teaching of English, 17*, 85–99.

van Dijk, T. A. (1980). *Macrostructures: An interdisciplinary study of global structures in discourse, interaction, and cognition*. Hillsdale, NJ: Lawrence Erlbaum.

Wall, S. (1983). *Revision in a rhetorical context: Case studies of first-year college writers*. Unpublished doctoral dissertation. University of Pittsburgh, Pittsburgh, PA.

Winograd, T. (1977). A framework for understanding discourse. In P. A. Carpenter & M. A. Just (Eds.), *Cognitive processes in comprehension*. Hillsdale, NJ: Lawrence Erlbaum.

Witte, S. P. (1980). Notes toward a model for research in written composition. *Research in the Teaching of English, 14*, 78–81.

Witte, S. P. (1983a). The reliability of mean t-unit length: Some questions for research in written composition. In A. Freedman, I. Pringle, & J. Yalden (Eds.), *Learning to write: First language/second language*. London: Longman.

Witte, S. P. (1983b). *Some causal properties of prior knowledge, goals, and text structure in revision*. Paper presented at the annual meeting of the Conference on College Composition and Communication, Detroit, MI.

Witte, S. P. (1983c). Topical structure and revision: An exploratory study. *College Composition and Communication, 34*, 313–341.

Witte, S. P. (1983d). Topical structure and writing quality: Some possible text-based explanations of readers' judgments of student writing. *Visible Language, 17*, 177–205.

Witte, S. P. (1984, April). *Knowledge integration during revision*. Paper presented at the annual meeting of the American Educational Research Association, New Orleans.

Witte, S. P., Cherry, R. D., Meyer, P. R., & Trachsel, M. (1984, April). *The effects of writing assignment variables on text structure*. Paper presented at the annual meeting of the American Educational Research Association. New Orleans.

Witte, S. P., Daly, J. A., Faigley, L., & Koch, W. R. (1983). The empirical development of an instrument for reporting course and teacher effectiveness in college writing programs. *Research in the Teaching of English, 17*, 243–261.

Witte, S. P., & Davis, A. S. (1980). The reliability of t-unit length: A preliminary investigation. *Research in the Teaching of English, 14*, 5–17.

Witte, S. P., & Faigley, L. (1981). Coherence, cohesion, and writing quality. *College Composition and Communication, 32*, 189–204.

Witte, S. P., & Faigley, L. (1983). *Evaluating college writing programs*. (Studies in Writing and Rhetoric, No. 1). Carbondale: Southern Illinois University Press.

Witte, S. P., Meyer, P. R., Cherry, R. D., & Trachsel, M. (in press). *Holistic evaluation of writing: Issues in theory and practice*. New York: Guilford.

Witte, S. P., Meyer, P. R., Miller, T. P., & Faigley, L. (1981). *A national survey of college and university writing program directors.* (Tech. Rep. no 2). Austin: University of Texas, Writing Program Assessment Project. (ERIC Document Reproduction Service No. 210 709)

Witte, S. P., & Sodowsky, R. E. (1984). *Topical structure, text type, and writing quality.* Paper presented at the annual meeting of the Conference on College Composition and Communication, New York.

Witte, S. P., Trachsel, M., & Walters, K. (in press). Literacy and the direct assessment of writing: A diachronic perspective. In K. Greenberg, H. Wiener, & R. Donovan (Eds.), *Writing assessment: Issues and strategies.* New York: Longman.

Witte, S. P., Walters, K., Trachsel, M., Cherry, R. D., & Meyer, P. R. (forthcoming). *Literacy and writing assessment: Issues, traditions, directions.* Norwood, NJ: Ablex.

Young, R.E. (1978). Paradigms and problems: Needed research in rhetorical invention. In C.R. Cooper & C. Odell (Eds.), *Research on composing: Points of departure.* Urbana, IL: National Council for Teachers of English.

Author Index

Italics indicate bibliographic citations.

Subject Index